Santa Fe's fabled *Super Chief* ran daily across the continent.

THE ILLUSTRATED ENCYCLOPEDIA OF

NORTH AMERICAN LOCOMOTIVES

A historical directory of over 150 years of North American rail power

BRIAN HOLLINGSWORTH

Black powder and human sweat dug this cut on the Overland Route.

PUBLISHED BY

SALAMANDER BOOKS LIMITED

LONDON

THE ILLUSTRATED ENCYCLOPEDIA OF

NORTH AMERICAN LOCOMOTIVES

A historical directory of over 150 years of North American rail power

BRIAN HOLLINGSWORTH

Engine of the *Hiawatha*, fastest steam train ever scheduled.

A Salamander Book

Published by Salamander Books Ltd.
129–137 York Way
London N7 9LG
United Kingdom

© Salamander Books Ltd. 1984, 1997

ISBN 0 86101 933 4

9 8 7 6 5 4 3 2 1

Credits

Editor: Ray Bonds

Designer: Philip Gorton

Colour artwork: © Salamander Books Ltd.: David Palmer, Clifford and Wendy Meadway, Terry Hadler and Dick Eastland.

Picture research: Diane and John Moore (full picture credits are given at the back of the book).

Filmset and monochrome reproduction: Rodney Howe Ltd. and Tempus Litho Ltd.

Printed in Spain

The Author

BRIAN HOLLINGSWORTH,
M.A., M.I.C.E.

Brian Hollingsworth has had an extravagant passion for railways ever since he can remember. After qualifying in engineering at Cambridge University, and after a brief excursion into the world of flying machines, he joined the Great Western Railway in 1946 as a civil engineer. Later, his mathematical background led him into British Rail's computers and also to a heavy involvement with BR's TOPS wagon and train control system.

He left British Rail in 1974 to take up writing and has published twelve major books on various aspects of railways, including Salamander's "The Illustrated Encyclopedia of the World's Steam Passenger Locomotives" and "The Illustrated Encyclopedia of the World's Modern Locomotives", besides contributing to technical railway periodicals.

He is a director of the Romney, Hythe and Dymchurch Railway and civil engineering adviser to the Festiniog Railway. He has a fleet of one-fifth full size locomotives which run on his private railway in his own "back garden" (actually a portion of a Welsh mountain!), and he owns the full-size LMS "Black Five" Class 4-6-0 No. 5428 *Eric Treacy*, which operates as a working locomotive on the North Yorkshire Moors Railway for tourists and rail enthusiasts.

Acknowledgements

The author wishes to express his grateful thanks to those who have assisted him in writing this book. Arthur Cook was responsible for 20 of the locomotive descriptions and he and his sons, Peter and David, helped with many of the others. Chistopher Bushell, who had the arduous task of checking the manuscripts, also made many valuable suggestions. Artists David Palmer, Clifford and Wendy Meadway, Terry Hadler and Dick Eastland, responsible for the beautiful and constructive artworks, have contributed in great measure to the book's merits. The work done by Diane and John Moore in tracking down photographs of rare subjects has been an essential ingredient, and to this I must add my thanks to the Association of American Railroads and to the many photographers whose work decorates these pages. Of the people at Salamander Books, it perhaps says enough that they have the gift of making chores of book production seem fun. Finally, I must thank Margot Cooper for the accuracy and efficiency of her typing which so much eased the burden of committing thoughts to paper.

Brian Hollingsworth

The luxurious *Panama Limited* departs Chicago for New Orleans.

Contents

Introduction	8
Stourbridge Lion 0-4-0	24
Best Friend of Charleston 0-4-0 Tank	24
Brother Jonathan 4-2-0	25
Tom Thumb 0-2-2	26
John Bull 0-4-0	26
De Witt Clinton 0-4-0	28
Grasshopper 0-4-0	28
"Mud-digger" 0-8-0	30
Campbell 4-4-0	30
Hercules 4-4-0	31
Lafayette 4-2-0	32
John Stevens 6-2-0	34
Camel 4-6-0	34
American Type 4-4-0	36
Consolidation 2-8-0	38
Mogul 2-6-0	38
El Gobernador 4-10-0	40
Lovatt Eames 4-2-2	40
C-16-60 2-8-0	42
The Judge	43
No.999 4-4-0	44
Cog Locomotive 0-4-2T	44
Nos. 1-3 Bo+Bo	46
Forney 0-4-4T	46
No.382 4-6-0	48
Camelback Class 4-4-2	48
I-1 Class 4-6-0	50
Class D16sb 4-4-0	50
Class Q 4-6-2	52
Class F15 4-6-2	52
Lyn 2-4-2T	54
Class E3sd 4-4-2	54
Class S 1-Do-1	56
Class 9700 Mikado 2-8-2	58
No.2400 0-6-6-0	58
Class EP-1 Bo-Bo	60
No.9 4-6-0	60
900 2-10-2	62
Class H4 4-6-2	62
DD1 2-B+B-2	64
Class T Bo-Bo+Bo-Bo	64
Fairlie 0-6-6-0	66
Class 1300 2-4-6-2	66
No.7 2-4-4T	68
No.14 2-8-2	68
Class 60-3 Shay B-B-B	70
K4 Class 4-6-2	72
MacDermot 4-6-2	74
Triplex 2-8-8-8-2	74
1201 2-6-2T	76
Nos. 1-67 HGe 2/2	77
USRA Light Mikado 2-8-2	78
Class E 2-10-0	78
800 2-10-10-2	80
4300 Class 4-8-2	80
Class EP-2 "Bi-polar" 1-B-D-D-B-1	82
No.24 2-6-2	84
Narrow gauge 0-10-0	84
No.1 Bo-Bo	86
K-36 2-8-2	88
M-300 Single-unit railcar	90
A-6 4-4-2	90
Class A 4-8-4	92
Class 0-1A 2-8-2	94
P-1 4-6-4	94
9000 4-12-2	96
Class J3a 4-6-4	98
Class Ps-4 4-6-2	100
Class F-2a 4-4-4	100
P-7 4-6-2	102
G5s 4-6-0	103
AC-4 Cab Forward 4-8-8-2	104
No.9000 2-Do-1	106
L.F. Loree 4-8-0	106
Pioneer Zephyr Three-car train	108
M-10001 Six-car trainset	108
GG1 2-Co-Co-2	110
Class A 4-4-2	112
Class F7 4-6-4	112
EMD "E" Series A1A-A1A	114
Royal Hudson Class 4-6-4	116
Class 3460 4-6-4	118
S-7 0-10-2	118
05A 4-8-4	120
Class E4 4-6-4	120
EMD "F" Series Bo-Bo	122
Galloping Goose railcar	124
5001 Class 2-10-4	124
FEF-2 Class 4-8-4	126
Class I-5 4-6-4	128
M-3 Yellowstone 2-8-8-4	128
Class J 4-8-4	130
Class GS-4 4-8-4	132
NW2 Bo-Bo	134
"Electroliner" Four-car trainset	134
Big Boy 4-8-8-4	136
H-8 Allegheny2-6-6-6	138
J1a 2-10-4	140
Class T1 4-4-4-4	140
Challenger Class 4-6-6-4	142
MacArthur 2-8-2	144
S-160 2-8-0	144
Class U-4 4-8-4	146
Class Ul-f 4-8-2	146
2900 Class 4-8-4	148
141R Liberation 2-8-2	150
NH/4 2-8-2	150
Niagara Class 4-8-4	152
S2 6-8-6	154
QR-1 4-8-4	154
PA Series A1A-A1A	156
M-1 2-1Co-2-1Co-Bo	158
W1 Bo-Do-Do-Bo	158
BL2 Bo-Bo	160
Little Joe 2-D-D-2	160
Y6b 2-8-8-2	162
L-2a Class 4-6-4	162
Centipede 2-Do-Do-2	164
RF16 "Sharknose" Bo-Bo	164
S-3 2-8-4	166
Selkirk Class 2-10-4	166
S1a 0-8-0	168
Class YP 4-6-2	168
EMD GP Series Bo-Bo	170
Gas Turbine Bo-Bo-Bo-Bo	172
Trainmaster H-24-66 CoCo	173
FL9 Bo-A1A	174
Mv A1A-A1A	174
U25B Bo-Bo	176
Krauss-Maffei C-C	178
RDC Single Railcar	180
Class WP 4-6-2	180
Metroliner Two-car Trainset	182
Highliner railcar	182
Class DD40AX "Centennial" Do-Do	184
Class X Co-Co	186
Class 2130 Co-Co	186
Colonel Teague	188
WDM2 Co-Co	188
C630 "Century" Co-Co	190
Class 92 1-Co-Co-1	190
Class Dx Co-Co	192
E50C Co-Co	192
EMD SD-40-2 Co-Co	194
F40PH Bo-Bo	196
Class E60CP Co-Co	198
Class AEM7 Bo-Bo	198
LRC Bo-Bo	200
SD-50 Co-Co	202
GF6C Co-Co	202
ACE 3000 4-8-2	204
Glossary	204
Index	206

Freight moves in the Rockies on the Canadian Pacific Railway.

Introduction

IN A CERTAIN sense, the story of the North American locomotive is the story of North America. Just a lifespan ago the steam railroad locomotive loomed large in our everyday lives. For most people in most places the only reasonable way to leave town—or come back to it—was by rail. In the United States alone there were an amazing 60,000 steam locomotives in service on 250,000 miles (400,000km) of track.

Yet two lifetimes ago travel by rail must have seemed as rare, as exciting and as perilous as travel in space does today. The railroad locomotive had then only just begun to revolutionize the lives of ordinary people.

Today, railroad travel has fallen to take only a minor share of the passenger-carrying market, and the railroads are so much in the background that their world is far removed from everyday life. Accordingly, many Americans think railroads are on the way out and as close to their final End of the Line as they were to their beginnings 150 years ago. Yet nothing could be further from the truth, for we enthusiasts know that a slimmed-down system 30 per cent less in extent than that existed in 1910 is now carrying over 30 per cent more traffic, using less than half the number of locomotives.

1. A few short years after people had travelled West in covered wagons and extreme discomfort, moving hotels with amenities as good as any static one became available. Here is the lounge car of the Northern Pacific's North Coast Limited in 1900.

2. America builds the railroads! A typical construction train from the boom years of railroad buildings. Note the 'Sky-scraper' dormitory cars and the soldiers to give protection from hostile Indians as construction forces advance to head of steel.

3. This famous photograph shows the scene on 5th May, 1869 when the golden spike was driven at Promontory, Utah, to celebrate the joining of East to West by a continuous line of rails. The site is now a museum where the ceremony is re-enacted.

4. Steam railroads went everywhere: a Forney 0-4-4T locomotive and single car pose for an official photograph at Oakley Boulevard on Chicago's brand new Lake Street Elevated Railroad in 1893. Note the appropriate name of the locomotive!

2

4

Origins of the Railroads

The first line in America to rely entirely upon locomotive power was the South Carolina Railroad, opened in 1835. It ran 135 miles (216km) from the port of Charleston to Hamburg, just across the River Savannah from Augusta, Georgia. It was then the longest railroad in the world and put the United States firmly in the position it has held ever since, of having the world's greatest rail mileage. Currently, the nearest rival is the Soviet Union with only half as much, but it must be said that the USSR puts over twice as much traffic on its trains as does the United States.

Expansion of North American railroads was extremely rapid from 1840 onwards. By 1870, the first full year in which the USA could be crossed by rail all the way, more than 50,000 miles (80,000km) were open for traffic. A brief 12 years later this huge figure was doubled and it was doubled again before the turn of the century. Several times more than 10,000 miles (16,000km) were completed in a single twelve-month period. It was an incredible achievement—America had built the railroads, and the railroads built America.

But there was one sad price to pay. As the huge task proceeded, the pressures of this phenomenal rate of expansion meant that there was no time for frills. So the beautifully finished, decorated and often named locomotives of the 1860s and '70s gave way to the plain, unkempt workhorses of the 1890s and after.

A similar rapid expansion occurred in the size of the locomotive fleet. In 1880 there were 18,000 units running, in 1890 30,000, in 1900 38,000 and in 1910 60,000. Over 6,000 were ordered in 1905 alone! But it was not a case of quantity at the expense of quality, for this great leap forward in system size was also one

1. The maps show (reading from top to bottom) the extent of the US railroad system in 1870, the same in 1966, and the AMTRAK passenger network in the 1970s.

2. In the great days of steam, a Denver & Rio Grande Western train pauses in the Royal Gorge of the Arkansas River for passengers to admire the scenery. Note the famous hanging bridge.

3. This picture of a Union Pacific passenger train taking water near Citadel Rock, Wyoming, shows the timber trestles and trusses used in the early days to produce quick results. Replacement with more durable earth fills and ironwork followed soon.

4. The railroads played a key role in the industrial and agricultural development of the United States. This picture, dating from the latter years of the last century, shows freight cars loaded with cotton in the yards of St Louis, Missouri.

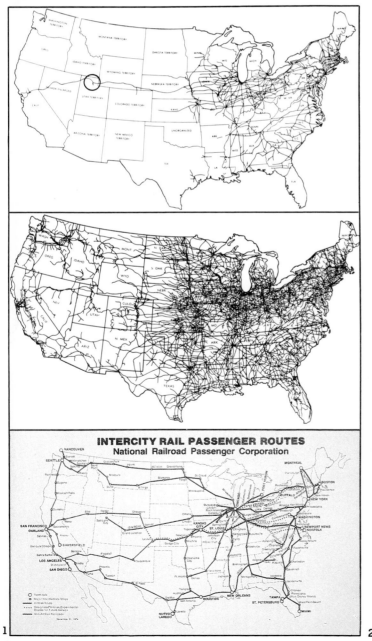

3

4

of great technical and operational advancement. The technical achievements are described in the body of the book, but the operational improvements were equally important.

The railroads were getting really good at the hauling of trains but were apt to forget that the stopping of them was just as essential. The only way to do this satisfactorily was to use an automatic braking system that acted on all the wheels of the train and was under the direct control of the engineer. It also had to go on automatically if the train broke in two and, furthermore, it had to be designed so that it could be applied from the train as well as the locomotive. Even more important than that, a compatible brake had to be chosen and then fitted to each of some million and a half cars belonging to hundreds of railroads in two (later three) independent countries.

The couplers by which one car was connected to another posed another problem which needed urgent solution. Before 1880 most couplings were of the link-and-pin type, notorious for chopping fingers off or even worse, because a man had to stand precariously between a pair of cars being coupled and hold up the link attached to one of them so that it would enter the socket in the other. By 1895 the US Association of Master Car Builders had produced the MCB

1. As common carriers, the railroads had to accept traffic however unwelcome. This view shows the ingenious way in which three early motor trucks could be loaded on a single flat car.

2. A dramatic portrayal of US railroading at its most spectacular period. A Great Northern Railway 4-8-4 takes the luxurious *Empire Builder* train over the Continental Divide near Summit, Montana, en route from Chicago to Seattle.

3. An early steam rotary snow-plough of the Central Pacific Railroad pauses for its picture on a timber trestle bridge high in the Sierra Nevada Mountains. This application of mechanical power revolutionised operations here in winter.

1

coupler which during the next decade would be fitted to virtually every rail vehicle in North America. Thereafter, both ends of every one of them would couple automatically to either end of every other.

During the same years that saw this revolution in operating methods caused by the Westinghouse Brake and the MCB coupler, the capacity of locomotives improved to take advantage of the resulting possibilities of heavier loads and faster speeds. Piston valves ousted slide valves, Walschaert valve gear replaced Stephenson, narrow fireboxes became wide ones and superheating became universal. Power, weight and size increased and the ability to do work more quickly made a fundamental contribution to the prosperity and success of the country. It was line clear ahead for the foreseeable future . . . . Or was it?

1. The cab of a steam locomotive. In the centre is the firehole door with left- and right-hand water gauges above. The throttle lever is on the right, hanging from the roof. Below that is the reversing screw with its circular notched latch plate.

2. Steam survives! The world's largest operable steam locomotive, a Union Pacific articulated "Challenger" 4-6-6-4, at the Sacramento Rail Fair, 1981. Note the two separate engines, each with its own cylinders and Walschaert valve gear.

3. The three-cylinder engine of a "Shay" logging locomotive, the speciality for many years of the Lima Locomotive Works. Shays ran on four-wheel trucks with all wheels driven through gearing and rode on steeper, rougher tracks than other types.

4. The prototype Fairbanks-Morse "Trainmaster" model TM-1 road-switcher diesel-electric locomotive is mounted on its trucks in the company's shops. Only two firms, General Motors and General Electric, now produce main-line locomotives in the USA.

The Automobile Competition

It was in 1909 that Henry Ford launched his Model "T" automobile on an unsuspecting world. His idea was to supply motor cars which were cheap enough to provide convenient transport for ordinary people, whereas previously they had just been playthings for the rich. By 1927 15 million examples of this one model alone had been made and motor cars and trucks were impinging seriously on the railroads' monopoly of mechanical passenger transport. No wonder that significant railroad expansion ceased in 1915, and has been followed by a gentle decline ever since.

In attempting to meet the competition of cars and trucks, the railroads were hampered by government regulations which had been designed to curb their actions at a time when rail transport had a monopoly. There were also problems caused by the Depression; traffic came down by 25 per cent, while locomotive acquisition fell to zero. Since the railroads were not allowed to merge or reduce their routes, they tried to cope with the situation and got at least some short-term advantage by permitting their physical plant to age beyond its economic lifespan. There was certainly no prospect of any such costly improvement as wholesale electrification.

1. Not all railroads had money to spend on equipment. This "Galloping Goose" railcar, built from bits of discarded motor cars, was an economical lash-up used by the fabled Rio Grande Southern RR in remote south-western Colorado during the 1920s.

2. Steam still exists strongly as an instrument of pleasure. A double-shotted tourist train of the narrow-gauge Cumbres & Toltec Scenic RR (once the Denver & Rio Grande) at grips with the hideous 4 per cent grade of the ascent to the Cumbres Pass.

3. A most prestigious train on a most prestigious railroad, the *Super Chief* of the Atchison, Topeka & Santa Fe Railway leaves Chicago for Kansas City and Los Angeles in 1952 behind a neatly assembled set of four General Motors "F" diesel-electric units.

1

2

3

So far as the railroads were concerned, then, World War II was fought with steam, but after it was over the replacements that had been due well before the war had now become urgent necessities. So the stage was set for a rapid replacement of all steam locomotives by diesel-electric units. In making a case for doing this the comparison was always made between brand-new diesels and worn-out steam locomotives. But when modern steam locomotives maintained with modern facilities existed, the case for change was a poor one. It must be admitted, though, that labour troubles in the coal mines did not help steam's cause at that period.

One factor in the equation, perhaps even the key one, was that railroads faced savage competition yet were still treated as a monopoly. Consequently, most were in poor financial shape and could borrow money more easily to buy a diesel fleet than to modernise their roundhouses. The diesels were at least portable assets, often carrying inconspicuous ownership plates reading something like "The Property of the XYZ Equipment Trust Co".

There is one thing that steam enthusiasts can comfort themselves with. If the railroads had modernised with steam instead of dieselising, there would have been just the same holocaust of their favourite classes. Certainly in no way would it have prevented the slaughter of railroad companies and names which has, since the end of World War II, changed things even more than the sad farewell to steam. The state of ▶

1. In the 1950s railroads tried to compete with road and air by introducing radically altered passenger trains but none succeeded. Chicago, Rock Island & Pacific's "Train of Tomorrow" (also known as *Aerotrain*) is now displayed at St Louis.

2. Coal-haulers but oil burners! Typical of American motive power today, a multiple-unit set-up of diesel-electric road-switchers of the Chessie System make ready at Hinton, West Virginia, to take an eastbound coal drag across the Alleghenies.

3. By the end of the 1960s it was realised that inter-state passenger trains could not continue unless funded nationally. Hence the National Railroad Passenger Corporation now marketed as AMTRAK. Here AMTRAK's *Southwest Limited* leaves Chicago for Los Angeles.

1

2

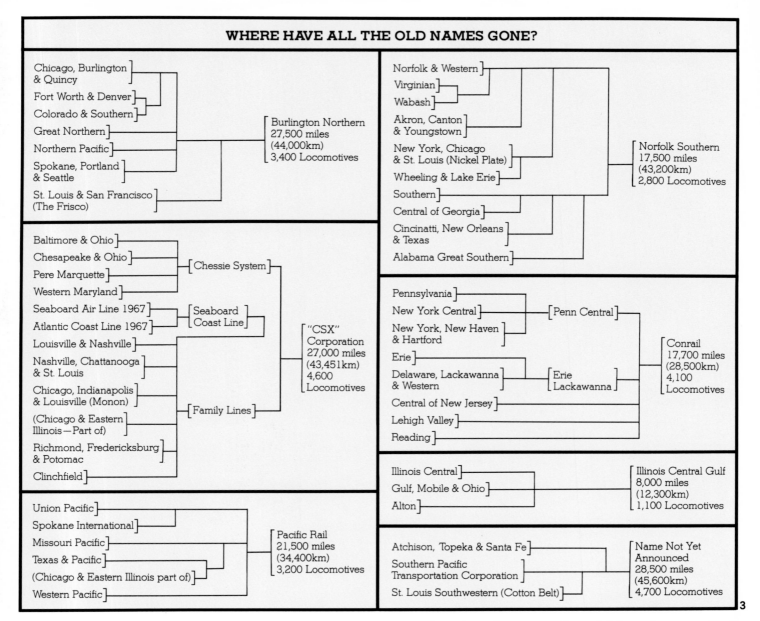

WHERE HAVE ALL THE OLD NAMES GONE?

Chicago, Burlington & Quincy
Fort Worth & Denver
Colorado & Southern
Great Northern
Northern Pacific
Spokane, Portland & Seattle
St. Louis & San Francisco (The Frisco)
→ Burlington Northern 27,500 miles (44,000km) 3,400 Locomotives

Baltimore & Ohio
Chesapeake & Ohio
Pere Marquette
Western Maryland
→ Chessie System

Seaboard Air Line 1967
Atlantic Coast Line 1967
→ Seaboard Coast Line

Louisville & Nashville
Nashville, Chattanooga & St. Louis
Chicago, Indianapolis & Louisville (Monon)
(Chicago & Eastern Illinois — Part of)
Richmond, Fredericksburg & Potomac
Clinchfield
→ Family Lines

→ "CSX" Corporation 27,000 miles (43,451km) 4,600 Locomotives

Union Pacific
Spokane International
Missouri Pacific
Texas & Pacific
(Chicago & Eastern Illinois part of)
Western Pacific
→ Pacific Rail 21,500 miles (34,400km) 3,200 Locomotives

Norfolk & Western
Virginian
Wabash
Akron, Canton & Youngstown
New York, Chicago & St. Louis (Nickel Plate)
Wheeling & Lake Erie
Southern
Central of Georgia
Cincinatti, New Orleans & Texas
Alabama Great Southern
→ Norfolk Southern 17,500 miles (43,200km) 2,800 Locomotives

Pennsylvania
New York Central
New York, New Haven & Hartford
→ Penn Central

Erie
Delaware, Lackawanna & Western
→ Erie Lackawanna

Central of New Jersey
Lehigh Valley
Reading
→ Conrail 17,700 miles (28,500km) 4,100 Locomotives

Illinois Central
Gulf, Mobile & Ohio
Alton
→ Illinois Central Gulf 8,000 miles (12,300km) 1,100 Locomotives

Atchison, Topeka & Santa Fe
Southern Pacific Transportation Corporation
St. Louis Southwestern (Cotton Belt)
→ Name Not Yet Announced 28,500 miles (45,600km) 4,700 Locomotives

3

1. Will electrification play a major part in the future of railroads here? On the only major electrified route on the American continent, an AMTRAK express runs into the Union Station at Washington, D.C., under a cat's cradle of catenaries.

2. The need to find an alternative to the motor car is encouraging the development of rapid transit systems in North America. Here passengers wait for a modern electric train of the Chicago Transit Authority to stop and take them into town.

3. The table shows schematically how the railroads of America have been consolidating into seven big groups during recent years. Some of the mergers still involve only common ownership rather than complete integration so a few old names survive for now.

▶affairs today is that almost 26,000 out of 28,000 US locomotives belong to a mere seven corporate organisations, which have absorbed more than 40 traditional railroads. The table shows how things have worked out.

A few traditional railroad names remain among the Class I railroads—Chicago & North Western, Florida East Coast, Denver & Rio Grande Western, Kansas City Southern, Missouri-Kansas-Texas (the Katy), Pittsburg & Lake Erie and the sad remains of the proud Chicago, Milwaukee, St. Paul & Pacific—but for how long? There are the subsidiaries of US Steel, Canadian National, Canadian Pacific and the various Government- or State-owned railroads like the Alaska RR, the Long Island RR and the National Railroad Passenger Corporation (AMTRAK). Three bankrupts

were abandoned, except for odd lengths parcelled out among their neighbours—New York, Ontario & Western, the Rutland RR and Chicago, Rock Island & Pacific.

The remaining locomotives belong to a multitude of smaller railroads which do not qualify for Class I status by having gross revenues greater than $50 million. They include smaller railroads, short lines as well as a host of new commuter train operating authorities. And we have not considered at all the switching fleets owned by industry.

These consolidations are the most conspicuous reflection of a new freedom for railroads to run their own affairs. This in its turn stems from their being now in the background rather than the foreground of people's lives. More directly it has resulted from some legislation—known as the Staggers Act—enacted in the late 1970s, which removed the crippling restrictions which dated from a century before, when Henry Ford and the Wright brothers were still mere boys, and all-powerful railroad barons said (and acted upon) things like "Let the public be damned".

So now, after more than 50 years of winter for the railroads of the United States, suddenly spring is coming out all over. And if their new freedom were not enough, vast sums in the way of tax rebates (brought about by certain favourable changes in tax legislation) have become available for rehabilitation. Furthermore, ▶

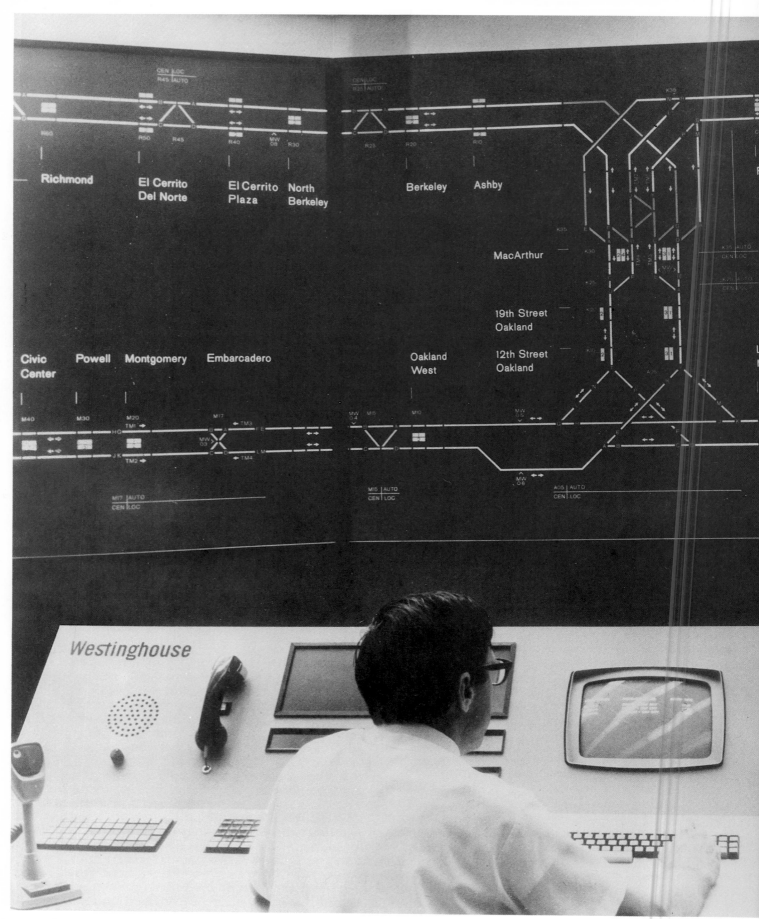

not only is traffic increasing but it is also the kind of traffic for which railroads were first built and are best at handling: huge quantities of coal are being mined in faraway places and need rail transportation.

Cheap and abundant coal also means the possibility of welcoming fundamental changes in the type of motive power the railroads use. Electrification — yes possibly. But there is even the thrilling prospect of our much-mourned friend, the steam locomotive, coming back to life. So the future, then, of the North American locomotive may not be certain, but without doubt it is going to be exciting.

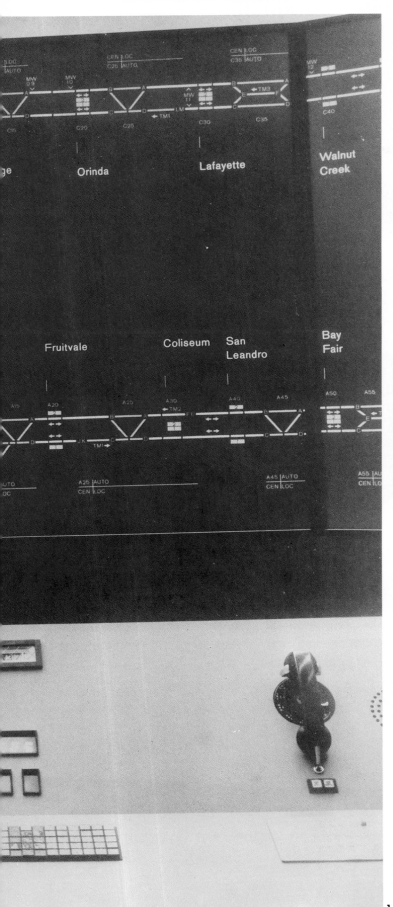

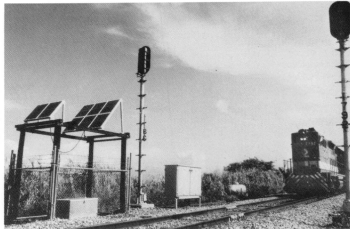

1. Much of North America's rail network is controlled remotely from panels like this one on the BART (Bay Area Rapid Transit) system in California. Here application of automation avoids human intervention more than is possible on regular railroads.

2. Solar power on the railroads. A battery of solar cells are used to power track signals on the Southern Railway.

3. The funding of commuter traffic is no longer the responsibility of the railroads. Here a train of New Jersey Transit passes through Harrison, N.J., for points west in 1982.

4. If they commute by a train of the Grand Trunk System (a subsidiary of Canadian National Railways.) into downtown Detroit, workers can walk to offices in the new Renaissance Centre.

Stourbridge Lion 0-4-0 Delaware & Hudson Canal Company (D&H), 1829

Gauge: 4ft 3in (1,295mm).
Axleload: 8,624lb (3.9t).
Cylinders: (2) 8½ x 36in (215 x 914mm).
Driving wheels: 49in (1,244mm).
Adhesive weight: 15,680lb (7.1t).*
Length overall: 12ft 10.5in (3,924mm).
* without tender.

Choosing the words with care, it must be stated that August 9, 1829 was the first day on which a locomotive intended to be used commercially made a run in America. This event occurred at Honesdale, Pennsylvania, on the light track of the 4ft 3in (1,295mm) gauge horse-operated tramway which belonged to the Delaware & Hudson Canal Company and connected the canal with mines at Carbondale. Horatio Allen, the company's young master mechanic, who had previously visited England to order the locomotive, later wrote describing his feelings as follows: "I took my position on the platform of the locomotive and with my hand on the throttle said, 'If there is any danger in this ride it is not necessary that the life and limb of more than one be subjected to danger'. The locomotive, having no train behind it answered at once to the movement of the hand... soon I was out of sight in the three miles ride alone in the woods of Pennsylvania. I have never run one since."

The locomotive was named *Stourbridge Lion,* and was an 0-4-0 built by Foster & Rastrick of Stourbridge, near Birmingham, England, in what was then the well-named 'Black Country'. It weighed over twice as much as had been promised by the makers when Allen visited them the previous year and so its effect on the track was such that it was decided not to put the *Lion* into service as a locomotive. Instead a use was found for it as a stationary engine. But Allen remained convinced that the future lay with steam, and when his advice was asked concerning motive power for the South Carolina Railroad he came down firmly on the side of mechanical power.

Stourbridge Lion had a sister—an almost identical twin in fact, named *Agenoria.* She was good enough to perform successfully on the Shutt End Railway near Stourbridge in England for over

Right: *D&H replica of the Stourbridge Lion now to be seen in Washington at the Smithsonian Museum.*

Left: *Stourbridge Lion as it might have looked on that memorable day in 1829. Gross overweight cut short what would surely have been a successful life on the track.*

Best Friend of Charleston 0-4-0 Tank South Carolina Railroad (SCRR), 1830

Gauge: 4ft 8½in (1,435mm).
Tractive effort: 453lb (206kg).
Axle load: 4,500lb (2t).
Cylinders: (2) 6 x 16in (152 x 406mm).
Driving wheels: 54in (1,371mm).
Steam pressure: 50psi (3.5kg/cm²).
Grate area: 2.2sq ft (2m²).
Water: 140gall (165 US) (0.64m³).
Adhesive weight: 9,000lb (4t).
Total weight: 9,000lb (4t).
Length overall: 14ft 9in (4,496mm).

History was certainly made on 15th January 1831, the day when the first full-size steam locomotive to be built in the United States went into service. This was *Best Friend of Charleston,* running on the New World's first commercial steam railway, the South Carolina Railroad. This little contraption foreshadowed the building of 170,000 further steam loco-

Gauge: 4ft 8½in (1,435mm).
Tractive effort: circa 1,023lb (464kg).
Axle load: 7,000lb (3.2t).
Cylinders: (2) 9½ x 16in (241 x 406mm).
Driving wheels: 60in (1,524mm).
Boiler: details not recorded.
Boiler pressure: circa 50psi (3.5kg/cm²).
Adhesive weight: circa 7,000lb (3.2t).
Total weight*: 14,000lb (6.4t).
Length overall*: 16ft 5½in (5,017mm).
*Engine only without tender.

As regards express passenger trains, certainly one of the great benefactors of mankind was John B. Jarvis, who in 1832 introduced the pivoted leading truck or bogie into the locomotive story, an idea suggested to him by Robert Stephenson when he visited England. Although very few particulars have survived, this little 4-2-0, originally known as *Experiment,* was the vehicle used. This pathfinding design of locomotive was built at the West Point Foundry in New York and delivered to the M&HRR.

Amongst the features of the locomotive, one notes that the boiler was rather small (copied from Robert Stephenson's "Planet" type) and that there was room for the connecting rods in the space between the sides of the firebox and the main frames, which were situated outside the driving wheels. These in turn were located behind the firebox, as on a Crampton locomotive.

None of these other features

Above: Brother Jonathan, *the first locomotive in the world to have a four-wheel leading truck or bogie.*

became the norm on the world's locomotives, but as regards express passenger locomotives, the four-wheel bogie certainly is much used. It will be found that all the classes of locomotive described in this book have leading four-wheel bogies according to the principle pioneered with *Brother Jonathan.* Incidentally, Brother Jonathan was then an impolite way of referring to the English; no doubt the name was a gesture of triumph at having thrown off any possible continued dependence on English technology.

The idea was to provide guidance by having two wheels pressing against the outer rail of curves as near as possible in a tangential attitude. For any particular radius, or even at a kink in the track, the bogie would take up an angle so that the three contact points between wheel and rail on each side would lie correctly on the curve. This was particularly important on the light rough tracks of the time.

This locomotive demonstrated very clearly that the principle was a sound one and for many years thereafter the majority of American locomotives of all kinds had the advantage of this device. *Brother Jonathan* itself was successful in other ways; converted later to a 4-4-0 it had a long and useful life.

Below: *A replica of* Brother Jonathan, *alias* Experiment.

---

a quarter of a century, so we know that *Lion* would have done well as a locomotive, if allowed to operate. Happily, *Agenoria* has survived and can be seen in London's Science Museum. The most conspicuous difference between the *Lion* and *Agenoria* was that the latter had a much longer smokestack.

The driving mechanism of the Stourbridge twins consisted of what amounted to a pair of single-cylinder beam engines. The beams and linkage effectively reduced the stroke of the cylinders from 36in to 27in. Loose eccentrics engaging with stops fixed to the rear axle worked the valves when running and there was provision to move them by hand for starting.

The design in fact owed much more to William Hedley of *Puffing Billy* fame than to the Stephensons. In 1829 *Puffing Billy* had been running for 16 years and so the *Lion* was built to a well-matured design, the result of a good deal of experience. But it was not to prevail over the direct-drive system which was to be the main feature of some 99 per cent of steam locomotives ever built. Some 120 years were to pass before locomotives with near-vertical cylinders and complicated transmission systems would supersede the Stephenson concept. An excellent replica of the *Stourbridge Lion* is kept at the Smithsonian Museum of Science & Technology at Washington, DC.

---

motives for service in the USA during the years to come. *Best Friend* was constructed at the West Point Foundry in New York in late 1830. Features included a vertical boiler, a well tank integral with the locomotive, four coupled wheels and two modestly inclined cylinders. It was built at the West Point Foundry in New York to the design of E.L. Miller, engineer of the South Carolina Railroad.

Although, apart from the coupled wheels, none of its principles of design were adopted generally, the locomotive was quite successful, but the next one built for this railroad followed the same principles only as regards mechanical parts—the later version had a horizontal boiler, the first to be built in America. Even so, the original design could

Left: Best Friend of Charleston. *Some contemporary accounts tell of additional cylinders driving the tender wheels.*

handle a train of five cars carrying more than 50 passengers at 20mph (32km/h).

In one rather tragic way, however, the locomotive did contribute to the story of steam traction development. The firemen had become annoyed with the noise of steam escaping from the safety valves and used to tie down the lever which controlled them. One day in June 1831 he did this once too often—and the boiler exploded and he was killed. In due time tamper-proof valves became the rule—people normally need shock before they take action.

Later, the locomotive was rebuilt with a new boiler and re-entered service, appropriately named *Phoenix.* By 1834, the South Carolina Railroad went the whole 154 miles from Charleston to Hamburg, just across the river from the city of Augusta, Georgia. When opened, this was by far the longest railway in the world.

Tom Thumb 0-2-2 Baltimore & Ohio Railroad (B&O), 1830

Gauge: 4ft 8½in (1,435mm).
Tractive effort: 820lb (372kg).
Axleload: 5,800lb (2.6t).
Cylinders: (1) 5 x 27in
(127 x 685mm).
Driving wheels: 30in (762mm).
Heating surface: 40sq ft (4m²).
Steam pressure: 90psi
(6.3kg/cm²).
Grate area: 2.7sq ft (0.3m³).
Fuel: 800lb (0.4t).
Water: 52 US gall (0.2m²).
Adhesive weight: 5,800lb (2.6t).
Total weight: 10,800lb (4.9t).
Length overall: 13ft 2in
(4,013mm).

These figures apply to the replica
built in 1927.

The first section of the Baltimore
& Ohio Railroad had been
chartered in 1827. The intention
was that it should be a horse-
worked line, at any rate for the
first section from Baltimore to

Ellicot Mills near Washington, but
after a short length of track had
been laid at the Baltimore end a
certain Peter Cooper offered to
demonstrate the use of steam
traction. His *Tom Thumb* locomotive was little more than a toy,
with a single-cylinder engine and
vertical boiler of which legend
states "the boiler tubes were made
from musket barrels". The tiny
machine pulled a single boat-
shaped car in which the directors
of the Baltimore & Ohio travelled,
and the event was staged as a
race with a horse-drawn vehicle,
on August 28, 1830.

Tom Thumb did fine on the
way out but lost the battle on the
return trip when the belt driving
the fan used to draw the fire

Right: *A replic of the* Tom
Thumb, *the first steam locomotive
to run on the Baltimore & Ohio
Railroad, on August 28, 1830.*

John Bull 0-4-0 (later 4-2-0) Camden & Amboy Railroad, 1831

Gauge: 5ft 0in (1,524mm).
Tractive effort: 765lb (347kg).
Cylinders: (2) 9 x 20in
(228 x 508mm).
Driving wheels: 54in
(1,371mm).

Heating surface: 300sq ft
(28m²).
Steam pressure: 30psi
(2.1kg/cm²).
Grate area: 10sq ft (0.9m²).
Adhesive weight: 44,080lb
(20t).
Length overall: 37ft 0in
(11,277mm).

Just as the world now goes to
General Motors Electro-Motive
Division's plant at La Grange,

Illinois, for locomotives, there was
a time when it went to the works
of George and Robert Stephenson
at Newcastle-upon-Tyne, England.
The little Camden & Amboy line,
an early ancestor of the giant
Pennsylvania Railroad, did just
that in 1830 for a little 0-4-0 based
on the Stephenson's supremely
practical 'Planet' design. Up until
then the portion of the railroad
that was open had relied on horse
power.

The *John Bull* arrived by sea at
Philadelphia in mid-1831 and, after
a further sea voyage to Bordentown,
New Jersey, was erected by the
C&A's young Master Mechanic
Isaac Dripps. This is someone
less-celebrated than he should
be, because it was this man who
first fitted to a locomotive not only
a bell and headlight but the cowcatcher or pilot as well. Although
only 22 when appointed, he had
had a good apprenticeship to

broke. Even so, steam won the war because the B&O management decided to become a steam railroad in the future, although as we shall see, vertical-boilered locomotives were used on their railroad for a considerable time.

The replica depicted here was made to entertain the crowds at the Baltimore & Ohio's 'Centenary Fair of the Iron Horse' in 1927. It was constructed in good faith and certainly demonstrated the principles of the original design, but various features of it do not correspond with contemporary accounts of the locomotive which have come to light since.

Thomas Cooper relates how at the last minute he decided that the natural draught of his little vertical boiler would not draw the fire sufficiently. "I screwed a crooked joint on the top of the smoke stack to hold my blower and carried a belt down over a

wheel on the shaft. . ." he told the Master Mechanics Association in 1875. In the replica there is no sign of the contrivance attached to the chimney, while the blower is down below on the platform. Amongst other differences it is now found that the original had a conspicuous A-frame to support the cylinder and also the platform was mounted much lower, so that the tops of the wheels protruded through.

The sequel to the run of *Tom Thumb* was that the B&O directors decided to set a competition for American manufacturers only, for the best practical steam locomotive to be decided by trials after the style of those which Stephenson's *Rocket* won at Rainhill, England.

Left: *The* Tom Thumb *replica on display for the opening of the California Railroad Museum, Sacramento, in 1981.*

Thomas & Holloway, makers of ships' steam engines. Dripps went on to become superintendent of motive power to the Pennsylvania Railroad at Altoona Shops.

John Bull made a demonstration trip on November 12, 1831, but steam operation did not begin on a regular basis for over a year. No doubt the track needed strengthening and improvement, while the locomotive was also modified. The bell which was first put on the

John Bull is still carried by all North American locomotives today while, until Dripps designed and introduced an oil-burning headlight, which would stand both the vibration and the weather, the only means of lighting the way ahead was a fire in a brazier carried ahead of the chimney. Dripps' pilot was quite different from today's, being carried on its

Above and left: John Bull, *built by George and Robert Stephenson of Newcastle, England, in 1831 for the Camden & Amboy Railroad, is now the oldest steam locomotive in the world still in operable state.*

own pair of wheels. It was a primitive kind of leading truck. The coupling rods with their outside cranks must have given some trouble for they were removed, making the engine into a 4-2-0. The cab now carried was a later addition—the 1830s was not a time when crew comfort was considered very seriously.

One non-Stephenson feature was present, the circular firebox similar to the design used by Edward Bury, locomotive engineer to the London & Birmingham Railway. This item and all the other 'Planet' features were very successful and the locomotive ran in service until 1866. It travelled to the Columbian Exposition at Chicago in 1893 under its own steam and, even more remarkably, the oldest operable locomotive in the World celebrated its own 150th anniversary with another run. *John Bull* can be seen in the Smithsonian Museum in Washington, DC.

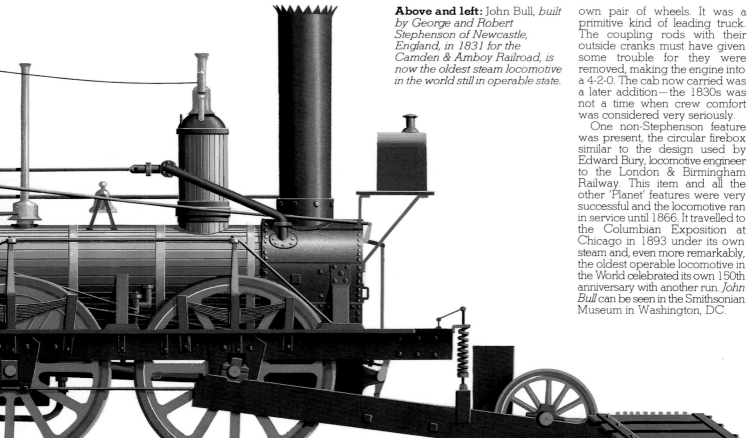

De Witt Clinton Mohawk & Hudson Railroad, 1831

Gauge: 4ft 8½in (1,435mm).
Axleload: 3,526lb (1.6t).
Cylinders: 5½ x 16in (140 x 406mm).
Adhesive weight: 6,750lb (3.1t).
Total weight: 6,750lb* (3.1t).
Overall length 19ft 8in (5,985mm).
*without tender.

In 1831 steam trains began running on the first section of what was one day destined to become the giant New York Central Railroad. The line in question was the 14-mile (22.5km) Mohawk & Hudson Railroad which ran between Albany and Schenectady. Previous operation had been with horses, but on June 25, 1831 the first steam locomotive was delivered by water up the Hudson River from the West Point Foundry at New York. The locomotive was the *De Witt Clinton*, the third locomotive built by this pioneer locomotive works. The previous locomotives, *Best Friend of Charleston* (previously described), and another locomotive *West Point*, had been for the South Carolina Railroad.

De Witt Clinton was designed by John B. Jervis, Chief Engineer of the M&HRR, and like other first attempts it needed some fine tuning. The boiler was domeless and

there was a tendency for water to 'prime', that is boil over and enter the cylinders; this was corrected by adding a dome. The exhaust pipes also needed some adjustment before they would draw the fire properly. But by August 9, all was ready for the first scheduled run. Five stage coach bodies mounted on railroad wheels were

provided, coupled together with chains to form a train. It is said that hundreds wanting to travel were turned away; perhaps it was as well, for the journey was more exciting than comfortable.

The slack action of the chains jerked the cars—particularly the rear ones—violently into motion and upset the passengers a

moment after the locomotive had started. Because of the problems with drawing the fire sufficiently to burn coal, wood was being burnt as a temporary expedient.

Below: *Replica of the 1831* De Witt Clinton *M&HRR in the Henry Ford Museum at Dearborn, Michigan.*

Grasshopper 0-4-0 Baltimore & Ohio Railroad (B&O), 1832

Gauge: 4ft 8½in (1,435mm).
Tractive effort: 4,245lb (1,926kg).
Axleload: 13,580lb (6.2t).
Cylinders: (2) 12 x 22in (304 x 558mm).
Driving wheels: 36in (914mm).
Heating surface: 204sq ft (19m²).
Steam pressure: 75psi (5.3kg/cm²).
Grate area: 11sq ft (1m²).
Fuel (coke): 800lb (0.4t).
Water: 300 US gall (1.1m³).
Adhesive weight: 27,160lb (12.3t).
Total weight: 27,160lb (12.3t).
Length overall: 14ft 7in (4,445mm).

With these so-called "Grasshopper" engines and their successors, the vertical-boilered steam locomotive was taken further on the Baltimore & Ohio Railroad than elsewhere. The name came from the form of the driving mechanism, which carried the *Stourbridge Lion* or *Puffing Billy* line a little further. Vertical cylinders raised and lowered beams connected first to a crankshaft which in its turn was geared to a jackshaft. Cranks on the end of this jackshaft drove the wheels by connecting rods, in the manner which many electric locomotives were to follow. It was the movement of the beams which gave the locomotives their name.

The earliest "Grasshoppers" were built by a firm called Davis & Gartner, one of whose founders was watchmaker Phineas Davis

who built the vertical-boilered locomotive *York*, and was thus the winner of the B&O locomotive competition held in 1831. His company became official locomotive builders to the B&O and completed their *Atlantic* at the Mount Clare Shops in September 1832. The locomotive was quite successful and regularly made a round trip of 80 miles (128km) daily between Baltimore and the inclines at Parr's Ridge. However, longevity was not yet a feature and together with the second "Grasshopper" called *Traveller*, also completed in 1832, *Atlantic* was retired in 1835. The replica *Atlantic*, currently in the B&O museum, is actually one of the later improved "Grasshoppers" (B&O No.7 *Andrew Jackson*) modified to take on the superficial

appearance of the earlier machine.

The first of the new breed was *Arabian*, B&O No.1, delivered in July 1834. By the end of "Grasshopper" production in 1837, 16 had been built. The details were improved and included such advanced ideas as a fan driven exhaust steam to draw the fire, and a feed-water heater, while later examples were more strongly built. This resulted in a weight which was nearly doubled and. was reflected in a life exceeding 50 years, latterly in switching service. Phineas Davis, who originated these engines, was tragically killed in an accident on the railroad in 1836, gave his name to No.9, amongst the Presidents and other famous men whose names decorated the others. After Davis' death, his company

Above: *Grasshopper 0-4-0 No.7* Andrew Jackson *in disguise as the original* Atlantic *together with replica train of the early-1830s for display at the Baltimore & Ohio's Railroad Museum.*

Right: *Replica Grasshopper* Atlantic *and preserved loco* Tom Thumb *outside the Mount Clare shops, Baltimore, where both were built. This is now the site of the Baltimore & Ohio's Railroad Museum.*

became Gillingham & Winans. No.8 *John Hancock* as well as the much altered No.7 survives in the B&O museum. No.8 also masqueraded for a time as No.3 *Thomas Jefferson*. The details given above refer to this locomotive.

So red hot fragments poured out of the chimney, the result being more havoc in the form of burn holes in the clothes of the passengers. Even so, it must have been fun doing the journey at a mind-bending speed of 25mph (40km/h) or so (the average speed was reportedly 18mph—28km/h), watching spectators' horses bolting and, perhaps, being aware that history was being made that day.

The *De Witt Clinton* was very lightly built. The boiler in fact was small enough for there to be room for the connecting rods between it and the timber frame, for the cylinders were mounted at the rear. The performance was excellent and no damage was caused to the wooden rails strapped with iron which formed the track, but the flimsy construction of the locomotive did not help with solving the problem of achieving longevity, for the locomotive was retired a year or two after going into service. A replica was built in 1893 for the World's Columbian Exposition held at Chicago and is now in the Ford Museum at Dearborn.

Right: *The replica* De Witt Clinton *re-enacting its inaugural trip from Albany to Schenectady on that memorable day in 1831.*

'Mud-digger' 0-8-0 Baltimore & Ohio Railroad (B&O), 1844

Gauge: 4ft 8½in (1,435mm).
Axleload: 12,925lb (5.9t).
Cylinders: (2) 17 x 24in
(432 x 610mm).
Driving wheels: 33in (838mm).
Adhesive weight: 47,000lb
(21.3t).
**Total weight* 47,000lb
(21.3t).**
Total weight*: 47,000lb (21.3t).
Length overall*: 49ft 10in
(6,045mm).
*Without tender.

Ross Winans was a horse-dealer who called on the Baltimore & Ohio Railroad in the early days with the idea of selling them motive power. He was not at all put out at finding they had gone over to steam and stayed on to sell and build iron horses instead. He was appointed assistant engineer of machinery in 1831 and four years later, as Gillingham & Winans, took over locomotive building in the B&O Mount Clare shops from Phineas Davis (Davis & Gartner). He completed his predecessors' 'Grasshopper' programme, but by 1837; had ready for production his own (patent) design known as 'Winan's Crab'.

Because of the adoption of horizontal cylinders, the Crabs came one short step closer to conventionality when compared with the Grasshoppers. The separate crankshaft gearing and crankshaft remained however, as well as a vertical boiler. Because of the gearing the cranks turned the opposite way to the wheels, hence the supposedly crab-like gait. Two 0-4-0 crabs, *McKim* and *Mazeppa,* were built by Gillingham & Winans for the B&O and were delivered in 1838. They

Campbell 4-4-0 Philadelphia, Germantown & Norriston Railroad (PG&NRR), 1837

Gauge: 4ft 8½in (1,435mm).
Tractive effort: 4,373lb
(1,984kg).
Axle load: 8,000lb (3.6t)..
Cylinders: (2) 14 x 15¾in
9356 x 400mm).
Driving wheels: 54in.
(1,370mm).
Heating surface: 723sq ft
(67.2m²).
Superheater: None.
Steam pressure: 90psi
(6.3kg/cm²).
Grate area: Circa 12sq ft (1.1m²).
Adhesive weight: 16,000lb
(7.25t).
Length overall:* 16ft 5½in
(5,017mm).
*Engine only — tender details not known.

Henry Campbell, engineer to the Philadelphia, Germantown & Norriston Railroad had the idea of combining coupled wheels, as fitted to *Best Friend of Charleston,* with the leading truck of *Brother Jonathan.* In this way he could double the adhesive weight, while at the same time have a locomotive that could ride

satisfactorily round sharp or irregular curves. He patented the idea and went to a local mechanic called James Brooks (not the Brooks who founded the famous Brooks Loco Works of Dunkirk,

New York) and he produced the world's first 4-4-0 in May 1837.

Although in fact this locomotive was intended for coal traffic, it has its place here as the prototype of perhaps the most numerous

and successful of all passenger-hauling wheel arrangements.

The layout of *Brother Jonathan* was followed, the additional driving axle being coupled to the first by cranks outside the frames. The cylinders were thus inside the frames, driving the leading coupled wheels by means of a crank axle, an arrangement which was to become popular on a few railways back in Europe, even if very rarely repeated in America. The high boiler pressure is notable for the time. Whilst this remarkable locomotive demonstrated great potential, the flexibility provided in order to cope with poorly lined tracks was not accompanied with flexibility in a vertical plane to help with the humps and hollows in them. In consequence, Campbell's 4-4-0 was not in itself successful.

Above: *The world's first 4-4-0, designed by Henry R. Campbell, engineer to the Philadelphia, Germantown and Norriston Railroad. It was built in 1837 by James Brooks of Philadelphia.*

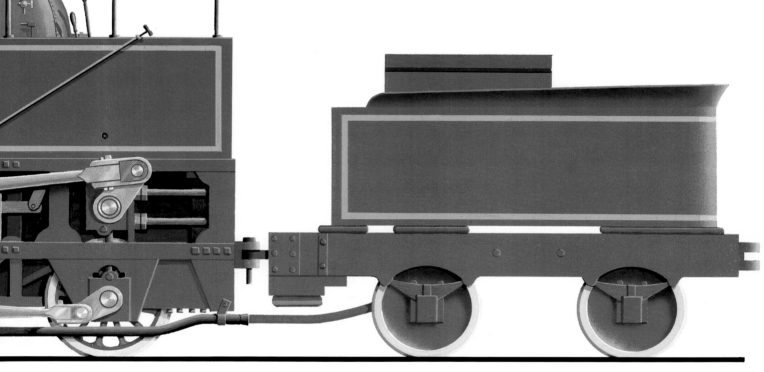

Below: *0-8-0 'Mud-digger' class locomotive, built by Gillingham and Winans for the Baltimore & Ohio Railroad, 1844.*

gave good service, lasting until 1863 and 1868 respectively.

Out of the Crabs came the relatively enormous 0-8-0 'Mud-diggers'. This time (after the first few which did not go to the B&O), a proper locomotive boiler was used, but the layout of the machinery was unchanged, apart from the two extra axles. The first one was appropriately named *Hercules* and there were 13 more, all built between 1844 and 1847.

Seven of the Mud-diggers were rebuilt completely on more conventional lines between 1853 and 1856, losing their names in the process. The remainder soldiered on for many years, the last (No.41

Elk) being retired in 1880.

The last of these locomotives to be built (No.49 *Mount Clare*) was rather different from the others. It was built by the B&O itself rather than Winans, had no geared drive and was inside-connected. The cylinders drove on to a jackshaft mounted between the second and third axles. The jackshaft was connected to the wheels by outside cranks and an additional pair of coupling rods. As regards the Mud-digger class as a whole, it was the outside cranks moving so close to the ground—where they were liable to stir up dirt, stones and mud—that produced the evocative name.

Hercules 4-4-0 Beaver Meadows Railroad, 1837

Gauge: 4ft 8½in (1,435mm).
Tractive effort: 4,507lb (2,045kg).
Axle load: circa 10,000lb (4.5t).
Cylinders (2) 12 x 18in (305 x 457mm).
Driving wheels: 44in (1,117mm).
Steam pressure: 90lb/sq in (6.3kg/cm²).
Adhesive weight: circa 20,000lb (9t).
Total weight: *30,000lb (14t).
Length overall: * 18ft 11in (2,564mm).
*Without tender—boiler and tender details not recorded.

In 1836, the Beaver Meadows Railroad ordered a 4-4-0 from Garrett & Eastwick, in nearby Philadelphia. The workshop foreman, Joseph Harrison, had become aware of the problems encountered by Henry Campbell in keeping all the wheels of his 4-4-0 pressing on the rail, yet he also remembered 4-2-0 *Brother Jonathan* of 1832 which sat on the rough tracks like a three-

legged stool on the floor. The saying "right as a trivet" comes vividly to mind, the three legs being, respectively, the two driving wheels and the pivot of the leading bogie or truck. There was also the example of one or

two early 4-2-0s by Norris, also of Philadelphia. Harrison had the idea of making his two pairs of driving wheels into a kind of non-swivelling bogie by connecting the axle bearings on each side by a large cast iron beam,

pivoted at its centre. The pivots were connected to the main-frame of the locomotive by a large leaf spring on either side.

In this way eight wheels were made to support the body of the locomotive at three points. It was a brilliant notion which solved the problem of running on rough tracks and was the basis of the three-point compensated springing system which was applied to most of the world's locomotives from simple ones up to 4-12-2s.

Hercules was well named and many similar locomotives were supplied. Joseph Harrison was made a partner in the firm which (since Garrett was retiring) became known as Eastwick & Harrison. The famous "American Standard" 4-4-0, of which 25,000 were built for the USA alone, was directly derived from this most innovative engine.

Above: Hercules, *built by Garrett & Eastwick of Philadelphia in 1836, marked an important step forward in locomotive development.*

Lafayette 4-2-0 Baltimore & Ohio Railroad (B&O), 1837

Below: *A typical standard Norris 4-2-0 locomotive is portrayed in this side view. The elementary controls of a locomotive of the 1830s can all be clearly seen. The horizontal handle behind the firebox is the throttle, while the* *vertical one alongside the firebox controls the "gab" reversing gear. The spring balance pressure gauge is above the firebox together with the whistle. A brake on the engine was regarded as a luxury.*

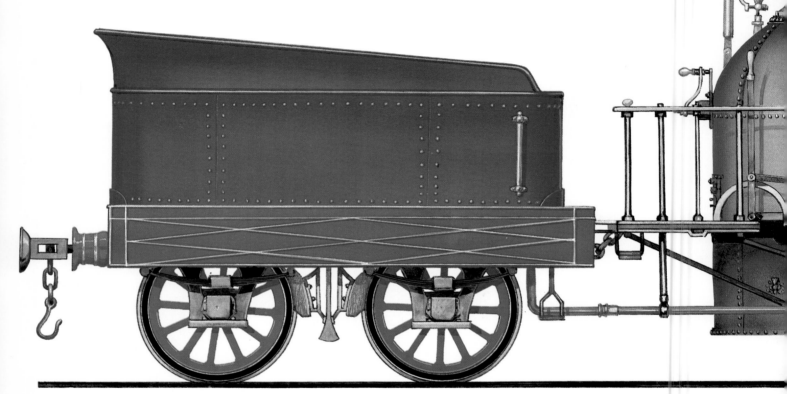

Gauge: 4ft 8½in (1,435mm).
Tractive effort: 2,162lb (957kg).
Axle load: 13,000lb (6t).
Cylinders: (2) 10½ x 18in (268 x 457mm).
Driving wheels: 48in (1,220mm).
Heating surface: 394sq ft (36.6m²).
Superheater: None.
Steam pressure: 60psi (4.2kg/cm²).
Grate area: 8.6sq ft (0.8m²).
Fuel (coke): 2,200lb (1t).
Water: 450gall (540 US) (2m³).
Adhesive weight: 30,000lb (5t).
Total weight: 44,000lb (20t).
Length overall: 30ft 40¼in (9,250mm).

The so-called Norris locomotives have a very important place in locomotive history, being a design which took steam-powered rail transport another great step forward.

William Norris had been building locomotives in Philadelphia since 1831. Although a draper by trade, after a few years in partnership with a Colonel

Stephen Long, he set up on his own and by the beginning of 1836 had produced some seven locomotives. In that year he built a 4-2-0 for the Philadelphia & Columbia Railroad called *Washington County Farmer*. In arrangement it bore some resemblance to *Brother Jonathan* with leading bogie, but the two cylinders were outside the wheels and frames and the valves were on top of the cylinders. The driving wheels were in front of rather than behind the firebox, so increasing the proportion of the engine's weight carried on them.

In this way the final form of the steam express passenger locomotive had almost arrived. *Northumbrian* had the locomotive-type boiler and two outside cylinders; *Planet* had the cylinders at the front while Forrester's *Vauxhall* had cylinders outside and at the front. Bury's locomotives had the bar frames and *Brother Jonathan* had the bogie. Now we find outside cylinders, bar frames and a leading bogie in combination.

In 1827, the Baltimore & Ohio Railroad was the first public railroad for passengers and

freight transport to receive a charter. It was opened for twelve miles out of Baltimore in 1830, but for a number of years horses provided haulage power—although there were trials with steam locomotives. Steam took over in 1834 in the form of vertical-boiler locomotives, which came to be known as the "Grasshopper" type.

The Ohio River was reached in 1842 via a route which then included a series of rope-worked inclined planes, but long before this more powerful locomotives than could be encompassed within the vertical-boiler concept were needed. The B&O management were impressed with Norris' *Washington County Farmer* and asked him to build a series of eight similar engines. The first was *Lafayette* delivered in 1837; it was the first B&O locomotive to have a horizontal boiler. Edward Bury's circular domed firebox and bar frames were there and the engine is said to have had cam-operated valves of a pattern devised by Ross Winans of the B&O. It says enough that later members of the class had the normal "gab" motion of the period.

In those high and far-off times all the Baltimore & Ohio's locomotives (indeed, this applied to most US railroads in those days) had names as well as numbers. So *Lafayette* was followed in 1838 by three more, *Philip E. Thomas*, *J.W.Patterson*, *Wm. Cooke*, and in 1839 by *Patapsco*, *Monocacy*, *Potomac* and *Pegasus*. *Pegasus* was the last to be retired, in 1863, although the *Philip E. Thomas*, which was rebuilt as a 4-4-0 in 1848, managed to survive until 1870.

After 1839 the B&O went on to buy 4-4-0 locomotives to serve a line which now extended 178 miles (285km) from Baltimore. Even so, within the limitation of the low adhesive weight implicit in a single driving axle, the Norris locomotives were a success, giving much better performance at reduced fuel consumption. They were also relatively reliable and needed few repairs. The same year Norris built a similar locomotive for the Champlain & St. Lawrence Railway in Canada. This was the first proper locomotive exported from America, and the hill-climbing ability of these remarkable locomotives was the main factor that

led to many further sales abroad.

The first Old World customer was the Vienna-Raab Railway and their locomotive *Philadelphia* was completed in late 1837. Before the locomotive was shipped it was put to haul a train weighing 200 tons up a 1 in 100 (1 per cent) gradient, a feat then described as the greatest performance by a locomotive engine so far recorded. Railways in Austria (not the small republic we know today but a great empire also embracing much of what is now Czechoslovakia, Poland, Roumania and Jugoslavia) were the best customers, but even before 1840 Norris had also sent his 4-2-0s to the Brunswick and Berlin & Potsdam Railways in Germany.

A large fleet of 15 locos went to the Birmingham and Gloucester Railway in Britain, where they had some success in easing the problems involved in taking trains up the 1 in 37 (2.7 per cent) Lickey Incline at Bromsgrove in Worcestershire.

The demand for Norris locomotives was so great that the firm was able to offer the design in a range of four standard sizes. Class "C" had a cylinder bore of

9in (229mm), class "B" 10½in (268mm), class "A" 11½in (292mm), class "A extra" 12½in (318mm). Grate areas were, respectively, 6.4, 7.3, 7.9 and 9.5sq ft (0.6, 0.69, 0.73 and 0.88m²) while engine weights were 15,750, 20,600, 24,100 and 29,650lb (7.1, 9.4, 10.9 and 13.45t).

The Norris locomotives which went to England were particularly interesting as of course the English railway engineers were more accustomed to sending engines abroad rather than importing them. Seventeen locomotives were sent from Philadelphia between March 1839 and May 1842 and they included examples of the three larger out of the four standard Norris sizes. There were nine B's, three A's and five A extras, the latter of which were used as bankers on the heavy grade.

Certain improvements were made to reduce what was originally a very high coal consumption on the arduous banking duties. All five A-extras were converted to tank locomotives and this saved hauling the weight of the tenders. Steam blown from the safety valves and some ex-

haust steam was turned back into the new saddle tanks. Copper fireboxes replaced iron ones and various other examples of rather shaky workmanship replaced. The result was that a coal consumption of 92lb/mile (26kg/km) which prevailed in 1841 was reduced by some 53 per cent by 1843.

The best of the Norris engines remained in service until 1856.

In his native America, Norris' list of other customers in the 1830s included 27 predecessors of the railroads of the great age of steam, situated in Connecticut, Georgia, Louisiana, Maryland, Massachusetts, New York State, North Carolina, Pennsylvania, Tennessee and Virginia. One of them, the Richmond, Fredericksburg and Potomac Railroad, is even still trading under the same name today. Norris went on to become for a time the largest locomotive builder in the USA, supplying 4-4-0s, 0-6-0s and finally 4-6-0s in addition to the 4-2-0s which made his name. On the other hand the success of these engines in Europe did not bring commensurate prosperity there. Although William Norris and his brother Octavius went to

Vienna in 1844 and set up a locomotive building plant, it was other builders who were to adopt Norris' ideas, eventually produce hundreds of locomotives based on them, and who therefore enjoyed the financial gain.

The first of the European builders who built Norris-type locomotives was John Haswell of Vienna. Others were Sigl, also of Vienna and Guenther of Austria, Cockerill of Belgium, Borsig, Emil Kessler and his successor the Esslingen Co of Germany. In Britain, Hick of Bolton and Nasmyth of Manchester also built 4-2-0s of this pattern. A 4-2-0 called *La Junta* supplied to Cuba circa 1840 was for many years preserved at the United Railways of Havana station in Havana. No reports have been received either of its survival or destruction. A full-size replica of an early Norris locomotive was constructed in the USA about 1941 and was reported to be preserved on the Tallulah Falls Railway in northern Georgia. A working replica of *Lafayette* herself is housed in the B&O museum in the old Mount Clare shops at Baltimore, Maryland.

John Stevens 6-2-0 Camden & Amboy Railroad, 1849

Gauge: 4ft 8½in (1,435mm).
Cylinders: (2) 13 x 34in (330 x 863mm).
Driving wheels: 96in (2,438mm).
Grate area: 15.2sq ft (11.4m²).
Total weight: 50,000lb (22.7t).*
Length overall: 29ft 8in (9,042mm).*
*without tender

In the 1840s a man called Thomas Russell Crampton had patented a strange type of locomotive which had just one pair of very large driving wheels, the axle of which was mounted behind the boiler. The idea was to keep rotational speed down, while also keeping a very low centre of gravity because the boiler no longer had to be above the wheels. He impressed many railway managers, particularly in Belgium and France, and about 320 locomotives were made to

his ideas. In France, the expression 'le Crampton' was slang for 'le train' over many years.

Robert Stevens, President of the Camden & Amboy Railroad, visited Europe in 1845 and came back enthused with Crampton's thinking. He soon arranged for several similar but even more amazing-looking contrivances to be built by Norris & Co. The first was completed in 1849 and was named after the John Stevens who in 1825 built a small model

demonstration locomotive which he ran on a short circular railroad on his estate at Hoboken, New Jersey. Seven 6-2-0s were built in all over the next three years.

Crampton engines were very fast but lacked adhesive weight so they were only really suitable for light trains, and because the trains were fast they were popular and so ceased to be light. Even so these particular examples lasted until the early-1860s, although by then some if not all had been

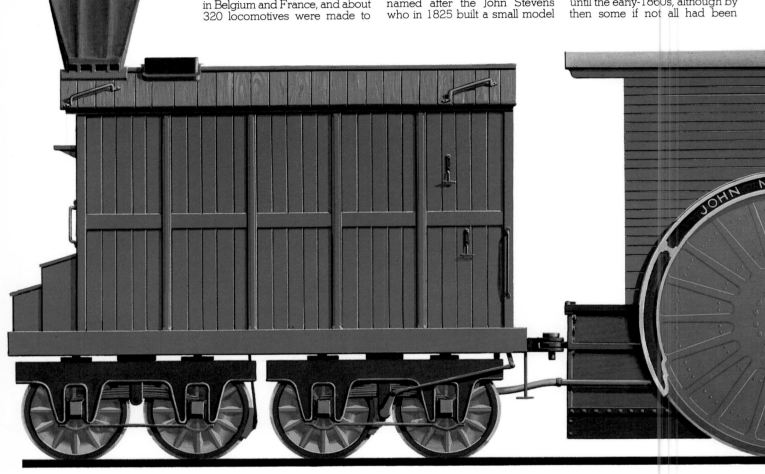

Camel 4-6-0 Baltimore & Ohio Railroad (B&O)

Gauge: 4ft 8½in (1,435mm)
Tractive effort: 6,775lb (3,074kg).
Axleload: 20,716lb (9.4t).
Cylinders: (2) 19 x 22in (482 x 558mm).
Driving wheels: 50in (1,270mm).
Heating surface: 881sq ft (82m²).
Steam pressure: 65psi (4.6kg/cm²).
Grate area: 17.2sq ft (1.6m²).
Fuel: 6,000lb (2.7t).
Water: 2,000US gall (7.6m³).
Adhesive weight: 56,500lb (25.6t).
Total weight: 77,100lb (35t).
Length overall: 52ft 5in (15,976mm).

It was 25 years after the Baltimore & Ohio Railroad received its charter that the line finally reached the Ohio River at Wheeling, Virginia. To handle the expected increase of traffic over sections which included grades up to 2.2 per cent (1-in-45), Samuel Hayes, who was "Master of Machinery",

devised these ten-wheeler 4-6-0s. They were a development of Ross Winans' 0-8-0 *Camel* design, of which some 20 had been built between 1848 and 1852. The 0-8-0s were prone to derail when asked to run at above coal-train speeds and so a leading truck was indicated, yet something with

more tractive effort and power than a 4-4-0 was also needed.

As on the older 0-8-0s, the firebox of the new engines was a long one situated behind the driving wheels. The fireman's platform was located low down and close to the wheels. He himself was separated from the engineer,

who conned his steed from a cab mounted on top of and half-way along the boiler. The big firebox was designed to be specially suitable for burning the anthracite coal then mined in huge quantities in the Eastern States.

The result was this unusual and impressive design of which 17

rebuilt into more conventional 4-4-0s.

John Stevens and his companions were intended to burn anthracite but both the grate area and the firebox would have been on the small size even for bituminous coal. So there were problems of steam generation as well as lack of adhesion. The boiler barrel was no larger in diameter than the wheels of the leading truck

and smaller than the amazing smokestack. At the same time, a notable feature was the valve gear operated by a return crank just as in a modern steam locomotive. There were also double valves to control admission and cut-off separately.

As regards looks, nothing quite as bizarre has ever been seen on rails either before or since. The designers may have copied Crampton's principles but they were certainly not followers when it came to matters of detail, possibly influenced by a wish to avoid infringing the Crampton patents. Hidden away were the spiral seams of the boiler barrel, but painfully obvious were those amazing 8ft driving wheels made of wrought iron with a wood in-fill between the spokes! Then there was the

connecting rod with wire bracing! And we hardly dare think of that garden shed on top of the boiler as a conning tower for the engineer—even Crampton never thought of that one! Such was the greatest locomotive joke in 170 years of railway history.

Below: *Was there ever a more curious-looking locomotive than John Stevens? But the strange design did incorporate some notable features, and the locos remained in service for more than 20 years.*

Left: *One of Ross Winans' 0-8-0 "Camels".*

Right: *A "Hayes' ten-wheeler" Camel 4-6-0.*

were built in 1853 and 1854. For the first time a whole locomotive class on the B&O failed to receive names. Even so, they were clearly excellent, several lasting in normal service for over 40 years. Another pointer to their qualities was that Hayes' successor, Henry Tyson, had another batch of nine built in 1857, similar in appearance but different in design, and these also had long lives. A further group of 109 was built between 1869 and 1875, under the regime of Master Mechanic J. C. Davies. One of these (No.217—to which the details given above apply) survives in the B&O museum at Baltimore, but No.173 of the original Hayes design is kept at the National Museum of Transport at St Louis, Missouri.

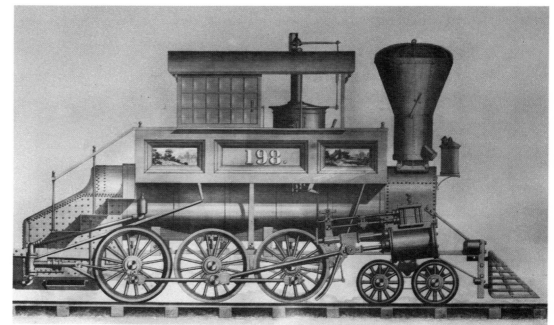

American Type 4-4-0 Western & Atlantic Railroad (W&ARR), 1855

Gauge: Various (see text).
Tractive effort: 6,885lb (3,123kg).
Axle load: 21,000lb (9.5t).
Cylinders: (2) 15 x 24in (381 x 610mm).
Driving wheel: 60in (1,524mm).
Heating surface: 98.0sq ft (91m²).
Superheater: None.
Steam pressure: 90psi (6.35kg/cm²).
Grate area: 14.5sq ft (1.35m²).
Fuel: (wood) 2 cords (7.25m³).
Water: 1,250 gall (2,000 US) (5.75m³).
Adhesive weight: 43,000lb (19.5t).
Total weight: 90,000lb (41t).
Length overall: 52ft 3in (15,926mm).

The *General* was built by Thomas Rogers of Paterson, New Jersey in 1855 and it is a wholly appropriate example of the most numerous and successful locomotive design ever to have been built. The reason is that Rogers was responsible for introducing most of the features which made the true "American" the success it was. The most significant development, so far as the USA was concerned was the general introduction of Stephenson's link motion, which permitted the expansive use of steam. This was in place of the "gab" or "hook" reversing gears used until then, which permitted only "full forward" and "full backward" positions.

In other aspects of design Rogers gained his success by good proportions and good detail rather than innovation. An example was the provision of adequate space between the cylinders and the driving wheels, which reduced the maximum angularity of the connecting rods and hence the up-and-down forces on the slide bars. A long wheelbase leading truck (in English, bogie) allowed the cylinders to be horizontal and still clear the wheels. This permitted direct attachment to the bar frames, which raised inclined cylinders did not.

To allow flexibility on curves, early examples of the breed inherited flangeless leading driving wheels from their progenitors, but by the late 1850s the leading trucks were being given side movement to produce the same effect. Naturally the compensated spring suspension system giving three-point support to the locomotive was continued. Wood-burning was also nearly universal in these early years of the type, and the need to catch the sparks led to many wonderful shapes in the way of spark-arresting smokestacks.

Within two or three years other makers such as Baldwin, Grant, Brooks Mason, Danforth and Hinkley began offering similar locomotives. To buy one of these locomotives one did not need to be a great engineer steeped in the theory of design—it was rather like ordering a car today. One filled in a form on which certain options could be specified and very soon an adequate and reliable machine was delivered.

Speeds on the rough light tracks of a pioneer land were not high—average speeds of 25mph (40km/h) start-to-stop, implying a maximum of 40mph (64km/h), were typical of the best expresses. Although the 4-4-0s were completely stable at high speeds, the increased power required meant

that by the 1880s a bigger breed of 4-4-0 as well as "Ten-wheelers" (4-6-0s) were taking over from the "American".

There was another revolution taking place too. The earlier years of the type were characterised by romantic names and wonderful brass, copper and paint work, but the last quarter of the nineteenth century was a time of cut-throat competition, with weaker roads going to the wall. There was no question of there being anything to spare for frills of this kind—so it was just a case of giving a coat of bitumen and painting big white running numbers in the famous 'Bastard Railroad Gothic' fount on the tender sides.

For most of the second half of the nineteenth century this one type of locomotive dominated railroad operations in the USA. It was appropriately known as the "American Standard" and

Above: *Union Pacific's 4-4-0 No.119, veteran of the Golden Spike ceremony, on show at the 1948 Chicago Rail Fair.*

about 25,000 of them were built, differing only marginally in design. The main things that varied were the decor and the details. They were simple, ruggedly constructed machines appropriate for what was then a developing country; at the same time a leading bogie and compensated springing made them suitable for the rough tracks of a frontier land.

The subject of the specification above is perhaps the most famous of all the 25,000. The *General* came to fame when hijacked by a group of Union soldiers who had infiltrated into Confederate territory during the American civil war. The idea was to disrupt communications behind the lines, in particular on the 5ft (1,524mm)

Below: *Typical United States "Standard" 4-4-0 illustrating the elaborate decor that was often applied in the early years of American railroading but which was abandoned in the 1880s.*

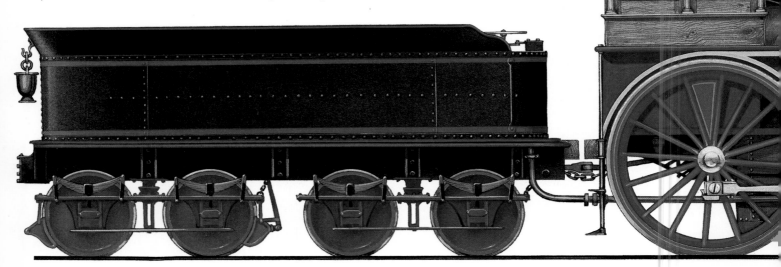

gauge line 135 miles (216km) long connecting Atlanta with Chattanooga. The Union forces were approaching Chattanooga after their victory at Shiloh and the Confederates were expected to bring up reinforcements by rail. There was a major trestle bridge at a place called Oostenabula and the intention was to steal a train, take it to the site and burn the bridge. A replacement would take weeks to build.

The Union force, twenty in number under the command of a Captain Andrews, having stayed overnight at a place called Marietta and having bought tickets to travel on the train, took over the locomotive at a place called Big Shanty, some 30 miles (48km) north of Atlanta, while the passengers and crew were having breakfast in the depot's eating house. The conductor of the train, whose name was Fuller, gave chase first on a handcart and then on a small private ironworks loco, the *Yonah*.

The raiders' intention was to cut telegraph wires behind them, remove the occasional rail and demand immediate passage at stations they came to in the name of Confederate General Beauregard. A problem Andrews faced was the presence of trains coming the other way on the single line and perhaps the game was lost at Kingston where he had to wait an hour and twenty five minutes until one divided into two sections had finally arrived.

In the end the *Yonah* arrived there only four minutes after Andrews and the *General* had left. Here Fuller took over another "American" 4-4-0, the *Texas* and after this Andrews never got enough time to block the track

before what had now become a Confederate posse came within rifle range. In the end, after eight hours and 87 miles the *General* expired when it ran out of fuel; the Union group then scattered into the woods. All were later captured and seven of the senior men shot.

Leaving out the human drama for a moment two qualities of the "American Standards" emerge from this affair. First, in spite of the rough track high maximum speeds of around 60mph (100 km/h) were reached during the chase and both locomotives stayed on the rails. The second thing was that the range between fuel stops was very short. A full load of two cords of wood fuel (a cord is 128cu ft or 3.62m²) would last for a mere 50 miles (80km).

Both the *General* and the *Texas* (or what purports to be them) have survived. The former, normally in store at Chattanooga, is occasionally run. Oil fuel is used, the tank being concealed under a fake woodpile. The *Texas*, as befits a Confederate conqueror, has an honoured place in Grant Park at Atlanta. Both were converted from the 5ft (1,524mm) gauge of the Western & Atlantic Railroad after the war was over.

The American Civil War was one of the first great wars to be

fought using railway transportation, most of which was provided on both sides by this "American" type. The earliest transcontinental railroads were first built and then operated by them; the well-known picture of the last spike ceremony at Promontory, Utah, has placed the Central Pacific's *Jupiter* and the Union Pacific No.119 second only to the *General* on the scale of locomotive fame. It is said that "America built the railroads and the railroads built America"; substitute "American 4-4-0" for "railroad" and the saying is equally true.

The "American" type was a universal loco; the only difference between those built for passenger traffic and those for freight was between 66in (1,676mm) diameter driving wheels and 60in (1,524mm). It also served all the thousands of railroad companies who then operated America's 100,000 miles (160,000km) of line, from roads thousands of miles long to those a mere ten.

The last "American" class in the USA did not retire from normal line service for more than a century after Rogers put the first on the rails in 1852. A few survive in industrial use in the remoter parts of the world even today. Numerous examples are preserved in museums and elsewhere all over North America, a few (a very few) perform on tourist railroads.

Above: *American Standard 4-4-0 as refurbished to resemble the Central Pacific RR's* Jupiter, *ready to re-enact the completion ceremony of the first transcontinental railroad at the Golden Spike National Monument, in Utah.*

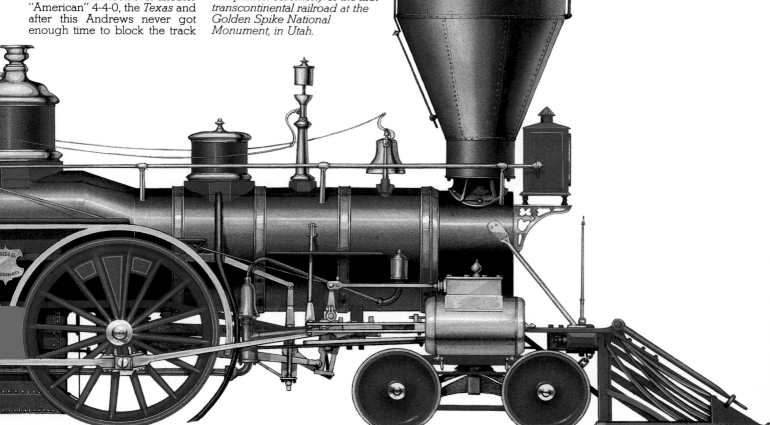

Consolidation 2-8-0 Lehigh Valley Railroad (LVR), 1866

Gauge: 4ft 9in (1,447mm).
Tractive effort: 21,061lb (9,556kg).
Axleload: 24,200lb (11t).
Cylinders: (2) 20x24in (508x609mm).
Driving wheels: 48in (1,219mm).
Heating surface: 1,281sq ft (119m²).
Steam pressure: 130psi (9.1kg/cm²).
Grate area: 27.6sq ft (2.6m²).
Adhesive weight: 88,000lb (39.9t).
Total weight: 100,000lb (45.4t).*
Length overall: 33ft 10in (10,312mm).*
*Locomotive only. Tender details not available.

Locomotives of the 2-8-0 wheel arrangement were built in the USA from 1866 onwards and by 1946 about 24,000 had been supplied to railroads all over the world. Tractive effort varied from 14,000lb (6,352kg) for narrow-gauge examples up to 94,000lb (42,650kg) for one fitted with a booster tender and built for the Delaware & Hudson Railway in the 1920s. They were all intended for freight work, with occasional use hauling passenger trains on steeply-graded lines.

The name "Consolidation", now universally applied to the type, came from the first of some heavy freight locomotives supplied to the Lehigh Valley Railroad in 1866, just as that company had been formed by means of a consolidation of a number of smaller railroads in the area. They were intended to work trains up the Mahoney Hill which had a grade of 2.5 per cent (1-in-40).

To traverse curves easily, the two centre pairs of driving wheels were flangeless. The connecting rods drove on to the third axle,

Mogul 2-6-0 Rogers Locomotive & Machine Works (Rogers), 1863

Gauge: 4ft 8½in (1,435mm).
Tractive effort: 13,055lb (5,923kg).
Axleload: 20,900lb (9.5t).
Cylinders: Two 16x24 (406x609mm).
Driving wheels: 48in (1,219mm).
Heating surface: 1,255sq ft (117m²).
Steam pressure: 120psi (8.4kg/cm²).
Grate area: 17sq ft (1.6m²).
Water: 2,880 US gal (10.9m³).
Adhesive weight: 57,000lb (25.9t).
Total weight: *7,000lb (31.8t).
Length overall: 55ft 0in (16,764mm).
*Locomotive without tender.

It is surprising to us, thinking 120 years later, that the name 'Mogul' should have been applied to the 2-6-0 type on account of its power. The idea was to have a locomotive the size of a 4-4-0 but with one guiding and three driving axles instead of two and two respectively. In principle there would then be 50 per cent greater adhesion and consequently the same amount more pulling ability. The basis was an idea of a New Yorker called Levi Bissel who in 1858 had patented a new kind of leading truck which could move sideways as well as swivel. Both two- and four-wheel trucks were

provided for. Inclined planes gave a self-centring action and in this way the two essential and previously incompatible elements of flexibility and stability could both be present.

William Hudson of the Rogers Locomotive Works, Paterson, New Jersey, developed the principle by replacing the inclined planes with swing links and also connected the truck springs to the main springs by a big compensating lever. This meant that the weight distribution would remain sensibly constant on rough tracks. Rogers were the first to build a proper Mogul in 1863, although a few 2-6-0s which were not true Moguls were made before that; usually the guiding wheels were mounted directly on the main frames with some side movement allowed.

Over the next 50 years 11,000 Moguls were built for US railroads. They filled a general-purpose role between 4-4-0 passenger locomotives and 2-8-0 freight units. It was sometimes

Above: *Put out to grass at Hillsboro, New Hampshire, in 1951 is Boston & Maine B-15 class Mogul No.1448.*

Right: *A loco engineer dwarfed by a 2-6-0 Mogul of the New York, Ontario & Western, about 1905.*

convenient to have motive power which could work, say, commuter trains during morning and evening and haul freight trains at other times.

the eccentric rods and links of the Stephenson link motion being shaped and positioned clear of the leading axles. Otherwise the successful US 19th Century recipe for the steam locomotive was applied in its entirety. One

important feature which became standard about this time was the casting of each cylinder integral with half the smokebox saddle. When bolted together, a very strong front end was produced.

At this time also, Baldwins had

begun making a great effort to standardise parts and fittings as between any particular locomotive and another similar one. It was a pet project of the founder,

Mathias Baldwin—who sadly died at the age of 70 in the same year that *Consolidation* was built—and was certainly a major factor in the dominant position in locomotive manufacture that his firm was to reach.

Below: Consolidation, *bearing the initials of the Lehigh Valley & Mahoney Railroad, and as delivered just as the two railroads had consolidated.*

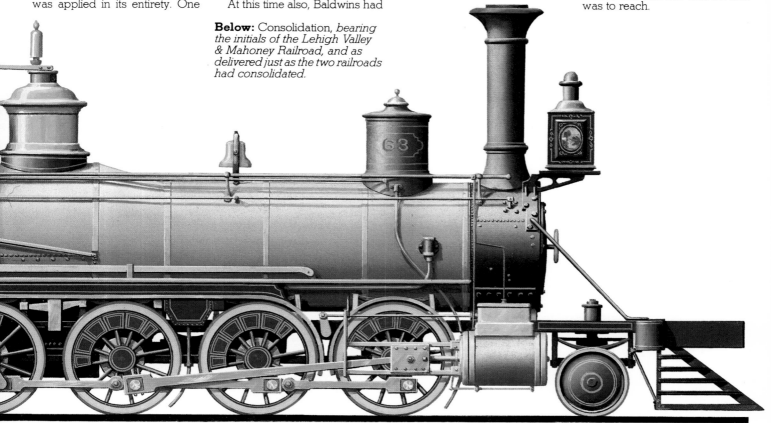

El Gobernador 4-10-0 Central Pacific Railroad, 1884

Gauge: 4ft 8½in (1,435mm).
Tractive effort: 34,546lb (15,674kg).
Axleload: 26,750lb (12.1t).
Cylinders: (2) 21 x 36in (533 x 914mm).
Driving wheels: 57in (1,448mm).
Steam pressure: 135psi (9.5kg/cm²).
Fuel: 10,000lb (4.5t).
Water: 3,000US gall (11.4m³).
Adhesive weight: 121,600lb (55t).
Total weight: 239,650lb (107.8t).
Length overall: 65ft 5in (19,939mm).

The Bill authorising the building of the original transcontinental railroad route was signed by President Lincoln on July 1, 1862. The Central Pacific Railroad,

founded by four Sacramento shop-keepers, was built from the California end. The infant company at once faced the worst obstacle of the whole route, the crossing of the Sierra Nevada mountain range. The grade was held to a maximum inclination of 2.77 per cent (1-in-36) but nothing could mitigate the tremendous height that had to be climbed from near enough sea level at Sacramento to 7,000ft (2,134m) at the Summit tunnel.

The first locomotive, 4-4-0 *Governor Stanford*, arrived in the summer of 1863, after a hazardous six-month 19,000-mile journey around Cape Horn by sailing ship. With the head of steel moving further and further inland towards the meeting point with the Union Pacific at Promontory Point, Utah, 700 miles (1,120km) from Sacramento, more and more motive

power was required. When the rails were joined on April 28, 1869, CP had nearly 200 locomotives. Most were standard 4-4-0s but ten-wheeler 4-6-0s also featured on the roster.

From 1872 onwards CP began building locomotives in its own Sacramento shops to the design of Master Mechanic A.J. Stevens. In 1882, to meet the demands of 'The Hill'—as the ascent of the

Sierras was known—Stevens introduced a twelve-wheeler or 4-8-0 called *Mastodon* and this well-named monster was sufficiently successful to be repeated many times.

In 1884, Stevens tried to go one step further with the superbly impressive 4-10-0 *El Gobernador*. This magnificent machine was on paper and at the time by far the largest and most powerful loco-

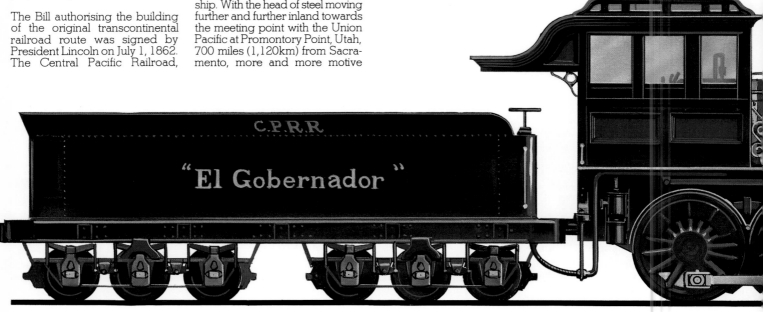

Lovatt Eames 4-2-2 Philadelphia & Reading Railroad (P&R), 1880

Gauge: 4ft 8½in (1,435mm).
Tractive effort: 11,000lb (4,991kg).
Axleload: 35,000lb (15.9t).
Cylinders: (2) 18 x 24in (457 x 609mm).
Driving wheels: 78in (1,981mm).
Heating surface: 1,400sq ft (130m²).
Steam pressure: 180psi (12.7kg/cm²).
Grate area: 56sq ft (5.2m²).
Fuel: 14,000lb (6.4t).
Water: 4,000 US gall (15.1m³).
Adhesive weight: 45,000lb (20.4t).
Total weight: 149,000lb (67.6t).
Length overall: 55ft 2in (16,814mm).

Baldwin's 5,000th locomotive was an unusual one but not really at all successful; even so, it had an extreme influence on practice elsewhere. It had the 4-2-2 wheel arrangement which was so rare in the United States that even though the type had a name (it was 'Bicycle'), this is hardly familiar currency even amongst the most expert historians. The locomotive was ordered by the Philadelphia & Reading railroad—better known to us simply as the 'Reading'—as power for

light high-speed trains, notably between Philadelphia and New Jersey. The single-driver arrangement had the advantage of simplicity—and, in addition, the fewer rods there were to thrash around at high revolutions the better. Against this there was the objection that the adhesion weight was limited to the amount allowable on a single axle.

However, there was an interesting device fitted to the locomotive which, by means of a steam servocylinder mounted between the frames, could move the effective central pivot position of the equalising levers connecting the driving wheels with the rear wheels. In this way the adhesive weight could be temporarily increased from 35,000 to 45,000lb to assist with traction whilst starting. Hopefully the engineer would reset the device before any speed was reached so that damage to the track did not result.

This device has (perhaps a little surprisingly) never found general adoption, but another feature applied to this locomotive became almost universal by the end of steam. This was the wide firebox, usually supported by a pair or pairs of small idle wheels underneath. Desirable for any type of fuel, a big grate was essential

when burning the anthracite coal which happened to be mined in the area served by the Reading Railroad.

Although the Reading went on to have other 4-2-2s generally similar to but larger than Baldwin's No.5000, they were temporarily unable to pay for the locomotive and accordingly it was recalled by the builders. In turn they sold it to the Eames Vacuum Brake Co, which had need of a light but speedy demonstration locomotive, naming it the *Lovatt Eames*.

The now familiar Westinghouse air-brake was about this time coming into general use on railways in North America, whilst the sponsors of the rival vacuum brake were being forced to find fresh fields to conquer. Both types of brake had the desirable automatic or 'fail-safe' qualities but the vacuum brake was very much simpler. On the other hand it had had problems associated with the fact that only some 12psi (0.8kg/cm²) of differential pressure (much less at any altitude) was available, whereas the air brake had six times as much and more. In the USA, then, the air brake became standard; abroad, however, there was still scope for extending the use of vacuum.

So the *Lovatt Eames* was sent across the sea to Britain and over a short trial period played a small part in influencing several companies in making the decision to adopt the vacuum brake.

In due time more British companies used vacuum than air and for many years the former was standard there. Only recently has the air brake been substituted. In an indirect way, therefore, and in due course, this marketing exercise led to adoption of vacuum brakes as standard in India, southern Africa and elsewhere as well as in Britain. Incidentally, the *Lovatt Eames* had as big a grate as was ever used in Britain up to the end of steam. Generally speaking steam coal of good quality was available and so large grates were not needed. The ultimate fate of the *Lovett Eames* is not recorded and it must be assumed that the engine was broken up after a few years.

Right: *The* Lovett Eames *was a 4-2-2 "Bicycle" type intended for the Philadelphia & Reading Railroad. Financial problems prevented delivery and the locomotive was used instead to demonstrate the Eames vacuum brake system in England.*

motive in the world. The most interesting feature was Stevens' own design of valves and valve gear for this locomotive. There were two valves to each cylinder, a main valve and a cut-off. The main valve was worked by a single eccentric rocking a link, while the cut-off valve was actuated by a connection with the crosshead. The amount of motion of the latter, and hence the cut-off, could be varied. Originally the double valves were rotary in form but more conventional slide valves were soon substituted.

Alas, the technology of the day had been pushed too far and *El Gobernador* was not a success as a haulage unit, although valuable in terms of publicity. It was not used very much except as an impressive switching unit at Sacramento, arranged to be in view when important passenger trains were in the depot. The engine is understood to have been broken up in 1894. It was the last locomotive on what in 1885 became the Southern Pacific Company to carry a name and was very soon outclassed in weight and power.

Below: El Gobernador *was too far ahead of its time to be successful, although the 4-8-0s upon which it was based were excellent. As a publicity stunt, though, it had some value (like certain other too-large pieces of hardware) as the world's biggest locomotive.*

C-16-60 Denver & Rio Grande Railroad (D&RG), 1882

Gauge: 3ft 0in (914mm).
Tractive effort: 16,800lb (7,623kg).
Axleload: 13,818lb (6.3t).
Cylinders: (2) 15 x 20in (381 x 508mm).
Driving wheels: 37in (939mm).
Heating surface: 834sq ft (77m²).
Steam pressure: 160psi (11,3kg/cm²).
Grate area: 14sq ft (1.3m²).
Fuel: 12,000lb (5.4t).
Water: 2,500 US gall (9.5m³).
Adhesive weight: 50,250lb (22.8t).
Total weight: 111,600lb (50.6t).
Length overall: 52ft 52¾in (17,189mm).

The idea that railroads built on an entirely different and smaller scale should be used not only for small local lines but also for larger operations in difficult country was an attractive one, owing much to the pioneering of the British narrow-gauge Festiniog Railway. So, when in the 1870s General William Jackson Palmer set out to build a vast railroad system radiating out of Denver to serve the length and breadth of Colorado, he decided on 3ft gauge.

Even though distracted from his main-line aspirations by the need to serve the booming mining camps of the Territory (as it was until 1876), he had soon taken these narrow tracks to the highest elevation then attained in the USA. Altitude of the line at La Veta pass was 9,400ft (2,865m), reached by a route which included 4 per cent (1-in-25) gradients and 30° (58m radius) curves. Stronger locomotives than the little 2-4-0s, 4-4-0s and 2-6-0s first supplied were then

Top: *Denver & Rio Grande G16 class No.278 on display at Montrose, Colorado. Built 1884, retired 1953.*

Right: *D&RG C-19 class No.346* Cumbres *at the Colorado Railroad Museum near Denver, Colorado.*

Below: *2-8-0 No.33 Silver Cliff was built by Baldwin in 1879; ceased work in 1908.*

found to be needed.

The solution came when, in 1877, Baldwin delivered to the Denver & Rio Grande their 22nd locomotive, one that was to found a whole dynasty of sturdy iron ponies. This pathfinder was 2-8-0 No.22, *Alamosa*. By the end of 1882, at the height of the silvermining boom, 130 similar locomotives had been delivered, mostly from Baldwin but a few from Grant. Diamond-pattern spark arrestors and other features gave an appearance such that, were trouble to come, one would instantly expect Gary Cooper or John Wayne to ride up out of the woods and put things right.

Most of the 2-8-0s had evocative names—*Roaring Forks, Shoshone, Old Rube, Treasury Mountain, Mosquito Gulch* and *Hardscrabble* were amongst the best. Apart from the narrow gauge the class was entirely orthodox, with slide valves above the cylinders and Stephenson's link motion between the frames. Many similar locomotives were supplied to narrow-gauge railroads at home and abroad. In later years the Denver & Rio Grande Western classified the majority of these locomotives as "C-16" (C = Consolidation; 16 = 16,000lb of tractive effort). There were also 20 of a stretched version known as "C-19".

Development of the system, and thus locomotive acquisition, came almost to a halt when in 1883 the narrow gauge reached Salt Lake City by a circuitous 771-mile (1,240km) route. General Palmer's resources were overstretched and he effectively lost control of his railroads. Conversion of the main line to accommodate standard-gauge trains followed in 1889-90, following which much of the narrow-gauge material was sold to other railroads, whilst the "C-16s" and "C-19s" soldiered on with much-rebuilt survivors still active 70 years later.

Many have been preserved, with No.346 *Cumbres* at the Colorado Railroad Museum, as well as Nos.400 *Green River* and 409 *Red Cliff* at Knott's Berry Farm near Los Angeles, both still operable and in 'daisy-picking' railroad service. When built both classes were ornately decorated with polished brass work, Russian iron boiler cladding and other elaborations applied by their devoted engineers. By the 1890s, however, all this had been dropped in favour of a coat of bitumen and plain white numbers in the traditional 'Bastard Railroad Gothic'.

Below: *The Colorado Railroad Museum steams and runs its precious No.346 on occasion.*

The Judge Chicago Railroad Exposition, 1883

Gauge: 3ft 0in (914mm).
Propulsion: Direct current at 75V fed via a central third rail to a traction motor of 20hp (15kW) which drove one axle by gearing and belt drives.
Weight: 9,000lb (4.1t).
Max. speed: 12mph (19km/h).

The first electric locomotive to haul traffic—in this case passengers—was operated at the Berlin Industrial Exhibition of 1879 and was the work of Dr Werner von Siemens, founder of the great German electrical engineering firm which still carries his name. However, his United States counterpart, Thomas Edison, was not far behind, with an experimental line at Menlo Park, New Jersey, constructed in 1880. A small experimental locomotive ran on this line and it is said that speeds as high as 40mph (64km/h) were run.

A man called Henry Villard, who was president of the Northern Pacific Railway Co., was impressed with Edison's work at Menlo Park. His railroad operated in country which could potentially produce ample amounts of electricity from water power. He made a contract with Edison to set an experimental line with a view to trying out this new form of propulsion on a 50-mile (80km) stretch of NP.

Two locomotives were built. Like the experimental one, they had insulated wheels so that the two running rails acted as the two conductors for the current. This simple method has had no followers in full-size practice, but is almost universal in the world of model railways. Alas, the Northern Pacific Railway project foundered when the customer became temporarily insolvent, but Edison, a most enterprising engineer, was not discouraged by this set back.

The concern known as the Electric Railway Company of the United States was formed in 1883 by Edison in conjunction with another pioneer, Stephen Field, and in June of that year they ran this little four-wheel tractor on a public train at the Chicago Railway Exposition. It was built for the 3ft gauge and over 20,000 passengers were carried on a 450yd (410m) circular track. Current was taken via a 'gripper' device which slid along a central third rail. One axle was driven by a single electric motor, transmission being via gears and belting.

The success of *The Judge* did not lead to immediate (or even subsequent) widespread adoption of electric traction by railroads; successful application to street car lines came first. A Belgian immigrant called Charles Van Depoele was responsible for the first fully-electrified one at Montgomery, Alabama, in 1886. It was only later, as we shall see, that the new technology was applied (and then only in a few selected cases) to main line railroads. Only today, a century later, is main-line electrification in North America being considered seriously on a wide scale, and even this idea has recently taken a back seat because the recession has been accompanied by a no doubt temporary glut of oil supplies.

Below: *Only sketches of* The Judge *exist but it is clear that its appearance was very similar to Edison's second and third locomotives, as shown in this picture, except that the wheels were enclosed by skirting boards and the car body was house-shaped rather than rounded. Note the arrangement of conductors on the insulated wheels, whereby current is conveyed from the wheel rims into the locomotive.*

No. 999 4-4-0 New York Central & Hudson River RR (NYC & HRRR), 1893

Gauge: 4ft 8½in (1,435mm).
Tractive effort: 16,270lb (7,382kg).
Axle load: 42,000lb (19t).
Cylinders: (2) 19 x 24in (483 x 610mm).
Driving wheels: 86in (2,184mm).
Heating surface: 1,927sq ft (179m²).
Superheater: None
Steam pressure: 190psi (12.6kg/cm²).
Grate area: 30.7sq ft (2.85m²).
Fuel: 15,400lb (7t).
Water: 2,950gall (3,500US) (13.5m³).
Adhesive weight: 84,000lb (38t).
Total weight: 204,000lb (92.5t).
Overall length: 57ft 10in (17,630mm).

When on 10 May 1893 New York Central & Hudson River Railroad No.999 hauled the Empire State Express at 112.5mph (180km/h) down a 1 in 350 (0.28 per cent) grade near Batavia, New York State, it was not only a world record for steam railways but for any kind of transport. The only problem is that it is not a question of "when" but of "if".

The conductor timed the train (presumably with his service watch) to travel between two marks a mile apart. With four heavy Wagner cars weighing 50-55 tons each, about 2,000 cylinder horse-power would be needed and this would seem to be just a little too much to expect; not so much as regards steam production at a corresponding rate, but in getting that steam in and out of the cylinders in such quantities. A speed of 102.8mph (166km/h) over 5 miles, timed the previous night, is a little more credible, but both must, alas, be regarded as "not proven".

The man responsible for this locomotive's existence was no great railroad tycoon, but an irrespressible patent medicine salesman called Daniels, taken on as the line's passenger agent in New York. He persuaded the management to run this exclusive Empire State Express between New York and Chicago during the period of the Colombian Exposition; the time of 20 hours for the 960 miles (1,536km) was

Cog Locomotive 0-4-2T Manitou & Pike's Peak (M&PP), 1890

Gauge: 4ft 8½in (1,435mm).
Tractive effort: 22,040lb (10,000kg).
Cylinders, HP: (2) 10 x 20in (254 x 508mm).
Cylinders, LP: (2) 15 x 22in (381 x 558mm).
Driving wheels: 22in (559mm).
Heating surface: 575sq ft (53m²).
Steam pressure: 200psi (14.1kg/cm²).
Grate area: 19sq ft (1.8m²).
Total weight: 52,700lb (23.9t).
Length overall: 22ft 7¼in (6,889mm).

Cog-wheel locomotives are almost as old as steam traction, for in 1812 John Blenkinsop had one built by Fenton, Murray & Woods of Leeds, England, for the Middleton Colliery Railway. This occurred the year before William Hedley built *Puffing Billy*, the world's first really-practical steam locomotive. It was soon shown that for normally-graded railways the bite of an iron wheel on an iron rail was sufficient and the world then put aside cog railways for half-a-century when this form of traction was used again for mountainous gradients.

The first rack-and-pinion railway which climbed mountains was built in the USA. This was the Mount

an unprecedented average speed for any journey of similar length.

This combination of speed and luxury was shortly to result in one of the most famous trains of the world, the legendary year-round "Twentieth Century Limited", running daily from New York to Chicago.

No.999 was specially built for the job and the train name was even painted on the tender. The NYC&HRR shops at West Albany turned out this single big-wheeled version of the road's standard 4-4-0s, themselves typical of the US locomotive of their day, with slide-valves, Stephenson's valve gear and more normal 78in (1,981mm) wheels.

On account of the record exploit, No.999's fame is world-wide; the locomotive even figured on a US two-cent stamp in 1900. Today, much rebuilt and with those high-and-mighty drivers replaced by modest workaday ones, No.999 is on display at the Chicago Museum of Science and Industry.

Below: *Despite the doubts surrounding No.999's record-breaking exploits in 1893, the locomotive has acquired a worldwide reputation and the name "Empire State Express" has passed into history. A pity, then, that the loco no longer sports its original 7ft 2in wheels.*

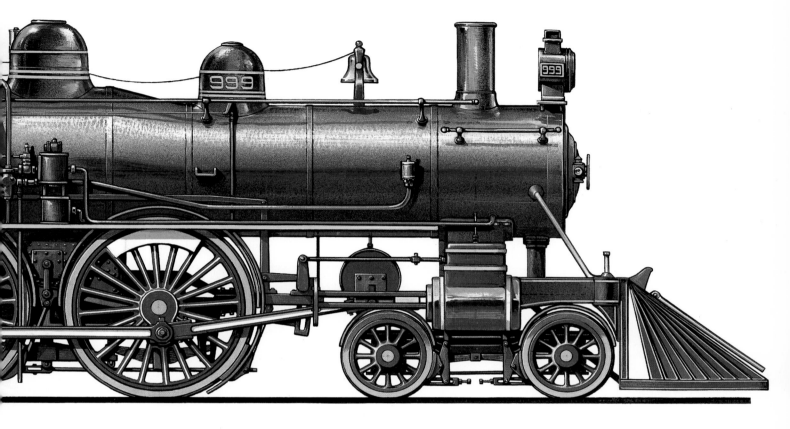

Washington line of which more later. In 1890 a railroad similar in principle but differing considerably in detail was completed. It ran from Manitou Springs, Colorado, to the 14,100ft (4,302m) summit of Pike's Peak. This altitude is the highest reached by a railway in North America. As regards the rest of the world, the title also applies except for South America. The 8.9 mile (14.3km) line is still open and runs daily (using diesel traction) throughout the season from May to October. The maximum grade is 25 per cent (1-in-4).

To work the line, the Baldwin Locomotive Works supplied in 1890 three six-pinion rack locomotives. The boiler was mounted sloping steeply downwards towards the front so that it would be acceptably level on 1-in-4 gradients. Steam was fed to two pairs of 17in bore by 20in stroke (432 x 509mm) cylinders which drove three double rack pinions mounted on axles separate from the rail wheels as the latter were not driven. There was a separate crankshaft driving the two rear

Left: *Preserved M&PP cog locomotive No.4 on display at the Colorado Railroad Museum.*

rack pinions directly through gearing with a 1:1 ratio. The leading rack-pinion was driven from the middle one by a pair of short coupling rods.

The arrangement did not prove satisfactory and in 1893 a further locomotive (No.4) was supplied and this had a different arrangement which could be described as an 0-4-2T. Vauclain compound cylinders drove on to a vertical arm which was also connected, giving a mechanical advantage of 1:1.5, to coupling rods which drove the main axles via outside cranks. The two double rack pinions were mounted on the two main axles, while the rail wheels revolved free. The original locomotives were then rebuilt to this model and one further new one (No.5) was built. No.6, built in 1906 was similar except that, instead of resembling an 0-4-2T, it was effectively a six-coupled 0-6-0T. No.6 had the greater mechanical advantage of 1:1.7 and correspondingly higher tractive effort.

Subsequently, in 1912, the whole fleet was again rebuilt to a uniform design, this time in the M&PP's own shops. A rocking lever, pivoted at the centre and as far distant from the cylinders

Above: *Manitou & Pike's Peak 0-4-2T cog locomotive as finally rebuilt in 1912.*

as possible, replaced the lever arm pivoted at its top and situated between the driving axles. The main driving rods were longer but their angular movement was less, while the mechanical advantage now became 1:1.55.

The M&PP used the Abt rack-and-pinion system, in which a rack consisting of two sets of teeth is mounted between the rails. The position of the teeth are staggered so that as cog teeth come in and out of mesh on one

side of the rack, they are fully engaged on the other.

Unlike most other compound locomotives which used the Vauclain principle, the unique arrangement with high-pressure and low-pressure cylinders driving the same crosshead was retained until the use of steam in normal service was ended. Locomotive No.4 has been retained and has recently been restored as a runner, thereby becoming what is thought to be the only operable Vauclain compound. Other steam locomotives from the Pike's Peak line are on show at Colorado Springs (No.1), Golden, Colorado (No.2), and Manitou Springs (No.5).

Nos. 1-3 B₀+B₀ Baltimore & Ohio RR (B&O), 1895

Type: Main line electric locomotive.
Gauge: 4ft 8½in (1,435mm).
Propulsion: Direct current at 675V fed via a rigid overhead conductor to four gearless motors of 360hp (270kW) each.
Weight: 192,000lb (87t).
Max. axleload: 48,488lb (22t).
Overall length: 27ft 1½in (8,268mm).
Tractive effort: 45,000lb (201kN).
Max speed: 60mph (96.5km).

The world's first main line electrification was installed on this section of the first public railway in America; it ran through the city of Baltimore and in particular through the 1¼-mile (2km) Howard Street tunnel, adjacent to a new main passenger station at Mount Royal. The tunnel was on a gradient of 1-in-125 (0.8 per cent) and trouble with smoke and steam therein was anticipated. The solution adopted was elec-

trification carried out by General Electric of Schenectady, New York State.

More remarkable than anything was the boldness of the decision —these B&O locomotives were over nine times heavier and nine times more powerful than their nearest rivals. It was upon such an enormous leap forward as this that the success of the whole vast investment in the new line was dependent, because a very different construction would have been necessary for steam traction.

Gearless motors were again used, but not mounted direct on the axle, although concentric with it. Torque was transmitted to the wheels through rubber blocks; this flexible drive was yet another feature many years ahead of its time. Each four-wheeled tractor

Below: *An about-turn indeed, as modern steam propels retired electric at the B&O centennial fair in 1927.*

unit was mechanically quite separate, although two were permanently coupled to form one locomotive. There were three double locomotives in all.

The locomotives were quite successful and had no problems hauling 1,630t (1,800 US tons) trains up the gradient. The load including the train's steam engine, which did no work in the tunnel. Trouble was encountered with corrosion of the unusual con-

Forney 0-4-4T Chicago & South Side Rapid Transit, 1892

Gauge: 4ft 8½in (1,435mm).
Axleload: 20,000lb (9.1t).
Cylinders, HP: (2) 9 x 16in (228 x 406mm).
Cylinders, LP: (2) 15 x 16in (381 x 406mm).
Driving wheels: 42in (1,066mm).
Heating surface: 555sq ft (52m²).
Steam pressure: 180psi (12.7kg/cm²).
Grate area: 19sq ft (1.8m²).
Water: 750 US gall (2.8m³).
Adhesive weight: 40,000lb (18.1t).
Total weight: 58,000lb (26.3t).
Length overall: 27ft 3in (8,305mm).

Mathias Nace Forney, engineer, railway journalist and inventor (born Hanover, Pennsylvania, 1935, died New York City, 1908) patented a type of 0-4-4 tank locomotive intended for sharply-curved city, suburban and local railways. Its main advantage was that it could turn on a dime, and so Forneys were used extensively

on both the New York and Chicago elevated lines while these were operated by steam. One of the last urban routes to be equipped with them was the Chicago & South Side Rapid Transit Railroad, which was opened in June 1892. Baldwins supplied 45 exceedingly neat little Vauclain compound Forneys and

Above: *Panorama of Victorian transport, with Forney-power on the New York elevated.*

one cross-compound to the South Side that year, the first 20 being shipped from Philadelphia to Chicago in one specially publicised train via the Lehigh Valley and Wabash railroads.

From all accounts they worked extremely well and the saving in fuel due to the compounding was claimed to be as unexpectedly high as 40 per cent, while there is no mention of any corresponding debit in respect of maintenance costs. Perhaps the fact that they were small engines which hauled light trains had something to do with this. Alas, nemesis in the form of multiple-unit electric traction which was even then waiting in the wings, threatened to displace these delightful little fire-chariots after at most six short years of operation. The steam-hauled cars were quickly fitted with trucks powered by electric motors and with third-rail current-collecting shoes, and by the turn of the century all the Forneys had been sold or scrapped.

The most important feature of these locomotives was that they should be able to negotiate 64° of curvature (27m radius) at street corners, hence the Forney configuration. They also represented one of the few successful applica-

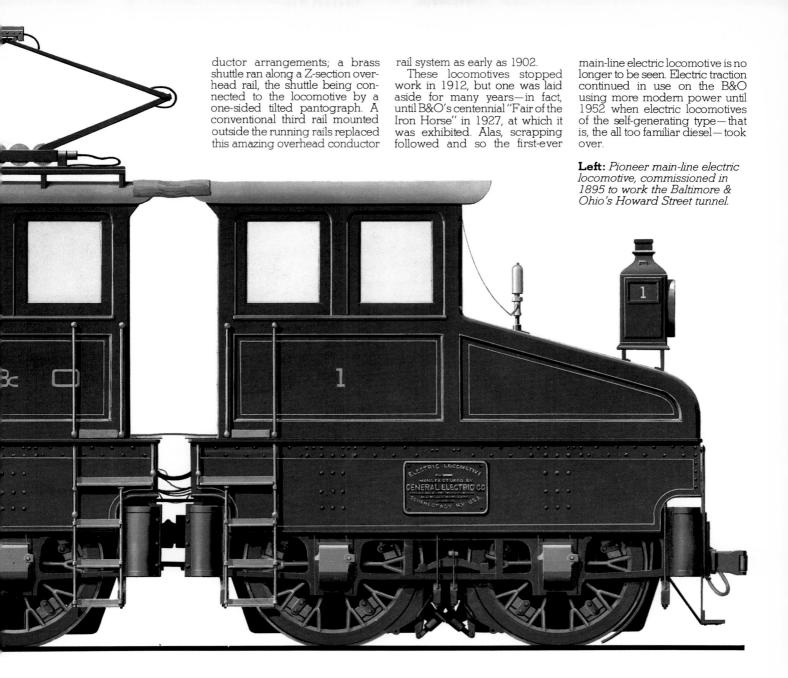

ductor arrangements; a brass shuttle ran along a Z-section overhead rail, the shuttle being connected to the locomotive by a one-sided tilted pantograph. A conventional third rail mounted outside the running rails replaced this amazing overhead conductor

rail system as early as 1902.

These locomotives stopped work in 1912, but one was laid aside for many years—in fact, until B&O's centennial "Fair of the Iron Horse" in 1927, at which it was exhibited. Alas, scrapping followed and so the first-ever

main-line electric locomotive is no longer to be seen. Electric traction continued in use on the B&O using more modern power until 1952 when electric locomotives of the self-generating type—that is, the all too familiar diesel—took over.

Left: *Pioneer main-line electric locomotive, commissioned in 1895 to work the Baltimore & Ohio's Howard Street tunnel.*

tions of the Vauclain compound arrangement, named after Samuel Vauclain, once head of Baldwins.

Vauclain compounds had pairs of large high and small low-pressure cylinders one above the other. They drove a common crosshead and each double cylinder needed only one set of valve motion. The problem with them seems to have been that the forces exerted by the two cylinders did not balance and the off-centre thrust which resulted led to excessive wear on the crosshead and slide bars. In this case the forces involved were small and satisfaction was achieved. An interesting feature of the South Side Forneys was that although the cylinders drove on to the second axle, the eccentrics for the Stephenson link motion were mounted on the leading axle and the eccentric rods drove links which were situated further to the rear, the reverse of the normal arrangement.

The final South Side steam locomotive, No.46, was a cross-

compound. In case readers are hazy as to the meaning of this, the explanation is that a large low-pressure cylinder is situated on one side and a smaller high-pressure cylinder on the other.

Mechanically, the arrangement is very simple, but for the locomotive to be able to start itself a by-pass valve is necessary for starting, to enable the low-pressure cylinder to receive live steam direct from

Above: *Prototype of the 45 short-lived South Side Forneys.*

the boiler and for the high-pressure cylinder to exhaust direct to atmosphere.

No. 382 4-6-0 Illinois Central Railroad (ICRR), 1896

Gauge: 4ft 8½in (1,435mm).
Tractive effort: 21,930lb (9,950kg).
Axleload: 36,923lb (16.8t).
Cylinders: (2) 19½ x 26in (495 x 660mm).
Driving wheels: 69in (1,752mm).
Heating surface: 1,892sq ft (176m²).
Steam pressure: 180psi (12.7kg/cm²).
Grate area: 31.5sq ft (2.9m²).
Fuel: 18,000lb (8.2t).
Water: 5,000 US gall (18.9m³).
Adhesive weight: 100,700lb (45.7t).
Total weight: 205,550lb (93.3t).
Length overall: 60ft 3in (18,364mm).

The most famous of all railroad songs tells the story of John Luther Jones who, one night in April 1900 at Memphis, Tennessee, 'mounted to the cabin with his orders in his hand, on his farewell trip to the Promised Land.' His locomotive, Illinois Central No.382, was a 4-6-0 which in reality would only be called (as she was in the song) a 'six-eight wheeler' by a Swiss. This accident would not really have been remarkable enough to go down to posterity were it not that Wallace Saunders, a labourer at the locomotive depot at Canton, Missouri, which was Casey's intended destination, made up the celebrated ballad often attributed to 'anon'. In those days train wrecks had the frequency, and consequently the status, that automobile accidents have today, so it was news when railroads did not have accidents rather than when they did. In this case the accident occurred at Vaughan, Mississippi, 174 miles

Below: *Casey's own locomotive, standard 4-6-0 No.382 in its original form, unsuperheated and with a most ornate cab.*

Camelback Class 4-4-2 Atlantic City Railroad (ACR), 1896

Gauge: 4ft 8½in (1,435mm).
Tractive effort: 22,906lb (10,390kg).
Axle load: 40,000lb (18t).
Cylinders: (4) see text.
Driving wheels: 84in (2,134mm).
Heating surface: 1,835sq ft (170m²).
Superheater: none.
Steam pressure: 200psi (14kg/cm²).
Grate area: 76sq ft (7m²).
Water: 3,300 gall (4,000 US) (15m³).
Adhesive weight: 79,000lb (36t).
Total weight: 218,000lb (99t).

The unusual appearance of these strange-looking but path-finding locomotives belied a capability well ahead of their time. The Atlantic City Railroad (ACR) ran them on fast trains which took people from the metropolis of Philadelphia to resorts on the New Jersey coast. It was a 55½ mile (90km) run from Camden (across the river from Philadelphia) to Atlantic City and there was intense competition from the mighty Pennsylvania Railroad which had direct access into the big city. In July and August, for example, it was noted that the booked time of 50 minutes was kept or improved upon each day. On one day the run is reported to have been made in 46½ minutes start-to-stop, an average speed of 71.6mph (115km/h). This certainly implies steady running speed of 90mph (145km/h) or more, but reports of 100mph (160km/h) (and more) speeds with these trains should be regarded as conjecture. The "Atlantic City Flier" was certainly the fastest scheduled train in the world at that time.

Apart from broad-gauge locomotives, here is the first appearance amongst the locomotives in this book of a feature which is in the future to become an integral part of most steam passenger express locomotives—the wide deep firebox, for which the 4-4-2 wheel arrangement is wholly appropriate. In this case it was adopted in order to allow anthracite coal to be burnt satisfactorily, but later it was realised that a large grate was also an advantage with bituminous coal and even with oil.

Two other features of these locomotives are fascinating but to some extent freakish. As can be seen they had pairs of compound cylinders on each side, driving through a common crosshead. The arrangement was named after Samuel Vauclain head of the Baldwin Locomotive Works, and his object was to attain the advantages of compounding without its complexities. In this case the high-pressure cylinders, 13in bore by 26in stroke (330 x 660mm), were mounted on top and the low-pressure ones 22in bore x 26in stroke (559 x 660mm) below. A single set of valve gear and a single connecting rod served

(278km) south of Memphis.

The train order system of operation, however satisfactory for a line carrying a few slowish trains, was very susceptible to human failure when used on such an important line as this trunk route from Chicago to New Orleans. The song states that Casey 'looked at his watch and his watch was slow'. Therefore it might be that, although his train was late by the public timetable,

Left: *Casey Jones in the cab of ICRR 2-8-0 No.638 just before his death in 1900.*

he could have been running ahead of the time set by his orders. Hence the cars he collided with might well have been legitimately still fouling the main track unprotected by a flagman. Since Casey habitually ran like the wind, and since no fixed signals existed, there was no prospect of stopping him and his ''Cannonball Express'' once his headlight had come into view.

The locomotive, which was very much a standard product of the day, was built by the Rogers Locomotive Works of Paterson, New Jersey. No.382 had outside

slide-valve cylinders, inside Stephenson valve gear and a narrow firebox boiler. Her most unusual feature was a handsome clerestory cab roof. After the accident she was repaired and gave many more years of service. It is said that further men were killed while running her. Later, No.382 was modernised with the original slide-valve cylinders adapted to have piston valves and with outside Baker valve gear replacing the original inside Stephenson's. She gained a superheater but, alas, lost that elegant cab.

Casey was buried at Mount Calvary Cemetery at Jackson, Tennessee, where a memorial was erected to him in 1947, paid for by that pair of incurable railroad romantics (and authors of many evocative books about trains) Lucius Beebe and Charles Clegg. Present at the dedication were Casey's wife Jane, his son Charles (also an Illinois Central employee), his grand-daughter Barbara and most remarkably, Casey's fireman Sim Webb, who had jumped clear just before No.382 struck on that fateful night in Mississippi nearly half-a-century earlier.

both cylinders of each compound pair. Alas, Vauclain compounds soon went out of fashion; as so often occurred, the work done by the HP and by the LP cylinders did not balance, and in the case of this arrangement it meant an offset thrust on the crosshead and consequent problems with maintenance.

The other oddity was the ''Camelback'' or ''Mother Hub-bard'' cab on top of the boiler for the driver. The fireman, of course, had to remain in the normal position and for him a second and very exiguous shelter was also provided. The object was to

Left: *Atlantic City Railroad ''Camelback'' class 4-4-2 locomotive No.1027, built in 1896. Note the high- and low-pressure cylinders mounted one above the other, the separate cab for the driver (engineer) on top of the boiler and the ornate decoration on the sides of the tender.*

improve visibility at the expense of separating the two members of the crew. The Philadelphia & Reading Railroad (later known simply as the Reading RR) which took over the ACR at this time went on to build many ''Camelbacks'' and the idea spread to other railroads in the area. But it was a practice which never became widely used.

Strangely enough, the name ''Atlantic'', which even today refers the world over to the 4-4-2 type, did not originate with these remarkable machines. Instead, it was first given to some rather prosaic 4-4-2s (without wide fireboxes) built in 1893 for the Atlantic Coast Line, a railroad which ran southwards towards Florida. Even if the ACR 4-4-2s did not give the type name to the world, the mighty Pennsy took note of the beating its competing trains received at their hands and adopted the principle involved with results described later in this narrative.

I-1 Class 4-6-0 Lake Shore & Michigan Southern Railroad (LS&MSRR), 1900

Gauge: 4ft 8½in (1,435mm).
Tractive effort: 23,800lb (10,800kg).
Axle load: 45,000lb (20.5t).
Cylinders: (2) 20 x 28in (508 x 711mm).
Driving wheels: 80in (2,032mm).
Heating surface: 2,917sq ft (271m²).
Superheater: None.
Steam pressure: 200psi (14.1kg/cm²).
Grate area: 33.6sq ft (3.1m²).
Fuel: 17,500lb (8t).
Water: 6,000gall (7,200 US) (27.2m³).
Adhesive weight: 135,000lb (61t).
Total weight: 300,000lb (136t).
Length overall: 62ft 3in (18,914mm).

As has been described, the "American Standard" 4-4-0 hauled most USA passenger

Class D16sb 4-4-0 Pennsylvania Railroad (PRR), 1895

Gauge: 4ft 8½in (1,435mm).
Tractive effort: 23,900lb (10,850kg)
Axleload: 52,000lb (23.5t).
Cylinders: (2) 20½ x 26in (521 x 660mm).
Driving wheels: 68in (1727mm).
Heating surface: 1400sq ft (130.1m²).
Superheater: 253sq ft (23.5m²).
Steam pressure: 175psi (12.3kg/cm²).
Grate area: 33.2sq ft (3.1m²).
Fuel: 26,000lb (11.8t).
Water: 4,660gall (5,600US) (21.2m³).
Adhesive weight: 98,500lb (44.7t).
Total weight: 281,000lb (127.4t).
Length overall: 67ft 0in (20,422mm).

By the end of the 19th century the Pennsylvania Railroad had established a reputation for large locomotives, mostly built in own Altoona shops, and characterized outwardly by the Belpaire firebox, a rarity in North America. Its 4-4-0 locomotives were no exception, and the high water mark of the type was reached with the "D16" class, introduced in 1895. With cylinders 18½ x 26in (470 x 660mm) and 185psi (13.0 kg/cm²) boilers, they were large engines for their day, and their appearance was the more impressive because the firebox was placed above the frames, making the boiler higher than was usual at this period.

Two varieties were built initially, one with 80 in (2,032mm) driving wheels for the more level divisions ("D16a"), and the other with 68 in (1,727mm) wheels for the hillier parts of the road ("D16"). The "D16a" engines soon established a reputation for high speed, as they were used in competition with the Atlantic City Railroad on the 58½mile (94km) "racetrack" between Camden and Atlantic City. On this service one famous driver was credited with covering an eight-mile stretch at 102mph (164km/h). On another occasion the same driver worked a Presidential special over the 90 miles (145km) from Philadelphia to Jersey City at an average of 72mph (116km/h).

The mechanical quality of the design was well demonstrated by engine No.816, which distin-

guished itself by covering 300,000 miles (483,000km) on the middle division of the PRR in three years and four months, without shopping or other heavy repair. This was a notable feat for its day.

A total of 426 engines were built in five sub-classes of "D16" between 1895 and 1910. Apart from the two driving wheel sizes, their main dimensions were identical as built. With the introduction of Atlantics and then Pacifics in the new century, the "D16"'s were displaced from the best

Below: *Former PRR Class D16sb (built in 1906) became Long Island Rail No.299, seen in shed at Morris Park, Jamaica, NY, in 1915.*

express trains from the 1850s until the 1880s. However, there came a time when loads began to outstep the capacity of locomotives with only two driven axles.

The obvious development was simply to add a third coupled axle, and this is what was done. Some of the best features of the 4-4-0 were retained in the 4-6-0 such as the bogie or leading truck to guide the locomotive, but in other ways problems arose. The ashpan was liable to get mixed up with the rear axle, for example, and the gap between the leading driving wheels and the cylinders, which on the 4-4-0 made the motion so easy to get at, became filled up. Even so, there was a period at the end of

Left: *I-1 class 4-6-0 No.604 at the head of the "Twentieth Century Limited".*

the 1800s when the 4-6-0 ruled the express passenger scene in the USA. About 16,000 examples went into service there all told, most between 1880 and 1910.

The high-wheeled example chosen to illustrate this famous type was built by the Brooks Locomotive Works of Dunkirk, New York State in 1900 for the Lake Shore & Michigan Southern Railroad. They were intended to take charge of the prime varnish trains of the Western part of the New York to Chicago main line belonging to what was soon to become the New York Central Railroad.

Kipling wrote of these great days in that evocative short story called "007" (collected in *The Day's Work*) but in fact they were to be brief. Wide fireboxes, piston valves and superheaters were shortly to replace narrow fireboxes, slide valves and the

use of saturated steam, so changing the world of steam for ever. In fact, the paint was hardly dry on these locomotives before the LS&MS ordered some 2-6-2s with wide fireboxes over the trailing pony trucks. However, the propensity of the flanges of the wheels of the leading single-axle pony truck of the 2-6-2s to ride up over the head of the rails at high speeds put these 4-6-0s back in charge of the legendary Twentieth Century Limited service running between New York and Chicago shortly after it was introduced on 15 June 1902.

The timing over the 960 miles (1,536km) between New York's Grand Central Terminal and La Salle Street station in Chicago was 20 hours, an average speed of 48mph (77km/h). This included several stops for servicing and changing locomotives and much slow running in such places

as Syracuse, where the main line in those days ran along the main street.

The train originally consisted of a buffet-library car, dining car and three sleeping cars, the last of which had an observation saloon complete with brass-railed open platform. The comforts offered were the equivalent of the highest grade of hotel.

One factor in all this comfort and luxury was the great weight of these 80ft (24.3m) Pullman cars even though there were only five of them. So soon enough it was necessary to increase the amount of accommodation provided and accordingly these 4-6-0s had to be replaced. But even if their days of glory were few, these locomotives with their 80-inch (2,032mm) drivers did wonders with what was acknowledged as one of the hardest schedules in the world.

---

trains, but the class was given a new lease of life from 1914 onwards when nearly half of them were modernised in line with the later engines. Slightly larger cylinders with piston valves were fitted, still with the inside Stephenson's valve gear, and the boiler was given a Schmidt's superheater, with the pressure reduced slightly. Most of the rebuilds were the smaller-wheeled engines, and these became "D16sb" (see the dimensions at the head of this article). In this form they settled down to

working numerous branch lines, and three of them were still engaged in this work early in World War II. One of these three, No.1223 built in 1905, was preserved on the Strasburg Rail Road in its native state.

Right: *On the Strasburg Railroad D16 4-4-0 No.1223 calls at Groff's Drove in July 1970.*

Below: *Preserved No.1223 again, this time with a short train of freight cars near Strasburg, Pennsylvania.*

Class Q 4-6-2 New Zealand Government Railways (NZGR), 1901

Gauge: 3ft 6in (1,067mm).
Tractive effort: 19,540lb (8,863kg).
Axle load: 23,500lb (10.5t).
Cylinders: (2) 16 x 22in (406 x 559mm).
Driving wheels: 49in (1,245mm).
Heating surface: 1,673sq ft (155m²).
Superheater: None.
Steam pressure: 200psi (14kg/cm²).
Grate area: 40sq ft (3.72m²).
Fuel: 11,000lb (5t).
Water: 1,700 gall (2,000 US) (7.7m³).
Adhesive weight: 69,500lb (31.5t).
Total weight: 165,000lb (75t).
Length overall: 55ft 4½in (16,872mm).

The year 1901 was marked by the construction of the first of a famous type—arguably *the* most famous type—of express passenger locomotive, which was to go on being built until the end of

steam. And it was not one of the great railway nations which was responsible for conceiving the idea (and to whose order it was built) but tiny New Zealand. A.W. Beattie, Chief Mechanical Engineer of the Government Railways, wanted a locomotive with a big firebox capable of burning poor quality lignite coal from South Island mines at Otago.

American manufacturer Baldwin suggested a "camelback" 4-6-0 with a wide firebox above the rear coupled wheels, but the New Zealander proposed a 4-6-0 with the big firebox carried by a two-wheel pony truck, making a 4-6-2. The 13 engines were quickly completed and despatched across the Pacific Ocean; and in this way a name was given to thousands of locomotives yet to be built. In due time the word "Pacific" entered that dialect of the English language used for describing railways.

Above: *Commissioning photo of Class "Q" prior to entering service on the South Island main line in 1901.*

Below: *NZGR class "Q"—she was the world's first class of Pacific locomotive when built in USA in 1901.*

Class F15 4-6-2 Chesapeake & Ohio Railway (C&O), 1902

Gauge: 4ft 8½in (1,435mm).
Tractive effort: 32,400lb (14,696kg).
Axle load: 52,500lb (24t).
Cylinders: (2) 23½ x 28in (597 x 711mm).
Driving wheels: 72in (1,829mm).
Heating surface: 2,938sq ft (273m²).
Superheater: None.
Steam pressure: 180psi (12.7kg/cm²).
Grate area: 47sq ft (4.4m²).
Fuel: 30,000lb (13.5t).
Water: 7,500 gall (9,000 US) (34m³).
Adhesive weight: 157,000lb (71.5t).
Total weight: 408,000lb (185t).
Length overall: 74ft 0in (22,555mm).

The Chesapeake & Ohio Railroad (C&O) can trace its corporate history back to 1785 when the James River Company received a charter. The first President was George Washington in person! Railroad operations did not begin until 1836 when the Louisa Railroad in Virginia was opened.

Only a few weeks after the Missouri Pacific RR got the first of their 4-6-2s, this historic company took delivery from the American Locomotive Company of the prototype of their famous "F15" class Pacifics. This time there was no ambiguity—the standard North American express passenger locomotive of the twentieth century had finally arrived. This path-finding C&O No.147 was also fitted with piston valves, but it still had Stephenson's

A feature which was also to appear on most of the world's steam locomotives built after this time was the type of valve gear used on these engines. Of 105 locomotives yet to be described in this book, 86 have Walschaert's valve gear. The invention was not new—a Belgian engineer called Egide Walschaert had devised it back in 1844 and a German called Heusinger had reinvented it since—but this application marked its entry into general use outside continental Europe. The gear gave good steam distribution, but the main advantage lay in its simplicity, as well as in the fact that it could conveniently be fitted outside the frames in the position most accessible for maintenance. In this case the gear was arranged to work outside-admission piston valves, which piston valves themselves were in the forefront of steam technology at the beginning of the century.

It should be said that this class of engine came closer than ever before to the final form of the steam locomotive. Only two fundamental improvements were still to be applied generally—inside-admission piston valves in place of outside, and superheating.

After some minor modification the "Q" class gave long and faithful service, the last of them not ceasing work until 1957. During their prime, in addition to working the principal trains on the South Island main line, some came to the North Island for use on the Rotorua Express, running between Auckland and the famous hot springs of the same name.

Right: *The splendid New Zealand Government class "Q" 4-6-2 No.343 as running in 1956 when nearing the end of more than 50 years service to this 3ft 6in gauge railway system which had adopted US practice for its locomotives.*

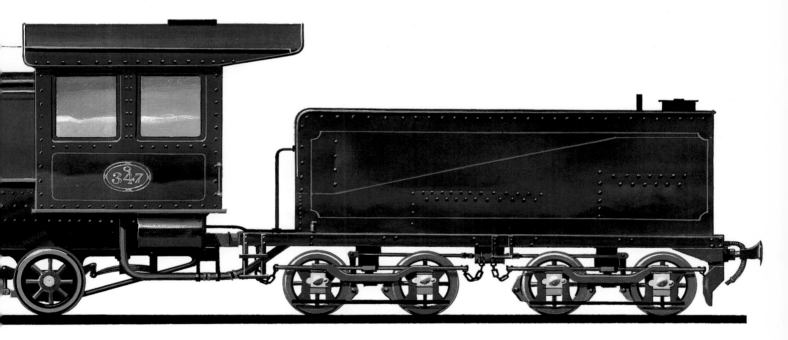

link valve motion between the frames. Naturally no superheater, but her size and power set a new standard. A further 26 followed during the years 1903-11. Most survived until the C&O turned to diesels in the early 1950s and, in a country that was not then given to hanging on to old machinery, that said a great deal for the qualities of the "F15" class. Of course, as the years went by, top-line express work was passed on to their successors, yet there

Left: *A latter-day Chesapeake & Ohio 4-6-2 of class "F16" introduced in 1937 and built by Baldwins of Philadelphia. The normal C&O trademark was the mounting of two duplex air pumps on the front of the locomotive smokebox.*

were routes whose weak bridges meant that these comparatively light engines continued being used on prime trains nearly to the end. During the 1920s all the "F15" locomotives were modernised with Walschaert's valve gear, superheaters, larger tenders, different cabs, mechanical stokers, new cylinders and, in some cases, even new frames; in fact, just in the manner of the legendary Irishman's hammer—"a hundred years old, only two new heads and three new handles".

In addition to setting the style for nearly 7,000 USA 4-6-2s to follow, the "F15" founded a dynasty on their own road. The "F16" 4-6-2s of 1913 represented a 34 per cent increase in tractive effort and a 28 per cent increase of grate area, while for the "F17"

of 1914 these increases were 45 per cent and 71 per cent respectively, in each case for a penalty of a 27 per cent increase in axle load. After World War I, classes "F18" and "F19" appeared, notable for 18,000 gallon 12-wheel tenders. These 61 4-6-2s handled all C&O's express passenger assignments until the coming of 4-6-4s in 1941.

It will be noted that these 4-6-2s showed something else. During the age of steam no major system outside North America ever had track strong enough to carry an axle load greater than 22½ tons, so these locomotives were as good an indicator as any that the USA, having come up from well behind, was now starting to go far into the lead in industrial might.

Lyn 2-4-2T Lynton & Barnstaple Railway (L&B), 1898

Gauge: 1ft 11⅝in (600mm).
Tractive effort: 7,415lb (3,364kg).
Axleload: 15,680lb (7.1t).
Cylinders: (2) 10 x 16in (254 x 406mm).
Driving wheels: 33in (838mm).
Heating surface: 379sq ft (35m²).
Steam pressure: 180psi (12.7kg/cm²).
Grate area: 7.7sq ft (0.7m²).
Water: 800 US gall (3.0m³).
Adhesive weight: 31,360lb (14.2t).
Total weight: 5,280lb (2.4t).
Length overall: 23ft 6in (7,162mm).

The two English-speaking locomotive-building countries were understandably reluctant to make use of each other's products. So this celebrated little treasure is also interesting as being one of the very few steam locomotives built in the USA for an English railway, which exceeded a reasonable quarter-century of working life. Narrow-gauge

common-carrier railways were rare in England, but a 19 mile (30km) line connecting the West Country seaside resort of Lynton with the inland town of Barnstaple, Devon, was completed in 1898. Shortly before the opening in May it was realised that an extra locomotive would be needed beyond the three 2-6-2 tanks originally ordered. There being at that moment full order books in Britain, Baldwin delivered this

2-4-2 tank in July 1898 at very short notice indeed. She bore no number, but the name *Lyn* (a local river) was carried; so the usual Baldwin numberplate on

the smokebox front had to have a blank centre.

In 1923 the Lynton & Barnstaple line came into the hands of the main-line Southern Railway, who later gave *Lyn* an overhaul at their main works at Eastleigh, Hampshire. The SR substituted a US-style 'stove-pipe' chimney for the British type of copper-capped

Class E3sd 4-4-2 Pennsylvania Railroad (PRR), 1901

Gauge: 4ft 8½in (1,435mm).
Tractive effort: 27,400lb (12,400kg).
Axleload: 64,500lb (29.3t).
Cylinders: (2) 22 x 26in (559 x 660mm).
Driving wheels: 80in (2,032mm).
Heating surface: 2,041sq ft (190m²).
Superheater: 412sq ft (38m²).
Steam pressure: 205psi (14.4kg/cm²).
Grate area: 55.5sq ft (5.2m²).
Fuel: 34,200lb (15.5t).
Water: 5,660gall (6,800US) (25.7m³).
Adhesive weight: 127,500lb (58t).
Total weight: 363,500lb (165t).
Length overall: 71ft 6in (21,640mm).

In the 19th Century the standard American passenger engine was the 4-4-0, but towards the end of the century the type was reaching the limit of size which was possible on eight wheels, and train loads were still increasing. A move to ten wheels was

inevitable, and there were two attractive alternatives, the 4-6-0 and the 4-4-2 or Atlantic. The former could have a greater adhesive weight, but the grate was restricted by the need to fit between the rear coupled wheels. The Atlantic had more restricted adhesive weight, but could have a very large grate. For the Pennsylvania Railroad the Atlantic was the obvious choice. The road was already laying exceptionally heavy rails, which could accept a very high axle load, whilst the locomotives had to be able to burn coal of moderate quality in great quantities.

In 1899 Altoona works produced its first two Atlantics, and they exploited the wheel arrangement to the full, with an adhesive weight of 101,600lb (46.1t) and a grate area of 68sq ft (6.3m²), more than twice that of the largest PRR 4-4-0. However, a third engine had a more modest grate of 55.5sq ft (5.2m²), and it was this size which became standard for all subsequent Atlantics, as well as for many other engines of the same period. With

this engine the pattern was set for the construction of 576 more Atlantics, all having the same wheel diameter, boiler pressure and grate area.

Although the basic dimensions were common to all the engines, successive improvements were made. The three prototypes had Belpaire tops to the fireboxes, in accordance with established Pennsylvania prac-

Above: *PRR E3sd Atlantic No.4170 with 22in cylinders, at Oyster Bay, NY, in 1938.*

tice, but the next two batches, totalling 96 engines, had the more usual round-topped firebox. Thereafter the Belpaire box reappeared, and was used on all subsequent engines. The two batches mentioned above differed only in their cylinder diameter,

smokestack fitted by Baldwin, and painted the locomotive in their own smart olive green livery. But in 1935 the L&B was closed and

Lyn was scrapped. Alas, if closure had been postponed even a short time, wartime gas (petrol) rationing would have bought survival for

several further years. By then the age of railroad preservation might well have ensured that the line would still be with us today. And

no doubt *Lyn*, too, would still be pounding up the lovely coombes of a particularly delightful stretch of British countryside.

Left: *Lyn, Southern Railway style after overhaul and repaint in the 1920s and numbered E762. The new stove-pipe chimney enhances the North American look of this unusual one-off locomotive.*

class "E2" having 20.5in (521mm) cylinders, and class "E3" 22in (559mm), the intention being to use the "E3"s on heavier work. All these engines had slide valves, but in the next series, starting in 1903, piston valves were used, at first with Stephenson's valve gear, but from 1906 with Walschaert's.

By 1913 a total of 493 engines had been built, all having a boiler with a maximum diameter of 65.5in (1,664mm). By that time the Pacific was well established on the railway, and it seemed that the heyday of the Atlantic had passed. However, Axel Vogt, the Chief Mechanical Engineer, was still averse to incurring the expense of six-coupled wheels if four would suffice, and in 1910 he built a further Atlantic with another type of boiler, having the same grate area as the earlier Atlantics, but a maximum diameter of 76.75in (1,949mm), almost as large as the Pacifics, and with a combustion chamber at the front. The new engine, classified "E6", developed a higher power than the existing

Pacifics at speeds above 40mph (64km/h). Two more "E6"s were then built, but with superheaters, and this made the performance even more impressive, and it was possible to increase the cylinder diameter to 23.5in (597mm).

After four years of intensive development work, a production batch of eighty "E6"s were built, having a number of changes from the prototypes, including longer boiler tubes. These engines were built at great speed between February and August 1914, that is, in the same year that the first of the famous "K4s" Pacifics was built. These engines took over the principal express workings on all the less hilly parts of the system, and during World War I they achieved prodigious feats of haulage for four-coupled engines. When large numbers of production "K4s" Pacifics appeared after the war, the "E6"s engines settled down to work on the less busy routes, mainly in New Jersey.

The smaller Atlantic soon established a reputation for high speed, but their full potential was

realised in 1905 when the Pennsylvania Special was accelerated to an 18-hour schedule from Jersey City to Chicago, giving an overall average speed of 50.2mph (80.1km/h), with an average of 57.8mph (92.9km/h) over the 189 miles (304km) from Jersey City to Harrisburg. It was on the first westbound run to this schedule that "E2" No.7002 was credited with exceeding 120mph (193 km/h), but the claim was based on dubious evidence. On this service the "E2" and "E3" engines kept time with up to eight wooden coaches, totalling about 360 (short) tons, but with the introduction of the heavier steel stock, double heading became common.

The "E6s" engines were able to handle trains of 800-900 tons on the New York-Philadelphia-Washington trains, but it was on lighter trains that they produced their most spectacular performances. Their greatest distinction was to haul the Detroit Arrow between Fort Wayne and Chicago, for in 1933 this was the world's fastest train, with a start

to stop average of 75.5mph (121.4 km/h) over the 64.1 miles (103km) from Plymouth to Fort Wayne and 75.3mph (121.1km/h) over 123 miles (198km) from Fort Wayne to Gary. On this service they hauled five or six steel coaches, weighing 300 to 350 tonnes.

Over the years many of the earlier Atlantics were modernised with superheaters and piston valves, making them into modern engines for light duties. Five of them survived until 1947, and one of them, by now classified "E2sd", was preserved. It was renumbered to 7002, thus purporting to be the engine of the 1905 record. The "E6s" engines survived well into the 1950s, and one of them, No.460, has been preserved. This engine had achieved fame by hauling a two-coach special from Washington to New York carrying news films of the return of the Atlantic flyer Lindbergh. The train averaged 74mph (119km/h); the films were developed en route and shown in New York cinemas before those carried by air.

Class S 1-D₀-1 New York Central & Hudson River Railroad (NYC&HR), 1904

Type: Electric passenger locomotive.

Gauge: 4ft 8½in (1,435mm).

Propulsion: 660V direct current collected from under-contact third rail supplying four 550hp (410kW) frame-mounted gearless traction motors with armatures on the axles.

Weight: 142,000lb (64.4t) adhesive, 200,500lb (91t) total.

Max. axleload: 35,500lb (16.1t).

Overall length: 37ft 0in (11,277mm).

Tractive effort: 32,000lb (145kN).

Max. speed: 70mph (113km/h).

A major development in electric traction occasioned by a collision between two steam trains—such was the electrification of New York Central's Grand Central terminal in New York and the surrounding lines. The smoke nuisance in this major city location had long brought criticism upon the railway, but it was the 2-mile Park Avenue tunnel on the app-roach lines which constituted an operating hazard. At busy times the tunnel was choked with smoke, and sighting of signals was imped-ed. After several collisions in the tunnel, the climax came in January 1902, when a train ran past a red signal and collided with a station-ary train, causing 15 deaths.

The New York Legislature thereupon passed an act pro-hibiting the use of steam south of the Harlem River after July 1, 1908. Since 1895 the Baltimore & Ohio had operated the Baltimore Belt line with electric traction, including the Howard Street tun-nel, so the legislation was not un-reasonable, but it had the addi-tional effect of forcing the issue of a major rebuilding of the terminal station.

The railroad adopted the third-rail system at 660V dc with under-contact current collection, and General Electric was appointed contractor. The great pioneer of electric traction, Frank Sprague, was one of the engineers to the project, and for commuter services on the electrified lines Sprague's multiple-unit system of control was applied to 180 cars. For haulage of long-distance trains, GE's engin-eer Asa Batchelder designed a 1-Do-1 locomotive of massive pro-portions, which incorporated a number of novelties of his devising. The principal feature of the design was the use of bi-polar motors, with the armature mounted on the axle and the two poles hung from the locomotive frame. The continuous rating was 2,200hp, and the short-term rating of 3,000hp gave a starting tractive effort of 32,000lb (145kN), which enabled the locomotive to accele-rate a train of 800 US tons at 1 mile per second per second (0.45m/s²), and maintain 60mph (97km/h) with 500 tons. The loco-motives were fitted with Sprague's multiple-unit control, so that they could operate in pairs with one driver, and they were the first locomotives to be so equipped.

The frames were outside the wheels to allow room for the armatures. The body had a central cab with a good all-round view, and with little more than the air compressors above floor level, the cab was very roomy. Other equipment was housed in the end hoods, including an oil-fired train-heating boiler.

The prototype locomotive, No. 6000, was completed late in 1904, and was tested exhaustively on a 6-mile (9.6km) stretch of the NYC main line near the GE works at Schenectady, which was electri-fied for the purpose. The test included side-by-side compara-tive runs with the latest steam engines, in which the steam engine usually gained an early lead, but was then overtaken and hand-somely beaten by the electric.

The success of No. 6000 was followed by orders for 34 similar locomotives, classified "T", which were delivered in 1906. One of them hauled the first electrically-worked train from the partially-completed Grand Central Station in September 1906. Full electric

Below: *The prototype 1-Do-1 electric locomotive, as built for the New York Central & Hudson River Railroad in 1904.*

working was instituted in 1907, but unfortunately three days later a train hauled by two "T" class locomotives derailed on a curve, causing 23 deaths. Although the cause of the derailment was not established definitely, the locomotives were rebuilt with end bogies, thus becoming 2-Do-2, and they were reclassified "S".

In regular service the electric locomotives showed savings in operating and maintenance costs compared with steam varying between 12 per cent in transfer service to 27 per cent in road service. In 1908-09 a further 12 locomotives were delivered. The entire class survived through half-a-century of service, ending their days on switching and empty coaching stock working. No. 6000 went to a museum after 61 years' service. Some of the class were still at work for Penn Central in the 1970s.

Left: *Sixty years on. Class S No.133 is still good for service in NYC's Bronx yard, New York, in November 1966.*

Class 9700 Mikado 2-8-2 Nippon Railway, 1897

Gauge: 3ft 6in (1,067mm).
Tractive effort: 27,928lb (12,672kg).
Cylinders: (2) 18½ x 24in (469 x 609mm).
Driving wheels: 45in (1,143mm).
Heating surface: 2,210sq ft (205m²).
Steam pressure: 180psi (12.7kg/cm²).
Grate area: 30sq ft (2.8m²).
Fuel: 12,122lb (5.5t).
Water: 3,000 US gall (11.4m³).
Total weight: 119,677.2lb (54.3t).
Length overall 56ft 2in (17,119mm).

The Mikado or 2-8-2 type of steam locomotive was built in far larger numbers than any other during the 20th Century. Like the Pacific the first one was a narrow-gauge (3ft 6in—1,067mm) example produced for export. In this case (as the name indicates) the customer for a batch of 20 was the Imperial government of Japan and the date was 1897. The builder was Baldwin and the aim was to produce an eight-coupled freight locomotive capable of making steam on inferior quality coal. A large grate area and a deep firebox of ample volume was needed, all of which added up to a small extra pair of pivoted carrying wheels at the hind end.

In other ways the first of the Mikados were typical of their day, with inside Stephenson valve gear and outside slide-valve cylinders. Exceptionally, they possessed handsome copper-capped smoke-stacks and inside bearings to the rear truck, plus the buffers, screw-couplings and vacuum brakes then used on the Nippon Railway. Originally they carried the numbers 530 to 547. Later the Japanese Government Railway renumbered the class (now designated "9700") 9700 to 9719. Automatic couplers of US pattern were substituted during a famous near-instantaneous conversion operation in the 1930s.

It is known that these locomotives were exceptionally successful and—imitation being the sincerest form of flattery—the Japanese went on to build themselves a huge fleet of 2-8-2s for home use, some being produced as late in the day for steam as 1962. There were also many standard-gauge examples built for use during the Japanese occupation of China. Many of these are still running there and some direct derivatives are even today being built. So the Japanese had some responsibility both for the first and for the last of the Mikados.

As regards the vast number of 2-8-2s which ran or were built in the USA, attempts were made during World War II to change the type name from 'Mikado' to 'MacArthur' but to no avail. Even so, the General's name was used for the fleet of 'Mikes' (this diminutive was common) built to bring supplies to the various land fronts opposing Japanese expansion, as will be told later.

Right: *The first 2-8-2 was for Japan's Nippon Railway, giving the name Mikado to the type.*

No. 2400 0-6-6-0 Baltimore & Ohio Railroad (B&O), 1903

Gauge: 4ft 8½in (1,435mm).
Tractive effort: 96,600lb (43,829kg).
Axleload: 61,325lb (27,8t).
Cylinders, HP: (2) 22 x 32in (558 x 812mm).
Cylinders, LP: (2) 32 x 32in (812 x 812mm).
Driving wheels: 56in (1,422mm).
Heating surface: 5,586sq ft (519m²).
Steam pressure: 235psi (16.5kg/cm²).
Grate area: 72.2sq ft (6.7m²).
Fuel: 30,000lb (13.6t).
Water: 7,000 US gall (26.5m³).
Adhesive weight: 335,104lb (152t).
Total weight: 477,500lb (216.7t).
Length overall: 67ft 2in (20,470mm).

Anatole Mallet was a Frenchman who took out a patent in 1884 for a locomotive with the front part hinged. He seems to have had in mind using the idea mainly in connection with small tank engines intended for sharply-curved local and industrial railways. The idea that his patent should be the basis of the largest, heaviest and most powerful locomotives ever built would have seemed strange, but so it was.

The Baltimore & Ohio Railroad had a problem in taking heavy trains up the Sand Patch incline, 16 miles (26km) long, graded at 1 per cent (1-in-100). There were sharp·7° curves (250m radius), and this limited the number of driving wheels which a straight unhinged locomotive could have. The idea was to replace the two 2-8-0 helpers necessary for a 2,000-ton train by a single locomotive. Looking at the problem with hindsight the answer now seems obvious, but at the time the proposal to introduce a relatively untried idea from Europe must have seemed bold to the point of rashness. Anyway, the B&O management took their courage in both hands and went to the American Locomotive Co for the first ever US Mallet compound. It was a turning point in US locomotive history.

This No.2400 launched another innovation as far as the USA was concerned—one which was to affect locomotive practice even more than the Mallet arrangement, for this pathfinding machine was the first significant US locomotive to have outside Walschaert valve gear. One set worked the inside-admission piston valves of the rear high-pressure cylinders and another had the slightly different arrangement appropriate to slide valves which are inherently outside-admission.

This simple, accessible and robust mechanism, which produced excellent valve events, was very soon to become the standard valve gear for most North American locomotives. Another feature to become standard later was the steam-powered reversing gear. With four valve gears, the effort required was too great for a manual arrangement. Later, the

Below: *The Great Northern Railway was an early Mallet user from 1906 on, as exemplified by this L class 2-6-6-0.*

mechanism of straight two-cylinder engines became so massive that power-reverse became general on all except the smallest.

The Mallet principle could be described as building a normal locomotive with a powered leading truck, for the frame of the rear high-pressure engine has the boiler attached rigidly to it. The large low-pressure cylinders can if required be placed in front of the smokebox, and thereby they can be freed of any restrictions on their size. The pivoting arrangements for the front engine are relatively simple, with a hinge at the rear and a slide at the front.

No.2400, known affectionately as "Old Maude" never had any sisters, but she numbered her descendants in thousands. They included virtually without exception all the world's largest, strongest and most powerful reciprocating steam locomotives ever built.

Above: *Baltimore & Ohio compound 0-6-6-0 No.2400 was the first Mallet articulated locomotive in the USA.*

Below: *By 1916 Baltimore & Ohio was building 2-8-8-0s much more powerful than No.2400, such as this EL-2 class articulated.*

Class EP-1 Bₒ-Bₒ New York, New Haven & Hartford Railroad (NY, NH & HRR), 1906

Type: Electric passenger locomotive.
Gauge: 4ft 8½in (1,435mm).
Propulsion: Alternating current at 11,000V 25Hz from overhead wires fed through transformer to four 240hp (180kW) bogie-mounted gearless traction motors with spring drive; alternative supply at 660V dc from third rail.
Weight: 204,000lb (92.6t).
Max. axleload: 51,000lb (23.1t).
Overall length: 37ft 6½in (11,440mm).
Tractive effort: 42,000lb (187kN).
Max. speed: 65mph (105km/h).

General Electric established an early lead in the supply of dc traction equipment in the United States, but in 1895 its main rival in the heavy electrical industry,

Westinghouse, began a long association with the Baldwin Locomotive Works. In that year an experimental locomotive was built at GE's East Pittsburgh Works, with mechanical components by Baldwin. This locomotive was used for experimental work on both dc and ac traction equipment.

By the turn of the century, the advantages of ac for electrical generation and transmission were well established, and early in the new century Westinghouse marketed a high-voltage single-phase ac traction system. The first application was in 1905, when a 41-mile (66km) line between Indianapolis and Rustville was electrified at 3,300V.

The New York, New Haven & Hartford Railroad had electrified various branches in New England from 1895 onwards, using dc with third-rail current collection.

In 1903 the law which compelled the New York Central to electrify its lines into Grand Central Terminal

Above: *Collector shoes and pantographs — the world's first dual-voltage loco.*

No. 9 4-6-0 Nevada-California-Oregon Railroad (NCO), 1909

Gauge: 3ft 0in (914mm).
Tractive effort: 17,800lb (8,076kg).
Axleload: 23,966lb (10.9t).
Cylinders: (2) 16 x 20in (406 x 508mm).
Driving wheels: 44in (1,117mm).
Steam pressure: 180psi (12.7kg/cm²).
Fuel (oil): 2,400 US gall (9.1m³).
Water: 5,000 US gall (18.9m³).
Adhesive weight: 65,360lb (29.7t).
Total weight: 165,150lb (74.9t).
Length overall: 53ft 11in (16,433mm).

By reason of its chance survival, in its later years this small

locomotive achieved considerable fame and, indeed, remains virtually intact to this day. Its origins lie in the 1880s when narrow-gauge disease spread across into the far west from Colorado. The route of the Nevada-California-Oregon Railway was constructed between 1880 and 1912. It ran 235 miles (378km), generally northwards, from Reno, Nevada, via Alturas in California to Lakeview, Oregon, incorporating the earlier Nevada & Oregon and Nevada & California railroads as well as other lines. Most of the mileage came into the hands of Southern Pacific by purchase in 1926 and was quickly altered to standard gauge.

NCO No.9 was one of four small oil-burning 3ft gauge ten-

wheelers delivered by Baldwin between 1907 and 1911. They pursued a busy but uneventful existence for 15 years or so until their new owner widened the gauge. However, SP had another narrow-gauge line not far away which had been effectively in its hands since 1900. The Carson & Colorado Railway ran from Mound House, Nevada, nearly 300 miles (483km) southwards to Keeler, California and the best of the NCO engines were moved there after 1928. By 1943 all but the southernmost 70 miles of the C&C had been abandoned or widened.

The remaining narrow-gauge tracks ran through the remote Owens Valley which, though once prosperous, had become

desolate following the abstraction of its water to supply the city of Los Angeles. Even so, once World War II was over, the fame of the slim gauge steam operations attracted hundreds of railfans who came both individually and by special excursions. Two of the 4-6-0s, Nos. 8 and 9, plus an ex-NCO 2-8-0 (No.18) soldiered on down the years. No.9 was the last steam locomotive to run, not only on the narrow-gauge but on the whole Southern Pacific system. This was in 1959 during a period of standby duty beginning in 1954 when a narrow-gauge diesel locomotive arrived. In 1960 the line was finally abandoned.

An unconventional feature of all three locomotives was the semi-circular tender, partitioned for oil

also applied to the New Haven, whose suburban trains used that station. The New Haven developed an even more elaborate scheme than the NYC. Rather than face the administrative and financial problems of a change from electric to steam working outside the area covered by the ban, the road decided to electrify to the limit of suburban territory at Stamford, 33 miles (53km) from Grand Central, making it the longest main-line electrification thus far undertaken. Having decided to go so far, the railroad then looked for a system of electrification which would be suitable for further extension along its very busy main line to New Haven, and even to Boston.

In 1905 GE and Westinghouse both submitted schemes for dc and ac systems. Despite the small experience of ac traction, the New

Haven surprised the railway world by announcing that the electrification was to be executed by Westinghouse using ac at 11,000V 25Hz with locomotive haulage. This was a bold step, but one which the road would have no cause to regret.

Design of the locomotives was difficult, for not only had novel problems in ac traction to be solved, but the locos had also to be able to work on 660V dc over the 12 miles of New York Central electrified line by which the New Haven gained access to Grand Central. The solution was a Bo-Bo design with commutator motors which could operate on both ac and dc, the ac being transformed to 660V. The motor casings were mounted on the bogies above the axles, and the armatures on hollow quills through which passed the axles. The quills were supported

in rigid bearings, and they were connected to the axles through spring connections. There was sufficient clearance in the quills for the axles to move vertically on their springs. The weight of the motor, including the armature, was thus fully spring borne, whereas in the GE bi-polar motors the weight of the armature was on the axle.

The size of the locomotives was suited to average trainloads, which included hauling expresses of 250 tonnes at up to 60 mph (97km/h), but to allow the locomotives to work in twos and threes on heavier trains, multiple-unit control was fitted. Current collection provision was generous, with two dc pick-up shoes on each side of each bogie, a small dc pantograph and two ac pantographs.

A total of 37 had been delivered by mid-1907. Some initial difficulties

were encountered, particularly with nosing of the bogies at high speed. This was solved by fitting a pair of guiding wheels at the outer ends of the bogies, making the wheel arrangement 1-Bo + Bo-1. After some electrical problems had been solved, the locomotives settled down to long and successful careers. By 1924 they had accumulated an average of 1¼ million miles (2 million km), much of it at high speed. At times they exceeded 80mph (129km/h), and on test a figure of 89mph (143km/h) was recorded. A further batch of six locomotives was built in 1908.

These locomotives were notable in being the first main-line ac units, as well as the first dual-voltage machines. Despite these innovations, several of them, including the prototype, were still in main line service in 1947.

and water supplies. Otherwise Nos. 8 and 9 followed normal turn-of-the-century practice. No.18 (supplied to NCO in 1911) was more modern, having outside Walschaert valve gear. It says enough of the fame of the line that three of its steam locomotives have survived—No.8 at Carson City, Nevada, No.18 at Independence, California and No.9 at Bishop, California.

Right: *NCO No.11 went to the Southern Pacific Coast Railroad in 1928, and then did war service in Hawaii.*

Below: *Unusual narrow-gauge survivor, former NCO 4-6-0 No.9 with its curious semi-circular tender.*

900 2-10-2 Atchison, Topeka & Santa Fe Railway (AT&SF), 1903

Gauge: 4ft 8½in (1,435mm)
Tractive effort: 62,560lb (28,385kg).
Axleload: 46,800lb (21.2t).
Cylinders, HP: (2) 19 x 32in (482 x 812mm).
Cylinders, LP: (2) 32 x 32in (812 x 812mm).
Driving wheels: 57in (1,447mm).
Heating surface: 4,817sq ft (488m²).
Steam pressure: 225psi (15.8kg/cm²).
Grate area: 59.5sq ft (5.5m²).
Fuel: 30,000lb (13.6t).
Water: 17,000 US gall (26.5m³).
Adhesive weight: 234,000lb (106.2t).
Total weight: 433,000lb (196.5t).
Length overall: 81ft 8in (24,892mm).

By the turn of the century, locomotive engineering had moved on apace since the failure of such early ten-coupled locomotives as Southern Pacific's *El Gobernador* (qv) of 1883. The Atchison, Topeka & Santa Fe Railway had an equal if not harder task in moving freight over the mountain barriers on its way to and from California. The approach to Santa Fe's Raton Pass was graded at 3.5 per cent (1-in-28½)

and two large Decapod 2-10-0s were built as pushers for use on this horrendous incline; they were very successful. The only problem occurred when running back down after helping a train up the hill; it was found that guiding wheels were advisable to assist the limited tracking qualities of the long rigid wheelbase. As a result the company asked Baldwin to build the world's first 2-10-2, and so history was made.

The 2-10-2 type, named "Santa Fe" after the first user, was built in big numbers—as many as 2,200 for US railroads over the next 40 years—and is even today in large-scale production for the Chinese Railways. The original examples were interesting in that they were 'tandem' compounds with each high-pressure cylinder sharing a common piston rod with the low-pressure ones. The problems of attending to the pack-

Above: *The very first "Santa Fe" or 2-10-2 type supplied to the Atchison, Topeka & Santa Fe Railway in 1903 by Baldwin, No.900 is seen at San Augustine, Texas, in April 1951.*

Right: *The 3800 class 2-10-2s were the final development of the Santa Fe type on the Santa Fe Railway. Introduced in 1924, they had a tractive effort 30 per cent more than the 900 class.*

Class H4 4-6-2 Great Northern Railway (GNR), 1909

Gauge: 4ft 8½in (1,435mm).
Tractive effort: 35,690lb* (16,193kg).
Axleload: 55,400lb (25.1t).
Cylinders: (2) 23½ x 30in (597 x 762mm).
Driving wheel: 73in (1,854mm).
Heating surface: 3,177sq ft (295m²).
Superheater: 620sq ft (57.6m²).
Steam pressure: 210psi (14.75kg/cm²).
Grate area: 53.3sq ft (4.95m²).
Fuel: 28,000 (12.7t).
Water: 8,000 US gall (30.3m³).
Adhesive weight: 151,200lb (68.6t).
Total weight: 383,750lb (174t).
Length overall: 67ft 3in (20,498mm).
*45,511lb (20,643kg) with booster.
†without tender.

The Great Northern Railway was the northernmost US transcontinental route to be completed between the Mississippi River and

the Pacific Ocean. It was a very different affair from those that had gone before, being a personal enterprise on the part of a legendary railroad tycoon called Jerome Hill. He had no government assistance and in the face of universal prophesies of disaster the GN was driven through to the Pacific coast in three short years. Even 'J.J.' himself was not present when the last spike—a plain iron one—was driven without ceremony on September 18, 1893, for he had

his sights on a day in December 1905, when his superbly de-luxe "Oriental Limited" would cross the continent to connect with his own steamship, the *SS Minnesota*, en route to China and Japan.

The GN section of the route ran 1,829 miles (2,926km) from St Paul to Seattle, and before all-steel equipment arrived in the 1920s, 4-6-2s were adequate as haulage units, with some assistance in the mountains. But it must not be thought that in the days when

It must be recorded (though one cannot expect readers to believe it straight away) that before disenchantment with complexity set in, Santa Fe in 1911 rebuilt 20 Class "900" 2-10-2s into 10 of the "3000" class 2-10-10-2 articulated locomotives which were then the most powerful in the world. They were not successful and were converted back to 2-10-2s in 1915, when, following changes in the top brass of the railroad, conversion was begun of all Santa Fe's compounds—numbering nearly 1,000 of many wheel arrangements—to simple propulsion.

The 2-10-2s had priority in this conversion and after World War II the fleet of this type was supplemented by more modern versions. As steam approached its end in the late-1940s nearly 300 of the 2-10-2s were still on the roster. Following improvements to the springing and side-control, and the dropping of compounding, the type had been found to be excellent workhorses for general heavy freight haulage, as well as on the helper duties for which the "900" class had originally been built. One "900" class (No. 940) is recorded as being preserved in Johnson Park, Bartlesville, Oklahoma.

ing of the glands between each pair of cylinders were assisted to some extent by providing a small crane on each side of the smokebox. Perhaps this illustrates part of the reason why Santa Fe's locomotive department, in their later and wiser days, never bought any locomotive, however huge, with more than two simple cylinders. Until, that is, diesel traction came along and the number of cylinders in a multi-unit locomotive came to be counted in dozens!

timber-bodied equipment was used on the "Oriental Limited" the train lacked anything in the way of luxury for its riders. The best food in America was to be found on the trains and certainly the Great Northern was no exception to this rule, until that sad day 60-odd years later when GN ceased to operate passenger service.

Delivery from the Baldwin Locomotive Works in 1909 of 20 new superheated "H-4" class Pacifics

coincided with running the "Oriental Limited" through from Chicago via the Burlington's route to St Paul. A further 25 came from Lima in 1913. Superheating was soon to become universal and this class was an early example of the technique. The arrangement used involved elements in the smokebox rather than in flue tubes and so was less efficient but still very creditable. The "H4s" burnt coal but some were later converted to oil-burning.

So all the elements had come together of the style of steam locomotive that would sweep the world. Cast frames, cylinders integral with the smokebox saddle, wide firebox, superheater, compensated springing with three point suspension, inside-admission piston valves and Walschaert valve gear proved an unbeatable combination. Steam locomotives currently in production in China are, as regards principles of design, exact copies.

The "H4s" had long lives of 40 years and over. Few alterations were made over the years, although boosters were fitted in the 1940s to some of the class to cope with wartime loads. Alas, none have been included amongst the handful of GN steam locomotives preserved for posterity.

Below: *The Class H4 4-6-2s were supplied by Baldwin and Lima to the Great Northern Railway between 1909 and 1913.*

DD1 2-B+B-2 Pennsylvania Railroad (PRR), 1909

Type: Electric passenger locomotive.
Gauge: 4ft 8½in (1,435mm).
Propulsion: Direct current at 600V fed via outside third rail (or by overhead conductors and miniature pantographs at places where third rail was impractical) to two 1,065hp (795kW) motors, each driving two main axles by means of a jackshaft and connecting rods.
Weight: 199,000lb (90.2t) adhesive, 319,000lb (145t) total.
Max. axleload: 50,750lb (23t).
Overall length: 64ft 11in (19,787mm).
Tractive effort: 49,400lb (220kN).
Max. speed: 80mph (129km/h).

The Pennsylvania Railroad gained entry to New York City and its new Pennsylvania Station by single-track tunnels, two under the Hudson River and four under the East River, and for the operation of these tunnels electrification was essential. The third-rail system at 650V was chosen, and between 1903 and 1905 three experimental four-axle locomotives were built, two B-Bs at the Pennsy's Altoona shops and a 2-B by Baldwin. The B-Bs had a separate motor for each axle, whilst the 2-B had a single 2,000hp (2,680kW) motor mounted on the main frame midway between the coupled axles. The motors of both types of locomotive drove through quills, an early version of the drive which

was to be used a quarter of a century later on the "GG1" electrics.

Test were made to determine the forces exerted on the rails by the two types of locomotive and by the most recent steam designs, and it was found that the 2-B, with its higher centre of gravity, exerted less than half the force of the B-B, with its low-slung motors. However, the force due to the 2-B was still twice as great as that from the heaviest steam engine. The next two electric locomotives therefore had the 2-B wheel arrangement, but to give the required power each one comprised two units permanently coupled back-to-back, giving the combined wheel arrangement 2-B-B-2. The important change in design from the experimental locomotive was in the drive to the axles, which incorporated a jackshaft mounted in bearings in the main frame of the locomotive, with connecting rods from the motor to the jackshaft and from the jackshaft to the driving wheels. The technical problems with the quill drive were left for solution at a later date.

With 72in (1,829mm) driving wheels, each half of the unit resembled the chassis of an express 4-4-0 steam locomotive. This similarity to steam design was apparent in a number of early electric engines, for example in Prussia, but unusually for such designs the Pennsylvania's was highly successful. It was capable of

Class T Bo-Bo+Bo-Bo New York Central Railroad (NYC), 1913

Type: Express passenger electric locomotive.
Gauge: 4ft 8½in (1,435mm).
Propulsion: Direct current at 660V collected from under-contact third rail supplying eight 330hp (246kW) gearless traction motors mounted on the bogie frames, with armatures on the axles.
Weight: 230,000lb (104.3t).
Max. axleload: 28,730lb (13.0t).
Overall length: 55ft 2in (16,815mm).
Tractive effort: 69,000lb (307kN).
Max. speed: 75mph (120km/h).

In 1913 the New York Central Railroad completed its Grand Central terminal, and in the same year it also completed an extension of electrification along the Hudson River main line to Harmon, 33 miles (53km) from Grand Central. The heaviest expresses would

80mph (129km/h), and there was no appreciable clanking of the rods. Maintenance costs were very low, and were helped by the design of the body. The whole casing could be removed in one unit to give access to the motors and control equipment. This feature was repeated in all subsequent PRR electric designs. A small pantograph was fitted to allow overhead current collection on complicated trackwork.

The first two rod-drive units appeared in 1909-10, the individual half-units being numbered from 3996 to 3999. They were followed in 1910-11 by a further 31, numbered from 3932 to 3949 and from 3952 to 3995. The Pennsylvania classified its steam

locomotives by a letter, denoting the wheel arrangement, followed by a serial number, letter "D" denoted 4-4-0. For electrics the road used the same system, the letter being doubled when appropriate, so that the 2-B+B-2, being a double 4-4-0, was a DD. The main production batch of 31 units was classified "DD1", and the two prototypes "odd DD".

The Pennsylvania Station project required seven years, from 1903 to 1910, for its execution, and electrification then extended from Manhattan Transfer, near Newark, New Jersey, to the carriage yards at Sunnyside, Long Island, a total of 13.4 route miles (21.5km). At Manhattan Transfer the change was made to or from

steam for the 8.8 miles (14.2km) between there and Pennsylvania Station. The heaviest gradient on the descent to the tunnels was 1-in-52 (1.93 per cent).

The "DD" locomotives worked all the express passenger services on this section of line until 1924 when newer types began to appear, but they continued to share the work until 1933 when overhead electrification reached Manhattan Transfer from Trenton, and the remaining section into Pennsylvania Station was converted to overhead. Third-rail current collection was retained between Pennsylvania Station and Sunnyside, because the Long Island Rail Road used this system.

After 1933 "DDs" continued

to work empty trains between Pennsylvania Station and Sunnyside for many years. After the arrival of newer power in 1924, 23 of the "DD1s" were transferred to the Long Island Rail Road, and these remained in service until 1949-51.

The "DDs" were a landmark in electric locomotive design, with exceptionally high power and unusual reliability for their day, but at the same time their design was conservative. Simplicity of design and the flexibility of the "double 4-4-0" chassis contributed greatly to their success.

Below: *Class DD1 electric loco for Pennsylvania Station-to-Manhattan Transfer traffic.*

now have some 20 miles of fast running with electric haulage, and a new type of locomotive was therefore commissioned, which would be both more powerful than the "S" class 2-Do-2 and also kinder to the track at high speed.

The new class was designated "T", thereby taking the letter vacated by the earlier locomotives when they were rebuilt. The most important change was adoption of an articulated layout in which every axle was motored, but at the same time the whole chassis was more flexible than in the earlier class. There were two sub-frames, each with two four-wheeled trucks pivotted to it. The trucks were connected by arms, and the sub-frames were hinged together at their inner ends and carried the couplers at the outer ends. The body rested on two pivots, one

Left: *New York Central Class T electric locomotive used to haul trains in New York City.*

on each sub-frame, and one pivot had some end play to allow for changes in geometry on curves. The whole assembly was therefore flexible, but with restraining forces on all its elements to discourage the build-up of oscillations. The wheel arrangement was Bo-Bo+Bo-Bo, and it was equivalent to two Bo-Bo locomotives hinged together.

Nominal power of the original motors fitted to Class "S" was 550hp (410kW), but in Class "T" the motor size was reduced to 330hp (246kW). This enabled the weight of the motors to be reduced, with a corresponding reduction in the forces on the track and with an improvement in riding. The new class was therefore allowed 75mph (121km/h), later reduced to 70 (113), compared with 60mph (97km/h) on Class "S". The motors were of the same bi-polar type as before, with almost flat pole faces to allow for the vertical movement of the axle

(and armature) on its springs.

Another change from Class "S" was that the motors had forced ventilation, which involved some complications of ducting to the bogies. As in the earlier units, in addition to pick-up shoes for the third rail, a small pantograph was fitted. This was used on complicated track layouts where there were long gaps in the third rail, and overhead wires were installed locally. There was an oil-fired train heating boiler, with supplies of water and oil. It seemed anomalous on an electrification introduced to eliminate the smoke nuisance that the locomotive should carry a small stack on its roof emitting oil exhaust!

The first locomotive was completed in March 1918; this was Class "T1a". Nine more, classified "T1b", were delivered later in the year. Sub-class "T2a" of 10 units came in 1914, a further 10 designated "T2b" in 1917, and a final batch of 10 in 1926; these were

"T3a". Successive batches differed mainly in the size of train-heating boiler and its fuel supplies, but the "T2s" and "T3s" were 20in (508mm) longer than the "T1s". The bodies of successive batches were a little longer, and the end overhang slightly less.

With a continous rating of 2,610hp at 48mph (77km/h), they were powerful locomotives for their day, and they were highly successful. They continued to work single-headed all express trains out of Grand Central until 1955, when some locomotives surplus from a discontinued electrification in Cleveland began to displace them. They could handle trains up to 980 US tons at 60mph (97km/h).

These locomotives established the practicability of the all-adhesion machine for high-speed work, and they showed that it was possible to avoid the heavy and complicated rod drives of many of their contemporaries.

Fairlie 0-6-6-0 Mexican Railway (FCM), 1911

Gauge: 4ft 8½in (1,435mm).
Tractive effort: 58,493lb (26,533kg).
Axle load: 46,000lb (21t).
Cylinders: (4) 19 x 25in (483 x 635mm).
Driving wheels: 48in (1,219mm).
Heating surface: 2,924sq ft (272mm²).
Steam pressure: 183psi (12.9kg/cm²).
Grate area: 47.7sq ft (4.43m²).
Fuel: 20,000lb (9t).
Water: 4,200 US gall (16m³).
Adhesive weight: 276,000lb (125t).
Total weight: 276,000lb (125t).
Length overall: 50ft 7¾in (15,435).

Right: A Mexican Railways "Fairlie" locomotive of the batch supplied by the Vulcan Foundry in 1911.

The Mexican Railway ran 264 miles (426km) from the port of Vera Cruz on the Atlantic Ocean to Mexico City, at an altitude of 7,349ft (2,240m). The summit of the route is at Acocotla, 8,320ft (2,536m), but in 108 miles (174 km) the line climbs to 8,050ft at Esperaza. The maximum gradient is a hideous 1 in 22 (4.5 per cent) and the sharpest curve is 325ft radius or 17½ degrees. Before electrification came in 1923, this superbly scenic but very difficult railway had not unexpectedly something rather special in the way of motive power.

The "Fairlie" articulated locomotive was invented by an English engineer called Robert Fairlie in 1864 and foreshadowed the majority of locomotives (other than steam) in service today by having a generator for the working fluid—steam in Fairlie's case, electricity in modern times—as part of the locomotive body; the body being carried on two power bogies which provided the traction. All the axles were therefore driven, so the total weight was available for adhesion, yet the whole vehicle remained extremely flexible. The arrangement made the locomotive an excellent proposition for sharply curved steeply graded mountain lines. Even so, "Fairlies" were never as popular

as the "Garratt" or "Mallet" articulated locomotive types, and their application for this British-owned Mexican line was certainly their greatest both as regard size of individual locomotives and their success as haulage units.

The first "Fairlie" came to Mexico in 1871 and by 1911 a total of 49 had been delivered, of which 18 were still in service in 1923 when electrification made them finally redundant. The last and largest of them was a batch of three supplied by Vulcan Foundry in 1911, carrying running numbers 183 to 185. The advantage of the "Fairlie" is best summed up by comparison with

Class 1300 2-4-6-2 Atchison, Topeka & Santa Fe Railway (AT&SF), 1909

Gauge: 4ft. 8½in (1,435mm).
Tractive effort: 53,700lb (24,365kg).
Axleload: 58,963lb (26.8t).
Cylinders, HP: (2) 24 x 28in (609 x 711mm).
Cylinders, LP: (2) 28 x 28in (711 x 711mm).
Driving wheels: 73in (1,854mm).
Heating surface: 4,756sq ft (442m²).
Superheater: 323sq ft (30m²).
Reheater: 728sq ft (68m²).
Steam pressure: 200psi (14.1kg/cm²).
Grate area: 52.7sq ft (4.9m²).
Fuel (oil): 4,000 US gall (15.1m³).
Water: 12,000 US gall (45.4m³).
Adhesive weight: 268,016lb (121.6t).
Total weight: 612,192lb (277.8t).
Length overall: 104ft 10¾in (31,973mm).

It has been related how the great Atchison, Topeka & Santa Fe Railway exchanged straight-forward locomotives for fairly complex ones and did not find the change satisfactory. The further solution was then to move from the fairly complex to some very complex machinery indeed. One of the first results of this policy was this really quite extraordinary 2-4-6-2 compound Mallet design, of which two prototype locomotives (Nos.1300-1) were supplied by Baldwin in 1909. They were intended for fast passenger traffic and to this end had the largest driving wheels ever used on a Mallet, plus a very low centre of gravity. The long, thin boiler was also complicated, with a corrugated firebox and plate stays rather than the usual staybolts. The boiler barrel was in two sections with a separate forward chamber which acted as a feed-water heater.

One modest but satisfactory complication, at this time becoming standard, was a superheater, but Santa Fe had to go one stage further and have a reheater as well. This feature is similar in form to a superheater, except that it is arranged to apply extra heating to the steam after it leaves the high-pressure cylinders and before going to the low-pressure engine. A small gain in thermal efficiency is achieved by its use, but, in contrast to normal superheating, in general railroads did not find the extra cost of maintaining reheaters worthwhile.

Aside from all the complications, the main problem with such locomotives as these was that the Mallet layout, as then being built, was a little too flexible for comfort at fast speeds. Violent oscillations were liable to occur and some very specific restrictions to the degree of freedom of the front engine had first to be devised

before these articulateds were suitable for anything but slow slogging freight trains.

In 1915, Nos.1300 and 1301 had their front engines and front boiler stages removed, and so with comparative ease they returned to service as simple two-cylinder 4-6-2s. At last their inherent high-speed capability could be used. Incidentally, after finding out that the two 2-4-6-2s were not going to work, Santa Fe had some 2-6-6-2 articulated locomotives with amazing flexible boilers that were even more complicated. This time, the front stage of the boiler was fixed to the leading chassis and was actually hinged to the rear part. Both concertina connections and ball-and-socket joints were tried, but to no avail.

Right: Complicated and short-lived, AT&SF's extraordinary Class 1300 compound Mallet.

a typical British main-line locomotive of the day. Compare, for example, these Mexican Railway locomotives with a LNWR type. For a penalty of 29 per cent in weight and 5 per cent in axleload, one obtained an 114 per cent increase in grate area, 220 per cent more adhesive weight and 190 per cent more tractive effort. The "Fairlie"'s were the most powerful locomotives built in Britain up to this time.

Although the speeds of trains on the Mexican Railway's inclines were severely restricted by traction limitations going up, and to 8mph (13km/h) for safety reasons coming down, the "Fairlie"'s had excellent riding and tracking qualities at high speeds. This was inadvertently discovered on one or two occasions when runaways occurred; speeds estimated at up to 70mph (113km/h) were achieved on sharp curves without derailment. The motion of these locomotives was quite conventional, with outside piston valve cylinders and Walschaert's valve gear. On the other hand the double boilers were very unusual indeed. The boiler barrels at both ends were nearly similar, but the firebox in the centre was common to both barrels. One big dome in the usual position for one half of the boiler (normally the uphill end) collected the steam for all four cylinders.

The expense involved in this double boiler was almost certainly the main reason why the "double Fairlie" articulated locomotive was never widely used. It is true there were some problems with the flexible pipes and joints which fed the steam from the boiler to the powered bogies, but experience and the improvement of details would have solved them. In fact this is just what has happened on the one railway left in the world that has "double-Fairlie" steam locomotives still in use, the Festiniog Railway in North Wales. Their 40 ton 0-4-4-0 tanks, are, however, a far cry from the 123-ton Mexican monsters.

"Single Fairlie"'s, however, went into quite extensive use. These locomotives had a normal boiler, a leading power bogie and a trailing un-powered bogie behind the firebox. An ability to negotiate absurdly sharp curves was the property that appealed and many (under various names, for Fairlie's patent was not recognised in the USA) were used on urban railways, particularly elevated lines which had to negotiate city street corners. But "single Fairlies" were only, as it were, half of what was a good idea.

No. 7 2-4-4T
Bridgton & Saco River Railroad (B&SR), 1913

Gauge: 2ft 0in (609mm).
Tractive effort: 10,072lb (4,570kg).
Axleload: 21,340lb (9.7t).
Cylinders: (2) 12 x 16in (304 x 406mm).
Driving wheels: 35in (889mm).
Steam pressure: 180psi (12.7kg/cm²).
Fuel: 3,000lb (1.4t).
Water: 1,000 US gall (3.8m³).
Adhesive weight: 38,800lb (17.6t).
Total weight: 69,700lb (31.6t).
Length overall: 34ft 7¾in (10,650mm).

This tiny locomotive from a tiny railway was nevertheless a pathfinder. It seems she was the first in the world to be restored for use as an instrument of pleasure after being withdrawn from normal commercial use.

Right: Edaville's No.7, forerunner of so many steam locomotives now preserved round the world. Baldwin was the builder in 1913.

The Baldwin Locomotive Works in 1913 delivered No. 7 to the 2ft gauge Bridgton & Saco River Railroad up in Maine. The locomotive followed the Forney style with the addition of a lead truck, making a 2-4-4T type, and had slide valves actuated by Walschaerts valve gear, vacuum brakes and an unsuperheated boiler. These features all helped by their simplicity to give this elegant little iron foal qualities of usefulness and reliability, leading to a long life and finally to survival beyond the end of the age of steam.

In 1930 the 35-mile B&SR had become the 27-mile Bridgton & Harrison, but traffic was miniscule and by the end of the decade

No. 14 2-8-2
East Broad Top Railroad (EBT), 1911

Gauge: 3ft 0in (914mm).
Tractive effort: 27,600lb (12,523kg).
Axleload: 29,700lb (13.5t).
Cylinders: (2) 19 x 24in (482 x 609mm).
Driving wheels: 48in (1,219mm).
Heating surface: 1,676sq ft (156m²).
Superheater: 357sq ft (33m²).
Steam pressure: 180psi (12.7kg/cm²).
Grate area: 36sq ft (3.3m²).
Adhesive weight: 108,000lb (49t).
Total weight: 244,750lb (1.111t).
Fuel: 18,000lb (8.2t).
Water: 5,000 US gall (18.9m³).
Length overall: 64ft 10in (19,761mm).

Narrow gauge was always rare east of the Mississippi and 30 years ago the only such system of any size still operating was the 33-mile (53km) 3ft gauge East Broad Top Railroad, with headquarters

at Orbisonia, Pennsylvania. The EBT was chartered in 1856, completed in 1874 and it spent its life doing mainly what it was built to do; that is, carrying coal from mines towards its far end to an interchange with the Pennsylvania RR at Mount Union.

It was a well-arranged operation; narrow gauge was no handicap because the coal had to be unloaded and reloaded at the Mount Union cleaning and grading plant anyway. Carload freight of other kinds was dealt with by replacing standard-gauge trucks with narrow-gauge ones for the ride over the EBT. Its long survival was due to these factors, as well as to the more fundamental point that coal-hauling was what railroads were first built for and were best at doing.

The EBT was also rare in that, by the early 1950s, it was still all-steam with a fleet of six reasonably modern Baldwin 2-8-2s which had been supplied one at a time

over the years 1911 to 1920. All were of similar appearance but the three later ones were larger and had piston instead of slide valves. Alas, in 1955 coal sales were at a very low ebb, and so it

Above: *Coal-hauling days are over for the East Broad Top 2-8-2s; now only tourists and railfans use the 10-mile (16km) preserved section of this 3ft (914mm) gauge line.*

abandonment was clearly not far off. On days when the train was not operating regularly, the manager would put on a special for a few dollars to satisfy visiting railfans. One group even went some way towards raising funds to buy the line. In the event, a scrap merchant put in a bid which the fans could not match.

In 1941 No.7 (plus sister No.8 and a number of pasenger and freight cars) was bought by a cranberry grower from Mass-achusetts called Ellis D. Atwood. As the war ended, Atwood began building a railroad on his farm. It was formed as a circuit 5½ miles (8.8km) in length, the dykes between the cranberry bogs providing a ready-made alignment on which he and his men could spike down the secondhand rails he had bought.

The idea was that the line should provide essential transport for the estate and only on high days and holidays be a pleasure line for himself and his friends. But it was not to be. People for miles around started to clamour for invitations, and soon enough the idea of opening the Ellis D. Atwood Railroad (Edaville for short) to the public was born. Monday, April 7, 1947 was the day when the golden spike was ceremonially driven, since when Edaville—and railway preservation round the world—has gone from strength to strength. The only sour note is that, after two changes of ownership, Edaville is having to move—its presence inconveniences modern methods of cranberry farming.

was no surprise that in April 1956 the last coal train ran and all these wonders seemed at an end.

Now the idea of preserving an operating commercial railroad as a tourist attraction had come to Pennsylvania in 1959, when the little Strasburg Railroad was saved from extinction in this way. Now, by a happy chance, the man who bought the East Broad Top for scrap was a railfan. Moreover, Nick Kovalchick had (as *Trains* magazine put it in 1960) "wanted to run a railroad ever since his parents couldn't afford to buy him a toy train years ago." And, since all the EBT locomotives had frames inside the wheel (instead of outside as was more typical of large narrow-gauge steam power), they looked for all the world like toy trains two-thirds full-size! So Kovalchick achieved his childhood dream and the rest of us rejoiced that the best part of this railroad treasure has survived for our enjoyment and pleasure. The new EBT, although rather remote in situation, still runs tourist trains northwards out of Orbisonia each weekend from June to October and daily during July and August.

Maintaining even narrow-gauge steam locomotives is a mighty task and in this regard the new EBT has been lucky in that the old EBT believed in do-it-yourself and had all the necessary tools.

Above: *Back in 1952, there was still hard work to be done by the Baldwin 2-8-2s. No.16 heads a train of empty hoppers at the Mount Union coal washery.*

Class 60-3 Shay B-B-B Sierra Nevada Wood & Lumber Co, 1913

Gauge: 3ft 0in (914mm).
Tractive effort: 36,150lb (16,402kg).
Axleload: 19,666lb (8.9t).
Cylinders: (3) 11 x 12in (279 x 304mm).
Driving wheels: 32in (812mm).
Heating surface: 881sq ft (82m²).
Superheater: 189sq ft (18m²).
Steam pressure: 200psi (14.1kg/cm²).
Grate area: 23sq ft (2.1m²).
Fuel (oil): 1,200 US gall (4.5m³).
Water: 3,000 US gall (11,4m³).
Adhesive weight: 118,000lb (53.5t).
Total weight: 118,000lb (53.5t).
Length overall: 50ft 2in (15,290mm).

The story of the Shay—a locomotive like nothing else on earth—is also the story of the Lima Locomotive Works of Lima, Ohio. Before 1880 it was just the Lima Machine Works, but in that year they built their first locomotive, a strange steam-driven flat car to the designs of a veteran logging man called Ephraim Shay. The first Shays had vertical boilers but later examples had locomotive-type ones. These were offset to one side of the centre-line in order to balance the two- or three-cylinder in-line steam engine with vertical cylinders mounted on the other side. This drove the axles via longitudinal shafts fore and aft, universal joints and bevel gears.

Below: *This oil-fired three-truck Shay, built in 1913, was originally produced for the Sierra Nevada Wood and Lumber Co.'s logging railroad.*

Above: *A Shay in untypically clean and polished condition, ready to take a trainload of tourists on the Roaring Camp & Big Trees RR, Felton, California.*

The basic Shay had two two-axle trucks but further powered trucks driven in the same way could be added at the rear. Three-truck Shays were common and four-truck ones were also built.

Because it had all wheels driven and because there was the maximum amount of flexibility along its wheelbase, and also because of its simplicity and robustness, the Shay pulled useful loads and held to the rails on crazy temporary tracks in forests which were being felled. It was also ideal for any steeply-graded and sharply-curved railroad. Over the next 65 years a total of 2,771 were sold, most of them in the first 35 or so. Their popularity was a clear indication of their usefulness and efficiency. The last one was delivered in 1944 by which time Lima had become a prestigous supplier of giant high-powered locomotives.

A valuable but by no means obvious feature was the short, fat, heavily-tapered boiler barrel which minimised the change in water level at the firebox end for different inclinations. This meant that Shays could run off and on to 10 per cent (1-in-10) grades without trouble. Their flexibility meant they could negotiate 76° (23m radius) curves with serious kinks and wildly varying cross-levels without derailing. In addition, they were available straight out of Lima's catalogue in all gauges and in sizes from 320,000lb total weight down to 50,000lb or less. They could burn coal, oil or forest waste and were easy and cheap

to maintain in primitive workshops. Perhaps one should add that, flat out at 12mph or so, they sounded like the "Overland Limited" setting alight the prairies at 90mph.

The example depicted here is the West Side Lumber Company's three-truck Class "60-3" Shay No.15, supplied by Lima, originally to the Sierra Nevada Wood & Lumber Company in 1913 as their No.9. West Side had one of the largest logging railroads with over 60 miles of main route based on Toulomne, California, where No.15 is preserved. Shays still run on several tourist railroads, notably at Cass, West Virginia; Tacoma, Washington State; Georgetown, Colorado; at Fish Camp and at Felton in California.

Above: *An oil-fired Shay logging locomotive of the Yosemite Mt. Sugar Pine Railroad at Fish Camp Railroad. A local law prohibits coal-burning steam locomotives to operate in California.*

K4 Class 4-6-2 Pennsylvania Railroad (PRR), 1914

Gauge: 4ft 8½in (1,435mm).
Tractive effort: 44,460lb (20,170kg).
Axle load: 72,000lb (33t).
Cylinders: (2) 27 x 28in (686 x 711mm).
Driving wheels: 80in (2,032mm).
Heating surface: 4,040sq ft (375m²).
Superheater: 943sq ft (88m²).
Boiler pressure: 205psi (14.4kg/cm²).
Grate area: 70sq ft (6.5m²).
Fuel: 36,000lb (16t).
Water: 10,000gall (12,000 US) (46m³).
Adhesive weight: 210,000lb (96t).
Total weight: 533,000lb (242t).
Overall length: 83ft 6in (25,451mm).

The Pennsylvania Railroad called itself the Standard Railroad of the World. This did not mean that the system was just average or typical, but rather that the railroad's status was one to which other lines might aspire, but a status that it was extremely unlikely that they would reach. The Pennsy's herald was a keystone, indicating the position the company felt it occupied in the economy of the USA. The famous "K4" 4-6-2s, introduced in 1914 and the mainstay of steam operations until after World War II, might well similarly be given the title Standard Express Locomotive of the World.

There were 425 of them, built over a period of 14 years, and they followed a series of classes of earlier 4-6-2s introduced previously. The Pennsy was normally exceedingly conservative in its locomotive engineering and its Pacific era was ushered in by a single prototype ordered from the American Locomotive Company in 1907, later designated class "K28". By 1910 the railroad felt it knew enough to start building some of its own and in a short time 239 "K2"s were put on the road. In 1912, quite late in the day really, superheating

was applied to these engines.

In 1913, the company went to Baldwin of Philadelphia for 30 "K3" 4-6-2s. These were interesting in that they were fitted with the earliest type of practical mechanical stoker, known as the "Crawford" after its inventor, D.F. Crawford, Superintendent of Motive Power (Lines West). This had been in use on the Pennsylvania Railroad since 1905 and by 1914 nearly 300 were in operation—but only 64 on 4-6-2s. Later designs of stoker used a

screw feed, but the principle used in the Crawford was to bring forward the coal by means of a series of paddles or vanes, oscillated by steam cylinders, which were feathered on the return stroke like the oars of a rowing boat. The coal was fed into the firebox at grate level, unlike later types of stoker, which feed on to a platform at the rear, for distribution by steam jets.

In addition, there was a further Alco prototype supplied in 1911, larger than the "K28" and desig-

Above: *Pennsy Class K4 speeds through Westbury, NY, during the winter of 1947.*

nated "K29". There was also the "K1" class, which was an "in house" project, designed but never built.

The prototype "K4" Pacific appeared in 1914; it was considerably larger than the "K2" class, having 36 per cent more tractive effort and 26 per cent more grate area at a cost of a 9 per cent increase in axle loading.

The design owed as much to that Apex of the Atlantics, the "E6" class 4-4-2 as to the earlier 4-6-2s.

The Pennsylvania Railroad was one of the very few North American lines to approach self-sufficiency in locomotive design and construction. It liked to build its own locomotives, designed by its own staff, in its own shops. One aid to this process was a locomotive testing plant at a place called Altoona — a hallowed name amongst the world's locomotive engineers. Altoona was then the only place in North America where a locomotive could be run up to full speed and power on rollers and where instrumentation could pick up exactly what was happening inside. In this way the designers' expectations could be checked under laboratory conditions and corrections applied.

The prototype "K4" was put to the question at Altoona soon after it was built, but few changes were needed as a result for the production version. The oil headlight and wooden pilot (cowcatcher) were not, however, repeated. By 1923, after more than 200 "K4"s had been built, power reverse replaced the hand-operated screw reversing gear of earlier engines. In due time the latter were converted, foreshadowing a date (1937) when hand reversing gear would be illegal for locomotives with over 160,000lb (72.7t) adhesive weight. The same edict applied to the fitting of automatic stokers to locomotives of such size and many (but not all) "K4"s were fitted with them during the 1930s. Before then the power output had been severely limited by the amount of coal a man could shovel. The last five "K4"s had cast steel one-piece locomotive frames. Another interesting box of tricks that also became general in the 1930s, was the continuous cab signalling system. A receiver picked up coded current flowing in track circuits and translated this into the appropriate signal aspect on a miniature signal inside the cab.

One could see signs of Pennsy's conservatism, for example, even in the later "K4"s the ratio of evaporative heating surface to superheater size was as low as 4.3, instead of the 2.2 to 2.5, more typical of the passenger locomotives which other North American railroads were using in the 1930s. There was also the modest boiler pressure, three-quarters or less of what was used elsewhere. It is not being suggested that such a policy was wrong, only that it was different. Low boiler pressures and modest degrees of superheat had a marked and favourable effect on the cost of maintenance and repair; perhaps the Pennsy, who could buy coal at pit-head prices, had done its sums in depth, trading some extra (cheap) coal for less (expensive) work in the shops.

Running numbers were allocated at random between 8 and 8378, although the last batches

Above: *Designer Raymond Loewy styled the streamlining of K4 No.3768, seen leaving Chicago on the "Broadway Limited".*

built during 1924-28 were numbered in sequence from 5350 to 5499. All were built at the PRR's Juanita shops at Altoona, Pennsylvania except Nos.5400 to 5474 of 1927 which came from Baldwin.

There were a few "specials" amongst the "K4" fleet. Two engines (Nos.3847 and 5399) were fitted with poppet valve gear, thermic syphons in the firebox, and improved draughting; so equipped they could develop over 4000hp in the cylinders instead of the 3000hp typical of a standard "K4". A number of other engines (designated class "K4sa")had less drastic treatment with the same end in view; in this case the firebox and exhaust improvements were accompanied by larger piston valves, 15in (381mm) diameter instead of 12in (305mm). One engine (No.3768) was fully streamlined

for a while; a number of others were partly streamlined and specially painted to match certain streamlined trains. Many types of tender were used, including a few which were so big they dwarfed the engine, but held 25 tons of coal and 23,500 US gallons (107m³) of water.

Until the coming of the Duplex locomotives after World War II, the "K4"s handled *all* Pennsy's express passenger trains outside the electrified area. During the winter of 1934 the *"Detroit Arrow"* was scheduled to cover the 64 miles (102km) from Plymouth to Fort Wayne, Indiana, in 51 minutes, an average speed of 75½mph (121km/h) and accordingly for a short time the fastest steam timing in the world. The cylinder limitations of the standard "K4"s did, however, mean much double-heading in driving Pennsy's great "Limiteds" across these long level stretches of the Lines West. The fact that these legendary locomotives were so economical in other ways more than balanced such extravagances as the use of two on one train.

In crossing the Allegheny mountains, such heroic measures as three "K4"s (or even, it is said, sometimes *four*) at the head end were needed to take, say, an unlimited section of the "Broadway Limited" up the 1 in 58 (1.72 per cent) of the Horseshoe Curve. Nowadays such things are only a memory, but a single "K4", presented to the City of Altoona, stands in a little park inside the famous semi-circle curve in remembrance of the monumental labours of one of the world's greatest express locomotives. Another (more accessible) is under cover in the Strasburg Railway's excellent museum in the town of that name.

Below: *One of the famous "K4" class 4-6-2s of the Pennsylvania Railroad. Between 1914 and 1928 425 were built, mostly at the road's own Altoona shops.*

MacDermot 4-6-2 Overfair Railroad, 1915

Gauge: 1ft 7in (483mm).
Tractive effort: 3,700lb (1,679kg).
Axleload: 5,544lb (2.5t).
Cylinders: (2) 8 x 9in (203 x 228mm).
Driving wheels: 26in (660mm).
Heating surface: 443sq ft (41m²).
Steam pressure: 200psi (14.1kg/cm²).
Grate area: 8sq ft (0.7m²).
Fuel: 1,000lb (0.5t).
Water: 300 US gall (1.1m³).
Adhesive weight: 15,120lb (6.9t).
Total weight: 24,080lb (10.9t).
Overall length: 28ft 1in (8,559mm).

The unlikely motivation for these delightful mini-locomotives was construction of the Panama Canal. To celebrate its completion in 1915, the Panama-Pacific-International Exposition was mounted at San Francisco. A wealthy and mechanically-minded young man, Louis MacDermot, secured a franchise to run an ambitious steam-operated line called the Overfair Railroad some 2½ miles long covering the length of the exposition site.

MacDermot made all his own drawings and had built machine- and erecting-shops in the grounds of his family's home in Oakland, California. Here an 0-6-0T and

Above and left: *Two views of one of the three 19in (483mm) gauge 4-6-2s built by Louis MacDermot in 1915 for the Panama-Pacific Exposition at San Francisco. Note how a seated engineer drives these locomotives, based on one-third of full-size practice.*

four 4-6-2s were built. Sixty cars with seats for 1,000 passengers were built, and there was also a freight train to be used for advertising purposes. Three trains were intended, but in the event only two were required. Allowing for one 4-6-2 in reserve, three were sufficient and the fourth was never quite completed.

The locomotives were perfect replicas of the classic passenger power of the day except that— quite incongruously—full-size air pumps were a rather too conspicuous feature of the left-hand side. The relatively massive coal-fired boilers produced saturated steam which was fed to conventional piston-valve cylinders. Walschaert valve gear was used, all the mechanism being one-third full size. It is a tribute to the elegant simplicity of the steam locomotive that there needed to be no compromise with correct functioning because of the reduction in size.

Triplex 2-8-8-8-2 Erie Railroad, 1915

Gauge: 4ft 8½in (1,435mm).
Tractive effort: 160,000lb (72,595kg).
Axleload: 69,813lb (31.7t).
Cylinders, HP: (2) 36 x 32in (914 x 812mm).
Cylinders, LP: (4) 36 x 32in (914 x 812mm).
Driving wheels: 63in (1,600mm).
Heating surface: 6,886sq ft (640m²).
Superheater: 1,584sq ft (147m²).
Steam pressure: 210psi (14.8kg/cm²).
Grate area: 90sq ft (8.4m²).
Fuel: 32,000lb (14.5t).
Water: 10,000 US gall (37.9m²).
Adhesive weight: 761,600lb (345.6t).
Total weight: 853,050lb (387t).
Overall length: 105ft 1in (32,029mm).

In December 1915, after 10 months of operation, the exposition and its railway closed. An unbusinesslike approach on the part of young MacDermot to the tedious matter of commercial arrangements led to his impoverishment, but his precious locomotives have since displayed a tenacity for continued existence typical of such rather special creations. MacDermot operated one of them in poor condition at Alameda Zoo in 1939.

MacDermot died a poor man in 1945, but all five of his superb locomotives still exist. Since then they have been in a number of hands and have seen occasional use, but only recently have they all come again into the same ownership with prospects of continued operation at Swanton, California.

Above: *This view of Swanton Pacific No.1913 shows how the original single clumsy Westinghouse air pump fitted by MacDermot in 1915 has been replaced by twin air pumps of a size more in keeping with the dimensions of the locomotive.*

By 1905 the Mallet articulated was here to stay but there was still a need for greater tractive effort for helper service on particularly steep grades. Limited drawbar strength made very high tractive efforts irrelevant for pulling trains, but for pushing at the rear the use of really substantial power was possible. The Erie Railroad's "Triplex" or triple Mallet articulated

Left: *The remarkable Erie Railroad 'Triplex' compound Mallet articulated 2-8-8-8-2 Matt. H. Shay, built by Baldwin in 1914. Three of these giants were built and were intended for helper service on the Erie's Gulf Hill grade. The centre unit took high-pressure steam from the boiler, while the two outer units were the low pressure ones.*

was a product of this thinking, intended to save locomotive expense in working heavy tonnage up Gulf Hill in the Susquehanna Division of the Erie Railroad. Baldwin offered the Erie a solution in the form of a compound Mallet with three engine units.

In fact, the locomotive was a 2-8-8-0 Mallet with an 0-8-2 steam-powered tender attached. The front and rear units were driven by four low-pressure cylinders, while the centre unit had two high-pressure cylinders. All six cylinders had the same bore and stroke. The leading unit exhausted up the chimney in the normal way, while the rear engine had its own separate exhaust at the back of the tender. The exhaust steam passed through a feed-water

heater beneath the tender en route.

Nominal tractive effort was substantially greater than that of Union Pacific's "Big Boy" and the weight on the drivers of these four locomotives (three were built for the Erie and one slightly different for the Virginian Railroad) was the greatest of any reciprocating steam locomotive type ever built, so that part of the objective was achieved. Alas, those responsible failed to match this with adequate steam generating capability. Since only low speeds were envisaged, the boiler was in principle big enough. However, only half the exhaust steam (and that at very low pressure) was available at the blastpipe and this seems to have been insufficient to produce enough smokebox

vacuum to ensure good steaming for the locomotive.

On test, the first "Triplex" (named *Matt. H. Shay* after one of the Erie's senior engineers) created a world record by hauling solo a 250-wagon train weighing 17,600 tons over a line which was generally uphill and included 0.9 per cent (1-in-110) adverse gradients. The distance was 23 miles (37km) and the average speed was 13½mph (21.6km/h). In service, though, there were difficulties and the Erie locomotives were withdrawn in 1925. So ended a remarkable experiment in extending the capability of the steam locomotive, which seems to have failed only through lack of attention to details of the combustion side of the design.

1201 2-6-2T British War Department, 1916

Gauge: 1ft 11⅝in (600mm).
Tractive effort: 6,252lb (2,837kg).
Axleload: 8,036lb (3.6t).
Cylinders: (2) 9 x 24in (228 x 609mm).
Driving wheels: 27in (685mm).
Heating surface: 264sq ft (25m²).
Steam pressure: 175psi (12.3kg/cm²).
Grate area: 5.4sq ft 0.5m².
Fuel: 1,680lb (0.75t).
Water: 475 US gall (1.8m³).
Adhesive weight: 23,400lb (10.6t).
Total weight: 38,281lb (17.4t).
Length overall: 22ft 1½in (6,743mm).

During World War I, trench warfare in France was sufficiently static to allow 2ft gauge military railways to be used to advantage in bringing up supplies and ammunition. With British industry hard-pressed, the War Department turned to the USA to supply motive power for such lines. The specification called for the simplest possible construction regardless of life expectancy. The American Locomotive Company's Cooke Works responded with 100 neat 2-6-2 tanks supplied during 1917 and 1918. They were intended to negotiate 50° (30m radius) curves, run on 20lb/yd (9.5kg/m) rail and had a maximum speed of 21mph (33.5km/h).

Few of these locomotives found long-term homes once peace came, but an exception was No.WD1265 (Alco No.57156), which fulfilled a humble role hauling trains of sugar beet during the season from Toury to the sugar factory at Pithiviers, a small town some 40 miles south of Paris. The Tramway Pithiviers à Toury numbered her 3.23.

Thirty years rolled by and No.3.23 defied the prognostications of the builders by long outlasting her contemporaries and indeed the majority of US-built steam locomotives. But, by the 1950s, industrial light railways had become unfashionable and the little locomotive was finally laid aside. This came to the notice of volunteers in the restoration of the 13-mile (21km) Festiniog Railway in Wales, a task which took over 25 years until its completion in 1982. The upshot was that the little Alco, now named *Mountaineer*, became in 1967 a member of the line's collection of famous narrow-gauge locomotives. Thus US motive power plays its part in carrying some 400,000 tourist passengers annually through beautiful Snowdonia on this spectacular railroad.

Following a recent major overhaul, *Mountaineer* (FR No.18), now fuelled mainly by waste oil collected by her admirers, is regarded as the pride of the fleet.

Right and below: *Distant in both time and surroundings from the World War I trenches,* Mountaineer *makes its final home in the Welsh mountains on the Festiniog Railway.*

76

Nos. 1-67 HGe 2/2

Panama Canal Company, 1912

Type: Rack-and-adhesion electric canal mule locomotive.
Gauge: 5ft 0in (1,524mm).
Propulsion: Three-phase current at 200V 25Hz fed via twin outside conductor rails to two 150hp (112kW) motors with pole-changing arrangements to give the fixed speeds. The rack pinions driven through gearing and the adhesive driving wheels via friction clutches.
Weight: 99,180lb (45t).
Overall length: 31ft 6½in (9,617mm).
Tractive effort: 28,600lb (127kN).
Max. speed: 5mph (8km/h).

Whilst handling ships passing through the Panama canal, these unique and fascinating machines for 50 years pulled heavier loads than any other railway locomotive in the world (as do their somewhat similar successors). They also climbed the steepest gradient of 1-in-1 (100 per cent) on the steps abreast of the lock gates—but not under load, as ships would at that moment be stationary in the lock. Elsewhere the running lines are level; the trackage extends to 20¼ miles (30km) of which 12 miles (17.7km) is equipped with Riggenbach "ladder" rack of a specially heavy pattern.

The braking system also has sufficient force to deal with the massive inertia of an ocean-going ship as well as being able to stop the locomotive in 10ft when descending a 1-in-1 (100 per cent) gradient at 3mph (4.8km/h). Locomotive power has to be provided at each of the four "corners" of a ship and there is a complex control system for the winch set between the cab units. Such is one of the most remarkable and unusual locomotives ever used in America.

Above: *A Panama Canal Company mule prepares to haul a ship through the Isthmus en route for Colon.*

Below: *Flexibility is the name of the game on the lock-side gradients that would tax even a rubber tyred vehicle.*

USRA Light Mikado 2-8-2 United States Railroad Administration (USRA), 1918

Gauge: 4ft 8½in (1,435mm).
Tractive effort: 54,700lb (24,817kg).
Axleload: 60,900lb (27.6t).
Cylinders: (2) 26 x 30in (660 x 762mm).
Driving wheels: 63in (1,600mm).
Heating surface: 3,783sq ft (351m²).
Superheater: 882sq ft (82m²).
Steam pressure: 200psi (14.1kg/cm²).
Grate area: 66.7sq ft (6.2m²).
Fuel: 30,000lb (13.6t).
Water: 12,000US gall (45.5m³).
Adhesive weight: 221,500lb (100.5t).
Total weight: 511,100lb 9232t).
Length overall: 97ft 5in (29,693mm).

Uncle Sam's own engines! During World War I, the railroads were taken over by a government agency known as the United States Railroad Administration (USRA). The idea was to avoid competition that was thought to involve wasteful duplication of effort, and replace it with co-operation in the best interests of the nation. From all accounts the results were a disaster, but one good thing did emerge—a range of excellent standard steam locomotives. Although these USRA designs were not to replace custom-built power, they certainly had great influence in encouraging railroads not to re-invent the wheel every time they went shopping for some new locomotives.

Twelve types of USRA locomotive were produced, consisting of 2-8-2s, 2-10-2s, 4-6-2s and 4-8-2s, each in both heavy and light versions, 0-6-0 and 0-8-0 switchers, as well as 2-6-6-2 and 2-8-8-2 Mallets. There were also 8,000, 10,000 and 12,000gall tenders which could be used on any of the types. Design was in the hands of an able team put together by the three major locomotive builders, Alco, Baldwin and Lima. The best practice of the day was adopted; two cylinders only (except for the Mallets), bar frames, superheaters, piston valves of adequate size, Walschaert or Baker valve gear and wide-firebox boilers. They represented standards of construction that lasted until the end of the steam.

Early in June 1918, only two months after the USRA takeover, details of the first design had been settled and Baldwin began work. A stupendous and successful effort was made to complete the locomotive, a light Mikado allocated to the Baltimore & Ohio, for public display on Independence Day. There are tales of parts travelling to Philadelphia by Pullman car as well as other extravagances, and the feat was certainly magnificent if not exactly commercial.

The three major builders then went on to build 624 of the same. The light Mikado was the most popular of all the USRA designs by a factor of more than two. They were allocated to 17 railroads and so well liked that a further 641 were produced in later years after the USRA programme came to an end. The first was designated Class "Q-3" by B&O and numbered 4500. Happily this historic locomotive has survived and is preserved at the B&O Museum in the original Mount Clare shops at Baltimore, Maryland.

Right: *A line of United States Railroad Administration "Light Mikado" 2-8-2s ready to leave the Baldwin Works, 1918.*

Class E 2-10-0 Imperial Russian Government, 1917

Gauge: 5ft 0in (1,524mm).
Tractive effort: 51,500lb (23,367kg).
Axleload: 39,644lb (18t).
Cylinders: (2) 25 x 28in (635 x 711mm).
Driving wheels: 52in (1,320mm).
Heating surface: 2,594sq ft (241m²).
Superheater: 569sq ft (53m²).
Steam pressure: 180psi (12.7kg/cm²).
Grate area: 64.7sq ft (6m²).
Water: 7,000 US gall (26.5m³).
Adhesive weight: 180,200lb (81.8t).
Total weight: 232,600lb (105.5t).
Length overall: 72ft 9in (22,174mm).

The story of this huge class of locomotive, over 3,000 strong, is almost incredible. The Imperial Russian government, hard-pressed for transport in the war with Germany, in 1915 ordered 400 big 2-10-0s from North American builders. Alco, Baldwin and the Canadian Locomotive Co shared the order and later, after some modifications had been made to the design, a further 475 were built. They became Russian Class "E," with sub-classes designated for the first 400 as "Ef" (Baldwin), "Es" (Alco) and "Ek" (Canadian). The subsequent 475 were all classified "E1".

Some became Japanese property and were converted to standard gauge (1,435mm) when

Above: *Preserved St. Louis San Francisco Railroad 2-8-0 originally built for Russia, at Kirkwood, Mo., in 1963.*

Below: *A US-built "Ye" class (in Russia "Y" is written "E") seen from the Trans-Siberian Express at Taldan, USSR, 1970.*

Above: *Soviet Railways "Ye" class 2-10-0, built by Baldwin in 1945, at Irkutsk, 1970.*

that country took over the South Manchurian Railway from Russia. Consequently this group later came into the hands of Chinese National Railways where they were classified "DK₂" ('DK' stands for Decapod), and until very recently some of them were still in use. Further orders were placed, but before they were completed the Russian revolution and the separate peace with Germany precluded delivery of the last

200. Eventually, they went to various US roads—the Erie had 75, Seaboard 40, Frisco 21, and 22 other lines had lesser quantities. This followed gauge conversion which involved little more than fitting new tyres to the driving wheels.

During World War II, the Soviet government was again facing major transport problems, and under lend-lease they asked for further large helpings of these rugged but rather out-of-date machines. Accordingly, 2,110 were supplied by Alco and Baldwin from 1944 onwards.

Locomotive classification was one thing that survived unchanged through the turmoil of the revolution and so the new engines became Class "Ea"; later various modifications led to sub-classes "Em" (modified leading driving axleboxes) and "Emb" (feed-water heaters plus the "Em" modification). A few that remained unshipped after the cold war began are believed to have been scrapped. One is recorded as having been sold to a short line, the Minneapolis, Northfield & Southern RR, with 75 miles (121km) of route in Minnesota.

Some of these locomotives were to be seen in use in the eastern part of Russia on switching duties until very recently, long after the official demise of steam in the Soviet Union. They seemed to have two qualities which were valued in that country. First, they had the rugged reliability of a familiar long-proven design, and secondly, there was a boost to the Communist system because officials could use them to demonstrate that the rival capitalists had made zero progress in the 20 years since the revolution.

800 2-10-10-2 Virginian Railroad (VGN), 1918

Gauge: 4ft 8½in (1,435mm).
Tractive effort: 176,600lb (80,127kg).
Axleload: 61,700lb (28t).
Cylinders, HP: (2) 30 x 32in (762 x 812mm).
Cylinders, LP: (2) 48 x 32in (1,219 x 812mm).
Driving wheels: 56in (1,422mm).
Heating surface: 8,605sq ft (799m²).
Superheater: 2,120sq ft (197m²).
Steam pressure: 215psi (15.1kg/cm²).
Grate area: 108.7sq ft (10.1m²).
Fuel: 24,000lb (10.9t).

Water: 13,000 US gall (49.2m²).
Adhesive weight: 617,000lb (279.9t).
Total weight: 898,000lb (407.4t).
Length overall: 99ft 8in (30,368mm).

Until 1918, Mallet articulated steam locomotives with more than 16 driving wheels had been fairly conspicuous by their lack of success. The Virginian Railroad, which faced serious haulage problems in the Appalachian Mountains, had been persuaded by Baldwin to have a Triplex 2-8-8-8-4, similar to those which were a failure on the Erie. Although attempts were made to give the new locomotive a better steam-raising capacity so as to satisfy the vast appetite of the three sets of machinery, it was not long before she was divided in two. So with one new boiler the VGN got two new locomotives, a 2-8-8-0 and a 2-8-0, both of which gave good service, but not in the way intended.

Nevertheless, the problem of hauling VGN's immense coal drags down to tidewater at Norfolk, Virginia, which first involved climbing the notorious 2.11 per cent (1-in-47) incline from the main collection point at Elmore, West Virginia, to Clark's Gap summit, remained unsolved. In 1917, with swollen wartime traffic round their necks, the management decided to have another go and ordered a batch of huge 2-10-10-2s from the American Locomotive Co. The dialogue between builder and customer was no doubt made more meaningful by the traumatic experiences of the recent past.

Be that as it may, the results were excellent. Small tenders made the "800s" less impressive

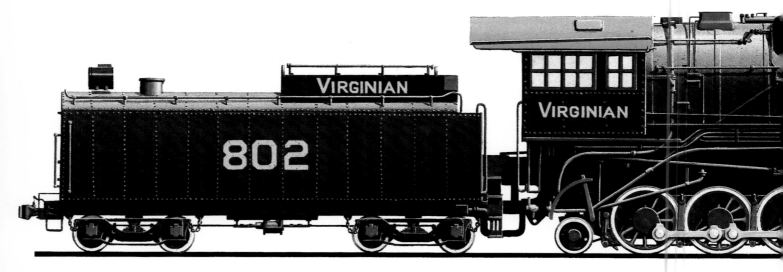

4300 Class 4-8-2 Southern Pacific Railroad (SP), 1923

Tractive effort: 57,100lb (25,907kg).
Axle load: 61,500lb (28t).
Cylinders: (2) 28 x 30in (711 x 762mm).
Driving wheels: 73½in (1,867mm).
Heating surface: 4,552sq ft (423m²).
Superheater: 1,162sq ft (108m²).
Steam pressure: 210psi (14.8kg/cm²).
Grate area: 75sq ft (7m²).
Fuel (oil): 4,000gall (4,700 US) (18m³).
Water: 13,300gall (10,000 US) (60m³).
Adhesive weight: 246,000lb (112t).
Total weight: 611,000lb (277.5t).
Length overall: 97ft 9in (29,794mm).

The 4-8-2 or "Mountain" type was appropriately named; its origins are a nice illustration of the difference between tractive effort and power. Locomotives with a high tractive effort are often described as powerful, but this is misleading. The 4-8-2 was developed from the 4-6-2 but, whilst the extra pair of drivers meant that a higher tractive effort could be exerted, the power output—which depends on the size of the fire—had to remain

than they actually were but their vital statistics were huge. For example, 4ft diameter low-pressure cylinders were the largest ever used on a locomotive. Their adhesive weight was 14 per cent greater than that of a Union Pacific "Big Boy" and the tractive effort 40 per cent greater when live steam was admitted to the low-pressure engine at starting. Naturally, power output was much lower, as one might expect from a machine intended for low-speed operation, but these iron mammoths did all that was expected of them and gave 30

years of good service to their owners. When working on their intended task, it was customary to have a 2-8-8-2 at the head of a 5,500 ton train, well able to handle this load other than on the 2.11 per cent (1-in-47) grade. Two 2-10-10-2s then pushed from the rear and the whole caravan moved upgrade noisily but steadily at some 5½mph (9km/h). It must have been one of the greatest sights and sounds in railroading.

The 800s were interesting in that the high-pressure cylinders had coventional piston valves,

but the huge, low pressure ones used old-fashioned slide valves. These were quite adequate for the lower temperatures involved on the L.P. side, while being easier to keep streamtight.

They are also thought to be the only successful class of locomotives in the world with as many as 20 driving wheels. Certainly the Mallet principle was

Below: *Almost a centipede! The Virginian Railroad's Mallet compound articulated 2-10-10-2 steam locomotives pushed coal drags up to Clark's Gap, Va.*

never carried further than with these giants, although the size and power of articulated loco-motives with few coupled wheels would in the end be even greater.

It is perhaps true to say that the problem of Clark's Gap was ameliorated rather than solved by the "800s". A few years later a real solution was found when this hilly stretch of line was the subject of an electrification scheme. The 2-10-10-2s were then given useful but less heroic work to perform elsewhere on the system and survived until the 1940s. Alas, none has been preserved.

Above: *Southern Pacific 4-8-2 No.4348 at Roseville Yard, California in May 1954.*

Left: *SP No.4360 ready to leave San Francisco for San José with a commuter train.*

limited because there was still only one pair of wheels to carry the firebox.

For climbing mountains a high

tractive effort is essential, but high *power* output only desir-able. These things were relevant to the Southern Pacific Railroad, for their trains leaving Sacramento for the east had the notorious climb over the Sierras to face, from near sea level to 6,885ft (2,099m) in 80 miles (128km).

So in 1923 SP went to the American Locomotive Co. of Schenectady for the first batch of

4-8-2 locomotives. The design was based on standard US prac-tice, the one feature of note being the cylindrical so-called Vander-bilt tender. A booster engine was fitted, driving on the rear carrying wheels, and this could give an extra 10,000lb (4,537kg) of trac-tive effort, provided the steam supply held out.

SP impressed their personality on the "4300"s by having them

oil-burning and by their trade mark, the headlight mounted *below* centre on the silver-grey front of the smoke box. The 77 engines of the class were very successful, all the later ones being built in SP's own shops at Sacra-mento. Some of the earlier batches had 8-wheel tenders of lower capacity, instead of 12-wheel ones. None of the class has been preserved.

Class EP-2
"Bi-polar" 1-B-D-D-B-1 Chicago, Milwaukee, St Paul & Pacific Railroad, (CM St P&P), 1919

Type: Express passenger electric locomotive.
Gauge: 4ft 8½in (1,435mm).
Propulsion: Direct current at 3,000V fed via overhead catenary to twelve 370hp (275kW) gearless motors mounted directly on the axles.
Weight: 457,000lb (207t) adhesive, 530,000lb (240t) total.
Max. axleload: 38,500lb (17.5t).
Overall length: 76ft 0in (23,165mm).
Tractive effort: 123,500lb (549kN).
Max. speed: 70mph (112km/h).

When the Chicago, Milwaukee, St Paul & Pacific Railroad was opened to Tacoma, Washington State, in 1909 (through passenger service did not begin until 1911) it was the last railway to reach the West Coast from the east. As a newcomer, then, the company had to try harder, and one of the ways in which it did this was to work the mountain crossings by the clean new power of electricity.

Catenary wires mounted on timber poles started to go up five years after the line was opened, and early in 1917 electric working began over the Rocky Mountain and Missoula divisions, between Harlowton and Avery, Montana, a distance of 438 miles (705km). Many miles of 100,000V transmission lines had to be built through virgin territory from hydro-electric power plants to rotary substations along the right-of-way. By 1919 the 230-mile (370km) Coast Division from Othello to Tacoma, Washington State, had been electrified also.

Electrification measured by the hundreds of miles was something quite new in the world, and the

North American railroad top brass watched with baited breath for the results. Technically, they were totally satisfactory: much heavier loads could be worked than with steam, energy costs were lower, faster running times—and hence better productivity—could be achieved. The system was reliable and one could have been forgiven for thinking that other railroads would quickly follow. Alas, the enormous costs involved proved too frightening at a time when railroads were beginning to feel the effects of competition from road transport. So, with one notable exception, in the USA main line electrification schemes were confined to shortish lengths of line.

The Milwaukee Railroad itself went bankrupt in 1925, and this caused a further ebb of confidence, although it was claimed

that the onset of bankruptcy was *delayed* rather than *caused* by the $24 million spent on electrification.

The original passenger locomotives (Class "EP1"), delivered from 1915 onwards by The American Locomotive Co and General Electric, were the same as those for freight, except that they had higher gearing and oil-fired train-heating boilers. They were formed as twin units, permanently coupled, of the 2-Bo-Bo + Bo-Bo-2 wheel arrangement and produced 3,440hp (2,570kW) for a weight of 288 tons. Their plain "box-car" style belied their ability to pull and go in an unprecedented manner. Thirty freight and 12 passenger locos were supplied.

When the wires were going up over the Cascade mountains in 1918, something more exotic was

Above: *"Bi-polar" No. E-2 as preserved at the National Museum of Transport, St Louis, Missouri.*

proposed; the result was these legendary "Bi-polars", created by General Electric. The name arose from using two-pole motors. The reason for this lay in a desire to simplify the mechanics of an electric locomotive. The ultimate in simplicity is to put the armatures of the motors actually on the driving axles, thereby doing away altogether with gearing, but it is then necessary to cater for vertical movement. Hence there can only be two poles, one on either side in a position where the critical air gap between poles and armature is not affected by vertical movement. The price of doing it this way is that the power of each motor is limited, partly because it

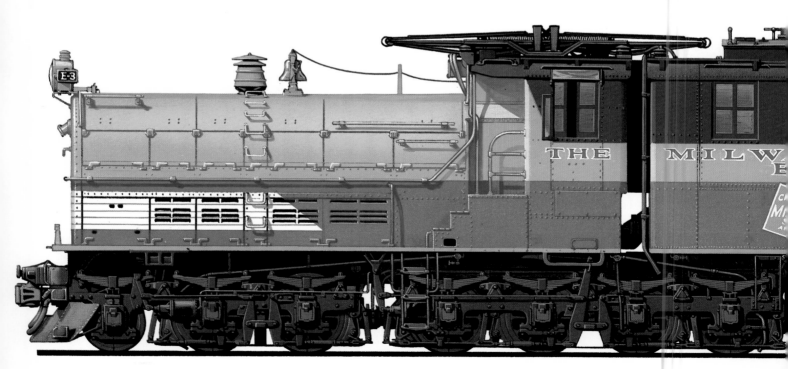

runs at the low speed of the wheels and partly because two-pole motors are less powerful than those with a more usual number of poles anyway.

The result was that, for a power output virtually the same as the "EP1s", the "EP2s" had half as many more driving wheels. The body was articulated in three parts, connected together by the four-axle trucks. All this made for a lot of locomotive, but the effect of size on the public was nothing compared with the impact of very impressive styling. The electrical equipment was contained in round-topped bonnets at each end of the locomotive and this simple change was what gave these engines that little extra the others hadn't got.

The designers were sensible enough to put the train-heating boiler, fuel and water tanks—all items that do not mix well with electricity—in the separate centre section. All things considered, the Cascade Division in 1918 found itself in possession of a reliable class of five locomotives that could haul 900t (1,000 US tons) trains up the long 1-in-45 (2.2 per cent) grades at 25mph (40km/h), as well as hold them back coming down. Some rather fine publicity stunts were arranged showing a "Bi-polar" having a tug-of-war with two big steam engines (a 2-6-6-2 and a 2-8-0) on top of a huge trestle bridge. The electric had no difficulty in pulling backwards the two steam engines set to pull full steam ahead.

Ten more passenger engines (Class "EP3") were delivered in 1921 by rival builders Baldwin

Below: *The Chicago, Milwaukee, St Paul & Pacific Railroad's Class EP-2 "Bi-polar", one of the most impressive locomotives of any form of traction ever to have been built.*

and Westinghouse, and these were more orthodox. Even so, 20 per cent more power was packed into a locomotive with only half the number of driving wheels, the wheel arrangement being 2-C-1 + 1-C-2. Their appearance was fairly box-like, although not quite as severe as that of the "EP1s".

So the "Bi-polars" were outclassed as well as outnumbered by nearly five-to-one soon after they were built, yet these legendary locomotives demonstrated very clearly the value of cosmetics, because they are the ones remembered and regarded as epitomising this longest amongst North American electrification schemes. The great engines gave excellent service, though, and soldiered on through the years. In the late 1950s they were moving the road's crack "Olympian Hiawatha" luxury express over the 438 miles (705km) of the Rocky Mountain Division in 10hr 40min, compared with 15 hours scheduled when the electrification was new.

Some modern electric locomotives of even greater power, built for the USSR but undeliverable on account of the so-called "Cold War", became available at this time. These "Little Joes" as they were known, were further nails in the coffins of the now ageing "Bipolars". In spite of a rebuild in 1953 which included the addition of multiple-unit capability, all five were taken out of service between 1958 and 1960. One (No. E2) is preserved at the National Museum

of Transport in St Louis, Missouri, but the others went for scrap.

In 1973, all electric operations on the Milwaukee came to end, a favourable price for scrap copper being one of the factors. The escalation in the price of oil which followed might have saved the day, although the existence of the whole railroad was soon to be in jeopardy, there being just too many lines in the area. It was no surprise, then, when in 1980 all transcontinental operations over the one-time electrified tracks ceased, and most have now been abandoned.

Below: *A "Bi-polar" in service under the 3,000 volt catenary wires of the Chicago, Milwaukee, St Paul & Pacific Railroad.*

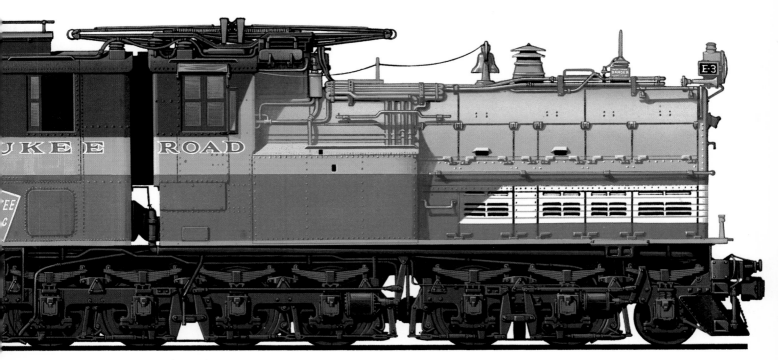

No. 24 2-6-2 Sandy River & Rangeley Lakes Railroad (SRRL), 1919

Gauge: 2ft 0in (609mm).
Tractive effort: 10,085lb (4,576kg).
Axleload: 5,400lb (7.0t).
Cylinders: (2) 12 x 16in (304 x 406mm).
Driving wheels: 33in (838mm).
Steam pressure: 170psi (12kg/cm²).
Fuel: 6,000lb (2.7t).
Water: 2,000 US gall (7.6m³).
Adhesive weight: 42,000lb (19.1t).
Total weight: 91,000lb (41.3t).
Length overall: 44ft 7in (13,589mm).

The Prairie or 2-6-2 wheel arrangement was first tried in any quantity around the turn of the century. It bore the same relationship to the 2-6-0 Mogul type as the 4-4-2 Atlantic bore to the 4-4-0 American standard. You could say that it was a Mogul with a much larger

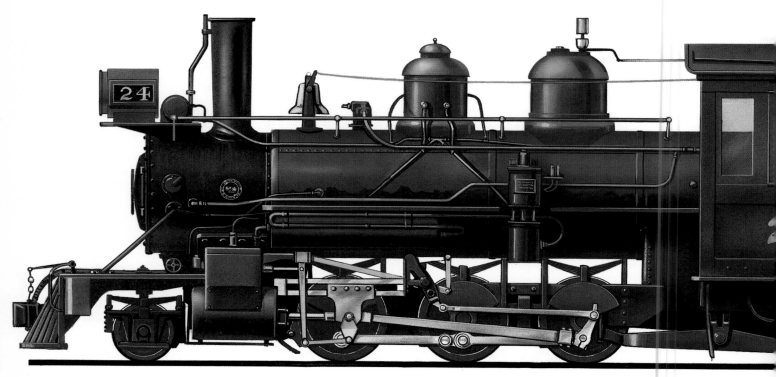

Narrow gauge 0-10-0 Ko Pei Railway (KPR), 1925

Gauge: 1ft 11⅝in (600mm).
Tractive effort: 14,700lb (6,670kg).
Axleload: 18,810lb (8.5t).
Fuel: 2,000lb (0.9t).
Water: 1,000 US gall (3.8m³).
Adhesive weight: 85,500lb (38.8t).

Somewhere in the world there had to exist the train lover's perfect line, the railroad to Shangri-La. This writer heard a murmur of it long ago when reading a book called *The End of the Line* (by Bryan Morgan) in which that Chinese railway which used 2ft gauge 0-12-0s was referred to in just such a throw-away fashion. The years rolled by, Bryan Morgan had died and eventually there were two visits to China, but extensive enquiry and research failed to offer any basis for

extrordinary locomotives with so many drivers on so few inches of track gauge. In fact, the existence of any narrow gauge in China was totally denied.

But suddenly, just as this book was being started, several unexpected sources came together to give the whole picture. These were a piece in *Trains* magazine, Mr H. L. Broadbelt's fabulous catalogue of Baldwin photographs, the French periodical *La Vie du Rail*, a correspondent in Australia and the last pages of an amazing Japanese five-volume picture book on Chinese railways.

It seems that a fleet of 16 little 0-10-0s (the traditional licence of the traveller's tale had made them 0-12-0s) were built by Baldwin in the 1920s for a little narrow-gauge railroad in the province of Yunnan which borders Vietnam,

Burma and Tibet. The Ko Pei Railway served tin mines. It was opened in November 1921 and extended in 1928. The ruling grade is 3 per cent (1-in-33) and there are curves as sharp as 28° (62m radius).

The 1980 Chinese Railways timetable indicates that passenger service is offered twice a day from JiJie, where there is interchange with a branch of the metre-gauge line which in more peaceful times connected Kunming, capital of Yunnan province with Ho Chi Min City in Vietnam. The public trains run 21 miles (34km) south to Gejiu. The journey takes more than two hours but photographs show that the scenery is wonderful.

The new locomotives were a godsend to the little railway. Being totally basic with slide valve cylinders, they were easy to main-

tain in a remote situation. At the same time, with the weight spread amongst so many wheels, there were no problems with light track laid with 33lb/yd (16kg/m) rails. Yet, the power was there and in comparison with the small tank locomotives used previously, train-loads could almost be doubled to a breathtaking 85 tons. Sixty years later even the same numbers are carried; the only significant changes are that the four-wheel tender has been replaced with a conventional eight-wheel one decorated by the People's Republic Railway tunnel-and-rail herald.

Right: *What was for long merely a legend of two-foot gauge 0-10-2s in China has proven to be fact now Ko Pei Railway No.26 is known to be running today on the People's Railways.*

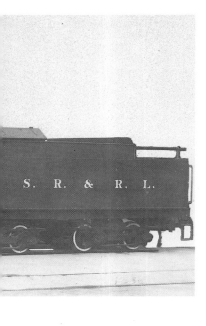

firebox, and hence more power without additional tractive effort. So it was eminently suitable for lines in the 'wide open spaces' of the mid-west, hence the name Prairie. But intense competition and a rapidly expanding economy meant a continuous search for increased productivity, and so the Prairie was quickly superseded by larger 4-6-2 Pacifics and 2-8-2 Mikados. So for main-line use the 2-6-2 was quickly eclipsed. It did however, find a niche on the short lines and by-ways of the US railroad system.

We have seen how the state of Colorado caught the 3ft version of narrow-gauge disease in the last decades of the 19th Century. Equally notable was the 2ft epidemic

Left: *2-6-2 No.24, the last locomotive supplied to the Sandy River & Rangeley Lakes RR.*

Below: *Sandy River & Rangeley Lakes Railroad No.24, supplied by Baldwin in 1919, ceasing work once the two-foot gauge line was taken up and sold for scrap in 1936.*

that swept the state of Maine at the same time. It resulted in construction of seven little narrow-gauge railroads, four of which were later consolidated into one system, which then became little only in respect of distance between the rails. This was the Sandy River & Rangely Lakes Railroad — a 46-mile main line with 60 miles of branches plus 16 locomotives and hundreds of freight cars. It interchanged traffic at Farmington, Maine, with the Maine Central Railroad. The narrow-gauge line eventually became the property of this 'big brother', although never formally incorporated into it.

The Sandy River's last locomotive (and the fifth 2-6-2 on the line) was this No.24 delivered by Baldwin in 1919. It is a reflection on the ways in which little railroads could 'design' their locomotives, that the superintendent would just jot down a few measurements for the builders to work to and send them off to Philadelphia. The tender tanks on the Sandy River line were typically 84in wide (even that was rather wide for a 24in gauge) but the boss's careless

handwriting led to Baldwin building one 8ft 4in wide. Not surprisingly, this overgenerous water cart overbalanced (unfortunately on a trestle) and had to have a slice taken out of its middle. But this tiny hunk of locomotive engineering was very soundly built — Walschaert valve gear, an unsuperheated boiler and slide valves making an excellent combination for ease of maintenance. 'Piston valves wear out, slide valves wear in' is the saying, whilst a little extra fuel consumption would hardly be noticed on such a small machine.

No.24 survived until the Sandy River line was abandoned in 1935. A railfan actually bought her for $250 (would this be the first ever purchase of a full-size locomotive for preservation by a private individual?) but, alas, problems of storage and finance forced him two years later to let the engine go for scrap. But memories of No.24 linger on in model form, while the railroad itself surely sets a record in the number of pages of print published per mile of railroad abandoned.

No.1 B₀-B₀ American Locomotive Co (Alco), 1924

Type: Diesel-electric switching locomotive.
Gauge: 4ft 8½in (1,435mm).
Propulsion: Ingersoll-Rand 300hp (224kW) 6-cylinder four-stroke diesel engine and GEC generator supplying current to four nose-suspended traction motors geared to the axles.
Weight: 120,000lb (54.4t).
Max. axleload: 30,000lb (13.6t).
Length: 32ft 6in (9,906mm).

The story of compression-ignition railroad motive power in this book begins with the first diesel-electric locomotives of more than very modest power to be commercially successful in public service. They were the result of co-operation between three well-known specialist manufacturers; Ingersoll-Rand of Phillips, New Jersey, produced the diesel engine, General Electric of Erie, Pennsylvania, the electric equipment, and the American Locomotive Company (Alco) of Schenectady, New York, the loco-

motive body and running gear. Both the principles of design and the configuration are the same as those used for the majority of today's locomotives. The difference is that for the same size and weight GE today could offer 1,000hp (746kW) instead of 300hp (224kW).

The diesel engine in the form in which it is now universally used is much less the work of Doctor Rudolph Diesel, of Germany, than of a Briton call Ackroyd-Stuart. In the 1880s he demonstrated an internal combustion engine in which the fuel was injected into the cylinder at the end of the piston stroke. This engine was turned into a practical proposition by Richard Hornsby & Co., of Grantham, England, later Ruston & Hornsby. Dr. Diesel's engine, demonstrated in 1898, used a high compression ratio typical of present day engines to obtain a big increase in thermal efficiency, but the fuel had to be injected by

a blast of compressed air at some 1,000psi (65kg/cm²). This involved heavy ancillary equipment.

In 1896 a small diesel locomotive, the first in the world and which one might more reasonably call an Ackroyd-Stuart locomotive, was built at Hornsbys. It was used for shunting purposes in the works. The first recorded use of a compression-ignition locomotive in public service seems to have occurred in Sweden, when a small railcar with a 75bhp (56kW) engine and electrical transmission was put into service on the Mellersta & Södermanlands Railway in 1913. Of course, this was hardly a greater output than would nowadays be installed in a medium-sized family car, and went no distance towards proving the diesel engine as suitable for rail traction.

As we all know from our motor cars, the problem of using internal combustion engines for traction is—in lay terms—that they need

to be going before they will go. This is in contrast to steam engines and electric motors which can produce a force while still at rest. For low powers, the familiar gearbox and clutch in the motor car can be used, but for hundreds—and certainly for thousands—of horsepower something more sophisticated is needed.

Experiments with a diesel engine driving an air compressor and feeding compressed air to a normal steam locomotive engine and chassis were not successful,

Below: *This was the first diesel-electric locomotive to be a commercial success. It was used for switching, from 1924 until it was scrapped in the 1950s. The trucks were similar to those found on existing electric trains. The drawgear had to be standard and otherwise only the sandpipes and the bell would be inherited from the age of steam.*

although the scheme was a simple one. The use of hydraulic fluid as a transmission medium has been reasonably satisfactory, but by far the majority of diesel locomotives ever built have, and have had, electric transmissions. A diesel engine drives an electric generator or alternator which feeds current to the motors of what amounts to an electric locomotive.

Because this concept of a diesel locomotive involved building, to start with, an electric locomotive complete with traction motors and control gear, and then adding to that a diesel-driven generator to supply current to the electric locomotive, it was not only expensive but complex. Furthermore, electrical equipment is not happy living in close company with the vibration and oil-mist which surrounds even the best-maintained diesel engines. Accordingly, in most places and for many years, diesel locomotives—however economical they might be as regards

fuel consumption and however efficient operationally—led rather unfulfilled and unhappy lives.

In respect of these drawbacks, the consortium took their courage in both hands and built a demonstrator early in 1924 by Ingersoll-Rand and General Electric. This machine put in over 2,000 hours showing off its abilities in various railroad yards and industrial premises. A feature of this unit was the spectacular all-round visibility available via seven large windows at each of the rounded ends. It had the appearance of a Pullman observation car on a train of the streamline era.

This trial locomotive led to a batch of five locomotives being built later that year for stock; 26 units in all were produced during the years 1924 to 1928. Customers included the Baltimore & Ohio (1), Central of New Jersey (1), Lehigh Valley (1), Erie (2), Chicago & North Western (3), Reading (2), and Delaware, Lackawanna &

Western (2). The remainder went to industrial buyers. There were also a few twin-engined models supplied, generally similar but longer and of twice the power. Seven were produced between 1925 and 1928. The railroads which had them were the Long Island and the Erie with two each, and the Great Northern with one. The others went to industrial customers. The weight was 200,000lb (90.7t) and each of the two engine-generator sets fitted were similar to those of the single-engined type.

Whilst the claim of commercial success was true in the sense that the makers did not lose money, it was not so for the buyers. All these customers had operations for which steam traction could not be used for some extraneous reason such as fire-risk or legislation, and so a more costly form of power was necessary. Amongst them was that famous ordinance whereby steam locomotives were

excluded from New York City. Useful experience was gained which eased the general introduction of diesel traction a quarter century later. It says enough, perhaps, of the technical success of these locomotives that, unlike so many firsts, they stood the test of time. Indeed, some were still giving service 35 years later although, like the legendary Irishman's hammer, they had no doubt acquired a few new heads and a few new handles in the meantime. Two units survive, one in the Baltimore & Ohio Railroad Museum at Baltimore, Maryland, and the very first, Central of New Jersey No. 1000, at the National Museum of Transport in St Louis, Missouri.

Alco no longer builds locomotives in the USA, although it does so in Canada. General Electric still produces diesel locomotives, including engines and the mechanical parts, and sells world-wide as well as in the USA.

K-36 2-8-2 Denver & Rio Grande Western Railroad (D&RGW), 1925

Gauge: 3ft 0in (914mm).
Tractive effort: 36,200lb (16,425kg).
Axleload: 39,558lb (17.9t).
Cylinders: (2) 20 x 24in (508 x 609mm).
Driving wheels: 44in (1,117mm).
Heating surface: 2, 107sq ft (196m²).
Superheater: 575sq ft (53m²).
Steam pressure: 195psi (13.7kg/cm²).
Grate area: 40sq ft (3.7m²).
Fuel: 16,000lb (7.3t).
Water: 5,000 US gall (18.9m³).
Adhesive weight: 143,850lb (65.3t).
Total weight: 286,500lb (130t).
Length overall: 68ft 3in (20,802mm).

The last proper steam railroad in the USA! For almost a decade from 1960 to 1968 the remaining Denver & Rio Grande Western 3ft gauge trackage in Colorado and New Mexico was just that. But eight years as the surviving one-thousandth of 250,000 miles of steam railroading was not the only reason why these 250 miles (402km) of lines attracted the attention of a railfan-infested nation to an unparalleled degree. If General Motors' Electro-Motive Division had finally been ousted by the traditional products of Lima, Baldwin, Alco, Roanoke and others, the Rio Grande narrow-gauge would have still made it to the top. It had the lot.

There were trestles, wyes, balloon loops, 10,000ft (3,000m) summits, deserts, snowsheds, 4 per cent (1-in-25) grades, mixed-gauge track, timber-lined tunnels, rotary snowploughs, open-platform passenger cars, steam pile-drivers, wooden gons and boxcars; not to speak of a fleet of vintage Alco and Baldwin mikes which, although bearing external signs of having been rolled down mountainsides on occasion, still had internals that could produce

exhaust sounds of unmatched crispness and precision. And those whistles! When the five chimes echoed round the mountains of Colorado, every eagle for miles left its nest in alarm.

For a long time, oil finds near Farmington, New Mexico, generated enough freight traffic to keep the line open. At the same time the prospects were not good enough to justify widening the gauge to standard or to dieselise. It was remarkable that this delicate

Right: *A Denver & Rio Grande Western K-36 2-8-2 takes on water at Alamosa, Colorado.*

Below: *K-36 2-8-2 No.481 hauls a trainload of tourists on the spectacular route from Durango to Silverton, Colorado.*

balance between modernisation and abandonment was maintained for so long. For this we all must be grateful, because when the end of freight operation came in 1968, railroad preservation had become fashionable and the states of Colorado and New Mexico bought the best 64 miles (103km) to run as a museum-piece tourist railroad. The preserved section, known as the Cumbres & Toltec Scenic Railroad, runs from Antonito, Colorado to Chama, New Mexico. With the mountain trackage came 124 cars of various kinds and, most important of all, nine narrow-gauge 2-8-2s of classes "K-36" and "K-37".

The "K-36" 2-8-2s ('K' indicates a 2-8-2; '36' means 36,000lb of tractive effort) were the third class of narrow-gauge Mikado supplied to the Rio Grande. The squat "K-27" "Mud-hens" of 1903 came first, followed in 1923 by 10 speedy "K-28" "Sports Models" from Alco, intended for passenger work. Three "K-28s" survive in tourist-train service on the Durango to Silverton line, also in Colorado. The 10 much larger "K-36s" came from Baldwins in 1925 and were entirely standard products of their day, apart from exceptional size and power for the slim gauge. The boilers and cylinders were the same as those of a typical 2-8-0 made for standard-gauge. With outside frames and cranks, the distance between the cylinder centre lines would be the same for the two gauges. Seven of the 10 built have been preserved, one on the Silverton line. They are rated to haul 232 tons on a 4 per cent (1-in-25) grade.

When further similar locomotives were needed a year or two later, the Rio Grande produced the "K-37" class 'in-house' from some surplus standard-gauge 2-8-0s, new frames and wheels being the only substantial pieces of hardware required. The old boilers, cabs, tender bodies, cylinders and most smaller fittings could be re-used. Although three have survived, boiler inspectors have been a little chary of certifying their boilers, dating from as early as 1902, for the hard work expected of locomotives working on the magnificent route of the Cumbres & Toltec Scenic Railroad.

Above: *Denver & Rio Grande Western K-36 2-8-2 No.481. Note the large snowplough on this classic narrow-gauge loco.*

Below: *The D&RGW class K-36 2-8-2s were built by Baldwin in 1923. Several like 487 survive on tourist railroads in the Rockies.*

M-300 Single-unit railcar Electro-Motive Company, 1924

Type: Petrol (gas) electric railcar for local passenger service.
Gauge: 4ft 8½in (1,435mm).
Propulsion: Winton 175hp (130kW) 6-cylinder four-stroke petrol (gas) engine coupled to a generator driving two rose-suspended motors on the leading bogie.
Weight: 70,000lb (32t) total, 35,000lb (16t) adhesive.
Max. axleload: 17,500lb (8t).
Overall length: 57ft 4in (17,475mm).
Max. speed: 60mph (96km/h).

Those who cut their teeth on developing these humble vehicles went on to found the company which in the end was responsible

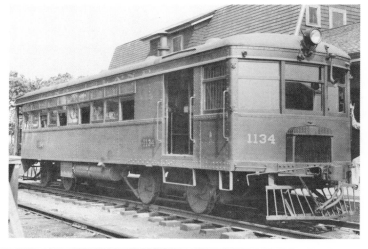

for displacing steam from most of the railways of the world. But, when Chicago Great Western 39-seat railcar No.M-300 was delivered in 1924, the Electro-Motive Company's assets consisted of hope, and a dream and a one-room rented office in Cleveland, Ohio. Sixty years later, as the Electro-Motive Division of General Motors Corporation, it had become the largest locomotive builder in the Western world.

The Winton petrol engine was basically a marine powerplant

Left: *A gas-propelled railcar of the Long Island Rail Road provides economical transport on the Sag Harbour Branch, 1935.*

A-6 4-4-2 Southern Pacific (SP), 1927

Gauge: 4ft 8½in (1,435mm).
Tractive effort: 41,360lb (18,766kg). *
Axleload: 33,000lb (15t).
Cylinders: (2) 22 x 28in (558 x 711mm).
Driving wheels: 81in (2,057mm).
Steam pressure: 210psi (14.8kg/cm²).
Grate area: 49,5sq ft (4.6m²).
Fuel (oil): 2,940 US gall (11.1m³).
Water: 9,000 US gall (34.1m³).
Adhesive weight: 62,000lb (28.1t).
Total weight: 465,900lb (211.4t).
Length overall: 78ft 8½in (23,990mm).
*29,860lb (13,094kg) without booster.

These delightfully elegant and simple locomotives have a very complex history, not being made any easier to understand by the fact that their owner ran three separately-administered railroad establishments. There was Southern

with added electrical equipment from General Electric; carbody. construction was by the St Louis Car Company, who also assembled the unit. One or two other builders had been supplying these gas-electric cars since 1910, but Electro-Motive quickly became the major supplier, just as they were to do in the diesel locomotive field a couple of decades later. By 1930, when the market for so-called "doodlebugs" collapsed, some 400 of these cars had been constructed, about 80 per cent of the total supplied by Electro-Motive to all US railroads.

Simplicity and standardisation was the secret of Electro-Motive's success then as now. Whilst it was not possible to dictate the

physical layout of the cars supplied to customers, most of the equipment was well-tried and easily available. For example, controls were only provided at the engine end, but this did not matter because wyes or turntables were generally available for turning.

Later, more powerful twin-engine cars with trailer-hauling capability came into being. They reached in excess of 500hp a weight of 160,000lb (72t) and 75ft length and used paraffin (distillate) rather than petrol (gasoline).

Left: *The gas-electric railcar of the preserved narrow gauge East Broad Top Railroad in Pennsylvania makes a run-past for photographic purposes.*

Pacific proper upon which the 75 4-4-2s built between 1902 and 1911 were numbered in chronological order from 3000 to 3074. Then, from time to time, some of them ran with different numbers on SP de Mexico or on the Texas & New Orleans (the 'Cotton Belt') Railroad. Both Mexico and Texas had hostile legislation concerning 'foreign' railroads on their territories and SP had to set up these nominally independent railroads to operate therein.

Further complications arise because the 4-4-2s were divided into five classes ("A-1" to "A-6" but not "A-4"). On top of that

Left: *Southern Pacific rebuilt class A-4 4-4-2 No.3025 on display at Traveltown, Burbank. Note below-centre position of headlight, an SP trademark.*

Below: *The class A-6 4-4-2s were produced in 1925 by rebuilding in Southern Pacific's own shops a number of older class A-3 4-4-2s which had been built in 1904-1906.*

each class—following various rebuildings—included differences as great or greater than between the separately-designated classes. The most obvious variations lay in the type of tender fitted; tubular 'Vanderbuilt' tanks of various sizes, ordinary 'box' pattern tenders as well as those with semicircular tanks could all be found on the 4-4-2s.

The illustration shows the "A-6" class of 1925, which was the last word as regards 4-4-2s on SP. The "A-6s" were produced in SP's own shops at Sacramento and Los Angeles by rebuilding four of the 51-strong "A-3" class built by Alco and Baldwin between 1904 and 1908. They took the numbers (No.3000-3003) of older 4-4-2s of Class "A-1" which had started life as Vauclain compounds and had by then been scrapped. Seven other members of the "A-3" class were given similar treatment, but were not reclassified. One of these latter machines, No.3025, is the sole survivor of the 4-4-2s and can be seen at Traveltown Museum in Burbank,

Los Angeles, California.

The great strength of the 4-4-2 steam locomotive lay in the big deep and wide firebox which it was possible to provide above the small rear carrying wheels; the great weakness, of course, lay in the limited adhesion possible with only four driving wheels. This problem was overcome by equipping the rebuilds with booster engines driving the rear wheels. At the same time, the new 'Delta' pattern cast-steel trailing trucks, which were needed to house this device, meant that the trailing wheels were converted from inside bearings to outside, and this had advantages too. Boosters were popular on the SP, being fitted also to over 300 4-8-2s, 2-8-4s, 4-8-4s, 2-10-2s and 4-10-2s.

The addition of a booster was the most important alteration made to the rebuilt Atlantics and it added 11,500lb (5,218kg) to the nominal tractive effort. It cut out automatically above 10mph (16km/h). In this guise the 4-4-2s could play their part in running SPs crack high-speed "Daylight" expresses and

two (3000-1) were painted in the special orange and black livery used on those trains. When loads exceeded the maximum permitted to a 4-8-4, a 4-4-2 would be attached as a helper on steeply-graded sections of the main coast line between Los Angeles and San Francisco.

A 4-4-2 on its own was assigned to the "Sacramento Daylight" on the independent section of its run. This was a portion of the "San Joaquin Daylight" which connected Los Angeles and San Francisco. Although the large driving wheels of the "A-6s" were a little smaller than the full 7ft of the "A-1s", they were totally adequate for the fast running necessary to keep time with these trains.

The rebuilding had involved improvements to the ports, passages and valve timing, quite apart from the substitution of Walschaert for Stephenson valve gear, thereby making it possible for the A-6s to run adequately fast to keep to schedule on such smartly-timed trains.

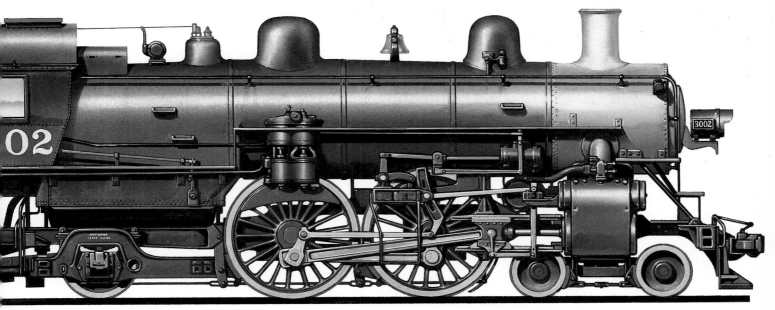

Class A 4-8-4 Northern Pacific Railroad (NP), 1926

Gauge: 4ft 8½in (1,435mm).
Tractive effort: 61,600lb (27,950kg).
Axle load: 65,000lb (29.5t).
Cylinders (2) 28 x 30in (711 x 762mm).
Driving wheels: 73in (1,854mm).
Heating surface: 4,660sq ft (433m²).
Superheater: 1,992sq ft (185m²).
Steam pressure: 225psi (15.8kg/cm²).
Grate area: 115sq ft (10.7m²).
Fuel: 48,000lb (22t).
Water: 12,500gall (15,000 US) (58m³).
Adhesive weight: 260,000lb (118t).
Total weight: 739,000lb (335t).
Overall length: 105ft 4⅜in (32,125mm).

The King of wheel arrangements at last! It needed 96 years for the 0-2-2 to become a 4-8-4, because all at once in 1927 4-8-4s quickly appeared on several railroads. But by a photo-finish the Northern Pacific's class "A" 4-8-4 was the first and hence the type-name

Northern was adopted. The Canadian National Railway, whose first 4-8-4 appeared in 1927 made an unsuccessful play for the name Confederation. Delaware, Lackawanna & Western put forward Pocono for their version. Other early members of the 4-8-4 Club—eventually to be over 40 strong in North America alone—were the Atchison, Topeka & Santa Fe and South Australia, the first foreign member.

The genesis of the 4-8-4 lay in the imbalance between possible tractive effort and grate area of its predecessor the 4-8-2. The Northern Pacific Railroad had a special problem in that its local coal supplies—known rather oddly as Rosebud coal—had a specially high ash content; hence the need for a big firebox and a four-wheel instead of a two-wheel truck at the rear.

And when we say a big firebox, we mean a *really* big one—measuring 13½ x 8½ft (4 x 2½m)—exceeding that of any other line's 4-8-4s. Northern Pacific themselves found their first Northerns so satisfactory

they never ordered another passenger locomotive with any other wheel arrangement, and indeed contented themselves with ordering modestly stretched and modernised versions of the originals—sub-classes "A-2", "A-3", "A-4" and "A-5"—right up to their last order for steam in 1943.

The originals were twelve in number and came from the American Locomotive Co of Schenectady. Apart from those enormous grates they were very much the standard US locomotive of the day, with the rugged features evolved after nearly a century of locomotive building on a vast scale. A booster fitted to the trailing truck gave a further 11,400lb (5,172kg) of tractive effort when required at low speeds.

The next 4-8-4 to operate on NP was another Alco product, built in 1930 to the order of the Timken Roller Bearing Co to demonstrate the advantages of having roller bearings on the axles of a steam locomotive. This "Four Aces" (No. 1111) locomotive worked on many railroads

with some success as a salesman. The NP was particularly impressed—not only did they buy the engine in 1933 when its sales campaign was over but they also included Timken bearings in the specification when further orders for locomotives were placed. On NP No. 1111 was renumbered 2626 and designated "A-1".

Baldwin of Philadelphia delivered the rest of the Northern fleet. The ten "A-2"s of 1934 (Nos. 2650-59) had disc drivers and bath-tub tenders, and the eight "A-3"s of 1938 (Nos. 2660-67) were almost identical. The final two batches of eight and ten respectively were also very similar; these were the "A-4"s of 1941 (Nos. 2670-77) and the "A-5"s of 1943 (Nos. 2680-89). These last two groups may be distinguished by their 14-wheel Centipede or 4-10-0 tenders of the type originally supplied for Union Pacific.

Below: *Biggest of the giants— "A-5" class 4-8-4 No.2685 starts "The Alaskan" out of Minneapolis in June 1954.*

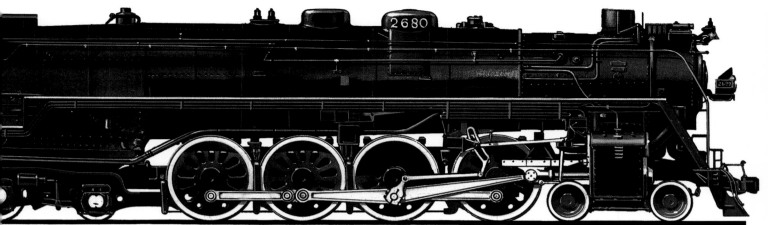

Above: *Northern Pacific Railroad class "A-5" 4-8-4 No. 2680 built by Baldwin in 1943. Note the "centipede" fourteen-wheel tender.*

This final batch is the subject of the art-work above. The amount of stretching that was done may be judged from the following particulars . . .

Tractive effort: 69,800lb (31,660kg).
Axle load: 74,000lb (33.5t)
Driving wheels: 77in (1,956mm)
Steam pressure: 260psi (18.3kg/cm).
Fuel: 54,000lb (24.5t)
Water: 21,000gall (25,000 US) (95m³).
Adhesive weight: 295,000lb (134t).
Total weight: 952,000lb (432t).
Overall length: 112ft 10in (34,391mm).

Other particulars are sensibly the same as the "A" class.

Northern Pacific had begun well by receiving a charter from President Abraham Lincoln in 1864 to build the first transcontinental line to serve the wide north-western territories of the USA. Through communication with the Pacific coast was established in 1883. By the time the 4-8-4s began to arrive it had established itself under the slogan "Main Street of the North West", and connected the twin cities of St Paul and Minneapolis with both Seattle and Portland.

The flag train on this run was the North Coast Limited, and the 4-8-4s assigned to it, after taking over from Chicago Burlington & Quincy Railroad power at St Paul, ran the 999 miles to Livingston, Montana, without change of engine. This is believed to be a world record as regards through engine runs with coal-fired locomotives. No doubt it was made possible by using normal coal in a firebox whose ash capacity was designed for the massive residues of Rosebud lignite.

Right: *One of the 1938 build of "A-3s", No.2664 eases a freight past the small depot at Manitoba Junction, Minn.*

Class 0-1A 2-8-2 Chicago, Burlington & Quincy Railroad (CB&Q), 1910

Gauge: 4ft 8½in (1,435mm).
Tractive effort: 58,090lb (26,355kg).
Axleload: 64,280lb (29t).
Cylinders: (2) 27 x 30in (686 x 762mm).
Driving wheel: 64in (1,626mm).
Heating surface: 4,178sq ft (388m²).
Superheater: 769sq ft (71m²).
Steam pressure: 200psi (14.1kg/cm²).
Grate area: 59sq ft (5.5m²).
Fuel: 38,000lb (17.25t).
Water: 10,000US gall (38m³).
Adhesive weight: 233,850lb (106t).
Total weight: 502,780lb (228t).
Length overall: 80ft 9in (24,613mm).

Herewith the typical 20th Century steam locomotive of North America! Supplied by the builder who made more steam locomotives than anyone else, with a wheel arrangement more common than any other, for a railroad of average size and situated in the geographical centre of the sub-continent, in the median year of steam construction during the 20th Century. So please welcome Chicago, Burlington & Quincy Class "01-A" 2-8-2 built by Baldwin in 1923.

Seventy Class "0-1" 2-8-2s came from Baldwin in 1910 and 1911, ever-growing traffic having out-classed the six-coupled power previously depended upon. A further 133 were supplied during the war years and immediately after, also by Baldwin. The "01-As" were a modestly modified version, the differences being hardly greater than those caused by alterations made from time to time to members of the original class. The Burlington also had some larger but less numerous 2-8-2s of classes "0-2", "0-3" and "0-4", the latter being the USRA heavy Mikado. There were both coal- and oil-burners amongst them.

Because the Burlington covered so much wheat-growing country

P-1 4-6-4 Wabash Railroad (WAB), 1925

Gauge: 4ft 8½in (1,435mm).
Tractive effort: 44,244lb (20,074kg).
Axleload: 72,009lb (32.7t).
Cylinders: (2) 26 x 28in (660 x 711mm).
Driving wheels: 80in (2,032mm).
Heating surface: 4,225sq ft (393m²).
Superheater: 1,051sq ft (98m²).
Steam pressure: 220psi (15.5kg/cm²).
Grate area: 71sq ft (6.6m²).
Fuel: 35,840lb (16.3t).
Water: 12,000 US gall (45.4m³).
Adhesive weight: 1,196,390lb (542.8t).
Total weight: 582,680lb (264.4t).
Length overall: 87ft 5in (26,644mm).

The Wabash Railroad Company had headquarters in St Louis and its tracks extended to Chicago, Kansas City, Omaha, Toledo and Detroit. With a route length of 4,000 miles, the Wabash was one of those medium-size lines which led a charmed life in spite of serving an area far too well provided with railroads. Its survival depended on the personal touch—that little extra bit of devotion on the part of the staff which made Wabash freight or passenger service just that critical amount better than its competitors. The personal touch was all that was available for the Wabash had for long been unable to afford much in the way of new equipment. Until dieselisation, the work was all done with a steam fleet which by the end of the war had no units less than 14 years old and included a high proportion built before World War I.

An urgent need for passenger locomotives in 1943 led to the rather drastic step of rebuilding six "K-5" class 2-8-2s into the road's first and only 4-6-4s, Class "P-1". A further "P-1" was produced in 1947 from a "K-4" 2-8-2. This remarkable piece of locomotive surgery was done in the Wabash Shops at Decatur, Illinois.

The original 2-8-2 locomotives were built by Alco in 1925 and, in accordance with the fashion of the moment, had a three-cylinder arrangement. The rebuilds had only two cylinders, three instead of four main axles, much larger driving wheels, two-axle instead of single-axle rear trucks, and roller bearings instead of plain ones. The boilers would also no doubt have needed renewal after 20 years service, so not too much of the originals could have been used.

One might wonder about the need for smallish, but fast new passenger engines in the middle of a war. The reason seems to lie in the fact that many Wabash passenger trains were light yet the only locomotives available to work them (apart from 40-year-old Class "J-1" 4-6-2s) were the large "M-1" and "O-1" 4-8-2s and 4-8-4s supplied in 1930-31. Even these had 70in (1,778mm) drivers—rather small for passenger services. So a batch of modest-sized roller-bearing 4-6-4s with high driving wheels, produced by rebuilding (in theory at least) some hard-to-maintain oldish 2-8-2s, would release bigger locomotives for freight and troop movements. At the same time the War Production Board's ban on new passenger locomotives would remain un-broken and the maintenance burden would be relieved by the

Right: *The Wabash Railroad produced these notable express passenger locomotives in 1943 by conversion from 2-8-2s.*

in Illinois, Iowa, Nebraska and Kansas, the 2-6-2s, which had suited the company for so long (and which had become the most numerous type on the system), were known the world over as 'Prairies'. However, by the 1920s the Mikados had ousted the Prairies from their premier position.

The "0-1s" and "0-1As" had no original features, but their extreme ordinariness was just what was needed to handle the everyday freight traffic of prairie towns, where the tracks were never out of sight of a grain elevator. In the end it was only the *force majeure* of dieselisation that led their owners to dispense with their services. Even so, several stayed on the roster into the 1960s, while "0-1A" No.4960 in particular became famous as a performer on railfan trips well on towards the end of the decade.

Left and right: *Burlington 0-1A 2-8-2 No.4960 performs for her fans near Hinckley, Illinois.*

up-to-date features of the rebuilds. Hence, benefits all round in a totally satisfactory way and the "Wabash Cannonball" would run to time.

The "P-1s" were semi-streamlined in a particularly handsome way, while the striking blue and white livery suited such excellent trains as the *Blue Bird* and *Banner Blue* between St Louis and Chicago. However, an obsolescent fleet of steam locomotives, expensive to run and to maintain, showed up badly against the diesel alternative. So all too soon after production of the last "P-1", the Wabash was to become an all-diesel line. Regrettably, none of these fine locomotives has been preserved.

Right: *Ready to go with the "Cannonball"! A blue-and-white 4-6-4 of the Wabash Railroad at St. Louis, Missouri, in 1946.*

9000 4-12-2 Union Pacific Railroad (UP), 1926

Gauge: 4ft 8½in (1,435mm).
Tractive effort: 96,650lb (43,852kg).
Axleload: 60,000lb (27.2t).
Cylinders: (2) 27 x 32in (685 x 812mm). (1) 27 x 31in (685 x 787mm).
Driving wheels: 67in (1,701mm).
Heating surface: 5,853sq ft (544m²).
Superheater: 2,560sq ft (238m²).
Steam pressure: 220psi (15.5kg/cm²).
Grate area: 108sq ft (10²).
Fuel: 42,000lb (19.1t).
Water: 15,000 US gall (56.8m³).
Adhesive weight: 355,000lb (161.1t).
Total weight: 782,000lb (354.8t).
Length overall: 102ft 7in (31,267mm).

Several times in this book the crossing of the Continental Divide by the Union Pacific Railroad will receive mention. The reason lies in the outstanding locomotive power needed to work ever-increasing tonnages over the grades involved. In the 1920s, traffic was being handled by 2-10-2s and 2-8-8-0 compound Mallets. The latter had adequate tractive effort but speeds above 25mph (16km/h) were not then possible with the Mallet arrangement, while the 2-10-2s had limited adhesion.

The idea of a 12-coupled engine was made possible by using the then new lateral-motion device developed by the American Locomotive Company. This arrangement enabled a long-wheelbase locomotive to negotiate sharp curves. Very few 12-coupled classes of steam locomotive then existed; apart from one or two singletons there were 24 narrow-gauge Class "61" 2-12-2Ts in Java, 44 of Class "59" 2-12-0s in Wurttemburg, Germany, and 10 0-12-0Ts in Bulgaria. Union Pacific had in mind something very much bigger than any of these. In fact the first 4-12-2 when it appeared from Alco in 1926 was well over

double the weight of its nearest 12-coupled rival.

The three-cylinder arrangement was adopted because otherwise the piston thrusts involved with a two-cylinder design would be greater than was considered feasible at the time. Tests indicated that No.9000 could take the same loads as the Mallets at very much

higher speeds and with much lower coal consumption. Production was put in hand at once and by 1930 the world's first and last class of 4-12-2s totalled 88.

Some of the "9000s" more unusual features did cause some trouble. Much was hoped for from the conjugated motion for the centre-cylinder which, being

Above: No.9032 of UP's unique class of 4-12-2s pauses at Topeka, Kansas, on a midsummer day in 1952.

Below: Ready for its next crack at the formidable Sherman Hill (40 miles of 1-in-66), Class 9000 No.9013 waits at Cheyenne in May 1953.

UNION PACIFIC 9000

rugged, simple and accessible, had apparently all the attributes. But, as also was found in Britain (its country of origin), the motion needed careful maintenance. There were two reasons—first, wear of any of the pins or bearings led to over-travel of the valve, and this in turn led to the middle cylinder doing more than its share of the work, often with dire results. The situation was particularly severe on the centre big-end bearing. A few engines were provided with separate third sets of Walschaerts gear set between the frames to operate the valves of the inside cylinder. This was driven from a second return crank mounted on the crankpin of the fourth axle on the right-hand side of the locomotive.

In order to encourage that 30ft 8in (9,347mm) of fixed wheelbase to perform as a contortionist, the leading and trailing coupled wheels were allowed 1in (25mm) sideplay either side of the centre line. The first locomotive originally had the centre (third) pair of driving wheels flangeless, but later examples had thin flanges. The sideplay was controlled against spring pressure, but no other devices such as spherical joints in the side rods were provided. The arrangements were entirely successful, so much so that the class as a whole would see steam out a quarter of a century later, although they were soon to be displaced from prime assignments and to other parts of the system by some greatly improved Mallet-type articulateds—the "Challengers"—introduced a few years later.

Only one of these unique locomotives is preserved; this is No.9004 at the Transportation Museum at Los Angeles.

Right: *Front-end clutter adds to the impressive proportions of the prototype Class 9000, built by Alco in 1926.*

Below: *Unique as a wheel arrangement, these 4-12-2s were also the longest non-articulated locos ever built.*

Class J3a 4-6-4 New York Central Railroad (NYC), 1926

Gauge: 4ft 8½in (1,435mm).
Tractive effort: 41,860lb (19,000kg).
Axleload: 67,500lb (30.5t).
Cylinders: (2) 22½ x 29in (572 x 737mm).
Driving wheels: 79in (2,007mm).
Heating surface: 4,187sq ft (389.0m²).
Superheater: 1,745sq ft (162.1m²).
Steam pressure: 265psi (18.6kg/cm²).
Grate area: 82sq ft (7.6m²).
Fuel: 92,000lb (41.7t).
Water: 15,000gall (18,000 US) (68.1m³).
Adhesive weight: 201,500lb (91.5t).
Total weight: 780,000lb (350t).
Length overall: 106ft 1in (32,342mm).

Some locomotive wheel arrangements had a particular association with one railway; such was the 4-6-4 and the New York Central. In 1926 the Central built its last Pacific, of Class "K5b," and the road's design staff, under the direction of Paul W Kiefer, Chief Engineer of Motive Power, began to plan a larger engine to meet future requirements. The main requirements were an increase in starting tractive effort, greater cylinder power at higher speeds, and weight distribution and balancing which would impose lower impact loads on the track than did the existing Pacifics. Clearly this would involve a larger firebox, and to meet the axle loading requirement the logical step was to use a four-wheeled truck under the cab, as was advocated by the Lima Locomotive Works, which had plugged engines with large fireboxes over trailing bogies under the trade name of Super Power. As the required tractive effort could be transmitted through three driving axles, the wheel arrangement came out as 4-6-4. Despite the Lima influence in the design, it was the American Locomotive Company of Schenectady which received the order for the first locomotive, although Lima did receive an order for ten of them some years later. Subsequent designs of 4-6-4s took over the type-name Hudson applied to these engines by the New York Central.

Classified "J1a" and numbered 5200, the new engine was handed over to the owners on 14 February 1927. By a narrow margin it was the first 4-6-4 in the United States, but others were already on the production line at Alco for other roads. Compared with the "K5b" it showed an increase in grate area from 67.8sq ft (6.3m²) to 81.5sq ft (7.6m²), and the maximum diameter of the boiler was increased from 84in (2,134mm) to 87⅜in (2,226mm). The cylinder and driving wheel sizes were unchanged, so the tractive effort went up in proportion to the increase in boiler pressure from 200psi (14.1 kg/cm²) to 225psi (15.8kg/cm²). The addition of an extra axle enabled the total weight on the coupled axles to be reduced from 185,000lb (83.9t) to 182,000lb (82.6t), despite an increase in the total engine weight of 41,000lb (22t). Improved balancing reduced the impact loading on the rails compared with the Pacific.

The engine had a striking appearance, the rear bogie giving it a more balanced rear end than a Pacific, with its single axle under a large firebox. At the front the air compressors and boiler feed pump were housed under distinctive curved casings at either side of the base of the smokebox, with diagonal bracing bars. The boiler mountings ahead of the cab were clothed in an unusual curved casing.

No.5200 soon showed its paces, and further orders followed, mostly for the NYC itself, but 80 of them allocated to three of the wholly-owned subsidiaries, whose engines were numbered and lettered separately. The latter included 30 engines for the Boston and Albany, which, in deference to the heavier gradients on that line, had driving wheels three inches smaller than the remainder, a rather academic difference. The B&A engines were classified "J2a", "J2b" and "J2c", the suffixes denoting minor differences in successive batches. The main NYC series of 145 engines were numbered consecutively from 5200, and here again successive modifications produced sub-classes "J1a" to "J1e". Amongst detail changes were the substitution of Baker's for Walschaert's valve gear; the Baker's gear has no sliding parts, and was found to require less maintenance. There were also changes in the valve setting.

From their first entry into service the Hudsons established a reputation for heavy haulage at high speeds. Their maximum drawbar horsepower was 38 per cent more than that of the Pacifics, and they attained this at a higher speed. They could haul 18 cars weighing 1,270 tonnes at an average speed of 55mph (88 km/h) on the generally level sections. One engine worked a 21-car train of 1,500 tonnes over the 639 miles (1,027km) from Windsor (Ontario) to Harmon, covering one section of 71 miles

Below: Standard Hudson or 4-6-4 of Class J3. The NYC had 275 locomotives of this type in passenger service and they monopolised the road's express trains for 20 years.

Below: *Nearing the end of its career as a mile-a-minute express locomotive, Class J3a No.5449 at East Albany, NY, in 1952.*

NEW YORK CENTRAL

(114km) at an average speed of 62.5mph (100.5km/h).

The last of the "J1" and "J2" series were built in 1932, and there was then a pause in construction, although the design staff were already planning for an increase in power. In 1937 orders were placed for 50 more Hudsons, incorporating certain improvements and classified "J3". At the time of the introduction of the first Hudson, the NYC, like the German engineers of the time, were chary of combustion chambers in fireboxes because of constructional and maintenance problems, but by 1937 further experience had been gained, and the "J3" incorporated a combustion chamber 43 in (1,092mm) long. Other changes included a tapering of the boiler barrel to give a greater diameter at the front of the firebox, raising of the boiler pressure from 225 psi (15.9kg/cmm²) to 275psi (19.3km/cm²) (later reduced to 265psi), and a change in the cylinder size from 25 x 28in (635 x 711mm) to 22½ x 29in (572 x 737mm). The most conspicuous change was the use of disc driving wheels, half the engines having Boxpok wheels with oval openings, and the other half the Scullin type with circular openings.

Above: *J1 4-6-4 No.5280 hauling the "Empire State Express" at Dunkirk, NY, in February 1950.*

The final ten engines were clothed in a streamlined casing designed by Henry Dreyfus. Of all the streamlined casings so far applied to American locomotives, this was the first to exploit the natural shape of the locomotive

Below: *The streamlined version of New York Central's famous J3 Hudsons. The designer of the casings was Henry Dreyfus.*

rather than to conceal it, and the working parts were left exposed. Many observers considered these to be the most handsome of all streamlined locomotives, especially when hauling a train in matching livery. Prior to the building of the streamlined "J3"s, a "J1" had been clothed in a casing devised at the Case School of Science in Cleveland, but it was much less attractive than Dreyfus' design, and the engine was rebuilt like the "J3"s; while two further "J3"s were given Dreyfus casings for special duties.

The "J3"s soon showed an improvement over the "J1"s both in power output and in efficiency. At 65mph (105km/h) they developed 20 per cent more power than a "J1". They could haul 1,130 tonne trains over the 147 miles (236km) from Albany to Syracuse at scheduled speeds of 59mph (95km/h), and could reach 60mph (96km/h) with a 1,640 tonne train. The crack train of the NYC was the celebrated 20th Century Limited. At the time of the building of the first Hudsons this train was allowed 20 hours from New York to Chicago. This was cut to 18 hours in 1932 on the introduction of the "J1e" series, and in 1936 there was a further cut to 16½ hours. Aided by the elimination of some severe service slacks,

and by the "J3" engines, the schedule came down to 16 hours in 1938, which gave an end-to-end speed of 59.9mph (96.3km/h) with 900-tonne trains, and with seven intermediate stops totalling 26 minutes. On a run with a "J3" on the Century, with 940 tonnes, the 133 miles (214km) from Toledo to Elkhart were covered in a net time of 112½ minutes, and the succeeding 93.9 miles (151km) from Elkhart to Englewood in 79½ minutes, both giving averages of 70.9mph (114km/h). A speed of 85.3mph (137km/h) was maintained for 31 miles (50km), with a maximum of 94mph (151km/h). The engines worked through from Harmon to Toledo or Chicago, 693 and 925 miles (1,114 and 1,487km) respectively. For this purpose huge tenders were built carrying 41 tonnes of coal, but as the NYC used water troughs to replenish the tanks on the move, the water capacity was by comparison modest at 18,000 US gallons (68.1m³).

Eventually the engines allocated to the subsidiaries were brought into the main series of numbers, and with the removal of the streamlined casings in post-war years, the NYC had 275 engines of similar appearance numbered from 5200 to 5474. It was the largest fleet of 4-6-4 locomotives on any railway, and constituted 63 per cent of the total engines of that wheel arrangement in the United States.

Although the Hudson had their share of troubles, they were generally reliable, and the "J3"s ran 185,000 to 200,000 miles (297,000 to 321,000km) between heavy repairs, at an annual rate of about 110,000 miles (177,000km).

After World War II the Niagara 4-8-4s displaced the Hudson from the heaviest workings, but as that class numbered only 25 engines, the Hudsons still worked many of the 150 trains daily on the NYC booked at more than 60mile/h (96km/h) start-to-stop. Despite rapid dieselisation the engines lasted until 1953-6, apart from an accident casualty.

Class Ps-4 4-6-2 Southern Railway (SR), 1926

Gauge: 4ft 8½in (1,435mm).
Tractive effort: 47,500lb (21,546 kg).
Axle load: 61,000lb (27.25t).
Cylinders: (2) 27 x 28in (686 x 711mm).
Driving wheels: 73in (1,854mm).
Heating surface: 3,689sq ft (343m²).
Superheater: 993sq ft (92.3m²).
Steam pressure: 200psi (14.1kg/cm²).
Grate area: 70.5sq ft (6.55m²).
Fuel: 32,000lb (14.5t).
Water: 11,600gall (14,000 US) (53m³).
Adhesive weight: 182,000lb (81t).
Total weight: 562,000lb (255.0t).
Length overall: 91ft 11⅞in (28,038mm).

Hundreds of classes of Pacific locomotives ran in America; to illustrate them the first choice was the earliest proper 4-6-2, of the Chesapeake & Ohio. Second choice was the Pennsylvania RR class "K4", as the 4-6-2 design built in the largest numbers. This locomotive, our third choice, is without any doubt the most beautiful amongst the Pacifics of America.

The history of the Southern Railway's Pacifics began in World War I, when the United States Railroad Administration, which had taken over the railroads for the duration, set out to design a standard set of steam locomotives to cover all types of traffic. One of these was the so-called USRA "heavy" 4-6-2. Based on this design, the American Locomotive Company built the first batch of 36 Class "Ps-4" 4-6-2s in 1923.

In 1925 President (of Southern Railway) Fairfax Harrison, visited

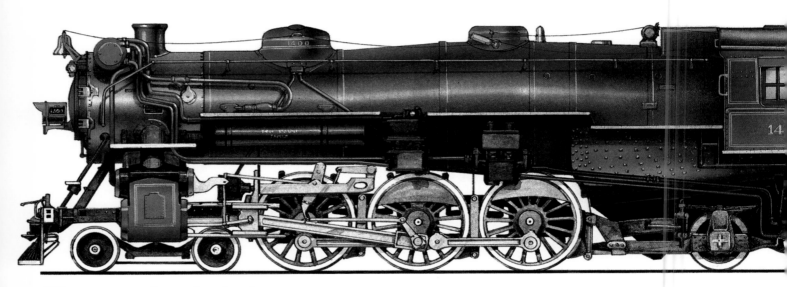

Class F-2a 4-4-4 Canadian Pacific Railway (CPR), 1936

Gauge: 4ft 8½in (1,435mm).
Tractive effort: 26,500lb (12,000kg).
Axle load: 61,000lb (28t).
Cylinders: (2) 17¼ x 28in (438 x 711mm).
Driving wheels: 80in (2,032mm).
Heating surface: 2,833sq ft (263m²).
Superheater: 1,100sq ft (102m²).
Steam pressure: 300psi (21kg/cm²).
Grate area: 55.6sq ft (5.2m²).
Fuel: 27,000lb (12t).
Water: 7,000galls (8,400 US) (32m³).
Adhesive weight: 121,000lb (55t).
Total weight: 461,000lb (209t).
Length overall: 81ft 2⅞in (24,762 mm).

In 1936 the Canadian Pacific Railway introduced four trains which were announced as a High-Speed Local Service. In each case the formation consisted of a mail/express (parcels) car, a baggage-buffet and two passenger cars. By North American

Above: *No.3002 of the original and larger batch of F-2as at Toronto, April 1952.*

standards they counted as lightweight, the weight being 200 tons for the four-coach train. Most American railroads would have found some hand-me-down locomotives discarded from first-line passenger service to work them, but that was not the CPR way. They ordered five new 4-4-4 steam locomotives, designated

the "Jubilee" type, from the Montreal Locomotive Works to work these trains—although spoken of as streamlined, they are better described as having a few corners nicely rounded. Running numbers were 3000 to 3004.

The new services for which this equipment was ordered comprised the "Chinook" in the West between Calgary and Edmonton (194 miles—310km—in 315 minutes including 22 stops) and the international "Royal York" between Toronto and Detroit (229 miles—366km—in 335 minutes with 19 stops) and two others between Montreal and Quebec. It was the sort of service for which a home-based British company might field a 100 ton 4-4-0 with perhaps 25sq ft (2.3m²) of grate area, but these "small" 4-4-4s weighed some 90 per cent more than this and had a fire-grate 120 per cent bigger.

Even if it was a case where the trans-Atlantic love of bigness might have been misplaced, the "F-2a"s were certainly magnificent. They had such sophisticated

his line's namesake in England and was impressed with its green engines. He determined that his next batch of 4-6-2s would make an equal if not better showing. He naturally chose a style very similar to the English SR except that a much brighter green was used together with gold—the small extra cost paid off quickly in publicity. Coloured locomotives were then quite exceptional in North America. A little later the earlier batch of locomotives appeared in green and gold also.

The 1926 batch of 23 locomotives had the enormous 12-wheel tenders illustrated here, in place of the USRA standard

8-wheel tenders on the earlier engines, and a different and much more obvious type (the Elesco) of feed water heater involving the large transverse cylindrical vessel just in front of the smokestack. Some locomotives from each batch had the Walschaert's gear, others had Baker's. A final batch of 5 came from Baldwin in 1928. These had Walschaert's valve gear and 8-wheel tenders of large capacity. All were fitted with mechanical stokers.

Southern had what it called an "optional equipment policy" whereby drivers were allowed to adorn their locomotives in various

ways, ways in fact that were similar to those of 70 years earlier. Eagles could be mounted above the headlights, themselves flanked by brass "candlesticks"; stars were fixed to cylinder heads, brass rings to smokestacks. Some locomotives were named after and by their regular drivers. A lot of this might be considered mere nonsense, but the end effect was that few steam engines anywhere were better maintained.

Of the 64 locomotives built, 44 were allocated to the Southern Railway proper, 12 to subsidiary Cincinnati, New Orleans & Texas Pacific and 8 to the Alabama Great Southern, although "Southern" appeared on the tenders of all. Running numbers were as follows:
SR proper—Nos.1366 to 1409.
CNO&TP—Nos.6471 to 6482.
AGS—Nos.6684 to 6691.

The CNO&TP engines had a device known as a Wimble smoke duct, by which the exhaust which otherwise would issue from the chimney could be led backwards to level with the sand dome and discharged there. The CNO&TP was a line with many timber-lined tunnels and a direct close-up vertical blast would have played havoc with the tunnel linings.

The "Ps-4" class was the last steam passenger locomotive type built for the Southern and they remained in top-line express work until displaced by diesels in the 1940s and 1950s. No.1401 is preserved and is superbly displayed in the Smithsonian Museum, Washington, D.C.

Alas, this involved erecting the display building around the locomotive, thereby preventing its use on special trains for railfans, a Southern speciality.

Left: *Diesels were beginning to displace the Ps-4s from the top trains when No.1406 was caught at Charlottesville, Va, in 1947.*

Below: *The glorious green and gold beauty of the livery applied to the Southern Railway (of USA) "Ps-4" class Pacific is superbly depicted below.*

features as mechanical stokers, feed-water heaters and roller bearings. One feature that was important for operation in Canada was an all-weather insulated cab, able to provide comfortable conditions for the crew in a country where the outside temperature could easily drop to minus 40°F (−40°C), 72 Fahrenheit degrees of frost.

A further series of similar and slightly smaller 4-4-4s, numbered from 2901 to 2929, were built in 1938, designated class "F-1a". The second series was easily recognisable by the drive on to the rear coupled axle, instead of on to the front axle as with the "F-2a". Nos.2928 and 2929 of this later series are preserved at the National Railway Museum at Delson, Quebec, and (currently but with future undecided) at Steamtown, Bellows Falls, Vermont, USA, respectively.

Right: *At the same location in Toronto is CPR's smaller 4-4-4, Class F-1a No.2928, now preserved.*

P-7 4-6-2 Baltimore & Ohio Railroad (B&O), 1927

Gauge: 4ft 8½in (1,435mm).
Tractive effort: 50,000lb (22,686kg).
Axleload: 68,000lb (30.9t).
Cylinders: (2) 27 x 28in (685 x 711mm).
Driving wheels: 80in (2,032mm).
Heating surface: 3,782sq ft (351m²)
Superheater: 950sq ft (88m²).
Steam pressure: 280psi (19.7kg/cm²).
Grate area: 70.2sq ft (6.5²).
Fuel: 39,000lb (17.7t).
Water: 11,000US gall (41.6m²).
Adhesive weight: 201,000lb (91.2t).
Total weight: 544,000lb (246.8t).
Length overall: 87ft 10½in (26,784mm).

The Baltimore & Ohio Railroad has used Pacifics for its principal passenger trains since 1906. For the start of through running by B&O locomotives from Washington to Jersey City in 1927, the eighth class of 4-6-2 was placed in service; these 20 Class "P-7s" were over 50 per cent more powerful than the original Class "P" of 20 years earlier.

This was also the year in which the B&O celebrated the centenary of the granting of its charter with an ambitious 'Fair of the Iron Horse' at Baltimore. One of the visitors to the fair was an elegant green and gold 4-6-0 called *King George V* which came from the Great Western Railway of England. The absence of visible plumbing and the stunning livery caused a sensation. As a result, imitation being the sincerest form of flattery, the "P-7" 4-6-2s not only took names from US presidents, but were painted a similar shade of green. It was many years since any B&O engine had been painted anything else but black. Incidentally,

the elegant simplicity of the British engine was no triumph of design—the plumbing really was simple. With no air pump, no sandboxes on top of the boiler, no bell, no power reverse, no feed-water pump, and no turbo-generator, anything but a clean outline was impossible. The "P-7s" had all these things, with mechanical stokers and water scoops as well.

The twenty-first "P-7", named *President Cleveland* and completed in 1928, was an experimental locomotive with a water-tube firebox and camshaft-driven Caprotti pattern poppet valves,

Right: *Baltimore & Ohio P-7 "President" class 4-6-2 No.5307 crosses the famous bridge at Harper's Ferry, Virginia in 1952.*

G5s 4-6-0 Long Island Rail Road (LIRR), 1928

Gauge: 4ft 8½in (1,435mm).
Tractive effort: 41,328lb (18,751kg).
Axleload: 63,000lb (28.6t).
Cylinders: (2) 24 x 28in (609 x 711mm).
Driving wheels: 68in (1,727mm).
Heating surface: 2,855sq ft (265m²).
Superheater: 613sq ft (57m²).
Steam pressure: 205psi (14.4kg/cm²).
Grate area: 55sq ft (5.1m²).
Fuel: 24,000lb (10.9t).
Water: 8,300US gall (31.4m³).
Adhesive weight: 178,000lb (80.8t).
Total weight: 409,000lb (185.6t).
Length overall: 70ft 5½in (21,475mm).

similar in principle to those used in automobile practice. The latter were not a success and were altered to the conventional Walschaert pattern the following year. Unlike the earlier engines, all of which came from Baldwin, this No.5320 was built in the B&O's own Mount Clare shops. Incidentally, the names were allocated in historical order beginning with No.5300 *President Washington*, one loco sufficing for both presidents named Adams.

The water-tube firebox, while not sufficient of an improvement to displace convention, did remain on the locomotive until 1945. In 1937 one other "P-7" No.5310 *President Taylor* was also treated in this way, with equally inconclusive results. These two locomotives were designated "P-9" and "P9b" respectively when running in this condition.

From 1937 to 1940 No.5310 was streamlined, painted blue and renamed *The Royal Blue* for working the train of that name. Because of the difficulty of allocating a specific locomotive to a particular train, the rest of the class were also painted blue and this matched the colour of new B&O trains then being put into service. Soon afterwards, the whole class ceased to carry names and in 1946 a further batch of four was streamlined for running the "Cincinnatian," following a rebuild which included provision of cast locomotive beds, roller bearings and bigger 12-wheel tenders.

Left: *P-7 class 4-6-2 No.5308 of the Baltimore & Ohio Railroad All were named after Presidents; this one is President Tyler.*

Below: *A "President" class 4-6-2 leans to the curve on this well ballasted stretch of the Baltimore & Ohio Railroad.*

These handsome locomotives must represent in this book all those built to carry people to and from the places where they earn their daily bread. Most railroads used superannuated main-line locomotives for this purpose, but the Pennsylvania Railward was not one of them, being then in the fortunate position of being able to afford the proper tools for the job.

Pennsy also followed the economical practice of do-it-yourself and 90 of these fine 4-6-0s, designated Class "G5s" were built in 1923, 1924 and 1925 in the road's own Juanita shops. The design owed a great deal to the "E6s" 4-4-2 class of 1910, thereby avoiding some of the expense of new tooling and patterns. An exception was the driving wheels which were 15 per cent smaller than those of the "E6s". Incidentally, the 'G' and the 'E' stood for the respective wheel arrangements, while 's' stood for 'superheated'.

The only important feature which was not standard North American practice was the Belpaire firebox. Invented by a Belgian engineer in 1864, the idea was to increase the surface area of the firebox and its

Below: *This Long Island G5s 4-6-0 was built in 1929, retired in 1955 and is now undergoing restoration.*

internal volume, whilst keeping plenty of room for water to circulate round it. The simplicity of the round-top firebox was lost because the change of section of the boiler made construction more complex. Further more, a good deal of additional staying was required, but improved steam generation was thought to make the extra costs worthwhile. Belpaire fireboxes were common in Europe but few other North American railroads used them.

Prosperous Pennsy had an immense freight business which could underpin essentially dubious commuter operations, but an orphan child in the household had no such advantage. This was the Long Island Railroad, owned by the Pennsylvania, whose whole basis of existence was bringing daily-breaders to and from the

Above: *Long Island Rail Road Class G5s 4-6-0 No.38 makes a fine display of smoke at Kings Park, New York, one day in 1950.*

city of New York. Between 1924 and 1929, a fleet of 31 "G5s" locomotives, identical to those on the Pennsy proper except that the keystone numberplate on the smokebox was originally replaced by a plain circular one, were built specially for the subsidiary railroad. Most of the shorter-distance Long Island traffic was operated electrically, so the new locomotives took the longer distance runs to the outer extremities of the island.

When diesels took over outside the electrified areas in the 1950s, the "G5s" were retired. One (No.5741) is preserved in the Railroad Museum of Pennsylvania at Strasburg.

AC-4 Cab Forward 4-8-8-2 Southern Pacific (SP), 1928

Gauge: 4ft 8½in (1,435mm).
Tractive effort: 124,300lb (56,397kg).
Axleload: 69,960lb (31.7t).
Cylinders: (4) 24 x 32in (609 x 812mm).
Driving wheels: 63.5in (1,612mm).
Heating surface: 6,470sq ft (601m²).
Superheater: 2,616sq ft (243m²).
Steam pressure: 250psi (17.6kg/cm²).
Grate area: 139 (12.9m²).
Fuel (oil): 6,100 US gall (23.1m³).
Water: 22,00 US gall (83.3m³).
Adhesive weight: 531,700lb (241.2t).
Total weight: 1,051,200lb (477t).
Length overall: 124ft 11in (38,074mm).

One of the most severe railway routes in the world is the Southern Pacific's 'Overland Route,' completed from Sacramento, California, to meet the Union Pacific at Promontory Point, Utah, on that notable day in railroad history, May 10, 1869. Travelling east, trains have to face the climb over the Sierras from what was effectively sea level to the summit at Donner Pass 7,000ft (2,135m) in altitude. The ruling grade had been eased from the original 2.77 per cent (1-in-36) to 2.42 per cent (1-in-41), but was still horrific. The ascent on the eastern side of the range from 4,500ft (1,370m) at Reno was equally severe although shorter. There was a greater deal of curvature, some as sharp as 12°.

Snow falls over the Sierras in vast quantities and in those early days the only reasonable solution was to roof over the track with timber. In the end 37 miles (60km) of snow sheds were built and in addition there were 39 tunnels. After the failure of 4-10-0 *El Gobenador*, already described, the Mallet principle was tried in the form of two compound 2-8-8-2s (then the most powerful locomotives in the world) built by Baldwin in 1909. As much as 1,300 tons could be handled over 'The Hill' by these machines, but the many miles of snowsheds and tunnels caused difficulties for their crews in finding air to breathe. The 2-8-0s and 4-8-0s, previously used in multiple, would be spread out down the train, which helped.

For some years oil fuel had been used, and this led to a suggestion for turning the locomotive round so that the cab came in front. The idea seems to have originated on a local Californian railroad called the North Pacific Coast, but was resuscitated by SP and Baldwin when, later the same year, 15 2-8-2s were built to this plan. They were otherwise very similar to the earlier 2-8-8-2s, and in fact the only significant change was due to the need for some assistance to persuade the oil to flow uphill a distance of some 100ft. This was done by making the tenders half-round in form, so enabling them to be pressurised with 5psi (0.5kg/cm²) of air pressure. By 1913 there were 46 of these locomotives, most of which were later

Below: *At Roseville, California, Class AC-4 No.4154 makes ready for a run "over the hill" to Sacramento with a heavy freight. The date is May 1954.*

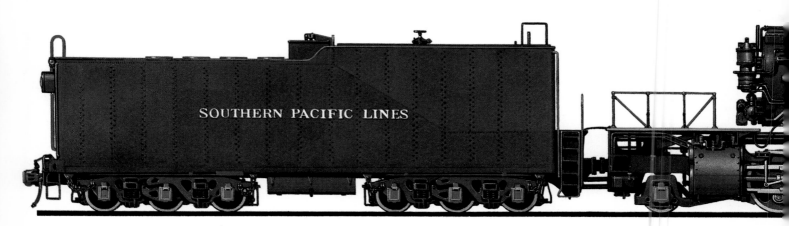

SOUTHERN PACIFIC LINES

converted from compound to simple.

Another detail involved the arrangement of the Walschaert valve gear. Since the locomotives usually ran in what on a normal engine would be reverse gear, this normally meant having the die-block at the top of the curved link rather than in the best position, giving a direct drive at the bottom. By moving the position of the eccentric crank through 180°, the engines of the 'cab-in-fronts' could have the best position of the motion in their normal direction of running.

Like other Mallets of the day, long before the idea of having a combustion chamber was evolved, the boiler of all these locomotives was in two parts. The rear section including the firebox was conventional, but in front was a separate section with its own fire tubes and tube plates, which acted as a feed-water heater. In due time modern single-stage boilers with a combustion chamber were substituted. One interesting device fitted to all the cab-in-fronts was a retractable longitudinal smoke-splitter which prevented the exhaust from impinging directly on to the vulnerable roofs of snowsheds.

By the end of 1913 three very similar batches of cab-in-front 2-8-8-2s had been built, designated classes "MC-2", "MC-4" and "MC-6", MC standing for 'Mallet-Consolidation'. Numbers ran in chronological order from 4002 to 4048.

Twelve 'Mallet-Mogul' cab-in-front 2-6-6-2s (later altered to 4-6-6-2s) were built in 1911 for passenger work, but they were not found suitable for passenger speeds and so were relegated to freight after a few years. As well as becoming unstable, one problem with a fast-running compound Mallet was getting the huge volume of low-pressure steam in and out of big low-pressure cylinders quickly enough. This led to the high-pressure Mallet-type articulated, with four HP cylinders, as pioneered by the Chesapeake & Ohio.

After converting an "MC-6" experimentally to simple working in 1927, SP in 1928 ordered a batch of 10 4-8-8-2s, classified

(partly inappropriately) as 'Articulated-Consolidation', or 'AC-4". SP then went on to have 185 more of these unique locomotives built by Baldwin, supplied in seven batches from 1929 to 1944. Locomotives of earlier "MC" classes were all converted to simple "AC" form, becoming classes "AC-1", "AC-2" and "AC-3", between 1928 and 1937, while the original two conventional Mallets, Class "MC-1" were converted to "AC-1" form. Similarly, the "MMs" became Class "AM-2" during the 1930s, making a final total of 257 cab-in-fronts on the Southern Pacific. They were used on several other lines besides the Overland Route.

The cab-in-fronts had one or two inherent weaknesses which caused problems from time to time. With the firebox at the leading end, the range of boiler water level for safe working was reduced when running uphill and thus steaming hard. There were more cases of boiler explosions than there should have been and this factor no doubt contributed. The other problem was that, because the furnace oil had such a long distance to flow, there was a tendency for the fire to go out and then relight explosively when the critical air-vapour mixture had been achieved. The dangers to the crews were accentuated by the totally-enclosed cabs. These and other combustion problems caused some difficulties and a few injuries, but in general the cab-in-fronts were very successful.

High speed was not their thing, 55mph (88km/h) being the maximum their modest riding qualities would permit. In the 1940s, three cab-in-fronts (one in front, one in the middle and one out

Above: *Baldwin's works photo of No.4159 shows clearly the massive proportions of the "cab-in-front" locomotives built for Southern Pacific.*

ahead of the caboose) would take a 5,000 ton load of perishables from Roseville Yard, 138 miles (216km) over 'The Hill' to Sacramento in just under 8 hours. This compared with 16 hours using five locomotives hauling a lighter load before the Mallets came 30 years before. Now, 30 years on, diesel traction has effected further modest improvement to 7 hours.

Below: *Though unique, Southern Pacific'c class AC 4-8-8-4s were successful enough to command a build totalling 257—not bad for a one-off design*

No. 9000 2-D₀-1 Canadian National Railways (CNR), 1929

Type: Main line diesel-electric locomotive.
Gauge: 4ft 8½in (1,435mm).
Propulsion: Beardmore 1,330hp (992kW) four-stroke V12 diesel engine and generator, originally supercharged, supplying direct current to four nose-suspended traction motors geared to the axles.
Weight: 255,644lb (116t) adhesive, 374,080lb (170t) total.
Max. axleload: 63,920lb (29t).
Overall length: 47ft 0½in (14,338mm).
Tractive effort: 50,000lb (222kN).
Max. speed: 75mph (120km/h).

The shape of things to come! These two locomotives—which usually worked coupled back-to-back as a pair—were the first main-line diesel units in North America. They were a joint product of the Canadian Locomotive Co and Westinghouse Electric. From all accounts they worked quite well when they were actually working—keeping time easily with 700 US tons on the "International Limited" between Montreal and Toronto, for example, on a schedule which involved an average speed of 44mph (70km/h) including 13 stops, some lengthy. Running costs were absurdly low, and yet the locomotives were not successful.

The problem lay in the difficulties of maintenance. CN's own maintenance department was almost entirely steam-orientated and so the basic infrastructure was not there. Secondly, the locomotives themselves had all the small faults typical of any unproven piece of equipment. Thirdly, none of the manufacturers involved nor CN had a stock of spare parts worthy of the name—almost all the parts needed had to be specially made to order, and many hand-fitted thereafter, a process which was both slow and expensive. No progress in dieselisation could be made until a package appeared which included a solution to these problems. This was shortly to happen, as will be seen.

On the other hand, both the overall technology, and the concept were good, one or two quite basic shortcomings being easily resolved. For example, in 1931 the engine manufacturer had to replace both crankcases with stronger ones nearly a ton heavier. This perhaps underlined the fact that an engine like the Beardmore, which was excellent in a submarine under the watchful eye of highly-qualified "tiffies" (Engine-room Artificer, 1st class, RN), was less satisfactory under railway conditions. Even so, the specific weight of the Beardmore engine at 24.5lb per hp (15kg/kW) had come a long way from the Ingersoll-Rand engines fitted to switchers a few years earlier, which turned the scales at double that figure. This must be considered against the background of present day North American diesel locomotives, which have engines of specific weights only half that of the Beardmore.

After trials with the locomotive as a twin unit, the two "ends"

L.F. Loree 4-8-0 Delaware & Hudson Railway (D&H), 1933

Gauge: 4ft 8½in (1,435mm).
Tractive effort: 75,000lb (34,029kg).
Axleload: 86,075lb (39.1t).
Cylinders, HP: (1) 20 x 33in (508 x 838mm).
Cylinders, IP: (1) 27½ x 33in (698 x 838mm).
Cylinders, LP: (2) 33 x 33in (838 x 838mm).
Driving wheels: 63in (1,600mm).
Heating surface: 3,351sq ft (311m²).
Superheater: 1,086sq ft (100m²).
Steam pressure: 500psi (35.2kg/cm²).
Grate area: 75sq ft (7m²).
Fuel: 30,000lb (13.6t).
Water: 14,000 US gall (53m³).
Adhesive weight: 313,000lb (142t).
Total weight: 658,000lb (298.5t).

Leonor F. Loree, President of the Delaware & Hudson Railway from 1907 to 1935, was the driving force behind one of the most thorough-going attempts ever made to improve the steam locomotive. The experiments began in 1923 when 4-8-0 No.1400 *Horatio Allen* took to the rails. The boiler was designed for a higher pressure than normal. This was too high to be withstood by the flat surfaces of a normal firebox, and so a water-tube arrangement was substituted. The steam pressure was also too high to be used to advantage with simple cylinders, and so No.1400 was arranged as a two-cylinder compound with a high-pressure cylinder on one side and a low-pressure unit on the other. As on some other D&H 2-8-0s there was also a booster engine on the rear tender truck, the axles of which were coupled by rods.

The new locomotive fulfilled its designer's promises by burning some 30 per cent less coal to do the same work, compared with a conventional 2-8-0. Alas, there was a penalty in increased cost of maintenance which outweighed (but only just) the savings due to reduced fuel consumption.

Two further experimental 2-8-0s followed, generally similar to No.1400 but using still higher pressures. No.1401 *John B. Jervis* used 400psi (27kg/cm²) and No.1402 *James Archbald* 500psi (35.2g/cm²). They were built in 1927 and 1930 respectively. Even greater savings in fuel consumption were achieved, but the debit of increased maintenance more than swallowed them.

Finally came the 4-8-0 No.1403 *L. F. Loree,* the subject of the figures above, which was designed as a unique triple-expansion compound locomotive with four cylinders. Two low-pressure cylinders were placed in the conventional position at the front, while the single intermediate-pressure and single high-pressure cylinders were placed beneath the cab on either side. All four drove on to the second coupled axle. Rotary-cam poppet valves of the Dabeg pattern distributed steam between the four cylinders. Bleed and by-pass valves enabled live steam direct from the boiler to be admitted to all cylinders for starting. Incidentally, this locomotive was the only one built in that depression year of 1933 for any US railroad.

No.1403 was a really superb technical achievement, showing an improvement in thermal efficiency which reduced coal consumption to less than half the amount a normal locomotive would burn on a given task. But once more the debits were even greater. For example, high temperature of the steam caused lubrication problems in the cylinders. Another problem was bearing failures in the main driving axleboxes, caused by taking the thrusts of all four cylinders on the same pair of wheels.

Even though Loree never took the steam locomotive beyond the Stephenson concept, the Delaware & Hudson during the same years pioneered several details which were also very important. The roller bearings fitted to the main axles of No.1403 were the result of an early application of such a feature to a D&H 4-6-2 in 1927. The first locomotive in the world to have roller bearings in the big ends of the connecting rods was another of the same class. The D&H also pioneered the cast-steel locomotive bed. All these items became commonplace when the last great pages of steam locomotive design came to be written.

Right: L.F. Loree *himself, the unique four-cylinder compound.*

were operated separately, being then renumbered 9000 and 9001. No. 9000 was scrapped in 1939, but during the war No. 9001 found a use in the west as a coastal defence train. Its body work was altered to give the appearance of a boxcar, as well as a modicum of armoured protection for the crew. After the war, No. 9001 worked for a short time in the east but was withdrawn in 1947. Even so, 20 years later, virtually all Canadian trains were to be hauled by locomotives of totally similar concept.

Right and below: *The first main line diesel-electric in North America, No.9000, built in 1929, and split into two units for operation following trial running.*

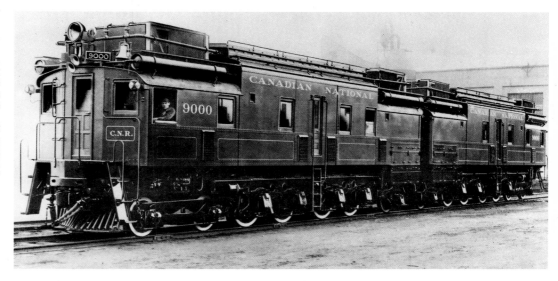

Pioneer Zephyr Three-car train
Chicago, Burlington & Quincy Railroad (CB&Q), 1934

Type: High-speed articulated streamlined diesel-electric train.
Gauge: 4ft 8½in (1,435mm).
Propulsion: Electro-Motive Type 201E 600hp (448kW) in-line two-stroke diesel engine and generator feeding two nose-suspended traction motors on the leading bogie.
Weight: 90,360lb (41t) adhesive, 175,000lb (79.5t) total.
Max. axleload: 45,180lb (20.5t).
Overall length: 196ft 0in (59,741mm).
Max. speed: 110mph (177km/h).

On May 25, 1934 the fastest train between Denver and Chicago (1,015 miles— 1,624km) was the "Autocrat", timed to do the run in 27hr 45min including 40 stops, an average speed of 37mph (59km/h). On May 26 a brand new stainless steel articulated streamlined self-propelled train reeled off the miles between the two cities in just over 13 hours at an average speed of 78mph (125km/h). As the little train triumphantly ran into its display position at the Century of Progress Exhibition in Chicago, US railroading had changed for ever.

Preparation for this triumph had begun in 1930 when mighty General Motors purchased both the Electro-Motive Company and their engine suppliers, the Winton Engine Co. GM concentrated their efforts on making a diesel engine suitable for rail transport. 'Softly, softly catchee monkey' was their policy and it was with considerable reluctance that after four years work they agreed to let an experimental engine out of their hands for this *Pioneer Zephyr*. The floodlight of publicity that illuminated its triumph could so easily have lit up a disaster

Right: *Leading end of the original Pioneer Zephyr train with powerful headlight to signal its approach.*

M-10001 Six-car trainset
Union Pacific Railroad (UP), 1934

Type: Diesel-electric high-speed passenger train.
Gauge: 4ft 8½in (1,435mm).
Propulsion: Electro-Motive 1,200hp (895kW) V-16 two-stroke diesel engine and generator supplying current to four 250hp (187kW) nose-suspended traction motors geared to the axles of the two leading bogies.
Weight: 143,260lb (65t) adhesive, 413,280lb (187.5t) total.
Max. axleload: 35,815lb (16.25t).
Overall length: 376ft 0in (114,605mm).
Max. speed: 120mph (192km/h).*

* Not operated in regular service above 90mph (144km/h).

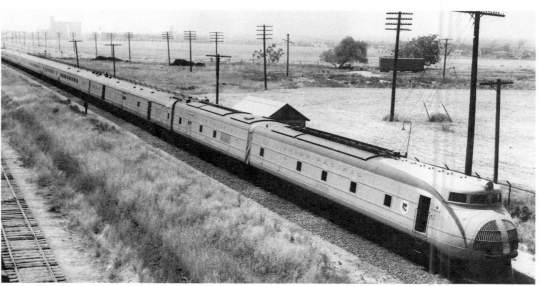

—indeed, electrical faults occurring during the trip, but bravely corrected by the staff whilst the equipment was still live, indicated that it was a very close-run thing indeed.

In some ways, of course, it was a nonsense. Naturally, the manufacturers pressed the view that the whole performance was due to diesel traction when it was really due to a different approach to long-distance passenger movement. Various railroads (notably the Chicago, Milwaukee, St Paul & Pacific and Southern Pacific) were quick to demonstrate that equal improvements were possible with steam, at much lower first cost. Of course, once they had been paid for, running costs of the new trains were much lower than with steam, but overall there was little in it. Incidentally, over one-third of the space available was devoted to the carriage of mail and parcels.

Extra comforts such as air-conditioning, radio reception, reclining seats, grill-buffet and observation lounge were very nice, but significantly little has ever been said about the riding of the *Pioneer Zephyr*. One must unkindly suspect, though, that compared with the heavyweight stock the new train replaced, a little was left to be desired. Even so, many other *Zephyr* trains—but never quite as lightly built as the original—were to go into service on the Burlington. It is true that the self-propelled concept was soon dropped in favour of separate locomotives, but the name is still commemorated today with Amtrak's "San Francisco Zephyr" running daily between Chicago and Oakland (San Francisco). The original little 72-seat train —later enlarged to four cars—ran over 3 million miles in traffic and is today enshrined in Chicago's Museum of Science & Industry.

Above: *The diesel era rushes in at an average of 78mph (125km/h): Pioneer Zephyr on its record-breaking run, May 26, 1938.*

Below: *Streamline Zephyr-style trainsets were adopted for many of the Burlington's prestige routes.*

Left: *Union Pacific's original 11-car version of the "City of Los Angeles" streamlined trainset at the time of its introduction between Chicago and Los Angeles in May 1936. A 17-car version followed.*

In February 1934 the famed Union Pacific Railroad only failed by a technicality to be the first in America with a diesel-electric high-speed train. A suitable diesel engine was not quite ready and UP's stunning train had to have a spark-plug engine using distillate fuel. This was the yellow and grey No. M-10000, consisting of three articulated streamlined light-alloy cars weighing including power plant 85t (93½ US tons), in total hardly more than a single standard US passenger car as then existing. The train was built by Pullman

Standard and seated 116 passengers in air-conditioned comfort; the leading power car included a 33ft (10m) mail compartment. After a coast-to-coast demonstration tour the train went into service as the "City of Salina" on one of UP's few short-distance daytime inter-city runs, that between Kansas City and Salina.

The success of the principles involved led to the first diesel-powered sleeping car train, the articulated six-car M-10001. This train was turned out also by Pullman in November 1934 and this time had a true diesel engine by Electro-Motive in the power car. At first a 900hp V-12 was installed, but later this was replaced by the V-16 engine mentioned above. Behind the power car was a baggage-mail car, then three Pullman sleepers and finally

a day coach with buffet. There was accommodation for 124 passengers.

On October 22, 1934, UP set its new train to capture the existing transcontinental record. The then existing coast-to-coast record was a run of 71½ hours by the Atchison, Topeka & Santa Fe route—described vividly by Rudyard Kipling in *Captains Courageous*—achieved by a special train put on in 1906 for railroad tycoon E. H. Harriman. In 1934, 508 miles (817km) from Cheyenne, Wyoming to Omaha, Nebraska were run off at an average speed of 84mph (135km/h) but no fireworks were attempted east of Chicago. To avoid breaking New York City's famous no-smoke law, a vintage 1904 New York Central electric loco (described earlier) had to

haul the train the final few miles. In spite of such handicaps and some quite lengthy stops for refuelling and servicing, No. M-10001 lowered the record to a so far unbeaten 57 hours for the 3,260 miles (5,216km) from Oakland Pier opposite San Francisco to Grand Central Terminal, New York.

The impact on the public was tremendous. In the following year the same train went into service as the "City of Portland" running the 2,270 miles (3,652km) between Chicago and Portland, Oregon, cutting 18 hours from the previous best schedule of 58 hours. More importantly, in succeeding years, the demand for travel by these trains was such that at first 11-car and then 17-car streamliners had to be put into service on such trains as the "City of Los Angeles" and "City of San Francisco".

GG1 2-C₀-C₀-2 Pennsylvania Railroad (PRR), 1934

Type: Heavy-duty express passenger electric locomotive.

Gauge: 4ft 8½in (1,435mm).

Propulsion: Medium-frequency alternating current at 15,000V 25Hz fed via overhead catenary and step-down transformer to twelve 410hp (305kW) traction motors, each pair driving a main axle through gearing and quill-type flexible drive.

Weight: 303,000lb (137t) adhesive, 477,000lb (216t) total.

Max. axleload: 50,500lb (22.9t).

Overall length: 79ft 6in (24,230mm).

Tractive effort: 70,700lb (314kN).

Max. speed: 100mph (160km/h).

The Pennsylvania Railroad devised a keystone herald to underline the position it justifiably felt it held in the economy of the USA. The keystone, displayed both front and rear of these superb locomotives, might equally well stand for the position they held in Pennsy's remarkable passenger operations. Since 1928, PRR had been pursuing a long-considered plan to work its principal lines electrically. The statistics were huge; $175 million in scarce depression money were needed to electrify 800 route-miles (1,287km) and 2,800 track-miles (4,505km) on which 830 passenger and 60 freight trains operated daily.

The medium-frequency single-phase ac system with overhead catenary was adopted. The reason lay in the fact that the dc third-rail system used in New York City was not suitable for long-distance operations and, moreover, since 1913 Pennsy had been gaining experience working its Philadelphia suburban services under

Below: *Pennsylvania Railroad Class GG1 electric locomotive in tuscan-red livery. These noble machines could also be seen in black or dark green.*

the wires on 25Hz ac. Only a corporation of colossal stature could have kept such a costly scheme going through the depression years, but by 1934 impending completion of electrification from New York to Washington meant a need for some really powerful express passenger motive power. There were two contenders for the prototype, the first being a 2-Do-2 which was based on the 2-Co-2 "P5a" class already in use. For comparison, a rather plain articulated locomotive of boxcar appearance and 2-Co-Co-2 configuration was borrowed from the neighbouring New York, New Haven & Hartford.

The latter proved superior, but first a further prototype locomotive was built. The main difference was a streamlined casing, which for production members of the class was stylishly improved by the famous industrial designer Raymond Loewy. Between 1935 and 1943, 139 of these "GG1s" were built; only very recently have they been superseded on prime express work.

Some of the "GG1s" were constructed in-house by the railroad's Altoona shops, others by

Baldwin or by General Electric. Electrical equipment was supplied by both GE and Westinghouse. The philosophy behind the design was the same as that of the railroad—solid, dependable and above all, well tried. For example, the arrangement of twin single-phase motors, the form of drive,

Above: *GG1 No.4835 restored to Pennsy black livery, ahead of two further GG1s and a modern E60P unit in Amtrak colours.*

Below: *A GG1 speeds through Glenolden, Pennsylvania, with the Chesapeake & Ohio RR's "George Washington" express.*

and many other systems were essentially the same as had been in use for 20 years on the New Haven. An interesting feature was the continuous cab-signalling system whereby coded track circuits conveyed information regarding the state of the road ahead, which was displayed on a miniature signal inside the "GG1" cabs. It was a remarkable tour-de-force for those days, especially considering that the rails also carried the return traction current.

At this time fortune was smiling on the Pennsy, because low traffic levels during the depression years meant that the physical upheaval of electrification was almost painless, while its completion (there was an extension to Harrisburg, Pennsylvania, in 1939) coincided with the start of the greatest passenger traffic boom ever known, that of World War II. The peak was reached on Christmas Eve 1944 when over 175,000 long-distance passengers used the Pennsylvania Station in New York. It was true that anything that had wheels was used to carry them, but coaches old and new could be marshalled in immense trains which the "GG1s" had no problem at all in moving to schedule over a route which led to most US cities from Florida to Illinois.

In numerical terms, a "GG1" rated at 4,930hp (3,680kW) on a continuous basis, could safely deliver 8,500hp (6,340kW) for a short period. This was ideal for quick recovery from stops and checks. In this respect one "GG1" was the totally reliable equivalent of three or four diesel units 30 or 40 years its junior. It is perhaps telling tales out of school, though, to mention an occasion when brakes failed on a "GG1" and it came through the ticket barrier on to the concourse of Washington Union Station. This was built for people not "GG1s", and the locomotive promptly descended into the basement!

Of the fate of the Pennsylvania Railroad in the post-war years, perhaps the less said the better. It is enough to state that the "GG1" fleet passed piecemeal to the later owners of the railroad, or parts of it—Penn Central, Conrail, Amtrak, and the New Jersey Department of Transportation. At this time it would have been laughable had it not also been tragic how various highly-advertised successors to what were now regarded as relics of a bad past failed to match up to these contemptible museum pieces. But finally, and very recently, the coming of Amtrak's "AEM7" class has put an end to the use of "GG1s" on main-line passenger trains.

Conrail also recently de-electrified the parts of the ex-Pennsylvania lines it inherited on the bankruptcy of Penn Central and so it too had no use for even a handful of "GG1s". Sadly, on October 28, 1982, the last "GG1" was withdrawn from service by the New Jersey DoT which had a few of these noble machines performing on a humble suburban operation.

Fortunately for rail fans, at least two "GG1s" survive in museums at Altoona and Strasburg, but no longer will it be possible to see one of these mighty people-movers effortlessly in action at 90mph (144km/h) plus, treating a 20-coach passenger train like a sack of feathers.

Above: *Superseded at last on main line duties by more modern motive power, a string of Amtrak GG1s await the next call to duty.*

Below: *Beautifully restored to its original black livery, GG1 No.4935 also sports full Pennsy regalia.*

Class A 4-4-2
Chicago, Milwaukee, St. Paul & Pacific Railroad (CMStP&P), 1935

Gauge: 4ft 8½in (1,435mm).
Tractive effort: 30,685lb (13,920kg).
Axle load: 72,500lb (33t).
Cylinders: (2) 19 x 28in (483 x 711mm).
Driving wheels: 84in (2,134mm).
Heating surface: 3,245sq ft (301.5m²).
Superheater: 1,029sq ft (96m²).
Steam pressure: 300psi (21kg/cm²).
Grate area: 69sq ft (6.4m²).
Fuel (oil): 3,300galls (4,000 US) (15m³).
Water: 10,800gall (13,000 US) (49.5m³).
Adhesive weight: 144,500lb (66t).
Total weight: 537,000lb (244t).
Length overall: 88ft 8in (27,026mm).

Class F7 4-6-4
Chicago, Milwaukee, St. Paul & Pacific Railroad (CMStP&P), 1937

Gauge: 4ft 8½in (1,435mm).
Tractive effort: 50,295lb (22,820kg).
Axle load: 72,250lb (33t).
Cylinders: (2) 23.5 x 30in (597 x 762mm).
Driving wheels: 84in (2,134mm).
Heating surface: 4,166sq ft (387m²).
Superheater: 1,695sq ft (157m²).
Steam pressure: 300psi (21kg/cm²).
Grate area: 96.5sq ft (9.0m²).
Fuel: 50,000lb (22½t).
Water: 16,700gall (20,000 US) (76m³).
Adhesive weight: 216,000lb (98t).
Total weight: 791,000lb (359t).
Length overall: 100ft 0in (30,480mm).

"Fleet of foot was Hiawatha" wrote Longfellow ... Intensive competition for the daytime traffic between Chicago and the Twin Cities of St Paul and Minneapolis

Right: *Class F7 No.101 darkens the sky over Milwaukee as it pulls out with Train No.101, the streamlined 13-coach "Afternoon Hiawatha".*

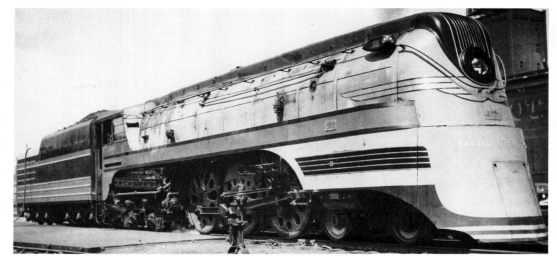

Left: *With only five cars for its 80mph (129km/h) sprint on the "Chippewa", Class A 4-4-2 No.1 near Deerfield, Ill, 1939.*

was the inspiration for the "Hiawatha" locomotives and trains, the fastest-ever to be run by steam. Three railroads were involved in the competition; first, there was the Chicago & North Western Railway; this line had a 408½ mile (657km) route which its "400" expresses traversed in 400 minutes. The "400"'s were formed of conventional equipment of the day, but specially refurbished and maintained. The Chicago Burlington & Quincy Railroad pioneered some stainless steel lightweight diesel-propelled "Zephyr" trains — fairly noisy in spite of their name — over a route 19 miles (30km) longer than the North Western one.

Lastly — and to us most importantly — there was the Chicago, Milwaukee, St Paul and Pacific Railroad, whose management decided to enter the lists with special matching high-speed steam locomotives and trains designed to offer a 6½ hour timing for the 412-mile (663km) route. For the first time in the history of steam locomotion a railway ordered engines intended for daily operation at 100mph (160km/h) and over.

The American Locomotive Company of Schenectady, New York, responded with two superb oil-fired and brightly coloured streamlined 4-4-2s. They were known as class "A" and received running numbers 1 and 2. In service they earned this prime designation by demonstrating that as runners they had few peers. They could develop more than 3000 horsepower in the cylinders and achieve 110mph (177km/h) on the level. It says enough about that success of these locomotives that they were intended to haul six cars on a 6½-hour schedule, but soon found themselves handling nine cars satisfactorily on a 6¼-hour one. These schedules included five intermediate stops and 15 per-

manent speed restrictions below 50mph (80km/h).

The design was unusual rather than unconventional; the tender with one six-wheel and one four-wheel truck, for instance, or the drive on to the leading axle instead of the rear one, were examples. Special efforts were made to ensure that the reciprocating parts were as light as possible — the high boiler pressure was chosen in order to reduce the size of the pistons — and particular care was taken to get the balancing as good as possible with a two-cylinder locomotive. Another class "A" (No.3) was delivered in 1936 and a fourth (No.4) in 1937.

Further high-speed locomotives were ordered in 1938 and this time the six 4-6-4s supplied were both usual *and* conventional. This time also the class designation "F7" and running numbers (100 to 105) were just run-of-the-mill. The 4-4-2s were superb with the streamliners but not at all suited to the haulage of heavy ordinary expresses. This restricted their utilisation; hence the 4-6-4s which combined heavy haulage powers with high-speed capability. The main concession to speed in the design was the big driving wheels, whilst the main concession to general usage

was a change back to coal-burning, in line with most Milwaukee steam locomotives. This in its turn necessitated a high-speed coal hopper and shoots at New Lisbon station, which enabled an "F7" to be coaled during the 2-minute station stop of the "Hiawatha" expresses there. The "F7"'s were also very successful engines, capable of 120 mph (193km/h) and more on level track with these trains.

Test running showed that such speeds could be maintained with a load of 12 cars, a load of 550 tons, and this makes the feat an even more remarkable one. There are also reports of maximum speeds of 125mph (200km/h) and it is a great pity that these cannot be authenticated, since if true would be world records. One did occur in 1940: a speed-up and re-timing produced the historic fastest start-to-stop run *ever* scheduled with steam power — 81¼mph (130km/h) for the 78½ miles (126km) from Sparta to Portage, Wisconsin. This was on the eastbound "Morning Hiawatha", for

Below: *No.3 of the original Class A 4-4-2s built for 100mph (161km/h) running. The striking livery was adopted for the streamline "Hiawatha" trainsets.*

Above: *Class F7 No.100, which with its sisters and the Class A 4-4-2s, monopolised the prestige "Hiawatha" express of the Milwaukee Road.*

by now a second daily run in each direction was operated. Also in 1940 came the "Mid-West Hiawatha" from Chicago to Omaha and Sioux Falls and it was to this train that the 4-4-2s gravitated, although one was usually held in reserve against a 4-6-4 failure on the Twin Cities trains.

Dieselisation came gradually; diesel locomotives made their first appearance on the "Hiawatha" trains in 1941, while steam did not finally disappear from the "Twin Cities Hiawatha" until 1946. The 4-4-2s held on two years longer on the Mid-West train. The last of both types were withdrawn — after a period on lesser workings or set aside — in 1951. It is a matter of considerable regret that none of these record-breaking steam locomotives has been preserved, especially now that the whole Milwaukee Road from Chicago to the Pacific is following them into oblivion.

Even so, models and memories keep these wonderful locomotives alive in the minds of those who admired them in their prime.

HIAWATHA

E Series A1A-A1A

Electro-Motive Division, General Motors Corporation (EMD), 1937

Type: Express passenger diesel-electric locomotive; "A" units with driving cab, "B" units without.

Gauge: 4ft 8½in (1,435mm).

Propulsion : Two EMD 567A 1,000hp (746kW) 12-cylinder pressure-charged two-stroke Vee engines and generators, each supplying current to two nose-suspended traction motors geared to the end axles of a bogie.

Weight: "A" unit 212,310lb (96.3t) adhesive, 315,000lb (142.9t) total. "B" units 205,570lb (93.3t) adhesive, 305,000lb (138.4t) total.

Max. axleload: "A" 53,080lb (24.1t), "B" 51,390lb (23.3t).

Overall length*: "A" 71ft 1¼in (21,670mm), "B" 70ft 0in (21,340mm).

Tractive effort: 53,080lb (236kN).

Max. speed: 85mph (137km/h), 92mph (148km/h), 98mph (157km/h), or 117mph (188km/h) according to gear ratio fitted.

*Dimensions refer to the E7 variant of 1945

In 1930 the General Motors Corporation made two purchases which were to have dramatic effects on the American locomotive scene. The first was the Winton Engine Co, a firm specialising in lightweight diesel engines. The second was Winton's chief customer, the Electro-Motive Corporation, an organisation established in 1922 to design and market petrol-electric railcars, which had sold some 500 units in 10 years. With the engine-building facility and the expertise acquired in

Below: *A 2,000hp E9 cab unit supplied to the Chicago, Rock Island & Pacific Railroad and specially painted in the livery of the line's "Rocket" express trains.*

these purchases, EMD was a major partner in the sensational pioneer streamlined trains introduced in 1934, and in the following year the firm produced its first locomotives. There were four Bo-Bo units with rectangular "boxcar" bodies, each powered by two 900hp (670kW) Winton 12-cylinder Vee engines. Pending the completion of its own plant, EMD had to employ other builders to assemble them.

In 1936 EMD moved into its own purpose-built works at La Grange, Illinois, and work commenced on the next locomotives. These were the first of the "E" series, known also as the "Streamline" series. Like the four earlier locomotives, they had two 900hp Winton engines, but the chassis and body were completely new. The body had its main load-

bearing strength in two bridge-type girders which formed the sides. The bogies had three axles to give greater stability at high speeds, but as only four motors were needed, the centre axle of each bogie was an idler, giving the wheel arrangement A1A-A1A. The units were produced in two versions, "A" units with a driver's cab and "B" units without. The Baltimore & Ohio was the first purchaser, taking six of each type to use as 3,600hp (2,690kW) pairs. Santa Fe bought eight As and three Bs, and the "City" streamliner roads bought two A-B-B sets for the "City of Los Angeles" and the "City of San Francisco". These latter at 5,400hp were the world's most powerful diesel locomotives when they appeared in 1937. The B&O units were classed "EA" and "EB", the

Above: *E8A survivor working out its time in push-pull service on Burlington Northern's Chicago area commuter lines.*

Santa Fe were "E1A" and "E1B", and the City units "E2A" and "E2B".

All these locomotives were an immediate success, not only by their performance but also by their reliability. The reliability was a striking tribute to the quality of the design, for there had been no demonstrator subsequent to the "boxcar" Bo-Bos. In multiple-unit working it was possible for some maintenance to be done on the road on the easier stretches, on which one engine could be shut down. With servicing assisted in this way, remarkable feats of endurance could be achieved. One of the B&O A-B sets gained

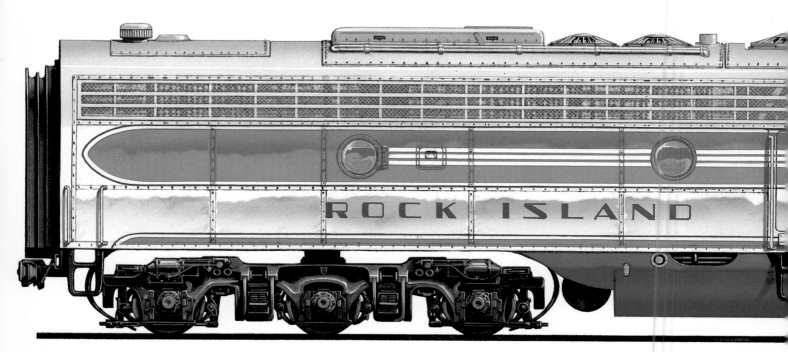

ROCK ISLAND

national publicity when it completed 365 continuous days of service between Washington and Chicago, covering 282,000 miles (454,000km) at an average scheduled speed of 56mph (90km/h).

Progress at La Grange was rapid. At 900hp the Winton engine was reaching its limit, and an EMD engine was therefore developed. Designated 567 (the capacity of a cylinder in cubic inches), it was available in three sizes with 8, 12, and 16 cylinders, giving 600, 1,000 and 1,350hp (448, 746 and 1,007kW). Simultaneously La Grange began to manufacture its own generators, motors and other electrical equipment.

The first all-EMD locomotives were an order from Seaboard Air Line for 14A and five B units, which appeared from October 1938 onwards. They had two 1,000hp engines and were operated as 6,000hp three-unit "lashups" (in the US jargon). These were the "E4s". "E3" and "E5" followed, the former comprising 18 units for the Sante Fe and the latter 16 for the Burlington.

So far each railroad's order had incorporated some individual variations—hence the different designations—but EMD aimed to gain the maximum benefits from production-line assembly of locomotives, to which end individual variations were to be discouraged. The next series, the "E6", which appeared in the same month in 1939 as the first freight demonstrator, was therefore a standard off-the-shelf unit, with the minimum of options. This was the start of real diesel mass production and 118 units had been built by the time the War Production Board terminated building of passenger locomotives in February 1942.

Construction of passenger locomotives was resumed in February 1945 with the first of the "E7" series. These locomotives bene-fited from the experience gained from both the "E" and the "F" series freight units. Improvements included a new and larger cooling system for the engine. Externally there was a noticeable difference in that the front of the body was sloped at 80° to the horizontal, as in the "F" series, instead of 70°, as in previous "E" series bodies. Apart from this change, there were few differences in external appearance throughout the range of "E" series, and most of them concerned windows and portholes.

With locomotive fleets rundown by wartime traffic, the railroads were even more eager to acquire passenger diesels, and Electro-Motive Division (as it had now become) settled down to a steady production of "E7s", averaging 10 per month for four years. During this time 428 A units and 82 B units were built, so that the "E7" outnumbered the passenger diesels of all other US makers put together. In general it was roads

Below: *A passenger train of the Gulf, Mobile & Ohio RR hauled by EMD E-series units.*

which had fast passenger services on easy gradients which bought "E7s"; for mountain work the all-adhesion "F" series was favourite.

Amongst "E7" buyers were the Pennsylvania and the New York Central. With 60 and 50 units respectively they had the largest numbers of any owner. On the NYC the most through comparison ever made between steam and diesel was conducted during October 1946. Two twin "E7" locomotives were tested against six of the new "Niagara" 4-8-4 steam engines working between Harmon, New York, and Chicago, 928 miles (1,493km). The "E7s" averaged 28,954 miles in the month and the 4-8-4s 27,221. Average operating costs per mile were $1.11 for the "E7" and $1.22 for the 4-8-4. However, a succession of coal strikes and then some trouble with the alloy steel boilers of the "Niagaras" ensured that the NYC did not allow its lingering love of steam to interpret the results in favour of the 4-8-4s, but the tests were still encouraging to steam enthusiasts in showing how small was the improvement when the best of

steam locomotives, intensively used and adequately serviced, were replaced by diesels. But on most roads the margin was much wider, and there was a handsome saving from diesels, quite sufficient to offset the greater capital cost.

In 1953 the 1,125hp (840kW) 567B engine was available, and this was incorporated in the next series, the "E8". By this time most of the principal passenger services were dieselised, so the impact of the "E8" was less spectacular than that of the "E7". By the time the final version appeared, the "E9" with 1,200hp (900kW) 567C engines, the need for passenger diesels had almost been met, and only 144 units were sold between 1954 and 1963, compared with 457 "E8s".

In the 1960s the American passenger train declined rapidly in the face of air and coach competition, and many of the later "Es" had short lives, being traded in against the purchase of new general-purpose locomotives.

The "E" series instituted the general conversion of the American passenger train to diesel operation, and they eventually saw many of the most famous trains out. In their heyday the US had an undisputed world lead in passenger train speeds. Geared for up to 117mph (188km/h), (although few roads operated them above 100mph (160km/h), the "Es" were the fastest diesel locomotives in the world, and yet their construction was rugged and straightforward. In particular they had nose-suspended traction motors, which the heavy North American rails with their close-spaced sleepers seemed able to accept without distress.

In 1980 Amtrak operated the last run of "E" locomotives in multiple and the ranks were very thin by this time. Fortunately the body of the first B&O unit is preserved.

THE ROCKET

645

Royal Hudson Class 4-6-4 Canadian Pacific Railway (CPR), 1937

Gauge: 4ft 8½in (1,435mm).
Tractive effort: 45,300lb (20,548kg).
Axle load: 65,000lb (29.5t).
Cylinders: (2) 22 x 30in (559 x 762mm).
Driving wheels: 75in (1,905mm).
Heating surface: 3,791sq ft (352m²).
Superheater: 1,542sq ft (143m²).
Steam pressure: 275psi (19.3kg/cm²).
Grate area: 81sq ft (7.5m²).
Fuel: 47,000lb (21t).
Water: 12,000gall (14,400 US) (54.6m³).
Adhesive weight: 194,000lb (88t).
Total weight: 659,000lb (299t)..
Length overall: 90ft 10in (27,686mm).

To be both Royal and North American is almost a contradiction in terms but, forty years ago, the Canadian Pacific Railway was as much British as it was Canadian. It had been incorporated by an Act of the British Parliament, and its east-most terminal was situated at Southampton, England. It was here in 1939 that King George VI and Queen Elizabeth set sail in the Canadian Pacific liner *Empress of Britain* for a tour of their largest Dominion. Once ashore, their home for much of the visit was a Royal train, at the head of which was a new 4-6-4, No.2850, specially turned out in royal blue and silver with stainless steel boiler cladding. The royal arms were painted on the tender and a replica crown was mounted on the running board skirt just ahead of the cylinders; later this crown was affixed to all 45 of CPR's famous 4-6-4s built between 1937 and 1945.

The genesis of these fine locomotives lay in a wish to improve upon the class "G-3" 4-6-2s which before 1931 had been the top-line power of the system, by increasing their steam-raising capacity a substantial amount. A fire-grate 23 per cent larger was possible if the 4-6-4 wheel arrangement was adopted and the boilers of the new locomotives were based on this. But in other

ways, such as tractive effort or adhesive weight, the new locomotives were little different to the old. Their class designation was H-1 and the running numbers were 2800 to 2819.

The boilers had large superheaters and combustion chambers (the latter an addition to the firebox volume, provided by recessing the firebox tubeplate into the barrel), as well as front-end throttles which worked on the hot side of the superheater. This enabled superheated steam to be fed to the various auxiliaries. There were arch tubes in the firebox and, necessary with a grate of this size, a mechanical stoker.

The first effect of the new locomotives was to reduce the number of engine changes needed to cross Canada, from fourteen to nine. The longest stage was 820 miles (1,320km)

from Fort William, Ontario, to Winnipeg, Manitoba; experimentally a 4-6-4 had run the 1,252 miles (2,015km) between Fort William and Calgary, Alberta, without change.

For five hectic months in 1931 the afternoon CPR train from Toronto to Montreal, called the "Royal York" became the world's fastest scheduled train, by virtue of a timing of 108 minutes for the 124 miles (200km) from Smith's Falls to Montreal West, an average speed of 68.9mph (111km/h). The record was wrested from the Great Western Railway of England, whose "Cheltenham Flyer" then had a timing of 70min for the 77¼ miles (124km), an average speed of 66.3mph. The 4-6-4s were normally assigned to this train. Subsequently the GWR dropped 3 minutes from their timing and took back the record.

An interesting feature, later provided on one of the "H-1"s, was a booster engine working on the trailing truck. One of the problems of a 4-6-4 was that only six out of 14 wheels were driven; this was no detriment while running at speed but starting was sometimes affected by the limited adhesion. The extra 12,000lb (5,443kg) of tractive effort provided by the booster came in very handy; the mechanism cut out automatically at 20mph (32km/h).

The 1930s were the period when streamlining was in fashion but when the time came to order some more 4-6-4s, H.B. Bowen, the CPR Chief of Motive Power, decided to compromise. He came

Below: *Ex-Canadian Pacific Royal Hudson Class No.2860 hauls a tourist train on the shores of Howe Sound, BC.*

to the conclusion that the shrouds which enveloped many contemporary designs made the mechanism inaccessible to an extent which smothered any savings attributable to reduced air resistance. On the other hand, he accepted that the public liked their trains hauled by locomotives which were a little easier on the eye than was then customary.

The result in 1937 was another batch of 30 Hudson type, Nos. 2820 to 2849 designated "H-1c", (the earlier ones had been delivered in two batches of ten, "H-1a" and "H-1b") which had not only softer lines but also sported a superb coloured livery, as our artist has tried to show. Very few mechanical changes needed to be made—although there were certain improvements or changes such as power-operated reversing gear, domeless boilers and a one-piece cast locomotive frame, while boosters were fitted to five of the locomotives. A further ten 4-6-4s, designated "H-1d" were delivered in 1938, while the last batch of five ("H-1e"), Nos. 2860 to 2864 of 1940, differed from the others in being oil burners. All the "H-1e"'s and five of the "H-1d"'s had boosters.

The last batch of 4-6-4s were intended to operate in the far west, between Vancouver and Revelstoke, British Columbia, where oil firing had been the rule for many years. After the war, when the big Canadian oil fields were being exploited, all the "H-1"'s operating over the prairies were also converted. This was made easier by the fact that it was customary to allocate a particular locomotive to a particular depot when they were built and they would then remain there for many years. This unusually stable approach to locomotive allocation also allowed the booster-fitted locomotives to be rostered for sections of line where their extra push was needed. For example, booster fitted "H-1c"'s allocated to Toronto could take the 18-car 1,300-ton "Dominion" express up the Neys Hill incline on Lake

Superior's north shore unassisted with booster in operation; otherwise a helper engine would have been an obvious necessity.

Like other lines which had excellent steam power, well maintained and skilfully operated, the Canadian Pacific Railway was in

Above: *Original Class H-1 No.2816 preserved far from home at Steamtown, Vermont.*

Below: *A head-on shot of 4-6-4 No.2860 as preserved and now running on the British Columbia Railway.*

no hurry to dieselise and, in fact, it was not until 1956 that the first 4-6-4 was scrapped. By mid-1960 all were out of service, but five have survived the scrap-men's torches. Standard Hudson No. 2816 is (at the time of writing) at Steamtown, Bellows Falls, Vermont, USA. Of the "Royal Hudson" types, No.2839 has recently been seen in operation in the USA on the Southern Railway, a line which regularly operates special steam trains for enthusiasts. No.2850 is in the Canadian Railway Museum at Delson, Quebec, No.2858 is on display at the National Museum of Science and Technology at Ottawa and, most famous of all, No.2860 works regular tourist trains on the British Columbia Railway between Vancouver and Squamish. No.2860 has visited Eastern Canada as well as steaming south as far as Los Angeles, hauling a show train intended to publicise the beauties of British Columbia.

Below: *The beautiful red livery of preserved 4-6-4 No.2860 was basically the same as used on these engines in Canadian Pacific Railway days.*

Class 3460 4-6-4 Atchison, Topeka & Santa Fe Railway (AT&SF), 1937

Gauge: 4ft 8½in (1,435mm).
Tractive effort: 43,300lb (19,640kg).
Axleload: 77,510lb (35t).
Cylinders: (2) 23½ x 29½in (597 x 749mm).
Driving wheels: 84in (2,131mm).
Heating surface: 4,770sq ft (443m²).
Superheater: 2,080sq ft (193m²).
Steam pressure: 300psi (21kg/cm²).
Grate area: 98.5sq. ft (9.2m²).
Fuel (oil): 7,000US gall (26.5m³).
Water: 21,000US gall (79.5m³).
Adhesive weight: 211,400lb (96t).
Total weight: 412,400lb (187t).
Length overall: 100ft 3in (30,556mm).

A decisive point in favour of diesel traction compared with steam, so it was said, was that trains could travel that much further without changing engines. It was convenient to forget the exploit of Atchison, Topeka & Santa Fe 4-6-4 No.3461, which in December 1937 brought an eastbound scheduled mail train all the way from Los Angeles to Chicago, a distance of 2,227 miles (3,583km). This still stands as a world record, although it must be said it was not one which any other single railroad in the USA had the length of route available to beat.

No.3461 was one of a small class of six 4-6-4s delivered from Baldwin in 1937. These were developed directly from (and numbered in series with) 50 4-6-2s delivered between 1919 and 1922, followed by 10 otherwise similar 4-6-4s in 1927. This "3400"

Above: *Santa Fe 4-6-4 fitted with a fortunately temporary sky-line casing as an attempt to improve locomotive decor.*

Below: *Atchison Topeka & Santa Fe Railway Class 3460 4-6-4 built by Baldwin in 1937 for long-distance passenger trains.*

S-7 0-10-2 Union Railroad (URR), 1936

Gauge: 4ft 8½in (1,435mm)
Tractive effort: 108,050lb (49,025kg).
Axleload: 71,300lb (32.4t).
Cylinders: (2) 28 x 32in (711 x 812mm).
Driving wheels: 61in (1,549mm).
Heating surface: 4,808sq ft (447m²).
Superheater: 1,389sq ft (129m²).
Steam pressure: 260psi (18.3kg/cm²).
Grate area: 85.2sq ft (7.9m²).
Fuel: 28,000lb (12.7t).
Water: 12,000US gall (45.4m³).
Adhesive weight: 343,900lb (156t).
Total weight: 644,360lb (292.4t).
Length overall: 83ft 5½in (25,436mm).

As must be clear from the treatment meted out to them in this book, the humble switcher was normally one of a forgotten army of has-beens, occupied well behind the scenes in the drudgery of putting cars together to make trains. But for companies like US Steel, whose Union Railroad connected steel plants in the Pittsburgh area, the switcher was king. So, as one might expect, the King of the Switchers was a Union RR loco-motive, holding the world record for every possible attribute for this category of motive power. A requirement for 100,000lb-plus tractive effort meant ten-coupled wheels plus a four-coupled booster. There had to be a wide firebox (with mechanical stoker) to provide an adequate source of power. There was also a limitation on

class was typical of its day and included coal-burning as well as oil-burning examples. They demonstrated very clearly that this great railway had finally thrown aside the thought of anything with a hinge in the middle or more than two cylinders. Not that big power was needed for much of Santa Fe's work; there are hundreds of miles of continuous level or near-level track between Chicago and Los Angeles as well as the more famous sections such as the ascents to the Cajon and Raton passes.

But it was considered that higher speeds could be run, and so in the 1930s the class went into the shops for a rebuild. This included replacing the 74in (1,880mm) spoked driving wheels with 79in discs, and a higher boiler pressure.

This was the period when Santa Fe's first streamline train—the now legendary "Super Chief"—was coming into service, and the idea of running other trains at faster speeds was important. Hence additions to the "3400s" were 4-6-4s rather than 4-6-2s and they had relatively enormous 84in (2,137mm) driving wheels, 19 per cent more tractive effort than the 4-6-2s and considerably bigger grates. Larger tenders were also attached both to the new 4-6-4s as well as to some of the rebuilt 4-6-2s, and this helped by reducing time spent taking on fuel and water.

The first of the new locomotives was streamlined and became the only Santa Fe steam loco to be so treated. This was No.3460, known colloquially as the 'Blue Goose'. The others well matched the standard heavyweight equipment used on such trains as the "Grand Canyon" and the "Santa Fe Chief," and could roll them at steamliner speeds over the long level miles of the midwest.

Right: *This impressive class of locomotive holds a world record as regards steam power for the longest run ever made.*

wheelbase length because it was necessary to use existing turntables.

This all added up to a new wheel arrangement, the 0-10-2, a type which was given the name 'Union'. However, the word has hardly entered the railroad vernacular, since unsurprisingly there have been no other takers. Those industries and few railroads which needed purpose-built switchers usually found the USRA 0-6-0 or 0-8-0 designs adequate for their needs, occasionally with minor adaptations. An occasional 0-10-0 could be found.

Baldwin delivered nine of these 0-10-2 monsters in 1936 and 1937.

Left: *This 0-10-2 or "Union" class of locomotive was built by Baldwin in 1936 for United Steel's Union Railroad.*

The Union Railroad classified them "S7" and they bore the brunt of wartime steel production traffic, but in 1949 dieselisation came in—switching was the first steam citadel to fall. Another home was found for these magnificent examples of steam's diversity, on the Duluth, Missabe & Iron Range RR. This was another of US Steel's lines, and it needed heavy-duty switchers for moving cars of iron ore in the port areas of Procter and Two Harbors. So the 0-10-2s saw out another 11 years in this new location; after retirement

Above: *A "Union" 0-10-2 now on the Duluth Missabe & Iron Range RR switches ore cars at Two Harbors, Minnesota, September 1957.*

in 1960, one was set aside for preservation.

O5A 4-8-4 Chicago, Burlington & Quincy Railroad (CB&Q), 1939

Gauge: 4ft 8½in (1,435mm).
Tractive effort: 67,500lb (30,626kg).
Axleload: 77,387lb (35.1t).
Cylinders: (2) 28 x 30in (711 x 762mm).
Driving wheels: 74in (1,879mm).
Heating surface: 5,225sq ft (485m²).
Superheater: 2,403sq ft (223m²).
Steam pressure: 250psi (17.6kg/cm²).
Grate area: 106.5sq ft (9.9m²).
Fuel: 54,000lb (24.5t).
Water: 18,000 US gall (68.1m³).
Adhesive weight: 281, 410lb (127.7t).
Total weight: 838,050lb (380.2t).
Length overall: 105ft 11in (32,283mm).

The Chicago, Burlington & Quincy Railroad, as its slogan but not its title indicated, served "Everywhere West". In steam days its tracks went far beyond the relatively local implications of its name, serving St Paul, Minneapolis, Kansas City, Omaha, Denver and St Louis. In addition a north-south axis of wholly-owned subsidiary lines con-

nected Billings, Montana, not far from the Canadian border, with Galveston, Texas, on the Gulf of Mexico.

In 1930 Baldwin supplied the Burlington with eight 4-8-4s intended for freight movement and classified "05". Subsequently in 1937 a further 13 of these giants were built. The locomotives

were all coal-burners and not specially remarkable, although they did have Baker valve gear. Their one optional complication was a Worthington feed-water heater, as power reverse and mechanical stoker were essential for locomotives of such size and power. In the following years the Burlington's shops turned out 15

Above: *Chicago, Burlington & Quincy 05A class 4-8-4 No.5632 heads a fan trip from Chicago to Denver after normal steam working had ceased.*

"Super 05s" designated "05A" Although they were dimensionally the same, a number of modern features were applied. There were

Class E4 4-6-4 Chicago and North Western Railway (C&NW), 1938

Gauge: 4ft 8½in (1,435mm).
Tractive effort: 55,000lb (24,798kg).
Axle load: 72,000lb (32.7t).
Cylinders: (2) 25 x 29in (635 x 737mm).
Driving wheels: 84in (2,134mm).
Heating surface: 3,958sq ft (368m²).
Superheater: 1,884sq ft (175m²).
Steam pressure: 300psi (21kg/cm²).
Grate area: 90.7sq ft (8.4m²).
Fuel (oil): 5,000gall (6,000 US) (22.7m³).
Water: 16,500gall (20,000 US) (75.5m³).
Adhesive weight: 216,000lb (98t).
Total weight: 791,500lb (359t).
Length overall: 101ft 9¾in (31,033mm).

These handsome locomotives of advanced design have the unhappy distinction of being the first to be superseded by the diesel-electric locomotive from the job for which they were built. The Chicago & North Western Railway had its own way of doing things; not for nothing did its trains run on the left-hand track, whereas most North American trains take the right. When, in 1935, the gloves came off for the fight between the Milwaukee, Burlington and C&NW companies for the daytime traffic between Chicago and the twin cities of St Paul and Minneapolis, the last-named was first into the ring with the famous "400" trains —named because they ran (about) 400 miles in 400 minutes. The C&NW stole this march over their competitors by running

refurbished standard rolling stock hauled by a modified existing steam locomotive, instead of trains brand new from end to end.

Soon enough, though, the C&NW had to follow their competitors' example. They chose to copy the style of the Milwaukee's "Hiawatha" rather than the Burlington's diesel "Zephyr" and accordingly the American Locomotive Company was asked to supply nine high-speed streamlined 4-6-4s.

The new locomotives, designated "E4" and numbered 4000 to 4008, were delivered in 1938, but in the meantime the C&NW management decided it had backed the wrong horse and went to General Motors Electromotive Division for some of the first production-line diesel loco-

motives. These took over the new streamlined "400" trains, leaving the new 4-6-4s to work the transcontinental trains of the original Overland Route, which the C&NW hauled from Chicago to Omaha.

Because of the arithmetic of design the basic physical statistics of the "E4" were very close to the "Hiawatha" 4-6-4s, yet it is very clear that lesser differences between the two meant two separate designs. So we have two classes of six and nine locomotives respectively, intended for the same purpose, built by the same firm at the same time, which had few jigs or patterns in common. Such was the world of steam railway engineering.

Amongst the advanced features of the "E4" may be mentioned Baker's valve-gear, oil

'Box-pok' disc driving wheels in place of spoked, and Timken roller bearings to all axles as well as to the pins of the valve gear. Later on, some of the locomotives were equipped for oil-burning.

Generally, 4-8-4s are regarded as passenger power, but the "05s" were classified as freight locomotives. One reason for this was that the CB&Q was the pioneer of diesel-electric streamlined trains and had been building up its fleet of such trains—the famous "Zephyrs"—ever since 1934. By 1939 all the principal routes were so operated by trains such as the "Denver Zephyr," "Twin Cities Zephyr" and others, so the need for powerful steam passenger locomotives was minimal. The other reason was that Burlington country was largely free from mountain grades. So a 4-8-4 had adequate adhesion for heavy freight haulage. The big firebox intrinsic to the type was needed for the high power output involved in running heavy long-distance trains at high speeds over straight alignments.

All except the first eight of the 36 "05s" and "05As" were built by the Burlington in their own shops at West Burlington, Iowa.

Though CB&Q was one of the few US railroads to do this, 'do-it-yourself' was common all over the world in the age of steam, when even quite small railways in almost wholly agricultural countries built their own locomtives. The passing of steam has left them completely in the hands of the two biggest of the big corporations.

For a time after complete dieselisation the CB&Q kept an "05A" (No.5632) in running order for special passenger trains. About 1967 this was ended, but four others are preserved as static exhibits. No.5614 is at St Joseph, Missouri, 5620 at Galesburg, Illinois, 5629 at the Colorado Railroad Museum, Golden and 5631 at Sheridan, Wyoming.

Right: *Do-it-yourself was a speciality of the Chicago, Burlington & Quincy Railroad. This 05A 4-8-4 was built at the West Burlington shops in 1938, ceasing work in 1960.*

Below: *A Class 05A of the Burlington Route. These fine locomotives were intended for freight traffic in spite of their 4-8-4 wheel arrangement.*

firing, roller bearings throughout and, particularly interesting, a Barco low water alarm. Boiling dry such a large kettle as a locomotive boiler is a very serious matter indeed and on most steam locomotives there is no automatic guard against the crew forgetting to look at the water-level in the gauge glasses.

Brash styles of painting were not the C&NW's way, and thus it is particularly sad that, when the time came in the early 1950s for the "E4"s to go to the torch, none of them was preserved. So, therefore, only in imagination is it possible to feast our eyes on their green and glided elegance.

Right: *Chicago & North Western Class E4 4-6-4 heads a mail train instead of a streamliner as was originally intended.*

"F" Series B₀-B₀ Electro-Motive Division, General Motors Corporation (EMD), 1939

Type: All-purpose diesel-electric locomotive, "A" units with cab, "B" units without.
Gauge: 4ft 8½in (1,435mm).
Propulsion : One EMD 5,67B 1,500hp (1,120kW) 16-cylinder pressure-charged two-stroke Vee engine and generator supplying current to four nose-suspended traction motors geared to the axles.
Weight: 230,000lb (104.4t) (minimum without train heating steam generator).
Max. axleload: 57,500lb (26.1t).
Overall length*: "A" 50ft 8in (15,443mm), "B" 50ft 0in (15,240mm).
Tractive effort: 57,500lb (256kN).
Max. speed: Between 50mph (80km/h) and 120mph (164km/h) according to which of eight possible gear ratios fitted.

*Dimensions refer to the "F3" variant of 1946

The railway locomotive leads a rugged existence, and only the fittest survive. Evolution has thus tended to move in moderate steps, and few successful developments have been sufficiently dramatic to merit the term "revolutionary". One such step was the pioneer four-unit freight diesel, No. 103, produced by the Electro-Motive Division of General Motors in 1939. When that unit embarked on a 83,764-mile (134,780km) demonstration tour on 20 major American railroads, few people, other than EMD's Chief Engineer Richard M. Dilworth, even imagined that it would be possible for the country's railroads to be paying their last respects to steam only 20 years later.

By 1939 EMD had some six years' experience of powering high-speed passenger trains by diesel locomotives tailored to suit the customer's requirements. Their

Below: *A pair of F3s supplied to the Baltimore & Ohio. The left-hand unit is a "cab" or "A" unit, while the right-hand unit has no driving cab, and is designated "B" or "Booster".*

ability to outrun the best steam locomotives had gained them acceptance in many parts of the country, but this was a specialised activity, and even the most diesel-minded motive power officer did not regard the diesel as an alternative to the ten, twelve or sixteen coupled steam locomotive for the heavy grind of freight haulage.

Dilworth had faith in the diesel, and his company shared his faith to the tune of a four-unit demonstrator weighing 912,000lb (414t) and 193ft (58,830mm) in length. Most of the passenger diesels built so far incorporated the lightweight Winton 201 engine, which EMD had acquired, but in 1938 EMD produced its own 567 series of two-stroke Vee engines (numbered from the cubic capacity of the cylinder in cubic inches). The 16-cylinder version was rated at 1,350hp (1,010kW), and this fitted conveniently into a four-axle Bo-Bo layout, with the whole weight thus available for adhesion.

Two such units were permanently coupled, an "A" unit with cab and a "B" or booster unit without; two of these pairs were coupled back-to-back by normal couplings. Multiple-unit control enabled one engineer to control all four units, but they could easily

be separated into pairs, or, with a little more work, into 1 + 3. Dilworth reckoned that a 2,700hp pair was the equal of a typical steam 2-8-2 or 2-10-2, and that the full 5,400hp (4,030kW) set could equal any of the largest articulated steam engines. As the combined starting tractive effort of his four units was almost double that of the largest steam engine, his claim had some substance. The demonstrators were geared for a maximum of 75mph (120km/h) but could be re-geared for 102mph (164km/h), producing a true mixed-traffic locomotive.

The units were built on the "carbody" principle, that is, the bodyshell was stressed and formed part of the load-bearing structure of the locomotive. The smooth streamlined casing was in sharp contrast to the Christmas-tree appearance of most large American steam engines, festooned as they were with gadgets. But this was one of the revolutionary ideas demonstrated by No. 103. Bright liveries on the passenger streamliners had attracted great publicity; now there was the possibility of giving the freight locomotive a similar image.

Despite the scepticism of steam locomotive engineers, 20 railroads

Above: *Boston's Massachusetts Bay Transportation Agency runs 38 diesel locos for the contract operation of its eight commuter lines. Amongst the fleet in 1979 was this "F" series unit.*

spread over 35 states responded to EMD's invitation to give No. 103 a trial, and everywhere it went it improved on the best steam performance by a handsome margin. From sea level to 10,240ft (3,120m), from 40°F below zero (−40°C) to 115°F (46°C), the story was the same. Typical figures were an average speed of 26mph (42km/h) over 98 miles (158km) of 1-in-250 grade with 5,400t, compared with 10mph (16km/h) by a modern 4-6-6-4, or an increase of load from 3,800t with a 2-8-4 to 5,100t. The booster units were equipped with steam generators for train heating, and this enabled No. 103 to show its paces on passenger trains. The impression it made on motive power men was profound.

Not least amongst the startling qualities of No. 103 was its reliability. Throughout the 11-month tour no failure occurred, and even when allowance is made for the close attention given by accompanying EMD staff, this was a remarkable achievement.

Production locomotives, designated "FT", followed closely on the heels of the demonstrator, and orders were soon received from all parts of the country. EMD's La Grange Works was tooled-up for quantity production, and over a period of six years 1,096 "FT" units were built, Santa Fe being the biggest customer with 320 units. The War Production Board was sufficiently impressed by the contribution which these locomotives could make to the war effort to allow production to continue with only a short break, despite the use of scarce alloys.

By the end of the war the freight diesel was fully accepted on many railroads, and total dieselisation was already in the minds of some motive power chiefs. The first post-war development was production of the 567B engine rated at 1,500hp (1,120kW) to replace the 1,350hp 567A model. After 104 interim units designated "F2", there came a four-unit demonstrator of the "F3" model, with a larger generator to suit the 1,500hp engine, and a number of other improvements based on six years' experience with the "FTs". Amongst these were automatically-operated cooling fans; the fans fitted to the "FTs" were mechanically-driven through clutches, and had manually-worked shutters. The fireman had a frantic rush to de-clutch the fans and close the shutters when the engine was shut down, particularly in severe cold when the radiators would freeze very quickly.

EMD proclaimed the "F3" as "the widest range locomotive in history", and the railroads seemed to agree, for new sales records were set with a total of 1,807 units sold in little more than two years up to 1949. Railroads took advantage of the scope which the smooth curved shape offered for imaginative colour schemes, and an EMD pamphlet showed 40 different liveries in which these locomotives had been supplied.

Simplicity of maintenance, and improvements in the engine to reduce fuel consumption, were two of EMD's claims for the "F3", and these same claims were re-

peated for the next model, the "F7", launched in 1949. The main change from the "F3" was in the traction motors and other electrical equipment. With the same engine power, the new motors enabled 25 per cent more load to be hauled up heavy grades. The model was offered with the usual options, including eight different gear ratios.

The "F7" proved to be a best-seller; 49 US roads bought 3,681 "F7s" and 301 "FP7s", the version with train-heating boiler, whilst Canada and Mexico took 238 and 84 respectively. They handled every type of traffic from the fastest passenger trains to the heaviest freight. Measured by sales, the "F7" was the most successful carbody diesel ever. "F7" production ended in 1953, to be replaced by the "F9". The main change was the 567C engine of 1,750hp (1,305kW). By this time the US market for carbody diesels was drying up, as "hood" units gained popularity, and only 175 "F9s" were built over a

Right: *A single "F" cab unit belonging to the Denver & Rio Grande Western Railroad at the head of a short train on the D&RGW's Moffatt Tunnel route.*

period of three years.

By the 1960s steam had been replaced totally, and diesel manufacturers were now selling diesels to replace diesels. Trading-in of old models became popular, and trucks in particular could be re-used. Many "Fs" were replaced in this way as the more powerful hood units became more popular, and the decline of passenger traffic helped the process. Nevertheless many units of the "F" series were still to be found at work in 1982, and the Canadian locomotives, in particular, could

Above: *"F" series unit in Maryland DoT livery for the Baltimore to Washington commuter operation.*

still be seen on important passenger trains.

The "F" series, more than any other model, showed that improvements in performance and economies in operation could be achieved in all types of traffic by dieselisation, despite the high initial cost compared with steam, and despite uncertainties about the life which could be expected from a diesel locomotive.

Galloping Goose railcar
Rio Grande Southern Railroad (RGS), 1933

Type: Home-made gasoline railcar for local passenger, mail and express traffic.
Gauge: 3ft 0in (914mm).
Propulsion: Pierce Arrow (later General Motors) gasoline engine driving the centre truck via clutch, manual gearbox, propeller shaft, gearing and chains.
Weights: 7,200lb (3.25t) adhesive, 14,770lb (6.7t) total.
Max. axleload: 3,600lb (1,65t).
Overall length: 43ft 3in (13,183mm).

Amongst all the famed narrow-gauge railroads of Colorado, the most spectacular, the bravest and the most impecunious was the Rio Grande Southern. It says enough that its 162-mile (260km) route connected terminals only 102 miles apart as the crow flies and that of 47 steam locomotives owned by the company during its 60 years of day-by-day struggle to survive all were acquired second-hand. Typically only two or three were required at a time so the idea was to buy worn-out machines and squeeze just one more drop of service from them before passing them on to even poorer lines.

In 1893, the year after the RGS

Above: *Early version of a "Galloping Goose" railcar with box car body, preserved at the Colorado Railroad Museum.*

Below: *Rio Grande Southern RR home-made "Galloping Goose" railcar as adapted for running scenic tours in summer 1951.*

5001 Class 2-10-4
Atchison, Topeka & Santa Fe Railway (AT&SF), 1938

Gauge: 4ft 8½in (1,435mm).
Tractive effort: 108,960lb (49,440kg).
Axleload: 81,752lb (37t).
Cylinders: (2) 30 x 34in (762 x 864mm).
Driving wheels: 74in (1,880mm).
Heating surface: 6,075sq ft (564m²).
Superheater: 2,675sq ft (249m²).
Steam pressure: 310psi (22kg/cm²).
Grate area: 121sq ft (11.25m²).
Fuel (oil): 7,100US gall (27m³).
Water*: 24,500US gall (93m³).
Adhesive weight: 371,600lb (169t).
Total weight*: 1,002,700lb (455t).
Length overall*: 123ft 5in (37,617mm).
*with 16-wheel tender.

The 2-10-4 type got the name 'Texas' from a group of locomotives built by Lima for the Texas &

Pacific Railroad in 1925. Yet the Atchison, Topeka & Santa Fe Railway had one earlier than that. In 1921 a Santa Fe type (2-10-2) had its rear truck replaced by a two-axle one. The railway got its second 2-10-4 (and its first designed as such) nine years later when new power was needed to hurtle vast freights across Kansas, Oklahoma, Texas and New Mexico along the southern and more easily graded of the two routes that ran southwest from Kansas City and joined at Belen, New Mexico, on the way to Los Angeles.

We have seen how Santa Fe's locomotive department promised itself, after traumatic experiences, never again to order locomotives with more than two cylinders. Within this limitation their own 2-10-2 type was the favourite, but fast running on moderate gradients needs a high power output in relation to tractive effort. This means

a high heat input, hence a large grate and a two-axle rear truck to carry its weight, making a 2-10-2 into a 2-10-4.

Above: *Santa Fe 2-10-4 No.5022, leased by the Pennsylvania Railroad for its last assignment at Columbus, Ohio, June 1956.*

opened, repeal of the Sherman Silver Purchasing Act of 1892 and the consequent collapse of the silver mining industry put the company in the Bankruptcy Court for three years. After a few years things got better, but in 1929 the line again found itself bankrupt as well as in very poor physical shape. A resourceful man called Victor A. Miller was appointed as receiver and amongst many measures adopted to reduce expenses was construction of these remarkable railbuses made from old motor cars. In his own words:

"A seven-passenger automobile sedan of Pierce Arrow manufacture, model 33, of the year 1926, is spread in the body to the ordinary width of a narrow-gauge car to give a carrying capacity of ten passengers, with the chassis remodelled to fit two four-wheel trucks of 36in gauge. A light metal trailer of box-car character and a capacity in excess of ten tons, running on a third narrow-gauge truck, is permanently affixed to the rear of the automobile."

As regards the name, it must be said that while geese in flight are the most graceful of God's creatures, ground movement is not something they do well. No.1 railbus appeared in June 1931 and was made from an old Buick. It was rather small and No.2 which came out three months later was similar but larger. No.3, also made this way, was a considerable advance on the earlier experiments. It seated 12 people and was the final solution, being sufficiently economical to pay back its cost in a few months. No.4, virtually a copy of No.3, followed in 1932 and No.5 in 1933. No.6 was used by the roadmaster to move materials and labour, while No.7 was a refrigerated unit provided to haul supplies to Civilian Conservation Corps camps.

Air brakes soon replaced mechanical ones and, aside from their helplessness in coping with frost and snow, the "Galloping Geese" did all that was asked of them and more in hauling mail, passengers and parcels in the mountains. After the war, (during which the RGS was busy with such traffic as the uranium ore used to produce the first atom bombs), surviving Geese Nos. 3, 4, and 5 were rebuilt with new General Motors engines and bigger bus bodies, but still accommodating 12 people. In 1950, after loss of the mail contract, the trailers of the remaining buses (which also included No.7) were rebuilt to seat parties of 20 tourists. Although nearly 2,500 sightseeing passengers had been carried in 1951, the first (and last) year that RGS catered seriously for tourists, it was to no avail and the railroad was abandoned at the end of the year. Through the efforts of their numerous admirers, four of these legendary creatures have been preserved and can be seen at Knott's Berry Farm, Los Angeles; Dolores and Telluride, Colorado, and at the Colorado Railroad Museum, Golden.

Because of the Depression the unremarkable prototype 2-10-4 No.5000 delivered in 1930 — built by Baldwin like almost all Santa Fe locomotives — remained a singleton for eight years, although it delivered the goods in a literal sense. In the meantime, however, the specification had grown to give for the first and only time in the history of steam a big-wheeled high-speed locomotive with as many as ten coupled wheels. Another way of getting speed was to cut out the need for fuel and water stops and the huge 16-wheel tender which resulted from this thinking brought the fully-loaded weight to over a million pounds, another record for a two-cylinder steam locomotive. More than 100,000lb of nominal tractive effort is also confined to a handful of examples.

These racing mammoths did all that was expected of them and more, being capable of developing

over 6,000hp (4,475kW) in the cylinders. This applied particularly to the second wartime batch (Nos. 5011 to 5035) which had roller bearings as well as larger tenders from the start.

Dieselisation came early to the Santa Fe, the first freight units arriving in 1940. Whilst the 2-10-4s showed up well against them, the older steam locomotives — then in the majority even on Santa Fe — did not. Moreover, in the west there were major problems in finding enough good water for steam locomotives; diesels eliminated much unproductive hauling in of water supplies. So, by the early 1950s, modern 4-8-4s and 2-10-4s were the only steam locomotives operating, and even these had ceased by August 1957.

Above: *Prototype 2-10-4 No.5000, known as "Madam Queen", preserved at Amarillo,*

Happily, four of these giants have been preserved in widely separated locations — No.5011 at St Louis, Missouri; 5017 at Green Bay, Wisconsin; 5021 at Belen, New Mexico; and 5030 especially appropriately at Santa Fe itself.

FEF-2 Class 4-8-4 Union Pacific Railroad (UP), 1939

Gauge: 4ft 8½in (1,435mm).
Tractive effort: 63,800lb (28,950kg).
Axle load: 67,000lb (30.5t).
Cylinders: (2) 25 x 32in (635 x 813mm).
Driving wheels: 80in (2,032mm).
Heating surface: 4,225sq ft (393m²).
Superheater: 1,400sq ft (130m²).
Steam pressure: 300psi (21kg/cm²).
Grate area: 100sq ft (9.3m²).
Fuel: 50,000lb (23t).
Water: 19,600gall (23,500 US) (90m³).
Adhesive weight: 266,500lb (121t).
Total weight: 908,000lb (412t).
Length overall: 113ft 10in (34,696mm).

The origin of the class occurred during the late 1930s, when rising train loads began to over-tax the 4-8-2s which were then the mainstay of UP passenger operations. One day in 1937 a "7000" class 4-8-2 had the temerity to demonstrate the lack of steaming power inherent in the type, on a train with UP President William Jeffers' business car on the rear. Even while the party was waiting out on the prairies for rescue, a dialogue by telegram went on with Alco in far-off Schenectady, with a view to getting something better.

The result in due course was this superb class of 45 loco-motives of which 20, numbered 800 to 819, were delivered in 1938. A further 15 (Nos.820 to 834) with larger wheels and cylinders as well as 14-wheel centipede tenders—instead of 12-wheel ones—came the following year and it is to these that the dimensions etc given above apply. This second batch was designated "FEF-2", the earlier ones becoming class "FEF-1". FEF stood for Four-Eight-Four!

A final batch of ten almost identical to the second one ex-cept for the use of some substitute materials, appeared in 1944. These were known as "FEF-3"s and were the last steam power supplied to UP. All the "800"s came from Alco.

The "800"s as a whole followed —like Northumbrian 108 years earlier—the standard recipe for success in having two outside cylinders only, the simplest poss-ible arrangement. That king of passenger locomotive wheel ar-rangements, the "Northern" or 4-8-4, was adopted and mis-givings originally felt regarding the suitability of eight-coupled wheels for very high speeds were found not to be justified. The negotiation of curves was made easier by the fitting of Alco's lateral motion device to the lead-ing coupled wheels.

The basic simplicity of so many US locomotives was often spoilt by their designers being an easy touch for manufacturers of com-plicated accessories. The UP managed to resist most of them with the pleasing result that the locomotives had a delightfully elegant uncluttered appearance, unmarred by any streamline shroud. On the other hand, they rightly fell for such excellent simplifications as the cast-steel locomotive frame, which replaced many separate parts by one single casting. Another example was the use of a static exhaust steam injector instead of a steam-driven mechanical water-pump and feed water heater. A compli-cation resisted by the UP was the provision of thermic syphons in the firebox; they held the view that on balance these quite com-mon devices were more trouble than benefit. Even so, both com-mon sense as well as Uncle Sam's rules meant power rever-sing gear and automatic stoking, whilst electric lighting was some-thing that certainly paid off in helping "800" crews to see what they were doing.

Perhaps the most original fea-ture and one which contributed a good deal to the success of the "800"s was the main motion. Aesthetically, the main rods were pure poetry but there was a

Above: *The last steam locomotive built for the Union Pacific Railroad, class "FEF-3" 4-8-4 No.844 (renumbered to 8444 to avoid confusion with a diesel unit).*

Below: *No.8444 smokes it up on a railfan special "Extra 8444". Note enthusiasts at the windows of the train.*

Above: *Preserved Union Pacific 4-8-4 No.8444 on parade. In addition to outings for the railfans, the loco is used to promote publicity.*

great deal more to it than that. Because of the speeds and forces involved, current technology was taken beyond the then accepted limits; at the same time, the magnitude of the stresses to which those whirling rods were subject are very different to evaluate with any degree of confidence.

What a triumph for the designers, then, that these lovely tapered coupling and connecting rods were a resounding success even though frequently moved at revolutions corresponding to running speeds above the 100mph (160km/h) mark. The main principle of the new design was that the pulls and thrusts were trans-

mitted from the connecting rods —and hence to three out of the four pairs of wheels—by separate sleeve bearings instead of via the main crankpins in accordance with convention. The result was that separate knuckle-joints in the coupling rods were replaced by making the centre pair of rods forked at both ends and combining the roles of crank-pins and knuckle-pins.

The results were superb and there are many reports of speeds being run up to the design limit of 110mph (176km/h). After the war there was a period when coal supplies were affected by strikes and, in order to safeguard UP passenger operations, the "800"'s were converted from coal to oil burning; a 6,000gall (27m³) tank was fitted in the bunker space. Otherwise only minor modifications were needed over

many years of arduous service, a fact which is also much to the credit of the designers.

Normally the 4-8-4s were entrusted with the many expresses formed of the then conventional heavyweight stock, but the new engines' arrival on UP coincided with the introduction of diesel-electric streamline trains on much faster timings. In those early days the new form of motive power was not too reliable and "800" class locomotives frequently found themselves replacing a multi-unit diesel at the head end of one of UP's crack trains. They found no problem in making up time on the tight diesel schedules sufficient to offset extra minutes spent taking on water.

The last service passenger train hauled by an "800" was caused by such a failure; it occurred when in autumn 1958,

the last one built took the "City of Los Angeles" over the last stretch of 145 miles (232km) from Grand Island into Omaha. No.844 gained time on the streamliner's schedule in spite of the crew's lack of recent experience with steam. A year later there came a time when all were out of service awaiting scrapping; it was a sad moment for all who admired these superb locomotives.

Since then No.844 (renumbered 8444 to avoid confusion with a diesel unit) has been put back into service by a publicity-conscious Union Pacific and frequently performs for her fans. No.814 is displayed across the Mississippi river from Omaha, at Dodge Park, Council Bluffs, and Nos.833 and 838 are also believed still to be in existence, the latter as a source of spares for No.8444.

Class I-5 4-6-4 New York, New Haven & Hartford (New Haven), 1937

Gauge: 4ft 8½in (1,435mm).
Tractive effort: 44,000lb (19,960kg).
Axle load: 65,000lb (29.5t).
Cylinders: (2) 22 x 30in (559 x 762mm).
Driving wheels: 80in (2,032mm).
Heating surface: 3,815sq ft (354m²).
Superheater: 1,042sq ft (97m²).
Steam pressure: 285psi (20kg/cm²).
Grate area: 77sq ft (7.2m²).
Fuel: 32,000lb (14.5t).
Water: 18,000 US gall (68m³).
Adhesive weight: 193,000lb (87.4t).
Total weight: 698,000lb (317t).
Length overall: 97ft 0¾in (29,585mm).

M 3 Yellowstone 2-8-8-4 Duluth, Missabe & Iron Range Railroad (DM&IR), 1941

Gauge: 4ft 8½in (1,435mm).
Tractive effort: 140,000lb (63,521kg).
Axleload: 74,342lb (33.7t).
Cylinders: (4) 26 x 32in (660 x 812mm).
Driving wheels: 63in (1,600mm).
Heating surface: 6,758sq ft (628m²).
Superheater: 2,770sq ft (257m²).
Steam pressure: 240psi (16.9kg/cm²).
Grate area: 125sq ft 11.6m²).
Fuel: 52,000lb (23.6t).
Water: 25,000 US gall (94.6m²).
Adhesive weight: 565,000lb (256.4t).
Total weight: 1,138,000lb (516.3t).
Length overall: 126ft 8in (38,608mm).

These fine locomotives are the ones which pulled the heaviest steam-hauled trains ever regularly operated in the world. They belonged not to one of the giant railroads of America but to a smallish concern in remote Minnesota known as the Duluth, Missabe & Iron Range. As the name implies its reason for existence was the transportation of iron ore some 70 miles (112km) to the Lake Superior port of Duluth.

Bulk movement is the task railroads are best suited to, and

These handsome engines were the first streamlined 4-6-4s in the USA to be delivered. They were also very much an example to be followed in that firstly, the desire to streamline was not allowed to interfere with access to the machinery for maintenance and secondly, they followed in all essential respects the simple Stephenson concept.

The New York, New Haven & Hartford Railroad (called the New Haven for short) had its

Left: *The New Haven to Boston section of NH's New York-Boston main line was the stamping ground of the 10 Class 1-5 4-6-4s delivered by Baldwin in 1937.*

main line from New York to Boston. This had been electrified in stages, beginning as early as 1905 and reaching its greatest extent at New Haven, 72 miles (115km) from New York in 1914.

There remained 159 miles (256km) of steam railroad from there to the "home of the bean and the cod". Trains such as "The Colonial" or the all-Pullman parlor car express "The Merchants Limited" heavily overtaxed the capacity of the existing class "I-4" Pacifics and, in 1936, after a good deal of research and experiment, ten 4-6-4s were ordered from Baldwin of Philadelphia. Running numbers were 1400 to 1409.

This "I-5" class with disc driving wheels, roller bearings and Walschaert's valve gear went into service in 1937. They certainly met the promise of their designers in that they showed a 65 per cent saving in the cost of maintenance compared with the 4-6-2s they replaced and, moreover, could handle 16-car 1100-ton trains to the same schedules as the Pacific could barely manage with 12.

Another requirement was met in that they proved able to clear the 1 in 140 (0.7 per cent) climb out of Boston to Sharon Heights with a 12-car 840-ton train at 60mph (97km/h). But, alas, the "I-5"s were never able to develop their no doubt formidable high speed capability because of a

rigidly enforced 70mph (113 km/h) speed limit. For this reason and because the line was infested with speed restrictions, the schedule of the "Merchants Limited" never fell below 171 minutes including two stops, representing an average of 55mph (89km/h). Forty years "progress" and a change from steam to diesel traction since the days of the "I-5"s has only succeeded in reducing this time to 170mins today.

None of the I-5s is preserved. Incidentally, nor is any other New Haven steam locomotive, except for an old 1863 American Standard 4-4-0, displayed in the State Fair Grounds at Danbury, Connecticut.

accordingly the little line prospered well enough to afford good equipment, which in its turn led to even better prosperity. A final stage of steam re-equipment was completed with eight of these superb million-pound-plus locomotives obtained from Baldwins in 1941. A further 10 came in 1943. The 1941 locomotives were designated Class "M3", the 1943 batch as Class "M4", but there were no significant differences between the two except for the use of some substitute material in wartime.

The 2-8-8-4 or Yellowstone wheel arrangement appeared first on the Northern Pacific Railway in 1928, hence a name appropriate to Northern Pacific territory. Use of low-quality coal mined on-line on NP led to these machines having grates as large as 180sq ft (17m²) in area, 20 per cent more than on the Union Pacific Big Boys, but for the DM & IR 10 per cent less would suffice with good Pennsylvania coal in their tenders. Even so, the "M3s" had a tractive effort significantly greater than UP's giants could exert, a world record for any non-compound class of steam locomotive and reflecting the requirements of hauling loads three times

Left: *A Duluth, Missabe & Iron Range 2-8-8-4 awaiting orders at Proctor, Minnesota.*

as great as the "Big Boys" did albeit on an easily-graded railroad.

In steam days, the Missabe moved up to 50 million tons each year, a period reduced by the length of time Lake Superior is frozen over. This implied a need to move over 200,000 tons each day to meet this target. A 2-8-8-4 could haul 190 ore cars with a gross weight of some 18,000 tons, carrying 13,000 tons of ore. Handling trains of this size was made easier by the fact that the railroad on the whole descended from the mines to the lakeside, although local grades of up to 0.3 per cent (1-in-330) faced loaded trains.

No reliance was placed on the locomotive to stop loads of this kind, but the ore cars had special differential systems whereby an

extra and larger brake cylinder was automatically brought into operation when the car was loaded with over twice its empty weight of ore. So the 2-8-8-4s would set out with their crews secure in the knowledge that brake force was available proportionate to the immense load behind, on down-grades as steep as 1.4 per cent (1-in-70).

In spite of excellent track with heavy rail and deep ballast, a major factor in the économical operation of the railroad was strictly enforced modest speed limits of 30mph (48km/h) for loaded cars and 35mph (56km/h) for empties. 'Safety First' was rightly incorporated in the herald displayed on DM & IR tenders. Incidentally, the DM & IR is one of the few railroads in the United

Above: *DM&IR 2-8-8-4 No.204 heads a farewell passenger train before retirement.*

States to run left-handed on double-track sections.

Articulation of the "M3s" and "M4s" was based on the Mallet layout as developed by US builders, although a true Mallet, of course, has compound cylinders. Comprehensive equipment included feed-water heaters, recording speedometers, radio and an ample-sized enclosed vestibule cab. Two have been preserved, at Proctor and Two Harbors respectively.

Below: *DM&IR 2-8-8-4 No.229, a fine example of the huge M3s, which were among the greatest steam heavy haulers.*

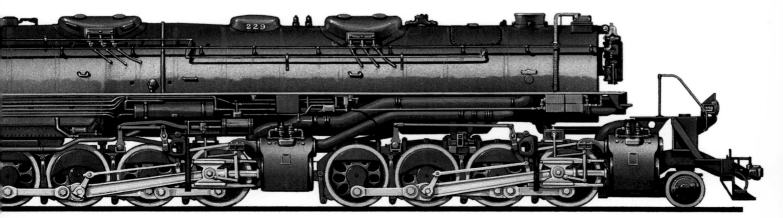

Class J 4-8-4 Norfolk & Western Railway (N&W), 1941

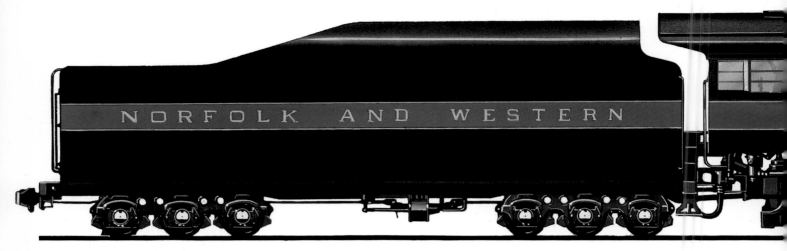

Gauge: 4ft 8½in (1,435mm).
Tractive effort: 80,000lb (36,287kg).
Axle load: 72,000lb (33t).
Cylinders: (2) 27 x 32in (686 x 813mm).
Driving wheels: 70in (1,778mm).
Heating surface: 5,271sq ft (490m²).
Superheater: 2,177sq ft (202m²).
Steam pressure: 300psi (21kg/cm²).
Grate area: 107.5sq ft (10m²).
Fuel: 70,000lb (31.75t).
Water: 16,700gall (20,000 US) (76m³).
Adhesive weight: 288,000lb (131t).
Total weight: 873,000lb (396t).
Length overall: 100ft 11in (30,759mm).

"Of all the words of tongue and pen, the saddest are 'it might have been'." In the USA, there was just one small (but prosperous) railroad that, on a long-term basis, came near to fighting off the diesel invasion. This was the Norfolk & Western Railway, with headquarters in Roanoke, Virginia, and a main line then stretching 646 miles (1,033km) from ocean piers at Norfolk, Virginia, to Columbus in Ohio. It had branches to collect coal from every mine of importance across one of the world's greatest coalfields. In the end steam lost the battle on the N&W and big-time steam railroading finally vanished from the United States—so dealing a fatal blow all over the world to the morale of those who maintained that dieselisation was wrong. But the Norfolk & Western's superb steam locomotives came close to victory; so let us see how it was done.

The principle adopted was to exploit fully all the virtues of steam while, rather obviously, seeking palliatives for its disadvantages. It was also a principle of N&W management that the maximum economy lay in maintaining the steam fleet in first-class condition, with the aid of premises, tools and equipment to match. All this is well illustrated by the story of the "J" class, Norfolk & Western's own design (and own

build) of express passenger super-locomotive.

Around 1940 the company's locomotive chiefs felt that it should be possible to have something better than the standard United States Railroad Association's design of 4-8-2 upon which N&W passenger expresses then relied. Very wisely, they accepted that Robert Stephenson had got the thermal and most of the mechanical principles right with the *Northumbrian*, but what needed attention was the cost and time involved in servicing and maintenance. This meant, for example, roller bearings to the axleboxes and throughout the motion, while an unparalleled number of subsidiary bearings, over 200 in fact, were automatically fed with oil by

a mechanical lubricator with a 24-gallon (110-litre) tank, enough for 1,500 miles (2,400km). Even the bearings of the bell were automatically lubricated!

There was another large lubricator to feed high-temperature oil for the steam cylinders; this is normal but the feeds from this lubricator also ran to the steam cylinders of the water and air pumps and the stoker engine. Hence the labour involved in filling separate lubricators at each of these was avoided. The basic simplicity of the two-cylinder arrangement with Baker's valve gear also had the effect of minimising maintenance costs.

Huge tenders enabled calls at fuelling points to be reduced to a minimum. Together with the usual

modern US features such as a cast-steel locomotive frame, all these things added up to a locomotive which could run 15,000 miles (24,000km) per month, needed to visit the repair shops only every 1½ years and had a hard-to-believe record of reliability.

During the period when steam and diesel were battling for supremacy on United States railroads, it was typically the case that brand new diesel locomotives were being maintained in brand new depots while the steam

Below: *A Class J 4-8-4 of the Norfolk & Western Railway climbs into the hills of Virginia with an express passenger train.*

Above: *First of the Class J streamliners turned out of Norfolk & Western's Roanoke shops in 1941.*

engines with which they were being compared were worn out and looked after in tumble-down sheds. Often much of the roof would be missing while equipment was also worn out and obsolete. The filth would be indescribable.

On the Norfolk & Western Railroad during the 1950s, locomotives were new and depots almost clinically clean, modern, well-equipped and well arranged. A "J" class could be fully serviced, greased, lubricated, cleared of ash, tender filled with thousands of gallons of water and many tons of coal, all in under an hour. The result was efficiency, leading to Norfolk & Western's shareholders receiving 6 per cent on their money, while those of the neighbouring and fully-dieselised and electrified Pennsylvania Railroad had to be content with ½ per cent.

In the end, though, the problems of being the sole United States railroad continuing with steam on any scale began to tell. Even a do-it-yourself concern like N&W normally bought many components from specialists and one by one these firms were going out of business. In 1960 this and other factors necessitated the replacement of steam and the "J"s plus all the other wonderful locomotives of this excellent concern were retired.

One feels that the "J"s were the best of all the 4-8-4s, but that is a matter of opinion; in matters of fact, though, they had certainly the highest tractive effort and, as well, the class included the last main-line steam passenger locomotives to be constructed in the United States. They were built as follows, all at N&W's Roanoke shops: Nos. 600 to 603, 1941; 604, 1942; 605 to 610, 1943; 611 to 613, 1950.

No.604 had a booster engine on the trailing truck.

Nos.605 to 610 were originally unstreamlined and ran for two years as chunky but attractive

locomotives in plain garb.

In spite of having driving wheels which were on the small side for a passenger locomotive, speeds up to 90mph (144km/h) were recorded in service and 110mph (176km/h) on test. The latter was achieved with a 1,000 ton trailing load of 15 cars and represented the development of a remarkable 6,000hp in the cylinders.

With such power and speed capability available, the fact that overall speeds were not high reflected the hilly nature of the country served. For example, the coach streamliner "Powhattan

Arrow" needed 15hr 45min for the 676 miles (1,082km) from Norfolk, Virginia to Cincinatti, Ohio, an average speed of 43mph (69km/h). Whilst this train was not a heavy one, the overnight "Pocahontas" which carried through cars from Norfolk to Chicago via Cincinatti and Pennsylvania Railroad, could load up to 1,000 tons which had to be handled on ruling grades up to 1 in 62 (1.6 per cent).

Norfolk & Western also acted as a "bridge road" and their 4-8-4s hauled limiteds such as the "Tennessean" and the

Above: *The 1943 batch of six Class Js were at first not fitted with streamline casing, but all were subsequently altered to match the superb line of the first five built.*

"Pelican"—the original Chattanooga Choo-choos—between Lynchburg and Bristol, on the famous journeys from New York to Chattanooga and points beyond. No.611 was preserved at the Transportation Museum in Roanoke, Virginia but it was being restored to working order in 1982-84.

Class GS-4 4-8-4 Southern Pacific Railroad (SP), 1941

Gauge: 4ft 8½in (1,435mm).
Tractive effort: 71,173lb (32,285kg).
Axle load: 68,925lb (31.25t).
Cylinders: (2) 25½ x 32in (648 x 813mm).
Driving wheels: 80in (2,032mm).
Heating surface: 4,887sq ft (454m²).
Superheater: 2,086sq ft (194m²).
Steam pressure: 300psi (21.1kg/cm²).
Grate area: 90.4sq ft (8.4m²).
Fuel (oil): 4,900galls (5,900 US) (22.3m³).
Water: 19,600gall (23,500 US) (89mm³).
Adhesive weight: 276,000lb (125.5t).
Total weight: 883,000lb (400.5t).

The "Daylight" express of the Southern Pacific Railroad was the third of three famous train services worked by matching streamlined express locomotives and coaches over a similar distance. The "Hiawatha" trains of the Milwaukee line between Chicago and the Twin Cities and the "Coronation" of the British London & North Eastern Railway between London and Edinburgh have been noticed elsewhere. Each of the three trains introduced new standards of speed, comfort and decor, and each train was spectacularly successful in attracting new traffic.

The 470-mile route between Los Angeles and San Francisco was much the hardest as well as the longest of the three. For example, there was nothing on either of the other lines to compare with the 1 in 45 (2.2 per cent) gradient of Santa Margharita Hill, north of San Luis Obispo. The "light-weight" 12-car "Daylight" express weighed 568 tonnes, nearly double the weight of the British train—though it must be said that as regards weight hauled per passenger carried, the latter came out at 15 per cent less than the former.

Because of the severe curvature of the line as well as the heavy gradients the 48.5mph (78km/h) average speed of the "Daylight" train was considerably less than that of the other two, although

the lessening of running times represented by all three of the new trains were roughly even. The gradients encountered by the "Daylight" nicely balanced out with the "Hiawatha" faster running, but certainly the "Daylight" was a far tougher haulage proposition than the British train. The motive power provided reflected this.

Eight-coupled wheels were needed and enabled the resulting "Daylight" 4-8-4 to have (with booster) 124 per cent more tractive effort than the LNER "A4" 4-6-2. As regards grate area, that is, the size of the fire, the increase was 119 per cent. The SP already had fourteen 4-8-4s (class "GS-1"), which came from Baldwin of Philadelphia in 1930. As with the LNER's but unlike the Milwaukee's, the SP's new locomotives (class "GS-2") were from a mechanical point of view based very closely on their immediate predecessors. Of course, the decor was something else again and it gave these four black, silver and gold monsters from the Lima Locomotive Works of Lima, Ohio, an appearance which could hardly be described as less than superb.

Like so many large North American locomotives of the time, the success of the "Daylight" type was due to the application of the excellent standard of US practice of the day. Amongst a

few special features worth recording was one that has almost no steam traction parallel elsewhere, that is the provision of electro-pneumatic brake equipment. With other forms of traction, the electro-pneumatic brake is commonplace today, especially for multiple-units. Application of the brakes on a normal air-brake system relies on a pressure change travelling down the brake pipe from the locomotive to switch on the brakes under each successive car. This involves a flow of air towards the driver's brake-valve and in consequence a delay of several seconds occurs before the brakes are applied to the wheels of the rear car. In contrast, with EP braking the signal to apply the brakes goes down the train with the speed of electric current. The thinking was that these few seconds—during which the train would travel several hundred feet—might in the case of a high-speed service be the difference between an incident and a disaster.

The curvature of the route was recognised by the provision of spring-controlled side-play on the leading coupled axle. In this way the wheels could "move-over" on a curve and allow the flange force to be shared between the two leading axles, with benefits to the wear of both rails and tyres. The hilliness of the line gave rise to a series of water

Above: *Last of the GS classes were the unstreamlined GS-6s, of which no.4466 hauls the "Klamath Express" at Dunsmuir, California, in June 1952.*

sprays to cool the tyres on engine and tender wheels during braking on the long descents. Air sanding gear was provided, fed from a tank under that boiler-top casing, which held a full *ton* of sand! With booster cut in, the "GS"'s could manage the standard "Daylight" consist on the 1 in 45 grades (2.2 per cent); but if any extra cars were attached a helper was needed.

Although the "Daylight" type held to the simple and world-standard concept of a two-cylinder locomotive with outside valve gear, the host of equipment provided did add a certain complexity. There were three turbo-generators, for example, and a feed-water heater and pump as well as injectors. It must be said that virtually all of this complication was made up of items of proprietary equipment each of which, as it were, came in a box and could be bolted on. Such fittings were apt to work well because

Below: *One of the original batch (class "GS-2") of Southern Pacific's "Daylight" 4-8-4s as delivered from the Lima Locomotive Works, Ohio, in 1937.*

Below right: *An improvement to Class GS-4 was fitting of fully-enclosed cabs. No.4449 of this batch has been preserved in the full Southern Pacific "Daylight" livery.*

competition kept the suppliers on their toes; and if problems arose a replacement could be fitted quickly. Even so, an electro-magnetic gadget—inside the boiler!—which sensed foaming and opened the blow-down cocks automatically, did not last.

Like most SP steam locomotives, the "Daylight"'s were fired with oil—indeed, SP were the United States' pioneers in this area—economy being achieved with a device called a "locomotive valve pilot" which indicated to the engineer what cut-off he should set to suit any particular speed and conditions of working.

Streamlined trains, worked by further batches of these magnificently-equipped locomotives, spread to all parts of SP's system and thus served such far distant places as Portland in Oregon, Ogden in Utah and New Orleans. Details of the 60 locos were as shown in the table.

The War Production Board refused to sanction the "GS-6" batch, but on being told that "GS" now stood for "General Service" rather than "Golden State", they accepted the proposal. Of an order for 16, six went to Western Pacific Railroad.

The first "GS" to be withdrawn was No.4462 in 1954 and in October 1958 No.4460 (now displayed at the Museum of Transportation at St Louis, Missouri) brought SP steam operations to a close with a special excursion from Oakland to Reno, Nevada. No.4449 also survived to haul the "Freedom Train" several thousands of miles across the USA in connection with the bi-centennial of independence in 1976. The locomotive is still able to run and has recently been restored to the original superb "Daylight" colours.

Designation	Date	Running Nos	Features
GS-2	1937	4410 to 4415	Driving wheels 73½in (1,867mm) dia instead of 80in (2,032mm)
GS-3	1937	4416 to 4429	
GS-4	1941-2	4430 to 4457	Fully enclosed cabs began with this batch
GS-5	1942	4458 to 4459	As GS-4 but with roller bearings
GS-6	1943	4460 to 4469	No streamlining — plain black

NW2 B₀-B₀ General Motors Electro-Motive Division (EMD), 1939

Type: Diesel-electric switching locomotive.
Gauge: 4ft 8½in (1,435mm).
Propulsion: Type 567 12-cylinder two-stroke 1,000hp (746kW) diesel engine and generator supplying current to four dc traction motors geared to the axles.
Weight: 250,160lb (113.5t).
Max. axleload: 62,540lb (28.4t).
Tractive effort: 62,500lb (278kN).
Overall length: 44ft 5in (13,540mm).

While General Motors' Electro-Motive Division were beginning their takeover of main-line rail movement from steam power, they did not forget humbler switching operations in yards and depots. We have seen how a reliable diesel-electric switcher had been developed by a consortium in the 1920s and this had led to unhindered acceptance of the concept. EMD's first essay into

this field was in 1935 with two demonstration switchers of 600hp (450kW) installed power. They were neat Bo-Bos known as model "SC", 'S' standing for 'switcher' and 'C' standing for 'cast-frame'. A production series followed, with alternative "SW" (switcher, welded-frame) and "SC" versions offered and more than 100 sold.

Many roads found that these machines had not quite enough muscle for the work, so a more powerful switcher with a 12-cylinder series 20/A engine followed in 1937. This was the "N" series, and versions "NC", "NC1" "NC2", "NW", "NW1", "NW3" and "NW4" were produced and sold a total of 50 between 1937 and 1939. The differences between the model numbers were connected with variations in the electrical equipment. Series production began in 1939 with the 1,000hp (746kW) "NW2" model, the subject of the details given above, which was the first EMD locomotive to use

EMD-made electrical equipment. This model also had a 12-cylinder version of EMD's famous standard '567' series engine. Over 1,100 examples were sold between 1939 and 1949 and many are still hard at work.

There were a few "NW3s" and "NW5s" built in 1942 and 1947 respectively which were road-switcher versions of the "NW2" extended to house steam generator equipment, used to pre-heat or pre-cool passenger trains before they began their journeys. These machines were equipped with EMD's 'road' trucks and larger fuel tanks. There were also 43 cab-less "TR", "TR2" and "TR3" booster units, intended to be used semi-permanently coupled to an "NW2" which was equipped with multiple-unit connections. These twin units were known as 'cow-and-calf' units, and EMD was the first manufacturer to offer this arrangement.

Since all EMD switchers by now had welded frames, "SW"

was taken in 1949 to mean 'switcher' and the "NW2" line was modified to become successively the "SW7" and then the "SW9" model. The 12-cylinder '567' engine continued to be used, but uprated to give 20 per cent more power. In 1954, the designation was again changed; from now on the model number was to indicate the horsepower, hence the "SW1200". "SW7"/"SW9"/ "SW1200" production totalled some 2,300 units all very similar to the "NW2" design, before a completely new series of switchers incorporating the later '645' series engine was introduced in 1966. A round 1,000hp could now be offered using an eight-cylinder engine and production of the "SW1000" and "SW1001" models (for freight clearances) continues to this day, while roads needing more powerful switchers can buy the 'Multi-Purpose' light road-switcher, model "MP15", with a 12-cylinder 1,500hp (1,125kW) engine.

"Electroliner": Four-car trainset

Chicago, North Shore & Milwaukee Railroad (North Shore), 1941

Type: High-speed articulated electric interurban train.
Gauge: 4ft 8½in (1,435mm).
Propulsion: Direct current at 550V (600/650V post-World War II) fed via trolley wire and poles (or 600V on third rail on the Loop) to eight 125hp (200kW) Westinghouse nose-suspended traction motors geared to the driving axles of all except the third of the five Commonwealth cast steel bogies.
Weight: 171,030lb (77.6t) adhesive, 210,500lb (95t) total.
Max. axleload: 21,380lb (9.7t).
Overall length: 155ft 4in (47,345mm).
Max. speed: 85mph (136km/h)*.

*after World War II

At a time when high-speed electric multiple-unit trains seem set to provide the inter-city transport of the future, it is worth considering that the United States has already developed and discarded a huge network, 18,000 miles (29,000km) in extent, of fast interurban electric trains. Some were faster than others but virtually all have now vanished. Some of the longest lasting, as well as the fastest and best, ran on the Chicago, North Shore & Milwaukee Railroad. On this line, travellers started their journeys at selected stops on the famous central loop of Chicago's elevated railway — which meant that trains had to be flexible enough to turn street corners on 90ft (27.5m) radius curves. This was achieved by making the cars articulated as well as rather short.

Only a few minutes later they would have to be rolling along at 85mph (135km/h) on the North Shore's excellent main line tracks. In Milwaukee, the trains made their final approach to the city centre terminal on street-car tracks, with all that that involves in control at crawling speeds. It was a superb feat of design to build rolling stock that was able to suit both such a high-speed as well as such a low-speed environment.

Below: *The legendary Chicago, North Shore & Milwaukee Railroad "Electroliner" trains consisted of five articulated cars of which the outer two pairs are depicted here. They were financed by employees' pay cuts, staving off closure until 1963.*

The famous trains that did all this so spectacularly had some unusual features, not least the fact that the line's employees had agreed to finance improvements to the line, including the "Electroliners" by taking a wage cut! This was because the trains were a last-ditch attempt to hold off abandonment.

St Louis Car built the trains,

Switching was the first steam citadel to fall and, while all the other diesel manufacturing firms offered similar locomotives, a high proportion of the railroads in the United States, Canada and Mexico, as well as many users in general industry, had these units on the roster.

In spite of the passing of the years and the availability of more up-to-date switching power, the "NW2s", built for tedious but essential chores far removed from the glamour of rolling vast trains across a continent, more than deserve their inclusion in this book. It surely says enough about these machines that a good many (and the youngest of them must be at least 35 years old) still perform their humble tasks with economy and reliability.

Right: *A newly painted Electro-Motive NW2 Bo-Bo switching locomotive of the Union Pacific Railroad at Pocatello, Idaho, in August 1981.*

using electrical equipment from Westinghouse. They seated 146 and boasted a tavern-lounge car. The two "Electroliner" trainsets were scheduled to make the 88-mile (141km) journey from Chicago to Milwaukee and return five times daily from February 9, 1941 until the flexibility of the motor car finally won out. The last full day on which the North Shore line operated was January 20, 1963.

The "Electroliners" were sold to the Red Arrow lines of the Southeastern Pennsylvania Transportation Authority in Philadelphia. In 1964 they went into service as "Liberty Liners" *Valley Forge* and *Independence Hall,* complete with a vivid maroon, white and grey colour scheme.

Right: *White flags indicate an "extra" worked by one of the North Shore's "Electroliners".*

Big Boy 4-8-8-4 Union Pacific Railroad (UP), 1941

Gauge: 4ft 8½in (1,435mm).
Tractive effort: 135,375lb (61,422kg).
Axleload: 67,750lb (30.7t).
Cylinders: (4) 23¾ x 32in (603 x 812mm).
Driving wheels: 68in (1,727mm).
Heating surface: 5,889sq ft (547m²).
Superheater: 2,466sq ft (229m²).
Steam pressure: 300psi (21.1kg/cm²).
Grate area: 150sq ft (13.9m²).
Fuel: 56,000lb (25.4t).
Water: 25,000 US gall (94.6m³).
Adhesive weight: 540,000lb (245t).
Total weight: 1,189,500lb (539.7t).
Length overall: 132ft 10in (40,487mm).

"Big Boy!" This evocative name is applied to what the world knows were the biggest, heaviest, most powerful and strongest steam locomotives ever built. In the one sense though, the world is wrong because the 25 "Big Boys" were surpassed (often substantially) in respect of most of the individual attributes mentioned above by other US steam locomotives described in these pages. Yet what the world says is completely correct if one considers the overall picture. If a magic figure could be produced which combined all these individual attributes, then the "Big Boys" would without doubt be No.1 in the world. Should one go further and add some measurement of success in respect of performance as economic and successful tonnage-moving instruments, then these

absolutely magnificent means of locomotion stand amongst those at the very top.

The genesis of the "Big Boys" lay in the recovery of the US economy during the late-1930s from the Depression of 1929 combined with increased spending on defense. In 1940 Union Pacific went, not for the first time, to the American Locomotive Company (Alco) for a locomotive to handle yet heavier trains across the mountainous Wyoming Division between Cheyenne, Wyoming and Ogden, Utah. Out of Cheyenne going west the ruling grade was until 1953 1.55 per cent (1-in-65) on the notorious Sherman Hill, with a maximum elevation of 8,013ft (2,443m) at Sherman Summit. Eastwards out of Ogden, the crossing of the Wahsatch Mountains involved

some 60 miles (96km) uphill, much of it at 1.14 per cent (1-in-88) as the rails climbed from 4,300ft altitude to 7,230ft (2,200m) at Altamont. The prime object of acquiring the new locomotives was to handle 3,600-ton trains unassisted on this latter section using the new locomotives.

A rapid-fire dialogue between UP's excellent mechanical department and Alco's equally experienced design teams led to design work being completed in an amazingly short time of six months or so. Such was the confidence of UP management in the work done that they ordered 201 locomotives straight from the

Above and below: *"Big Boy" in elevation and in perspective. Six out of twenty-five built are preserved for posterity.*

drawing board. The price was $265,174 each.

Legend states firmly that a shopman at Alco chalked the name "Big Boy!" on the smoke-box of an early member of the class. There are tales of UP's efforts to counter it with more solid suggestions such as "Wahsatch". But, whatever its origin, media publicity was such that the "Big Boy" name was clearly with us for good even before the first one arrived at Omaha early in September 1941, about a year after the order was placed.

Before this memorable day much preparatory work had to be done, including replacement of lighter rails with new 130lb/yd (65kg/m) steel and new 135ft (41m) turntables at Ogden and Green River. Many curves had to be realigned, not so much because these surprisingly flexible monsters could not get round them but rather that excessive overhang might mean contact with trains on adjacent lines. The front of the boiler swung out some 2ft (600mm) sideways from the centre of the track on a 10° (134m) radius curve! In fact, the maximum curvature that could be negotiated was as sharp as 20° (87m) and few locations on main tracks are as sharply curved as that. On good alignments the maximum speed of a "Big Boy" was about 70mph (112km/h).

The engineering of the "Big

Above: *UP "Big Boy" 4-8-8-4 at the head of freight extra X4019 conveying Pacific Fruit Express refrigerator cars through Echo Canyon, Utah. In accordance with UP practice, the train number of the extra is also that of the locomotive.*

Right: *The impressive front end of Union Pacific articulated "Big Boy" 4-8-8-4 No.4002, built by the American Locomotive Company in 1941.*

Boys" was massive but wholly conventional. Such up-to-date features as cast-steel locomotive beds and roller bearings were adopted as a matter of course. All were coal burners except No.4005 which for a time burned oil. They are recorded as developing 6,290 horsepower (4,692kW) in the cylinders, consuming some 100,000lb of water and 44,000lb of coal per hour whilst doing it. As the years went by, experience gained allowed loads to be increased. Towards the end of their lives, with the aid of the new line which reduced the grade to 0.82 per cent (1-in-122), the "4000s" were taking 6,000-ton trains up Sherman Hill. It says enough that a "Big Boy" had the unique distinction for a steam locomotive of appearing on the cover of *Time* magazine! Six are preserved at widely-spread locations from California to New Hampshire, but none are operable.

H-8 Allegheny 2-6-6-6 Cheapeake & Ohio Railway (Chessie), 1941

Gauge: 4ft 8½in (1,435mm).
Tractive effort: 110,200lb (50,000kg).
Axleload: 86,350lb (39.2t).
Cylinders: (4) 22½ x 33in (571 x 838mm).
Driving wheels: 67in (1,701mm).
Heating surface: 7,240sq ft (673²).
Superheater: 3,186sq ft (296m²).
Steam pressure: 260psi (18.3kg/cm²).
Grate area: 135sq ft (12.5m²).
Fuel: 50,000lb (22.7t).
Water: 25,000 US gall (94.6m³).
Adhesive weight: 471,000lb (213.7t).
Total weight: 1,076,000lb (488.2t).
Leigh overall: 130ft 1in (39,653mm).

The most powerful locomotives ever built! And for once this barely needs qualifying in any way, except to say that only prime-movers are included. Several times in this narrative we have discussed the search for ever more economic means of bringing coal across the Allegheny Mountains. This was spurred on by the fight between competing roads, upon which cheap energy and therefore United States' industrial might depended. Just as the USA entered World War II in December 1941, the Lima Locomotive Works delivered to the Chesapeake & Ohio—'George Washington's railroad'—the first of the most super of all their celebrated 'super-power' designs. The design involved a unique 2-6-6-6 wheel arrangement and was totally modern and totally successful.

During the traumatic years which followed, 59 more were built, the last batch as late as 1948. The class was designated "H-8" and carried road numbers 1600 to 1659. A further eight were built for the nearby Virginian Railroad.

Power output from a steam locomotive depends on the size of the fire and so the most important feature of the "H-8" was the huge deep firebox made possible by having that six-wheeled rear truck. The area of the grate was 11 per cent less than that of a Union Pacific "Big Boy", but the "H-8" firebox, not being situated above the rear driving wheels, was much deeper. Moreover, West Virginian coal was of better quality than that used on UP. Hence the "H-8s" could steam at higher rates, corresponding to a record drawbar-horsepower just short of 7,500 (10,000kW). However, high horsepower involves high speed as well as a heavy pull, but it was some time before these vast machines—which took their name from the mountains they first conquered—had arrived in sufficient numbers to be used elsewhere and so prove their speed capabilities. About a third of the "Alleghenies" were fitted with steam connections for use on passenger work, on which their ability to reach 60mph (100km/h) was useful.

On the climb from Hinton, West Virginia, eastward up to the 2,072ft (631m) summit at Allegheny tunnel, inclined at 0.57 per cent (1-in-175) two "H8s", one at each end, could manage an immense train of 140 cars weighing 11,500 US tons. An important feature in this remarkable capability was the high adhesive weight upon which all hauling ability depends. A total of 254 tons was carried on the six driving axles, corresponding to an unprecedented axleload of well over 40 tons, a 37 per cent increase over that of their predecessors, the "H-7a" 2-8-8-2s.

This was a world record for any major common-carrier railroad and only made possible because of Chessie's superb well-maintained heavy-duty permanent way. Even so, a great deal of track strengthening and tunnel enlargement had to be undertaken before the weight and bulk of the "H-8s" could be accommodated. The comparatively large driving wheels also helped in preventing

Below: *No diesel fumes in the air yet as Allegheny No.1648 takes water at Russell, Kentucky, May 1949.*

CHESAPEAKE & OHIO   1603

rail-head failures—too small wheels carrying too large loads are liable (in lay terms) to 'sink in' and cause shelling-off of the running surfaces.

Every possible well-tried modern feature was applied to the "Alleghenies" in order to improve their efficiency and availability. Cast-steel locomotive beds with integral cylinders, roller bearings on all main axles, Worthington feed-water heaters, Baker valve gear and very sophisticated counter-balancing of the reciprocating parts all contributed. More ancient devices, such as a totally adequate sand supply from four great sandboxes situated each side of the top of the boiler, were not forgotten. Sand could be put just ahead or just behind each driving wheel; there were also steam jets to wash it off, so keeping the train wheels rolling with minimum friction on clean smooth rails.

Also notable was the C&O trademark, known as the 'flying pumps', whereby both brake pumps were mounted on the smokebox front. In typical Mallet fashion, the headlight was fixed to the leading articulated engine in order that its beam should follow the line of rails more closely. Unusually the tender had a six-wheel leading truck plus an eight-wheel trailing one; the engine and tender just squeezed on to existing 115ft (35m) turntables.

It is sad but almost incredible to relate that, with the newest "H-8s" a bare four years old, in 1952 the C&O had begun to replace them by diesels. Four years later all 60 has been laid aside. Only two survive. No.1601 is preserved well outside their territory at the Henry Ford Museum, Dearborn, Michigan, while No.1604 is in the Transportation Museum at Roanoke, Virginia.

More than a quarter of a century later, with the relative cost of coal and oil changed so considerably, it is scant comfort that a new and much enlarged Chessie, along with other coal-hauling railroads, is reconsidering ordering steam locomotives, as will be related.

Above: *Lifeblood of steam! A Chesapeake & Ohio H-8 2-6-6-6 articulated locomotive has its 25,000 gallon tank filled from a convenient water crane alongside the tracks.*

Below: *Equally at home with fast passenger or heavy freight trains, the H-8s were the final flowering of steam traction on Chessie.*

J1a 2-10-4 Pennsylvania Railroad (PRR), 1942

Gauge: 4ft 8½in (1,435mm).
Tractive effort: 108,750lb (49,342kg); 93,750lb (42,536kg) without booster.
Axleload: 83,116lb (37.7t).
Cylinders: (2) 29 x 34in (736 x 863mm).
Driving wheels: 70in (1,778mm).
Heating surface: 6,568sq ft (610m²).
Superheater: 2,930sq ft (272m²).
Steam pressure: 270psi (191kg/cm²).
Grate area: 122sq ft (11.3m²).
Fuel: 60,000lb (27.2t).
Adhesive weight: 377,800lb (171.4t).
Total weight: 984,100lb (446.5t).
Length overall: 117ft 8in (35,864mm).
* 93,750lb (42,536kg) without booster.

During the 1940s the Pennsylvania Railroad was making what turned out to be a disastrous attempt to develop a dynasty of duplex-drive locomotives. Soon after the war began, however, there was an urgent and immediate need for heavy, powerful freight locomotives. As a result of this attempt to carry the state of the art a stage further, the 'standard railroad of the world' was rather short of efficient locomotives that were merely up-to-date. So, because the war could not wait, they had to pocket their pride and take a package from their neighbours and rivals, Chesapeake & Ohio.

The Chessie had an excellent series of 40 2-10-4s known as Class "T-1", capable of moving 13,000-ton coal trains at a respectable speed over the less heavily-graded sections of their road. The "T-1s" were one of the Lima Locomotive Company's well-known 'Super-power' designs and dated from 1930. In the event a "T-1" was lent for evaluation, the blueprints followed, and immediately the Pennsylvania's great Altoona Shops set about mass-producing a modified version to the tune eventually of 125 examples, more than three times the number of the originals.

The Pennsy classified their new

Class T1 4-4-4-4 Pennsylvania Railroad (PRR), 1942

Gauge: 4ft 8½in (1,435mm).
Tractive effort: 64,700lb (29,300kg).
Axle load: 69,000lb (31.5t).
Cylinders: (4) 19¾ x 26in (501 x 660mm).
Driving wheels: 80in (2,032mm).
Heating surface: 4,209sq ft (391.0m²).
Superheater: 1,430sq ft (131.9m²).
Steam pressure: 300psi (21.1kg/cm²).
Grate area: 92sq ft (8.5m²).
Fuel: 85,000lb (38.5t).
Water: 16,000gall (19,000 US) (72.5m³).
Adhesive weight: 273,000lb (124t).
Total weight: 954,000lb (432.7t).
Length overall: 122ft 10in (37,440mm).

In the 1930s there was a notable increase in the use of 4-8-4 locomotives in the United States, both for freight and passenger service. There were, however, some problems with the very high piston thrust in these engines, and the resultant stresses in crank pins, while the balancing of the heavy reciprocating parts for high speeds also caused difficulties. All the problems could be solved, but R.P. Johnson, chief engineer of The Baldwin Locomotive Works suggested that they could be avoided by dividing the driving wheels into two groups in a single rigid frame, with separate cylinders for each, thus making the engine into a 4-4-4-4. Compared with the 4-8-4, piston loads were reduced, and it was easier to provide valves of adequate size, but the rigid wheelbase was increased by the space required to accommodate the second set of cylinders. This increase was in itself sufficient to discourage some roads from further consideration of the proposal.

The first road to build a duplex engine was the Baltimore and Ohio, which made a 4-4-4-4 with an experimental water-tube firebox in 1937, but it was the Pennsylvania which first built a locomotive with a conventional boiler for this layout. In 1937, with the principal passenger services still worked by the "K4" Pacifics of 1914 design, the road's engineers embarked on the design of a locomotive to haul 1,090 tons at 100mph (160km/h), which was well beyond the capacity of any existing 4-8-4.

Johnson put the case for the duplex engine, and this appealed to the PRR men, but for the size of the engine required 16 wheels were insufficient, and the PRR took one of its most spectacular steps by adopting the 6-4-4-6 wheel arrangement. The locomotive was designed and built at Altoona, and it was the largest rigid-framed passenger engine ever built. It was numbered 6100 and classified "S1", and with driving wheels 84in (2,134mm) in diameter, a grate area of 132sq ft (12.3m²), and a boiler some 15 per cent greater than that of any 4-8-4, it was essentially an engine for developing high power at high speed. With a streamlined casing design by fashionable stylist Raymond Loewy, its appearance was a striking as its dimensions.

No.6100 appeared early in 1939, but it spent much of 1939 and 1940 on display at the New York World Fair and it was not until December 1940 that it entered revenue service. Although intended for use throughout the main line from Harrisburg to Chicago, in the event its great length led to its prohibition from the curved lines in the east, and this prohibition was further extended because the maximum axle load came out at 73,880lb (33.5t) against the figure of 67,500lb (30.5t) which had been stipulated to the designer.

As a result the engine was limited to the 283-mile Crestline to Chicago division, on which it proved capable of hauling 1225 tons at an average speed of 66mph (106km/h). With smaller loads it achieved very high speeds, and although the PRR and its official locomotive historian were silent on the subject, it was

Above: *A new shape in steam. Pennsylvania Railroad class T1 4-4-4-4 in new condition at the Baldwin Locomotive Works.*

widely believed to have exceeded 120mph (193km/h) on many occasions. There were, however, problems, particularly with slipping, not helped by the fact that only 46 per cent of the total engine weight was carried on the driving wheels, compared with 65 per cent in a "K4" Pacific.

Despite the limited and variable experience gained so far with the "S1", the PRR ordered two more duplex locomotives from Baldwin in July, 1940. The performance requirement was reduced to the haulage of 880 tons at 100mph (160km/h) and this could be met by a 4-4-4-4, with 80in (2,032mm) driving wheels, and a grate area of 92sq ft (8.5m²). The maximum

Left: *J1 class 2-10-4 with a freight train at Belleview, Ohio, in June 1956.*

acquisitions "J-1" and "J1a"—the numbers ran from 6150 to 6174 and 6401 to 6500. In spite of the fact that they were quite different in various fundamental ways from anything else in the stable, Pennsy

found them very good. For example, round-top fireboxes (instead of Belpaire with square corners), Baker valve gear and the provision of booster engines were almost unknown on the PRR.

The modifications made to the C&O design were almost all superficial, but even so they changed the appearance of these

Above: *Massive J1 No.6168 makes slow and noisy progress up the fabled Horseshoe Curve.*

chunky hulks of machinery almost beyond recognition. The 16-wheel tenders were of the unusual-looking standard Pennsy 210-F-84 type and that, combined with a cab having partially-rounded windows,

took care of the C&O look at the rear. At the other end, solid rounded pilots with couplers normally dropped to a flush position, a high-mounted headlight and, of course, a smokebox numberplate cast in the form of the famous keystone herald in place of the 'flying pumps', did the same for the front end.

---

axle load was 69,250lb (31.4t) compared with 73,880lb (33.5t) of the "S1". The two engines, classified "T1" and numbered 6110 and 6111 differed only in that 6111 had a booster. Apart from the inclusion of certain PRR standard fittings, Baldwin was given a free hand in the design. Franklin's poppet valves were fitted at PRR insistence, as these had produced a notable increase in the power of "K4" Pacific. Roller-bearings, light-weight motion, and disc wheels were amongst the modern equipment and the engine was clothed in a casing designed by Raymond Loewy, but quite different from that of No.6100. They were delivered in April and May 1942.

In 1944, No.6110 was tested

on the Altoona testing plant and it produced a cylinder horsepower of 6,550 at 85mph (137 km/h) with 25 per cent cut-off. In service the engines worked over the 713 miles between Harrisburg and Chicago, but despite these long runs they built up mileage slowly and spent an undue amount of time under repair. Slipping was again the main trouble, although in these engines 54 per cent of the total weight was adhesive.

At this point the road took a fateful step. Ignoring its old policy of testing and modifying a prototype until it was entirely satisfactory, it ordered 50 almost identical engines. Nos.5500-24 were built at Altoona and 5525-49 by the Baldwin Works and delivered be-

tween late 1945 and early 1946.

With a shorter rigid wheelbase than the "S1" and a smaller maximum axle load, the "T1"s were allowed over the full steam-worked part of the PRR main line from Harrisburg to Chicago, and they worked through over the whole 713 miles. They took over all the passenger work on this route, including the 73.1mph (117.5km/h) schedule of the Chicago Arrow over the 123 miles (198km) from Fort Wayne to Gary, and four other runs at more than 70mph (112.5km/h). At their best they were magnificent, with numerous records of

Below: *Pennsylvania Railroad J1 class 2-10-4 with freight train at Belleview, Ohio, in June 1956.*

100mph (160km/h) with 910-ton trains, including a pass-to-pass average of 100mph over 69 miles of generally falling grades with a load of 1,045 tons. They rode smoothly, and when all was well they were popular with the enginemen, but slipping remained a major hazard, not only slipping at starting but violent slipping of one set of wheels at high speed.

At this time the motive power department of the PRR was at a low ebb, both in equipment and in morale, and compared with the simple and well-known "K4" Pacifics, the "T1" was a complex box of tricks, particularly its valve gear. Maintenance of the big engines proved to be a difficult job, and their appearances on their booked workings became less and less regular. The faithful "K4"s were out again in force.

Various modifications were made to ease maintenance, mainly by the removal of parts of the casing, but one engine was rebuilt with piston valves. Eight engines had their cylinder diameter reduced in an attempt to reduce the tendency to slip but the problem was never solved. As time passed, the worsening financial state of the railroad led to the ordering of mainline diesels.

It was intended that the "T1"s should have a full economic life before succumbing to diesels. In the event, the serious and intractable problems with them had the effect of accelerating dieselisation, and by the end of 1949 most of them were out of service. So ended what is considered the most expensive locomotive fiasco of the century.

Challenger Class 4-6-6-4 Union Pacific Railroad (UP), 1942

Gauge: 4ft 8½in (1,435mm).
Tractive effort: 97,400lb (44,100kg).
Axle load: 68,000lb (31t).
Cylinders: (4) 21 x 32in (533 x 813mm).
Driving wheels: 69in (1,753mm).
Heating surface: 4,642sq ft (431m²).
Superheater: 1,741sq ft (162m²).
Steam pressure: 280psi (19.7kg/cm²).
Grate area: 132sq ft (12.3m²).
Fuel: 56,000lb (25.4t).
Adhesive weight: 406,000lb (184.3t).
Total weight: 1,071,000lb (486t).
Length overall: 121ft 11in (37,160mm).

On virtually all counts this locomotive was the largest, heaviest, strongest and most powerful one which ever regularly handled express passenger trains. Its existence was only possible because it was an articulated locomotive, that is, there was a hinge in the middle.

Articulated locomotives were introduced early in locomotive history, but it was not until the full flowering of the narrow-gauge railway late in the 19th century that they were built in quantity. Many designs were tried, but the most popular was that of Anatole Mallet, a French consulting engineer. Mallet was an early advocate of compounding, and from 1876 a number of two-cylinder compound locomotives were built to his designs. In 1884, to cater for larger locomotives, he proposed an articulated design in which the rear set of driving wheels were mounted in the main frame, which supported the firebox and the rear part of the boiler. The front set of driving wheels were in a separate frame, the rear end of which was hinged to the front of the main frame. The front of the boiler rested on the hinged frame, and as the boiler swung across this frame on curves, a sliding support was needed. The high-pressure cylinders drove the rear set of wheels and the low-pressure cylinders the leading set. High-pressure steam was thus entirely on the rigid part of the locomotive,

and hinged steam pipes were needed only for the steam to and from the low-pressure cylinders.

The European engines built to this design were mostly for narrow-gauge railways. However, in 1903 the first American Mallet was built. Here the aim was to get the maximum adhesion, and as there were difficulties in designing a locomotive with six driving axles in a rigid frame, articulation was an attractive proposition at this stage. The American engine was an 0-6-6-0 built for the Baltimore and Ohio Railroad. It was the largest locomotive in the world and thereafter that distinction was always held by an American member of the Mallet family.

More American Mallets followed, at first mainly for banking duties, but then for road work. However, with their huge low-pressure cylinders and the tortuous steam pipes between the cylinders, these engines were unsuitable for speeds above 30-40mph (50-65km/h). Above these speeds oscillations of the front frame developed leading to heavy wear on locomotive and track.

In 1924 the Chesapeake and Ohio Railroad ordered twenty 2-8-8-2 locomotives with four simple expansion cylinders. Although the main reason for this was that the loading gauge of C&O could not accommodate the large low-pressure cylinders of a compound, the change

brought the further benefit that more adequate steam pipes could be provided, and the engines were capable of higher speeds. Some intensive work was needed to develop flexible joints suitable for carrying high-pressure steam to the leading cylinders.

From this time onwards American interest centred on the four-cylinder simple Mallet and successive improvements were made which upgraded the type from banking duties to main line freight work and, eventually, on a few roads, to express passenger

Below: *"Challenger" class 4-6-6-4 No.3985 at Cheyenne awaiting restoration to working order in 1981.*

UNION PACIFIC 3977

A favourite racing ground for these monsters was the main line, mostly across the desert, between Salt Lake City, Las Vegas and Los Angeles, where they regularly ran at up to 70mph (112km/h) on passenger trains.

In 1952 coal supplies were interrupted by a strike and a crash programme for further conversions to oil-burning was put in hand, but the strike ended after eight engines had been converted. Rather perversely, in 1950 ten of the original series had been converted back to coal-firing, but in less than a year had been changed yet again to oil. Dieselisation gradually narrowed the field of operation of the "Challengers", but they continued to take a major share of steam working up to 1958 when the delivery of a large batch of diesels rendered them redundant.

The numbering of the Challengers was extremely complicated due to the practice of renumbering engines when they were converted from coal-burning to oil-burning or vice versa. Thus the original engines were renumbered from 3900-39 to 3800-39 and the three batches of the second series were numbered successively 3950-69, 3975-99 and 3930-49, so that 3930-9 were used twice but 3970-4 not at all. Furthermore, eighteen of the second series which were converted to oil-burning were renumbered from 3700-17.

Several other roads bought engines of the 4-6-6-4 wheel arrangement, generally similar to the "Challenger" and they also were used on some passenger work, but it was on the UP that the articulated locomotive had its most important application to passenger work, and a "Challenger" hauling 20 or more coaches was a regular sight. Fortunately one of the engines, No.3985 was preserved as a static exhibit, but in 1981 it was restored to working order, making it by far the largest working steam engine in the world.

work. Amongst changes introduced were longer travel valves and more complete balancing of the moving parts, but most important were the changes made to the connection between the leading frame and the main frame, and to lateral control of the leading wheels. It was these latter alterations which eliminated the violent oscillations which had limited the speed of earlier Mallets.

The Union Pacific acquired 70 compound 2-8-8-0s with 59in (1,500mm) driving wheels between 1918 and 1924. These were essentially hard-slogging, modest speed engines and in 1926, for faster freight trains, the railroad introduced a class which was remarkable in several respects. It was a three-cylinder 4-12-2 with 67in (1,702mm) driving wheels, and was the first class with this wheel arrangement. It was also one of the few American three cylinder engines and the only one to be built in quantity, a total of 88 being built. They were highly successful, but with their long rigid wheelbase and heavy motion they were limited to 45mph (72km/h), and with growing road competition a twelve-coupled engine was needed capable of higher speeds than the 4-12-2.

Experience with the compound Mallets had led to the decision to convert them to simple expansion and the way was then set for the railroad to make another impor-

tant step forward in 1936 by ordering 40 simple-expansion 4-6-6-4s with 69in (1,753mm) driving wheels. They were numbered from 3900 to 3939 and designated "Challenger". The leading bogie gave much better side control than a pony truck and the truck under the firebox assisted the fitting of a very large grate. The engines were distributed widely over the UP system and were used mainly on fast freight trains, but the last six of the engines were ordered specifically for passenger work. The most obvious difference between these earlier "Challenger" locomotives and those depicted in the art-work above was the provision of much smaller 12-wheel tenders. Much of the coal which the UP used came from mines which the railroad owned.

In 1942 pressure of wartime traffic brought the need for more large engines and the construction of Challengers was resumed, a total of 65 more being built up to 1944. A number of changes were made, notably an enlargement of the grate from 108sq ft (10.0m²) to 132sq ft (12.3m²), cast steel frames in place of built-up frames, and an increase in the boiler pressure to 255psi (17.9kg/cm²) accompanied by a reduction in cylinder size of one inch, which left the tractive effort unchanged.

A less obvious but more fundamental change from the earlier engines was in the pivot between

Above: *Now unchallenged as the biggest working steam locomotive in the world, Union Pacific "Challenger" class 4-6-6-4 No.3985 at the head of a train of steam enthusiasts.*

the leading unit and the main frame. In the earlier engines there were both vertical and horizontal hinges, but in the new engines, following the practice adopted in the "Big Boy" 4-8-8-4s, there was no horizontal hinge. The vertical hinge was now arranged to transmit a load of several tons from the rear unit to the front one, thus evening out the distribution of weight between the two sets of driving wheels, and thereby reducing the tendency of the front drivers to slip, which had been a problem with the earlier engines. With no horizontal hinge, humps and hollows in the track were now looked after by the springs of each individual axle, as in a normal rigid locomotive.

All the engines were built as coal-burners, but in 1945 five of them were converted to oil-burning for use on passenger trains on the Oregon and Washington lines. Trouble was experienced with smoke obstructing the driver's view so these five engines were fitted with long smoke deflectors, and they were also painted in the two-tone grey livery which was used for passenger engines for a number of years, as depicted above.

Below: *Union Pacific Railroad "Challenger" 4-6-6-4 depicted in the two-tone grey passenger livery used in the late 1940s.*

MacArthur 2-8-2 US Army Transportation Corps (USATC), 1942

Gauge: 3ft 3⅜in* (1,000mm).
Tractive effort: 20,100lb (9,120kg).
Axleload: 20,000lb (9.1t).
Cylinders: (2) 16 x 24in (406 x 609mm).
Driving wheels: 44in (1,117mm).
Heating surface: 1,371sq ft (127m²).
Superheater: 374sq ft (35m²).
Steam pressure: 185psi (13kg/cm²).
Grate area: 28sq ft (2.6m²).
Fuel: 18,000lb (8.2t).
Water: 5,000 US gall (18.9m²).
Adhesive weight: 80,000lb (36.3t).
Total weight: 216,000lb (98t).
Length overall: 61ft 8½in (18,808mm).
*And other gauges—see text.

Above: *Veteran of the Burma campaign, now Indian Railways Class WD, at Agra Fort, 1974.*

In World War II there was no requirement for light minimum-gauge locomotives to support armies engaged in trench warfare, as had been needed in the previous conflict. But the second war was much more widespread and much of the fighting was in countries whose railroads were not built to standard gauge but instead mostly to gauges between 3 and 3½ft (900 to 1,067mm). A need for locomotives to suit these lines was soon identified and late in 1942 the first of 800 little narrow-gauge Mikados—often referred to as 'MacArthurs'—first saw the light of day at the Alco plant in Schenectady.

The basic design work on the 'MacArthurs' (more prosaically, the "S-118" class 2-8-2s) was done by Alco, while production was shared by them and Baldwin, the Davenport-Besler Corporation at Davenport, Iowa, H.K. Porter of Pittsburgh and the Vulcan Iron Works, Wilkes-Barre, Pennsylvania. They had a minute axleload of 20,000lb (9t), could be easily fitted with side or central buffers and screw couplings, 'chopper' combined buffers and couplings, or various types of normal couplers.

They could have air brakes, or steam brakes combined with vacuum control of the brakes on the train. Oil-burning equipment could also be fitted. They were really models of our familiar friend the USRA light Mikado built to a scale of about two-thirds full size. The overall height was only 11ft 3in (3,429mm) and this meant there were virtually no systems in the 3ft to 3ft 6in gauge range upon which they were unable to work.

The biggest group—about 375 in number—went to work on the metre-gauge tracks of the Indian Bengal & Assam Railway to help in bringing up supplies for the Burma campaign then being fought desperately in north-eastern India. Metre-gauge lines in Iraq and also in other parts of India, whose traffic had risen greatly on account of the war, also received large numbers. As the campaign proceeded some were used in Burma itself. A relatively small number—about 32 in all—were used in North Africa behind the

S-160 2-8-0 US Army Transportation Corps (USATC), 1942

Gauge: 4ft 8½in (1,435mm).
Tractive effort: 31,500lb (14,292kg).
Axleload: 35,000lb (15.9t).
Cylinders: (2) 19 x 26in (482 x 660mm).
Driving wheels: 57in (1,447mm).
Heating surface: 1,765sq ft (164m²).
Superheater: 471sq ft (44m²).
Steam pressure: 225psi (15.8kg/cm²).
Grate area: 41sq ft (3.8m²).
Fuel: 20,000lb (9.1t).
Water: 6,500 US gall (24.6m³).
Adhesive weight: 140,000lb (63.5t).
Total weight: 276,500lb (125.5t).
Length overall: 61ft 0in (18,592mm).

Until World War II no single North American-built class of locomotive on any railroad had exceeded the thousand mark in number. But during that conflict two classes of locomotive each attaining well over 2,000 in number were built in four short years, an incredible achievement for an industry whose average production over the previous four years had been counted in dozens. The 2-10-0s built for the USSR, which were copies of those built for Czarist Russia in World War I, have already been described. More familiar, especially to Europeans of the older generation, are these

little 2-8-0s, known as Class "S-160". Simplicity and adaptability were the keynotes of the design, which could be fitted with various types of braking and coupling systems, could be altered easily to oil-burning, and even altered in gauge.

The specification called for a locomotive capable of running anywhere in Europe, and with commendable promptitude the first of the 2,120 built emerged from Alco's plant in late-1942. Alco, Baldwin and Lima shared the orders. Most of those first built went to Britain to help the hard-pressed railways there during the build-up for the invasion of Europe on D-Day. Others were stored in Britain ready to work in Europe. Similarly, following Operation Torch in North Africa, 250 were sent there and later worked in Italy, Greece and southern France. Later examples went direct to Europe.

Other actual or potential theatres of war also received batches; 60 adapted to 5ft 6in (1,676mm) gauge went to India, 200 of 5ft (1,524mm) gauge went to the USSR and 12 standard-gauge examples went to Alaska. They did the job intended very well indeed. One weakness was that simplification had been taken

Right: *Ex-US Army 2-8-0 now working on Keighley & Worth Valley Tourist Railway in Britain.*

lines of the battles there.

Railroads of other countries needed additional motive power for wartime traffic and 3ft 6in (1,067mm) gauge MacArthurs, went to Nigeria (20), the Gold Coast (Ghana) (11), and Queensland Government Railways in Australia (20). The 3ft gauge version was rarer, but 11 went to the White Pass & Yukon Railway which began in Alaska but ended in the Canadian Yukon.

After the war was over, most railroads who had had them managed to keep some, but many were distributed to or bought by railroads and countries whose motive power had been depleted by the war. Sixty-eight went to Siam, 28 to Malaya, 8 to Tanzania, 10 to the French Camerouns. All these were metre gauge; 3ft 6in (1,067mm) gauge examples went to the Philippines and to the United Fruit Company's lines in Costa Rica and Honduras. Post-war copies (metre-gauge) of this remarkable design went to India, Greece and Ethiopia. About 40 are unaccounted for and were probably scrapped unused. A few of these locomotives can still be seen working in regular service—those in India certainly and those in Iraq possibly.

Right: *MacArthur Class 2-8-2 locomotive at Tnung Song Junction, Thailand, January 1974.*

a little too far as regards the boiler-staying arrangements; several boiler failures were to occur before a simple modification solved the problem.

At the war's end, the locomotives were first stored and then turned over to UNRRA (United Nations Relief & Rehabilitation Administration) which supplied them to many countries whose locomotive fleets had been devastated during the conflict. Substantial long-term use was made of them by the following countries: Australia (Class "956") 30; China (Class "KD6") 25; Czechoslovakia (Class "456") 80; Greece (Class "THg") 52; Hungary (Class "411") 500 plus;

India (Class "AWC") 60; Italy (Class "736") 243; Jugoslavia (Class "37") 65; Poland (classes "Tr.201" and "Tr.203") 500 plus; South Korea (Class "C52") 100 plus; Soviet Union (Class "Wa") 200.

Others were lost at sea, a few remained in the USA and as many as 175 are unaccounted for. Small numbers stayed in Tunisia and post-war copies went to Peru, Jamaica, Spain and Mexico. Those in China and Poland are the only ones known to be still in service, apart from one or two in the USA and one in Britain (on the Keighley & Worth Valley Railway) used on steam-for-pleasure lines.

Above: *"Big Jim" leaves Haworth on the Keighley & Worth Valley Railway, May 1983.*

Below: *S-160 class 2-8-0 ex-US Army at Kastanas, Greece, in April 1980.*

Class U-4 4-8-4 Canadian National Railways (CN), 1936

Gauge: 4ft 8½in (1,435mm).
Tractive effort: 52,457lb (23,794kg).
Axle load: 59,500lb (27t).
Cylinders: (2) 24 x 30in (610 x 762mm).
Driving wheels: 77in (1,956mm).
Heating surface: 3,861sq ft (322.5m²).
Superheater: 1,530sq ft (142m²).
Steam pressure: 275psi (19.5kg/cm²).
Grate area: 73.7sq ft (6.8m²).
Fuel: 40,000lb (18t).
Water: 11,700gall (14,000 US) (35m³).
Adhesive weight: 236,000lb (107t).
Total weight: 660,000lb (300t).
Length overall: 95ft 1in (28,990mm).

During the steam age the longest railway in America was not located in the USA, for Canadian National Railways held the title. Around 60 years ago Canada suffered from the sort of railway problems that the United States is in the throes of now and the Government had perforce to take over 24,000 miles of bankrupt lines. The task ahead was formidable and one of the most remarkable railwaymen of all time was engaged to take charge. This was Sir Henry Thornton, who had learnt his trade on the Pennsylvania Railroad and its notorious subsidiary, the Long Island Railroad. In 1914 he was appointed general manager of the British Great Eastern Railway. During World War I he became a brigadier-general in charge of rail movement in France, and received a knighthood.

It was a far cry from 0-6-2 tanks on Thornton's famous jazz service which so much eased the lot of commuters homeward bound from London's Liverpool Street station, to the Trans-Canada Limited running 2,985 miles (4,776km) across a great continent, but he took it in his stride. Adequate tools for the job was very much a Thornton principle. It should, therefore, have been no surprise that CN was right in the vanguard of roads in ordering that ultimate of passenger types, the 4-8-4.

The Canadian Locomotive Company delivered No.6100—named *Confederation* to celebrate the 60th anniversary of the Canadian Confederation—just seven months after Northern Pacific received its 4-8-4s. By the end of the year, CN and its US subsidiary Grand Trunk Western, had a fleet totalling 52 of these great machines. This made CN by far the greatest 4-8-4 owner in the world, a position which was retained until the USSR took the lead in the mid-1950s. Running numbers were 6100-39 and 6300-11, classes "U2" and "U3", for CN and GTW respectively.

Further batches, generally similar, built in 1929 and 1936 brought the numbers up to 77 and then in 1936-38 a high-speed streamline version was built. This "U-4" class, the subject of the dimensions given on this page, had larger driving wheels and a less than typically ugly shroud, but was also very much the same locomotive basically. Running numbers were 6400-4 (CN) and 6405-11 (GTW).

Yet more standard 4-8-4s followed in 1940 and 1944 until finally the total reached 203. All the CN locomotives were built in Canada either by the Montreal Locomotive Works or by the Canadian Locomotive Company also of Montreal, while (no doubt because of import duties) those for GTW were built by US builders.

It is no disparagement to say that the CN engineers were not keen on innovation, and so the class was very much the standard North American product. CN's trade marks were the cylindrical Vanderbilt tenders and, on those built up to 1936, a prominent transverse feed-water heater placed just in front of the chimney. Naturally, such improvements as roller bearings and cast-steel locomotive frames were adopted as they became available.

One locomotive (No.6184) was

Right: *CNR "O2-h" 4-8-4 No.6247, built in 1943.*

Class U1-f 4-8-2 Canadian National Railways (CN), 1944

Gauge: 4ft 8½in (1,435mm).
Tractive effort: 52,500lb (23,814kg).
Axle load: 59,500lb (27t).
Cylinders: (2) 24 x 30in (610 x 762mm).
Driving wheels: 73in (1,854mm).
Heating surface: 3,584sq ft (333m²).
Superheater: 1,570sq ft (146m²).
Steam pressure: 260psi (18.3kg/cm²).
Grate area: 70.2sq ft (6.6m²).
Fuel: 40,000lb (18t).
Water: 11,500gall (9,740 US) (53m³).
Adhesive weight: 237,000lb (107.5t).
Total weight: 638,000lb (290t).
Length overall: 93ft 3in (28,426mm).

It was in 1923, very soon after the formation of Canadian National Railways, that eight-coupled locomotives were first introduced into passenger service there. This was the original "U1-a" a batch consisting of 16 locos, built by the Canadian Locomotive Company. Then 1924 and 1925 brought the "U1-b" and "U1-c" batches of 21 and five from Canadian and from Baldwin respectively. The latter were for CN's Grand Trunk Western subsidiary in the USA. In 1929 and 1930 there followed five "U1-d" and 12 "U1-e" from Canadian and from the Montreal locomotive works.

Thus in seven years, fifty-nine 4-8-2s, numbered from 6000 to 6058, became available, although by now the class had become overshadowed by the 4-8-4s introduced in 1927, described on this page. There were also four 4-8-2s acquired by the Central Vermont

tried with poppet valves and in later years when Canada struck oil, many 4-8-4s changed over to that method of firing. Withdrawals began on a small scale in 1955 and grew slowly until the final holocaust of the last 159 took place in 1960. The sadness felt by Canadian railwaymen at the 4-8-4s departure from the scene is well expressed by Anthony Clegg and Ray Corley, in their excellent book *Canadian National Steam Power,* by quoting the following verse chalked on a withdrawn 4-8-4:

"In days gone by this junk pile now
Was a grand sight to behold
On threads of steel it dashed along
Like a Knight in armour bold. . . ."

For a period Canadian National operated certain 4-8-4s in excursion service. This has now finished, but eight have survived; two, including streamliner No. 6400, are on display at Ottawa in the National Museum of Science and Technology.

Railway, another CN subsidiary but one which did not then number or classify its locos as part of the main CN fleet. It did use the CN method of classification, though, so these 4-8-2s were also Class "U1-a". In fact they were rather different in design, having been acquired from amongst a flood of 4-8-2s which the Florida East Coast Railroad had ordered but found itself unable to pay for.

The 6000s performed with *élan* on the then highly competitive express trains between Montreal and Toronto; speeds up to 82mph (131km/h) have been noted with 700 tons or so. Later, the same engines operated well in pool

Left: *Canadian National Railways Class "U1-f" 4-8-2 No.6071 depicted at Toronto in April 1952.*

service in conjunction with Canadian Pacific.

In 1944, a further twenty 4-8-2s were delivered from Montreal, of the "U1-f" batch illustrated here. They were brought up to date by having cast-steel locomotive frames, disc wheels and other improvements. Some were oil-burners and all had Vanderbilt cylindrical tenders and outside bearings on the leading bogies. Most significant was a major simplification consisting of the replacement of the boiler feed pump and feed-water heater, by a device called an exhaust steam injector. Injectors are usually tucked away tidily under the side of the cab but in this case the device was hung outside the driving wheels, the large pipe which supplied the exhaust steam adding to its conspicuousness.

Like other injectors but more

so, exhaust steam injectors are remarkable conjuring tricks in the application of natural laws. It is difficult to believe that exhaust steam at, say 10psi (0.7kg/cm²) could force water into a boiler containing steam and water almost 30 times that pressure. However, an arrangement of cones turns a high velocity jet of low pressure steam into a low velocity high-pressure flow of water, which has no difficulty in forcing its way past the non-return clack valves into the boiler.

With just a few exceptions, CN steam locomotives were totally utilitarian, but with these excellent engines, efforts were made to make them good looking too. Side valences, a flanged British-style smokestack, green and black livery, brass numbers and placing the dome and sand container in the same box all contributed to

the clean lines. The result is so good that one can almost forgive the designers that bullet nose to the smokebox!

Canadian National is amongst that superior class of railway administrations who offer steam for pleasure, as exampled by the fact that a total of six of these locomotives are preserved. No. 6060 of class "U1-f" does the honours and in addition No.6069 is displayed at Bayview Park, Sarnia and No.6077 at Capreol, Ontario. Of the elder CN Mountains, No.6015 is at the Museum at Delson, Quebec, No.6039 (Grand Trunk Western) was at Steamtown, Bellows Falls, Vermont, and No.6043 at Assinboine Park, Winnepeg.

Below: *Artist's impression of Canadian National Railways class "U1-f" 4-8-2 as built.*

2900 Class 4-8-4 Atchison, Topeka & Santa Fe Railway (AT&SF), 1944

Tractive effort: 79,960lb
(36,270kg).
Axle load: 74,000lb (33.5t).
Cylinders: (2) 28 x 32in
(711 x 813mm).
Driving wheels: 80in
(2,032mm).
Heating surface: 5,313sq ft
(494m²).
Superheater: 2,366sq ft
(220m²).
Steam pressure: 300psi
(21kg/cm²).
Grate area: 108sq ft (10m²).
Fuel (oil): 5,830galls (7,000 US)
(26.5m³).
Water: 20,400gall (24,500 US)
(93m³).
Adhesive weight: 294,000lb
(133t).
Total weight: 961,000lb (436t).
Length overall: 120ft 10in
(36,830mm).

The Atchison, Topeka & Santa Fe Railway (Santa Fe for short) was remarkable in that it was the *only* railroad company which connected Chicago with California. Odder still perhaps that it was named after three small places in the southern Mid-West, while so many railroads with Pacific in their titles never got there. Even now it remains as it was in the great days of steam — solvent, forward-looking and with its physical plant in first-class condition. With a main line stretching for 2,224 miles (3,580km) across America (or 2,547 miles (4,100km) if you let the Santa Fe take you as far as San Francisco Bay) together, once upon a time, with some of the world's finest and most prestigious passenger services, you might think that the company's steam power must have been remarkable — and you would not be wrong.

Nearly all Santa Fe's steam locomotives came from Baldwin of Philadelphia. At one time it included briefly such exotic items as 2-4-6-2 and 2-6-6-2 super-heated express Mallet locomotives with 73 and 69in (1,854 and 1,753mm) diameter driving wheels respectively. Six of the class of 44 of the 2-6-6-2s even had *boilers* with a hinge in the middle! Experience with these and a few other wild ideas

brought about a firm resolve to stick to the Stephenson path in the future and almost without exception all subsequent steam locomotives built for Santa Fe were "straight" (ie non-articulated) "simple" (ie non-compound) and with two cylinders only. The results of the slow-and-steady policy were magnificent.

The Santa Fe main line crossed the famous Raton Pass in the New Mexico with its 1 in 28½ (3½ per cent) gradient, as well as the less impossible but still severe Cajon Pass in eastern California. East of Kansas City across the level prairies 4-6-2s and 4-6-4s sufficed until the diesels came, but for the heavily graded western lines Santa Fe in 1927 took delivery of its first 4-8-4s. It was only by a small margin that the Northern Pacific Railroad could claim the first of the type as its own. These early 4-8-4s (Nos. 3751 to 3764) were remarkable for having 30in (762mm) diameter cylinders, the largest both in bore or volume in any passenger locomotive, apart from compounds.

This first batch burnt coal, subsequent 4-8-4s being all oil-burners. More 4-8-4s (Nos.3765 to 3775) came in 1938 and a further batch was built in 1941. The final group (Nos.2900 to 2929) on which the particulars

given in this description are based, were constructed in wartime. Quite fortuitously, they also became the heaviest straight passenger locomotives ever built, because high-tensile steel alloys were in short supply and certain parts — in particular the main coupling and connecting rods — had to be much more massive when designed to be made from more ordinary metal. They managed this feat by a very small margin, but when those immense 16-wheel tenders were included and loaded there were no close rivals to this title. The big tenders were fitted to the last two batches; and as well as being the heaviest passenger locomotives ever built, they were also the longest.

Above: *No.2925 of the final batch of AT&SF 4-8-4s built for heavy hauls in the west.*

It must be said that Santa Fe would have preferred diesels to the superb last batch of 4-8-4s, but wartime restrictions prevented this. The company had been early into the diesel game with the now legendary streamlined light-weight de luxe "Super Chief" train, introduced in 1937, as well as the equally celebrated coach-class streamliner "El Capitan". But thirty years ago there were still trains such as the "California Limited", "The Scout" and the "Grand Canyon Limited" and, of course, the original "Chief", still formed of standard equipment.

Below: *Santa Fe "2900" class 4-8-4. Note the chimney extension in the raised position, the handsome tapered connecting* rods *and the enormous tender with two eight-wheel bogies. Eight of these magnificent engines survive, but none is now steamable.*

Above: *Another 3700 loco tops Cajon summit with the Chicago-Los Angeles "Super Chief".*

Left: *On home ground in the Cajon Pass, Class 3700 No.3769 and train in June 1946.*

Above: *The impressive front end of No.2925, preserved at Belen, New Mexico.*

They were often then run in two or more sections each and all needed steam power at the head end.

Apart from the early diesel incursions, these 4-8-4s that totalled 65 ruled the Chicago-Los Angeles main line from Kansas City westwards. It was normal practice to roster them to go the whole distance (1,790 miles—2,880km—via Amarillo or 1,760 miles—2,830km—via the Raton Pass); in respect of steam traction these were by far the longest distances ever to be scheduled to run without change of locomotive. Speeds up in the 90-100 mph (140-160km/h) range were both permitted and achieved.

This journey was not made without changing crews. In this respect feather-bedding union rules based on the capacity of the "American" 4-4-0s of fifty years earlier applied and crews were changed 12 times during the 34 hour run. Water was taken at 16 places and fuel nearly as often, in spite of the enormous tenders.

These magnificent examples of the locomotive builder's art were conventional in all main respects. One unusual feature was the 'hot hat' smoke-stack extension shown on the picture above; absence of overbridges and tunnels over many miles of the Santa Fe route meant that this could be raised for long periods with beneficial effect in keeping smoke and steam clear of the cab. Another detail concerned a modification to the Walschaert's valve gear on some of the 4-8-4s. To reduce the amount of swing— and consequent inertia forces— needed on the curved links, an intermediate lever was introduced into the valve rod. This was so arranged as to increase the amount of valve travel for a given amount of link swing.

Santa Fe was generous in handing out superannuated 4-8-4s as not always properly appreciated gifts to various on-line communities. These included Modesto and San Bernadino, California; Pueblo, Colorado; Fort Madison, Iowa; Kingsman, Arizona; Albuquerque, New Mexico; and Wichita, Kansas. No.2903 is displayed in the Chicago Museum of Science and Industry, while No.2925 is still in the roundhouse at Belen, New Mexico. There was a rumour a year or so ago that Santa Fe might have intentions of entering the steam-for-pleasure business with this locomotive, like neighbour Union Pacific, but nothing came of the proposal.

141R Liberation 2-8-2 French National Railways (SNCF), 1945

Gauge: 4ft 8½in (1,435mm).
Tractive effort: 44,500lb (20,191kg).
Axleload: 48,510lb (22t).
Cylinders; (2) 23½ x 28in (596 x 711mm).
Driving wheels: 65in (1,651mm).
Heating surface: 2,699sq ft (251m²).
Superheater: 704sq ft (65m²).
Steam pressure: 20psi (1.4kg/cm²).
Grate area: 55.5sq ft (5.2m²).
Fuel: 24,000lb (10.9t).
Water: 8,000 US gall (30.3m²).
Adhesive weight: 176,400lb (80t).
Total weight: 413,800lb (187.7t).
Length overall: 79ft 3¼in (24,161mm).

Of all the different schools of steam locomotive engineering in the world, no two were further apart than the American and the French. Most French mainline locomotives were complex four-cylinder compounds of an arrangement developed by Alfred de Glehn (in spite of his name and his place of work, de Glehn was an Englishman) in the early-1900s. Between the wars, when there was no money for new construction, that genius amongst locomotive engineers, André Chapelon, had modernised many of the de Glehn compounds with startling effect, giving both a thermal efficiency and a power-to-weight ratio unmatched elsewhere at any time.

For such outstanding performance there was, however, a price to pay in high maintenance costs. Furthermore, the men who drove French locomotives were not promoted from firemen but instead had first to qualify as skilled mechanics; in short, French engineers had also to be

Right: *Oil-fired No.141R 1043 pilots No.141C 19 on a freight at Angers, June 1967.*

Below: *Few concessions to Gallic principles on the Class 141R—the loco that set SNCF back to work after the war.*

NH/4 2-8-2 Scindia State Railway (ScSR), 1948

Gauge: 2ft 0in (609mm).
Tractive effort: 13,300lb (6,034kg).
Axleload: 14,987lb (6.8t).
Cylinders: (2) 12 x 18in (304 x 457mm).
Driving wheels: 33in (838mm).
Heating surface: 433sq ft (40m²).
Superheater: 141sq ft (13m²).
Steam pressure: 200psi (14.1kg/cm²).
Grate area: 17sq ft (1.6m²).
Fuel: 6,000lb (2.7t).
Water: 3,000 US gall (11.4m³).
Adhesive weight: 54,500lb (24.7t).
Total weight: 121,800lb (55.3t).
Length overall: 55ft 11½in (17,056mm).

In addition to showing how remote corners of the world even now depend on steam locomotives made in the USA, these four delightful little locomotives demonstrate a rare last word in the application of modern steam technology to the narrow gauge. They were supplied to the 2ft gauge Scindia State Railway of India in 1949 by Baldwin and were amongst that great firm's final steam products.

The Scindia State Railway consisted of three routes, totalling 254 miles (407km), radiating from Gwalior, the State capital; two of the three lines still survive. At Gwalior there is interchange with the Bombay to Delhi broad-gauge main line. A fleet of some 25 locomotives existed and were used indiscriminately on passenger, freight and mixed trains. Power for this system, very extensive for such a narrow gauge, had in the past come traditionally from Britain but, in spite of a shortage of dollars, the urgent need to replace older machinery led to this order being placed with a country whose steam locomotive-building capacity was not fully utilised at the time.

The result had a simplicity which would have pleased George Stephenson himself. Notable is the absence of any form of continuous brake for the train, stopping being wholly dependent on an elementary steam brake on the locomotive, plus the possibility of whistling for the guard (conductor), in his brake van (caboose) at the rear of the train, to screw down his handbrake. Even so, we see a wide firebox suitable for poor quality coal, superheater, piston valves and Walschaert valve gear.

Steam traction is totally suitable for such lines as these, of which India has many. Isolated as they are in the railroad sense, a high element of do-it-yourself in the little maintenance shops is a necessity. The possibility of ordering spares from Philadelphia has long since vanished, but steam locomotive bits and pieces are so few and so relatively simple compared with diesel equivalents, that ancient and primitive machine tools in the hands of resourceful men can produce them 'in-house' without difficulty. This continues today, even though the Scindia State Railway has long been a part of Indian Railway's Central Railway.

Incidentally, there was a second and equally famous freight-handling railroad at Gwalior. This was the one which on great

engineers in the technical sense. Thus they had the understanding to enable them to run compound locomotives with complex controls. For example, there were two reversers and two throttles.

Towards the end of World War II, even before the Allies had landed in France, the French government took steps to solve the urgent problem of replacing the large number of locomotives destroyed in the war, which would amount to 80 per cent of the fleet. Orders were placed in the USA and Canada for 1,340 2-8-2s based on (but slightly smaller than) the standard USRA light Mikado design.

For use in France the builders fitted buffers and screw couplings, squeaky high-pitched whistles, left-hand drive and oil lubrication instead of grease. Lima supplied 280, Baldwin and Alco 460 each, Montreal Loco Works 100 and Canadian Loco Co 40. The number series ran from 141R 1 to 141R 1340 and all were shipped between August 1945 and the end of 1947. Seventeen went

down with the vessel *Belpamela* which foundered in a mid-Atlantic storm, but the others survived to do great things.

Later examples of the 141Rs were more up-to-date than the first ones to be delivered. Delta cast rear trucks replaced the built-up Cole pattern, Box-pok wheels replaced spoked ones, cast locomotive beds replaced separate frames and cylinders, and roller

bearings were fitted. Many of the later locomotives were delivered as oil burners and others were converted to combat a severe shortage of coal which developed in France as reconstruction progressed.

US principles of design were totally vindicated by the excellent performance and overall economy of *les Americains* and it says enough that the 141Rs outlasted

Above: *It's 1968 and steam is still in charge in Northern France. No.141R 611 hurries a freight near Boulogne.*

compound 4-6-2s and 2-8-2s and eventually became the last mainline steam locomotives in normal service on SNCF. Several have been preserved and it is the intention that one of these should return to the USA.

occasions was laid round the Maharajah's banqueting table and its task was to serve sauces and condiments to the guests. The

rails, locomotive and the cars were mainly of solid silver and the train stopped automatically when someone lifted the lid of a dish to

partake of a delicacy! An official visitor recently had the rare privilege of seeing this remarkable line in action.

Above: *An example of US influence in India: Baldwin's clean and simple design for the Scindia State Railway.*

Niagara Class 4-8-4 New York Central Railroad (NYC), 1945

Gauge: 4ft 8½in (1,435mm).
Tractive effort: 61,570lb (27,936kg).
Axle load: 70,000lb (32t).
Cylinders: (2) 25½ x 32in (648 x 813mm).
Driving wheels: 79in (2,007mm).
Heating surface: 4,827sq ft (4.48m²).
Superheater: 2,060sq ft (191m²).
Steam pressure: 275psi (19.3kg/cm²).
Grate area: 100sq ft (9.3m²).
Fuel: 92,000lb (42t).
Water: 15,000gall (18,000 US) (82m³).
Adhesive weight: 274,000lb (124t).
Total weight: 891,000lb (405t).
Length overall: 115ft 5½in (35,192mm).

Something has already been said of the New York Central Railroad's speedway from New York to Chicago, arguably in steam days the greatest passenger railway in the world, in terms of speeds run and tonnage moved. By the 1940s these speeds and loads were beginning to be as much as the famous Hudsons could cope with and the Central's chief of motive power, Paul Kiefer, decided to move on a step. He proposed a 4-8-4 with above 30 per cent more adhesive weight and tractive effort than the 4-6-4, together with a fire grate 25 per cent bigger. His aim was a locomotive which could develop 6,000hp in the cylinders for hour after hour and could do the New York-Chicago or Chicago-New York run of 928 miles day after day without respite.

The American Locomotive Company at Schenectady, proposed what was to be the last really new design of passenger locomotive to be produced in the USA. It owed something to the Union Pacific's "800" class; dimensionally, the two designs were very close and, in addition, the design of the 14-wheel Centipede or 4-10-0 tender was certainly based on the UP one. The NYC engines had something else unusual for America, in common with the "800"s — a smooth and uncluttered appearance but with no false streamlining or air-smoothing.

Because the NYC structure gauge only allowed rolling stock to be 15ft 2in (4,623mm) tall instead of 16ft 2in (4,928mm) as on the UP, the smokestack had to be vestigial and the dome little but a manhole cover. There were other differences such as Baker's valve gear instead of Walschaert's but in general the adoption of standard American practice led to similarities.

Naturally, the foundation of the design was a cast steel integral locomotive frame — nothing else could have stood up to the punishment intended for these engines. Also, as one might expect, all axles, coupling rods and connecting rods had roller bearings. Baker's valve gear has the advantage that it has no slides, so all its moving parts could, as in this case, be fitted with needle bearings. While speaking of the valves, an interesting detail was that the edges of the valve-ports were sharp on the steam side, but slightly rounded on the exhaust side. This eased the sharpness of the blast beats, thereby evening out the draught on the fire.

Although fundamentally the same design as that fitted to the UP locos, the tender had some interesting differences. The fact

Below: *Regarded by many as the Ultimate Steam Locomotive, the last of the Niagara 4-8-4s of the New York Central Railroad.*

that the NYC was one of the very few American railroads equipped with track pans (in Great Britain water troughs) meant that less water could be carried conveniently, leaving more capacity for coal. This in its turn enabled the New York-Chicago run to be done with just one intermediate coaling, while an improved design of power-operated pick-up scoop reduced delays by allowing water to be taken at 80mph (128km/h). Special extra venting avoided bursting the tenders (there had been cases!) when some 1,600cu ft (45m³) of incompressible fluid enters the tank all in a few seconds. Incidentally, the overhang of the tank over the running gear at the rear end was to allow the engines to be turned on 100-foot turntables by reducing the wheelbase.

Allocating the number 6,000 to a locomotive whose target was that amount of horse-power as well as that number of miles run per week might seem to be tempting providence, but all was well. The prototype had the subclass designation "Sla", while the 25 production models (Nos. 6001-6025) were known as "S16" and there was also a single poppet-valve version known as "Slc" (No.5500). This greatest of steam locomotives got the classname "Niagara" and when the word is uttered, no steam man worthy of the name ever thinks of a waterfall! Both targets were

Above: *First of the production batch of NYC Niagaras, No. 6001 leaves Albany, NY, on a heavy southbound train in April 1952.*

achieved — 6,700hp on test and an average of 26,000 miles run monthly.

The original idea was that the prototype should be tested and then a production order confirmed, but before work had gone very far instructions were given for all 27 to be put in hand. This was reasonable because in fact the Niagaras were very much a standard, if slightly stretched, product of the industry, whereas what really needed attention was the ground organisation to enable the mileage target to be met. And this, of course, could not be tested until a fleet was available.

By an ordinance of the City of New York, steam locomotives were not allowed inside city limits. Trains therefore left Grand Central Station behind third-rail electric locos for Harmon, 32 miles out in the suburbs. It was here, then, and at Chicago that the Niagaras were, in their great days, kept in first-class condition for what was without doubt one of the hardest services ever demanded of steam, or for that matter, of any motive power.

World records are not achieved without extreme efforts, but excellent organisation allowed quick and thorough servicing. The

NEW YORK CENTRAL

power production part of the locomotives had to be just-so to give such a remarkable performance out on the road and to achieve this the fire was first dropped with the engine in steam. Than a gang of "hot men" in asbestos suits entered the firebox — the size of a room — and cleared tubes and flues, did any repairs required to the brick arch, grate etc. Good water treatment ensured that no scale built up in the heating surface, preventing the heat reaching the water inside the boiler. On many railways steam locomotives were allocated one "shed day" each week for these things to be done, but running the 928 miles from Harmon to Chicago or *vice versa* each night, the Niagaras needed to do a week's work in one 24-hour period.

In those days there were 12 daily trains each way just between New York and Chicago — the Chicagoan, the Advance Commodore Vanderbilt, the Commodore Vanderbilt, the Advance Empire State Express, the Empire State Express, the Lake Shore Limited, the Mohawk, the North Shore Ltd, the Pacemaker, the Water Level, the Wolverine and, greatest of all, the 16-hour Twentieth Century Limited.

Even the most fanatical steam enthusiast would admit that other factors have contributed, but nevertheless the Day of the Niagaras did mark a peak. So low have things fallen that the best time by diesel traction today on this route between New York and Chicago is 19hr 50min and there is only one train.

The Niagaras also demonstrated once again that modern well-maintained steam power could be more economical than diesel. Alas, in those days, coal supplies controlled by miners' leader John L. Lewis were less reliable than oil supplies; moreover, most of New York Central's steam power was neither modern nor well-maintained. So, having run more miles and hauled more tons in their short lives than most locomotives which run out their term to obsolescence, the Niagaras went to their long home. None has been preserved.

Above: *Smoke effects aplenty at Dunkirk, NY, as a Niagara accelerates away with a west-bound passenger, March 1952.*

Below: *No.6001 again, this time on shed at Harmon, NY, waiting its next turn of duty.*

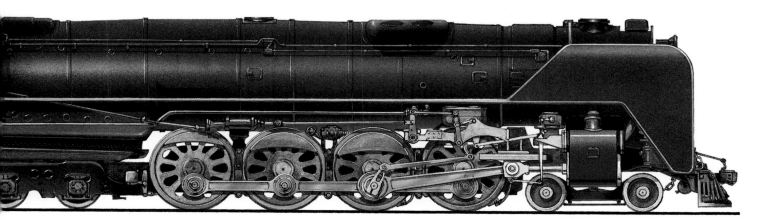

S2 6-8-6 Pennsylvania Railroad (PRR), 1944

Gauge: 4ft 8½in (1,435mm).
Tractive effort: 70,500lb (31,987kg).*
Axleload: 65,000lb (29.5t).
Driving wheels: 68in (1,727mm).
Heating surface: 3,860sq ft (359m²).
Superheater: 2,050sq ft (190m²).
Steam pressure: 310psi (21.8kg/cm²).
Grate area: 120sq ft (11.1m²).
Fuel: 85,000lb (38.6t).
Water: 19,500US gall (73.8m³).
Adhesive weight: 260,000lb (118t).
Total weight: 1,020,000lb (462.8t).
Length overall: 122ft 7¼in (37,369mm).
*In forward gear. Tractive effort in reverse is 65,000lb (29,484kg).

Steam turbines had been for so long the normal motive power for ships and electricity generation, that many locomotive designers in the 1930s reasoned 'why not try one out on a locomotive?' It is feasible to use turbines directly geared to a locomotive's wheels, and British, German and Swedish examples of this arrangement ran in normal service during that period. The Swedish examples belonged to the Grängesberg-Oxelösund Railway which had several in service hauling mineral trains. The British example was more in the public eye as it was a turbine version of the London, Midland & Scottish Railway's famous "Princess" class 4-6-2s. The 'Turbomotive' ran regularly between London and Liverpool for many years, working the fastest trains. Once any of these locomotives had gained speed, thermal efficiency was higher than with reciprocating engines, but when running slowly or starting, steam consumption was very high.

Just before World War II, the Pennsylvania Railroad entrusted Baldwin and Westinghouse jointly with construction of a locomotive of this type, but altogether bigger. Compared with the British example, the weight was 2.8 times as much, the grate area 2.7 times larger, and nominal tractive effort 1.75 times greater, but the principles of design were the same.

As a mechanism, the locomotive was simple even by the standards of normal steam locomotives, for it had no cylinders, pistons, valve gears, crossheads, connecting rods or other reciprocating parts, and the control system was also very simple. A single lever was arranged to turn on steam flow to a series of nozzles in succession until finally, at the full-open position, steam was issuing from all of them. There was a separate small turbine for reversing, normally disconnected from the main mechanism.

The main turbine was rated at 6,900hp (5,150kW), adequate for heavy trains at up to 100mph (160km/h) and this remained constantly engaged. The 1,500hp (1,120kW) reverse turbine would give sensibly the same tractive effort, but was only engaged for manoeuvring at up to 22mph (35km/h). The clutch for doing this was hydraulically operated. The main turbine was of the impulse type and had six stages. The latest technology was applied throughout with roller bearings to the coupling rods as well as the axles, and of course a cast-steel locomotive bed. The locomotive was completed in 1944, but not seriously tried until the war was won. Even then, whilst it worked well, significant and sufficient advantages over other forms of engine did not materialise.

Excepting one of the least successful entries to the Baltimore & Ohio's locomotive trials of 1829, this was the first direct-drive turbine locomotive to enter service in the USA. The 6-8-6 wheel arrangement was unique.

Right: *The direct-drive 6-8-6 steam turbine locomotive built for the Pennsylvania Railroad by a consortium of Baldwin and Westinghouse in 1944. This immensely powerful machine was successful as an experiment but not commercially.*

QR-1 4-8-4 National Railways of Mexico (NdeM), 1946

Gauge: 4ft 8½in (1,435mm).
Tractive effort: 57,000lb (25,826kg).
Axleload: 63,000lb (28.6t).
Cylinders: (2) 25 x 30in (635 x 762mm).
Driving wheels: 70in (1,778mm).
Heating surface: 4,185sq ft (389m²).
Superheater: 1,721sq ft (160m²).
Steam pressure: 250psi (17.6kg/cm²).
Grate area: 77.3sq ft (7.2m²).
Fuel (oil): 6,000US gall (22.7m³).
Water: 15,000US gall (56.8m²).
Adhesive weight: 240,000lb (108.9t).
Total weight: 632,000lb (286.8t).
Length overall: 98ft 11in (30,150mm).

It is remarkable that in North America, from southern Mexico to Hudson Bay and even Alaska, virtually any freight car can couple to another. Cars can also run to any destination over some quarter-of-a-million miles of railroad. Of the partners in the world's greatest railroad union, Canada and the USA share much besides a common language; this leaves Mexico which shares little with the other two save track gauge, couplers and braking systems.

The first railway in Mexico was British-owned and followed Cortez's trail of conquest from the port of Vera Cruz to Mexico City. It involved a climb of 7,350ft in its 264-mile (425km) length and took 28 years to build from 1845 to

Right: *A Class QR-1 4-8-4 of the Mexican National Railways taking water at Esobedo, New Mexico, July 1966.*

Above: *A freight train passes Lecharia, Mexico, in March 1966 hauled by 4-8-4 No.3036, built by Baldwin in 1946.*

Right: *A QR-1 4-8-4 moves on to the turntable at the Valle de Mexico depot at Mexico City, July 1964.*

1873. Shortly after its completion, President Diaz began a 35-year period of office and his encouragement during that time led to a forty-fold increase in route length to substantially the same 12,500 miles (20,000km) as exists today. This huge programme was carried through in spite of severe restrictions on foreign ownership or the appointment of foreign officials.

Even so, US equipment and practices have been dominant in Mexico for many years. Steam locomotives followed very closely trends set across the border and indeed many were acquired second-hand from various US railroads which were modernising their fleets. Long after the previous owners had gone over to diesel, such treasures as Florida East Coast 4-8-2s, Nickel Plate 2-8-2s and Illinois Central 4-6-0s could be found at work.

Of the locomotives built new for the National Railways of Mexico

(NdeM), pride of place must go to a batch of 32 4-8-4s constructed during 1946 at the American Locomotive Co's works in Schenectady. Their power and size was small in comparison with 4-8-4s built for home use in the USA, but restrictions of weight and size south of the border led to these limitations. Standard US practice with oil firing, two cylinders, Walschaert valve gear, a wide firebox and few frills made for a reliable product for a railroad system which lacked the resources to maintain anything too complex.

Unlike contemporary steam power built at that time for US railroads, the "QR-1s" were allowed to live out long lives, it being possible to find them at work as recently as 1966. There is no record of any being preserved in Mexico, but one (No.3028) has returned for restoration at its birthplace in New York state.

PA Series A1A-A1A
American Locomotive Company (Alco), 1946

Type: Diesel-electric express passenger locomotive; "A" units with cab, "B" units without.
Gauge: 4ft 8½in (1,435mm).
Propulsion: One Alco 244 2,000hp (1,490kW) 16-cylinder turbocharged four-stroke Vee engine and gearbox, supplying four nose-suspended traction motors geared to the end axles of the bogies.
Weight: 204,000lb (92.6t) adhesive, 306,000lb (138.8t) total.
Max. axleload: 51,000lb (23.1t).
Overall length: "A" unit 65ft 8in (20,015mm), "B" unit 63ft 6in (19,350mm).
Tractive effort: 51,000lb (227kN).
Max. speed: 80mph (129km/h), 90mph (145km/h), 100mph (160km/h), or 117mph (188km/h) according to gear ratio fitted.

The American Locomotive Company was mainly a builder of steam locomotives until the end of World War II, but it had already achieved considerable success with diesel shunters (switchers), and in 1940 had produced a 2,000hp (1,490kW) twin-engine passenger locomotive, of which 78 were built before construction ceased during the war. In the following year Alco produced a 1,500hp (1,120kW) road-switcher, but the railroads were not yet accustomed to the idea of a locomotive which could combine two functions. All these locomotives had engines made by specialist firms, but in 1944 Alco produced its own engine, designated the 244, the last two digits indicating the year in which it first ran. It was a turbocharged Vee engine made in two versions, one with 12-cylinders producing 1,500hp (1,200kW) and the other 16 cylinders giving 2,000hp (1,490kW).

With these two engines Alco launched three models in 1945, a 1,500hp "Bo-Bo combination switching locomotive" (in the terminology of the day), a 1,500hp road freight locomotive, and a 2,000hp A1A-A1A passenger locomotive. The first of these was a hood unit, and the others were "cab" or "carbody" units. All three had GE electrical equipment and were marketed as Alco-GE brand. Great emphasis was laid on the fact that 98 per cent of the electrical parts and 96 per cent of the mechanical parts were interchangeable between the three types.

The freight locomotives, the "FA" cab units and the "FB" booster units—note that "cab" is used to denote a locomotive with a driver's (engineer's) cab as well as any locomotive with a totally enclosed body—appeared at the end of 1945, and the passenger locomotives, the "PA" and "PB" series, in September 1946. With high cab windows and a projecting bonnet, both types bore a resemblance to existing EMD and Baldwin designs, but the front and the roof were flatter. The bonnet of the "PA" was quite distinctive. The first units were for the Santa Fe and were finished in a remarkable livery of red, orange and silver, which earned them the nickname of "warbonnets". The three-axle trucks were unusually long, and these combined with the long bonnets to give an appearance of great length, although in fact the locomotives were 5ft (1,525mm) shorter than the corresponding EMD "E" type.

Over the next three years a total of 170 A units and 40 B units were sold, designated "PA1" and "PB1". There was then a pause in production until the "PA2" and "PB2" series appeared in 1950 with the engine uprated to 2,250hp (1,680kW). Finally there came the third version, "PA3" and "PB3", also with the 2,250hp engine, but with a number of detail changes. The last of these was built in 1953, and although a 2,400hp (1,790kW) version was offered, none was built. The day of the carbody was over, and passenger trains were in decline. There was also an export model, which looked very similar but was usually a Co-Co. Some of these were built by Alco licencees in the country concerned.

Above: *Nickel Plate PA/PB unit hurries an eastbound train through Dunkirk, NY, in the early days of 1952.*

Below: *Atchison, Topeka & Santa Fe PA-series A1A-A1A diesel-electric locomotive No.51 supplied by the American Locomotive Co. in 1946.*

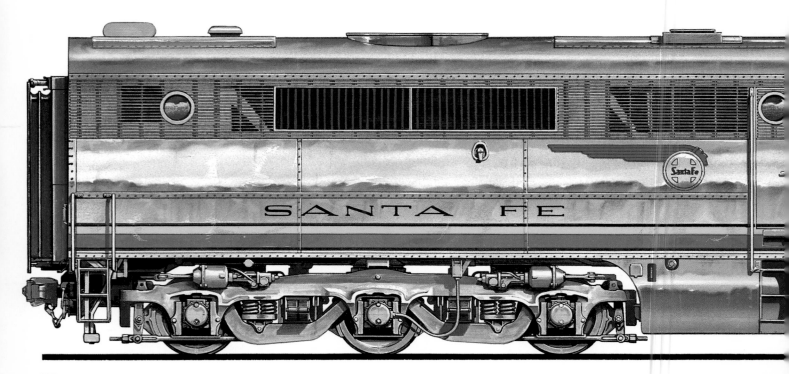

The 244 engine had a number of troubles, particularly the 2,000hp version when used intensively on long-distance passenger trains. The "PA" locomotives had several protective devices to prevent damage to the electrical equipment, and at times these were over-protective, giving false warnings. Compared with their EMD competitors, the Alco "PAs" had the simplicity of one engine, whereas the EMD passenger units had two, but the "PAs" never equalled the reliability of the EMD locomotives. Although 16 roads bought them, and used them on the best passenger trains, they were usually outnumbered by EMD units. As passenger traffic declined, the "PAs" were either withdrawn from service or transferred to freight work, often with altered gear ratios. The large GE traction motors could take a heavy overload, and were well suited to freight work. A few "PAs" were re-engined with EMD 1,750hp (1,305kW) engines, but none received the later Alco 251 engine.

The last four "PAs" ended their days in Mexico, having been leased by the Delaware & Hudson to the National Railways (NdeM) in 1978. The "FA" freight series, by contrast, of which a total of 1,072 were built, were still active in the 1980s in the United States, Canada and Mexico.

Above right: *A 6,000hp three-unit loco formed of Alco PA, PB and PA units climbing to the summit of the Cajon Pass, California, with a Santa Fe train bound for Los Angeles.*

Right: *Last of the PAs ending their days far from home. Three of the four leased to the National Railways of Mexico by D&H on shed at San Luis Potosi in January 1979.*

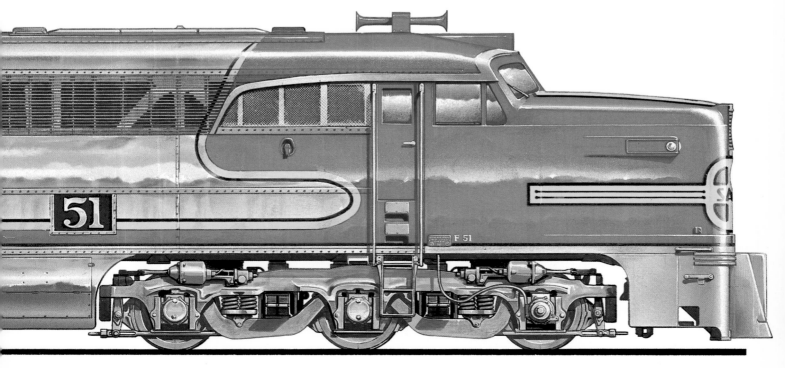

M-1 2-1C₀-2-1C₀-B₀ Chesapeake & Ohio Railway (C&O), 1947

Type: Steam turbo-electric express passenger locomotive.
Gauge: 4ft 8½in (1,435mm).
Propulsion: Coal-fired fire-tube boiler supplying steam at 310psi (21.8kg/cm²) to a 6,000hp (4,475kW) turbine coupled to two generators, providing current for eight axle-hung motors.
Weight: 508,032lb (230.5t) adhesive, 1,233,970lb (560t) total*.
Max. axleload: 63,475lb (28.8t).
Tractive effort: 98,000lb (436kN).
Overall length: 154ft 1in (46,965mm).
Max. speed: 100mph (160km/h).
*Including tender

Almost since its earliest constituent, the James River Company, got its charter and had George Washington himself as President, the Chessie (as the Chesapeake & Ohio RR has long been affectionately known) has had coal for its life-blood. Small wonder then that it resisted a change to diesel oil as a fuel.

Most electric current is generated by steam-driven turbines and in 1945 there seemed no good reason why locomotives should not with advantage be powered that way. Accordingly, in that year Chessie ordered from Westinghouse Electric and the Baldwin Locomotive Works, three of what were to become the heaviest and largest steam loco ever built.

The intention was to use the

W1 B₀-D₀-D₀-B₀ Great Northern Railway (GN), 1947

Type: Mixed-traffic electric locomotive for mountain grades.
Gauge: 4ft 8½in (1,435mm).
Propulsion: Alternating current at 11,500V 25Hz, fed via overhead catenary to two motor-generator sets supplying direct current to twelve 275hp (205kW) nose-suspended traction motors geared to the axles.
Weight: 527,000lb (239t).
Max. axleload: 43,917lb (20t).
Overall length: 101ft 0in (30,785mm).
Tractive effort: 180,000lb (900kN).
Max. speed: 65mph (104km/h).

The fourth great transcontinental railroad to reach the West Coast of the USA was the Great Northern Railway, built by famed railroad tycoon James J. Hill. The "Big G" crossed the Cascade mountains beneath the Stevens Pass, named after GN's Chief Engineer. After seven years of trouble with a temporary alignment involving 4 per cent grades, the first 2.6 mile (4.2km) Cascade tunnel opened in 1900. In 1909, working through the tunnel was electrified on the three-phase system, the only example in North America. In 1927, three-phase was abandoned and single-phase electrification installed; this time the approach ramps were included, as well as a new Cascade tunnel, at 7.8 miles (12.5km) the longest railway tunnel in America, eliminating the most exposed part

of the route. The scheme covered 73 miles (117km) from Wenatchee to Skykomish, Washington State.

In its principles, this electrification was far ahead of its time, for the single-phase current was converted to dc for use in the traction motors of the locomotives. Of course, solid-state devices for this purpose were still in the future and rotary convertor sets, consisting of synchronous motors coupled to dc generators, had to be used. The technology had been placed in two locomotives constructed in of all places the Ford Motor Works, but equipped electrically by Westinghouse for use on a railroad (the Detroit, Toledo & Ironton) that Henry Ford owned. The GN electrification had four "Y1" 1-C-C-1s and twelve

turbines on a proposed high-speed streamliner to run between Washington and Cincinnati. Mountainous terrain en route gave advantages to a locomotive with a high proportion of its axles powered and this could be arranged to order on any locomotive with electric transmission. Incidentally, the driven axles on the "M-1s" were not the obvious ones; three axles out of the four on each of the central rigid trucks, plus both axles of the rear guiding truck,

Left: *M-1 No.501 at speed with "The Sportsman", Waynesboro, Virginia, July 1948.*

Below: *Striking livery and finish accentuated the huge proportions of the M-1s.*

were the ones motored. The locomotive-type boiler with a grate area of 112sq ft (10.4m²) was placed so that the firebox was at the leading end, the opposite of normal practice, while right at the front of the engine was a bunker

holding some 27t of coal. The tender was for water only, no condenser being provided.

The "M-1s" were expensive to run and maintain, offering no serious competition to conventional steam, let alone diesel trac-

Above: *Largest of all the giant steamers, the hybrid turbo-electric Class M-1 of C&O.*

tion. Al three were scrapped in the early 1950s after only a few years' service.

Left: *Only two of the huge W1 class electrics were built; 3,300hp was a very modest output for such bulky units.*

"Z1" 1-D-1s; the latter again heralded the future of US railroading by virtue of their multiple-unit capability. Put another way, they were building blocks from which locomotives of any desired power could be assembled.

The final fling of this little system was purchase of the very large "W1" class, of which two examples were constructed by General Electric in 1947. Modest power, combined with the huge tractive effort possible with all axles motored, was appropriate to a locomotive confined to the mountains. They could be run in multiple both with each other and with the "Y1s" and "Z1s". As with all the GN electric fleet, regenerative braking of trains on the down grades could provide a proportion of the current needed for other trains climbing. The electrification was totally successful but even so, in 1956, after new ventilating equipment had been installed in the second Cascade tunnel, diesels took over. One "W1" was rebuilt as a gas-turbine locomotive for the Union Pacific Railroad, but all the others were scrapped.

Left: *A Class W1 hauls an eastbound freight at Cascade tunnel, Washington State.*

Right: *GN No.5019 in typical Cascade surroundings.*

BL2 B₀-B₀ Bangor & Aroostook Railroad (BAR), 1949

Type: Diesel-electric locomotive originally intended for passenger and freight traffic on branch lines but now used for freight traffic generally.
Gauge: 4ft 8½in (1,435mm).
Propulsion: Type 567B 16-cylinder 1,500hp (130kW) two-stroke diesel engine and generator supplying current to four traction motors geared to the axles.
Weight: 217,600lb (99t).
Max. axleload: 54,000lb (24.7t).
Tractive effort: 54,420lb (241kN).
Overall length: 57ft 8in (17,575mm).
Max. speed: 70mph (112km/h).

Shortly before General Motors Electric-Motive Division swept the board with their "GP7" road-switcher, they had put on the market a similar product but very differently packaged. This was the "BL2" which never reached 60 units sold, whilst "GP7" sales were counted in thousands. One reason perhaps was that BL stood for 'Branch Line', and branch line was a naughty word in the railroad industry at the time, being synonymous with accounts written in red ink.

These controversial units had the same 567B engine and running gear as the contemporary best-selling "F3" cab unit. The shape of the bodywork concealed the trusses upon which the unit's strength depended, while at the same time it allowed good visibility in both directions from the cab. A steam boiler for heating and cooling passenger trains was an optional extra, but it found few takers. Incidentally, there was a "BL1" which was a single demonstrator unit completed in February 1948, but this was no different from the "BL2" production series.

Because the machinery was the same as the "F"-series units, and because the "BLs" could be run in multiple with other units, there were no difficulties in keeping them running or finding them work. So most lived out normal lives, being in due time traded-in for the latest model in true automobile fashion. Many of their parts could then be what EMD called 're-manufactured' for resale.

Other "BL2s" have shown quite extraordinary powers of survival, such as a clutch which even today protects some of the operations of another surprising survivor, the 463-mile (746km) Bangor & Aroostook Railroad in north-eastern Maine, close to the Canadian (New Brunswick) border. The BAR once ran its romantically-named "Potatoland Special"

Above: *At North Maine Junction in 1980, a 30-year-old diesel-electric displays some smart new paintwork.*

Right: *Bangor & Aroostook veteran Electro-Motive BL2 "Branch Line" pattern diesel-electric locomotive at Oakfield, Maine in July 1980.*

complete with sleeping and buffet cars along the length of its well-maintained main line. Nowadays it's freight-only, still independent and very much a branch line in its own right. And long may it continue to be so.

Little Joe 2-D₀-D₀-2 Soviet Railways (SZD), 1947

Type: Heavy duty mixed traffic electric locomotive.
Gauge: 5ft 0in (1,524mm).
Propulsion: Direct current at 3,000V fed via overhead catenaries to eight 470hp (350kW) traction motors geared to the main axles.
Weight: 440,800lb (200t) adhesive, 535,572lb (243t) total.
Max. axleload: 55,100lb (25t).
Tractive effort: 110,750lb (490kN).
Overall length: 88ft 10in (27,076mm).
Max. speed: 70mph (112km/h).

Before the 'Cold War' between West and East began in the late-1940s, General Electric had begun work on an order for 20 giant 3,300V dc 2-Do-Do-2 electric locomotives. These were intended for the Soviet Union, then involved in the first stages of implementing Lenin's own pet project for railroad electrification on an immense nation-wide scale. When the time came for delivery, however, an embargo existed and for a time the locomotives which had been completed languished at the GE works. Later, the whole order was completed and offered for sale, the later units having been finished to standard

Right: *Chicago; Milwaukee St Paul & Pacific "Little Joe" No.E20 at Deer Lodge, Montana, in 1952.*

Above left: *2-Do-Do-2 "Little Joe" originally destined for the Soviet Union waits for an assignment under the 3,000v catenaries of the Milwaukee Road's electrification.*

Above: *The fierce-looking front end of a not-so-little "Little Joe" at Deer Lodge, Montana, in May 1962. Electric working began here in 1915 and ended in 1974.*

gauge (1,435mm) instead of the 5ft (1,524mm) gauge used in the Soviet Union.

The obvious buyer was Chicago, Milwaukee, St Paul & Pacific which used the same voltage and current and had not acquired any new locomotives for over 20 years. After a trial of a completed unit, this railroad in 1948 made an offer to purchase all 20, but the sum offered was considered too low. Before long, three were bought by the interurban-cum-freight railroad Chicago, South Shore & South Bend and five (involving conversion to 5ft 3in

(1,600mm gauge), went to the Paulista Railway of Brazil.

Eventually in 1950, the remainder—now blessed with the name "Little Joes" after the unlamented ruler of the country for which they were built—did reach the Milwaukee's electrified divisions. During a distinguished 24-year career amongst the mountains of the north-west, the "Little Joes" already provided with regenerative braking, were modified to run in multiple even with diesel-electrics. By the mid-1960s, they were sole electric power to run regularly over the electrified sections, normally acting

as helpers in the mountains. Alas, in 1972 the Milwaukee ceased using electric traction and the "Little Joes" were retired.

The "Little Joes" which were converted to broad gauge and for the vacuum-brake, side-buffer and screw-coupling environment in Brazil were luckier. All five are still running on the Paulista

Railway's successor FEPASA (Sao Paulo State Railway) but have now reverted to US-style braking and coupling arrangements. The three which went to the South Shore were modified to run on that system's 1,500V dc current and lived long lives, although all have now been retired.

Y6b 2-8-8-2 Norfolk & Western Railway (N&W), 1948

Gauge: 4ft 8½in (1,435mm).
Tractive effort: 152,206lb (69,059kg).
Axleload: 75,418lb (34.2t).
Cylinders, HP: (2) 25 x 32in (635 x 812mm).
Cylinders, LP: (2) 29 x 32in (736 x 812mm).
Driving wheels: 58in (1,473mm).
Heating surface: 5,647sq ft (525m²).
Superheater: 1,478sq ft (137m²).
Steam pressure: 300psi (21.1kg/cm²).
Grate area: 106sq ft (9.8m²).
Fuel: 60,000lb (27.2t).
Water: 22,000 US gall (83.3m³).
Adhesive weight: 548,500lb (248.9t).
Total weight: 990,100lb (449.2t).
Length overall: 114ft 11in (35,026mm).

When people talk of the great days of steam, Norfolk & Western is a name that is often heard. Already we have read here of the road's superb passenger engines, but there were only a handful of them. Because of what was usual elsewhere 40 years ago, unbelievers might wonder if there was not a different story to tell regarding the way N&W went about their proper business, that is hauling coal from pits to port. But they would be wrong.

After gaining experience—some of it traumatic—with other people's Mallets for this work, Norfolk & Western in 1918 had built by their own shops at Roanoke, Virginia, a really successful coal-mover in the form of a 2-8-8-2 compound articulated steam locomotive. This "Y2" class received wholesale recognition because, later the same

Above: *N&W Class Y6b No. 172 on a westbound freight at Shaffers Crossing, Roanoke, Va.*

Below: *Final version of the extensive Y class of 2-8-8-2s, the Y6b—last in the long line of US heavy steam power.*

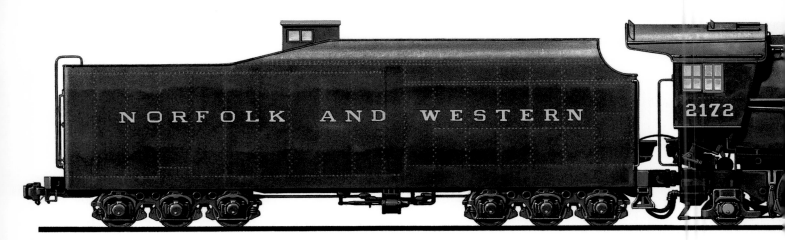

L-2a Class 4-6-4 Chesapeake & Ohio Railway (C&O), 1948

Gauge: 4ft 8½in (1,435mm).
Tractive effort: 52,1000lb (23,639kg).
Axle load: 73,500lb (33.5t).
Cylinders: (2) 25 x 30in (635 x 762mm).
Driving wheels: 78in (1,981mm).
Heating surface: 4,233sq ft (393m²).
Superheater: 1,810sq ft (168m²).
Steam pressure: 255psi (17.9kg/cm²).
Grate area: 90sq ft (8.4m²).
Fuel: 60,000lb (27.5t).
Water: 17,500gall (21,000 US) (80m³).
Adhesive weight: 219,500lb (100t).
Total weight: 839,000lb (381t).
Length overall: 108ft 0in (32,918mm).

It was a case of "last orders please" when in 1947 the Chesapeake & Ohio Railway went to Baldwin of Philadelphia for five 4-6-4s and to the Lima Locomotive Co of Lima, Ohio, for five 4-8-4s. They were to be the last steam express passenger locomotives supplied for home use by any of the big USA constructors, although naturally neither the customer nor the builders realised it at the time.

The C&O divided its routes into mountain and plains divisions and the eight-coupled engines were for the former, the six-coupled ones for the latter. There was, therefore, scope for the 4-6-4s, both north-west of the Allegheny mountains on the routes to Louisville, Cincinnati, Chicago and Detroit, as well as south-east of them in the directions of Washington and Richmond, Virginia.

In 1947 a man called Robert R. Young was in charge at C&O headquarters at Richmond and he believed the passenger train had a future. The Chessie ran through the big coalfields and at that time hauled more coal than any other railroad. It was therefore unthinkable that anything but coal-burning power should be used. Amongst his plans was one for a daytime streamline service actually to be known as The Chessie—and three steam-turbine locomotives with electric drive and 16 driving wheels were built in 1947-48 to haul it on the main stem and over the mountains. Conventional steam was to haul connecting portions and provide back-up. Alas, those whose concept it was had thrown away the steam locomotive's best card, that is simplicity, and in a short two years the turbo-electrics (Class "M-1", Nos.500-502) had been scrapped as hopelessly uneconomic.

In the meantime the whole C&O streamline project had been scrapped, but not before some older 4-6-2s (the "F-19" class) had been converted into stream-lined 4-6-4s to handle the new train over part of its route. Furthermore, in the grand manner of a great and prosperous railroad, C&O considered hand-me-downs not be good enough for a prestige train and so had ordered these "L-2a" Hudsons, intending them to be streamlined. Running numbers were 310 to 314 and fortunately they were as trouble-free as the turbines had been troublesome.

On various important counts the 4-6-4s were the top six-coupled locomotives of the world—in engine weight, at 443,000lb (201t), 7½ per cent above those of the nearest rival, Santa Fe. In tractive effort, both with and without their booster in action, the latter worth 14,200lb

year, the United States Railroad Administration based their standard 2-8-8-2 on this excellent design. N&W were allocated 50 by USRA, who were then running the nation's railroads. The new locomotives, classified "Y3", came from Alco and Baldwin. In 1923 they were augmented by 30 more, designated "Y3a" and a further 10 in 1927, Class "Y4". The "Y4s" were the last new steam locomotives not to be built by N&W at Roanoke; they came from Alco's Richmond Works.

N&W policy was to move forward slowly, not forgetting to consolidate the gains already made. So the successive improvements made between the "Y2", "Y3", "Y3a" and "Y4" classes were modest. For example, provision of feed-water heaters began with the "Y3as", but earlier locomotives were altered to bring them into line so that operationally the group of classes could be regarded as one.

In 1930 the first of an enlarged version, Class "Y5", was produced. Thus was founded a dynasty of coal-moving and coal-consuming power which would bring the science of steam locomotive operation to a never-to-be-repeated peak. Over the next 22 years modern developments were successively introduced through classes "Y6", "Y6a" and "Y6b" and, as before, the earlier locomotives were rebuilt to bring them into line so that the fleet was kept uniformly up-to-date. The last "Y6b", completed in 1952, was the last main-line steam locomotive to be built in the USA.

This time, some of the improvements passed on were not so minor. The introduction of cast-steel locomotive beds with integrally-cast cylinders on the "Y6s" was followed by rebuilding of the "Y5s" to match. The old "Y5" frames were then passed on to the "Y3"/"Y4" group, by now relegated to local mine runs. One problem with the older Mallets was that they tended to choke themselves with the large volume of low-pressure steam because of inadequately-sized valves, ports, passageways and pipes. This was corrected in the "Y5" design and these locomotives now had the freedom to run and pull at speeds up to 50mph (80km/h), which can be considered an exceptional figure for a compound Mallet.

Roller bearings came on the "Y6s" of 1936, and with the "Y6bs" of 1948 was booster equipment for extra power, whereby a modicum of live steam, controlled by a reducing valve, could be introduced to the low-pressure cylinders while still running as a compound. It was quite separate from the conventional simpling valve used for starting. An interesting feature was the coupling of auxiliary tenders behind locomotives in order to reduce the number of water stops.

It says enough of the efficiency of these engines that following a line relocation they displaced in 1948 N&W's pioneer electrification in the Allegheny Mountains. In due time though, Norfolk & Western became the only railroad which saw a long-term future for steam and this position became untenable in the later 1950s. With reluctance, then, the Company was forced to follow the crowd and the last "Y6" set out on the last mine run in the month of April 1960. One is preserved in the National Museum of Transportation at St Louis.

Below: *Steam still supreme in 1951, Class Y6b No.2181.*

(6,443kg) of thrust, and adhesive weight, the figures are records. The massive qualities of C&O track are illustrated by the fact that their adhesive weight is also unmatched elsewhere.

Technically the engines represented the final degree of sophistication of the American steam locomotive that came from nearly 120 years of steady development of practice and details upon the original principles. The "L-2a" class was developed

Above: *Chessie's last express passenger type, Class L-2a.*

from the eight "L-2" class 4-6-4s of 1941 (Nos.300-307) and differed from them mainly in having Franklin's system of rotary-cam poppet valves instead of more conventional Baker's gear and piston valves. These locomotives also were notable for having unusually clean lines. The C&O once even had liked to hang a pair of air-pumps in the most prominent possible position on the smokebox door; now even the headlight was cleared away and mounted above the pilot beam.

The advantages of poppet valves have been mentioned elsewhere in this narrative, as have the problems involved in their maintenance. It would appear, though, as if manufacturers on both sides of the Atlantic had begun in this respect to offer a viable product—now that it was just too late to affect the outcome of steam's struggle for survival.

By 1953 Chessie's passenger service had become 100 per cent dieselised.

Centipede 2-D₀-D₀-2 Seaboard Air Line (SAL), 1945

Type: Diesel-electric locomotive for express passenger trains.
Gauge: 4ft 8½in (1,435mm).
Propulsion: Two Baldwin Model 608SC eight-cylinder 1,500hp (1,120kW) four-stroke diesel engines and Westinghouse generators supplying current to eight nose-suspended traction motors geared to the main axles.
Weight: 409,000lb (186t) adhesive, 593,700lb (269t) total.
Max. axleload: 51,200lb (23.25t).
Tractive effort: 102,250lb (46,380kg).
Overall length: 91ft 6in (27,889mm).
Max. speed: 93½mph (150km/h).

Baldwin Locomotive Works, like some other famous steam locomotive builders, was slow to recognise that the main-line or road diesel posed a genuine threat to the future of steam. In 1939 the company launched a range of diesel shunters designed by a new diesel group which was almost independent of the firm's steam designers. One of this group, a Swiss named Max Essl, took out some patents for road diesels which were to be powered by small Vee-type engines mounted athwartships, the num-

ber of engines being varied to suit the power output required. It was with a demonstration locomotive built to one of Essl's patents that BLW eventually entered the road diesel field.

The unit was of the 2-DoDo-2 layout, although the maker designated it 4-8-8-4 in steam terminology. There were two massive frames, each with four rigid motored axles and an end truck to lead the unit into curves. The frames were hinged together in the manner of a Mallet steam locomotive. Compared with con-

temporary conventional diesels it had a lower axleload and took more kindly to rough track. It was intended to have eight engines giving a total power of 6,000hp, in token of which it was numbered 6000. The unit was designed to reach 120mph (193km/h), and to haul 14 80-ton (72.6-t) cars at 100mph (160km/h). The concentration of so much power in one unit was attractive because, amongst other reasons, there was uncertainty as to whether the labour unions would demand an engine crew on each unit of a

Above: *A pair of Pennsylvania Railroad Baldwin "Centipede" diesel-electric 2-Do-Do-2 units at Harrisburg, Pa, in May 1952.*

multiple-unit "lash-up". Wartime restrictions delayed completion of the locomotive, but eventually in 1943 it was able to make some successful trial runs fitted with four engines.

By this time the firm's accountants had totalled the cost of the unit and decided that they could not hope to compete pricewise with a conventional double-bogie

RF16 'Shark-nose' B₀-B₀ Baldwin Locomotive Works (BLW), 1949

Type: Diesel-electric freight locomotive.
Gauge: 4ft 8½in (1,435mm).
Propulsion: Baldwin Model 608A eight-cylinder 1,600hp (1,194kW) four-stroke diesel engine and Westinghouse generator supplying current to four nose-suspended traction motors geared to the axles.
Weight: 248,000lb (112.5t) adhesive and total.
Max. axleload: 62,000lb (28t).
Overall length: 54ft 11in (16,739mm).
Tractive effort: 73,750lb (33,462kg).
Max. speed: 70mph (113km/h).

The Baldwin Locomotive Works, in conjunction with the Westinghouse Company, kept trying for a number of years in the diesel-electric age to regain the position held for so long in steam days, of being the world's largest producer of locomotives.

As we have seen, the earliest offerings in this direction were exotic beasts such as the 'Centipede' diesels (described above) which were not wholly successful. But by 1949 satisfactory units were on the market and found takers amongst several of the larger eastern railroads. The earliest of these were EMD look-alikes, except for the larger front windows which earned them the nick-name 'baby-face'.

When production got under way, the appearance was changed

to what was described as 'shark-nose' outline. As with the General Motors range, there were passenger A1A-A1A and freight Bo-Bo units offered in both cab and booster forms. The shape of the front end was based on that of the Pennsylvania Railroad's "T1" class 4-4-4-4 steam locomotives. In fact, Pennsy was the first and only customer for the A1A-A1A 'shark-nose' passenger sets, taking 18 cab and 9 booster units in 1948. These were known respectively as models "DR-6-4-20" and "DR-6-4-20B", meaning that they were Diesel Road Units with 6 axles, 4 of which were driven, 2,000hp and B if Booster. To give this power, two 6-cylinder engines were used.

The freight units were at first classified "DR-4-4-15" and

"DR-4-4-15B" and 105 were sold between 1947 and 1950. The last 68 of these (34 cabs, 34 boosters) were shark-nose style and went to the Pennsylvania Railroad. The model "RF-16" (Road Freight, 1600hp) appeared in 1950, and 160 (including 50 boosters) were sold between then and 1953 to the New York Central, Pennsylvania, Baltimore & Ohio and Monongahela, Delaware and Hudson railroads. At last Baldwin had a rugged, reliable and saleable product, but it was to no avail, for there were no further takers. It says enough that locomotive production at what had now become the Baldwin-Lima-Hamilton corporation ceased in 1956 after 120 years.

Baldwin used the De La Vergne marine diesel engine for loco-

Above: *A Pennsylvania RR loco formed from three "Shark-nose" units at Cresson, Pa, May 1949.*

Right: *Baldwin "Shark-nose" unit as operated by the Delaware & Hudson Railway, 1977.*

motives. This differed greatly from the General Motors model 567 engines, being four-stroke instead of two-stroke. It also revolved at only three-quarters of the speed and had 12¾ x 15½in (324 x 394mm) cylinders instead of 8½ x 10in (216 x 254mm). Unlike those of other manufacturers, Baldwin diesels would not work in multiple with any except their own kind. This kept the sets neat, but aesthetic considerations do not play a part in the economical movement of freight trains!

diesel. Furthermore, agreement by the unions that only the leading unit of a "lash-up" need have a crew reduced the interest in large diesels, and No.6000 was laid aside, never having become more than "3000". BLW then turned to production of more conventional road diesels.

In 1945 Seaboard Air Line was troubled with EMD diesels damaging the track on curves at high speed, and this prompted Baldwin to rescue the big locomotive from the scrap line and rebuild it with two 1,500hp engines of a new design; it was designated 4-8-8-4 "1500/2 DE1". Seaboard bought the locomotive in December 1945 and was sufficiently impressed to order 13 more. In the meantime two other roads, which were already buying BLW A1A-A1A diesels, also placed orders for the 4-8-8-4. Pennsylvania Railroad was attracted by the high power, and ordered 12 double units to work back-to-back. Nacionales de Mexico was interested both in the high power and in the ability to run fast on indifferent track; they ordered a double unit, but later cancelled. BLW completed this pair as a demonstrator, but it won them no more orders; the conventional layout prevailed.

Delivery of these orders was

delayed by strikes at BLW's Eddystone plant and at suppliers' works, so delivery was slow by BLW standards; 53 units were delivered between March 1947 and July 1948.

Despite the intention that the locomotives should work express passenger trains, they all moved fairly quickly to freight work. At their best they were good, but all BLW road diesels suffered from the firm's late entry into this field, and much of the detail design was troublesome, particularly pipework. The engines also gave

trouble. The NdeM locomotives were sent back to the maker in 1953 for rebuilding, and in their improved condition some of them remained in service until 1971. Their US counterparts spent much of their time on helper (banking) duties, where their lack of dynamic (rheostatic) braking and inability to work in multiple with other types was little of a disadvantage, and their unusually high starting tractive effort could be exploited. The Seaboard locomotives were withdrawn by 1961 and all the

Above: *Intended for express passenger trains, Seaboard Air Line's No.4500 hauls freight. The original design was referred to as a 4-8-8-4.*

Pennsy units were withdrawn in 1962. By this time conventional diesels had reached 3,000hp.

Although technically unsatisfactory there was no doubt that the big Baldwin diesels were impressive, if only for the densely-packed wheels, which earned them their unofficial nickname of "Centipede."

S-3 2-8-4 Nickel Plate (NKP), 1949

Gauge: 4ft 8½in (1,435mm).
Tractive effort: 64,100lb (29,083kg).
Axleload: 73,158lb (33.2t).
Cylinders: (2) 25 x 34in (635 x 863mm).
Driving wheels: 69in (1,752mm).
Heating surface: 4,772sq ft (443m²).
Superheater: 1,932sq ft (179m²).
Steam pressure: 245psi (17.2kg/cm²).
Grate area: 90.3sq ft (8.4m²).
Fuel: 44,000lb (20t).
Water: 22,000 US gall (83.4m²).
Adhesive weight: 266,030lb (120.7t).
Total weight: 808,810lb (367t).
Length overall: 99ft 1¼in (30,206mm).

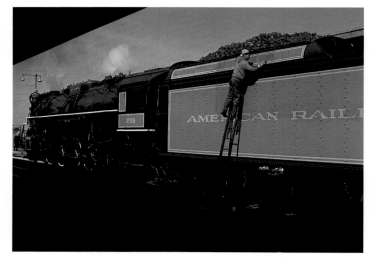

The Nickel Plate Road—in law the New York, Chicago & St Louis—never got near to New York, but it sent out tentacles from its Cleveland, Ohio, headquarters to Buffalo and Peoria as well as to the two other cities in its title. There was, too, a healthy absence of unremunerative branches. In the end, though, it was one of those small but efficient railroads that are easy meat for the carnivores of the industry, and so it was no surprise when in 1964 it was eaten by an expanding Norfolk & Western, now itself absorbed into mega-railroad Norfolk Southern.

The story begins 50 years ago

Above: *Gorgeous blue and black livery for the preserved NKP Class S-3 No.759, one of six that escaped the blowtorch.*

when NKP was in bad trouble with huge sums owing and due for repayment. The traffic was there but the problem was how to haul it fast and economically over generally fairly level but largely single-track routes. Big, fast trains were hauled by a fleet of excellent USRA light 2-8-2s, but it was considered that a more powerful 2-8-4 with larger firebox carried by a two-axle rear truck could manage bigger and faster ones.

In 1934 thought became reality with delivery of 15 Class "S" 2-8-4s Nos. 700-714 from Alco. Compared with the Mikados, the grate area had increased by 35 per cent, while tractive effort at starting (with booster in operation on the 2-8-2s) was sensibly the same. In addition to such modern features as cast-steel locomotive beds, they had large tenders which precluded the need to take coal or water between crew-change points. The 25 "S-1" 2-8-4s which followed from Lima in 1942-43 were generally similar, but the 1944 batch of 30 had roller bearings to the main axles, as well as other minor improvements. Numbering in the 700 series followed in chronological order.

The easy-to-maintain Berkshires—the name which was

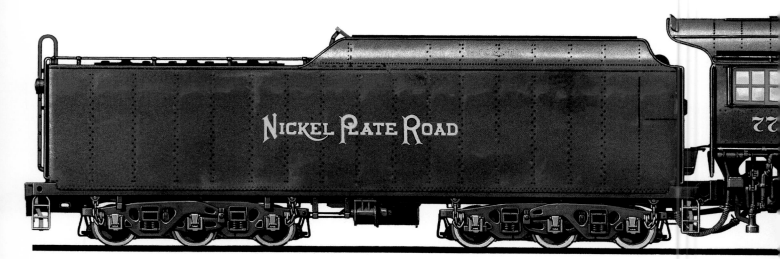

Selkirk Class 2-10-4 Canadian Pacific Railway (CPR), 1949

Gauge: 4ft 8½in (1,435mm).
Tractive effort: 76,905lb (34,884kg).
Axle load: 62,240lb (28.25t).
Cylinders: (2) 25 x 32in (635 x 813mm).
Driving wheels: 63in (1,600mm).
Heating surface: 4,590sq ft (426m²).
Superheater: 2,055sq ft (191m²)m².
Steam pressure: 285psi (20kg/cm²).
Grate area: 93.5sq ft (8.7m²).
Fuel (oil): 4,100gall (4,925 US) (18.6m²).
Water: 12,000gall (14,000 US) (54.5m³).
Adhesive weight: 311,200lb (141t).
Total weight: 732,500lb (332t).
Length overall: 97ft 10⅝in (29,835mm).

Ten-coupled locomotives were used in most parts of the world for freight movement; in fact, the only steam locomotives in quantity production in the world today are 2-10-2s in China. Because the length of a rigid wheelbase has to be limited, five pairs of coupled wheels implies that they are fairly small ones and this in turn means (usually) low speeds. It is true that British Railways had some superb 2-10-0s that were occasionally used on passenger trains "in emergencies" and, in spite of having only 62in (1575mm) diameter wheels, were timed up to 90mph (145km/h) whilst so doing, but these were exceptional. Perhaps the ten-coupled engines with the best claim to be considered as express passenger locomotives were the 2-10-4 "Selkirk" class of the Canadian Pacific Railway. Not only were they streamlined (in the way CPR understood the term) but the coloured passenger livery was also used for them; also, of course, they handled CPR's flag train, then called the "Dominion", across the Rockies and the adjacent Selkirks.

The overall story was very similar to that of the CPR "Royal Hudson". First came the slightly more angular "T-la" batch; 20 (Nos.5900 to 5919) were built in 1929. A further ten ("T-lb") with softer and more glamorous lines were built in 1938 and, finally, another six ("T-lc") came in 1949. No.5935 was not only the last of the class but the last steam locomotive built for the company and, indeed, for any Canadian railway. The "Royal Hudson" boiler was used as the basis, but enlarged and equipped for oil-burning, since all locomotives used on the mountain division had been fired with oil since 1916.

When one crossed Canada by CPR the whole 2,882 miles (4,611km) from Montreal to Vancouver was reasonably easy going apart from a section along the north shore of Lake Superior and, more notably, the 262 miles (420km) over the mountains between Calgary and Revelstoke. Until the 1950s CPR's flag train, the "Dominion", could load up to 18 heavyweight cars weighing some 1,300 tons and to haul these up the 1 in 45 (2.2 per cent) inclines required some fairly heroic measures. There was very little difference in the timings and loadings of the various types of train, even the mighty "Dominion" made 23 stops over this section.

The 2-10-4s were permitted to haul loads up to about 1,000 tons on the steepest sections. Typically when hauling a capacity load up a bank of 20 miles mostly at 1 in 45, (2.2 per cent) the average speed would be 10mph. The

generally applied to 2-8-4s after the country they first conquered in the hands of the Boston & Albany Railroad—were well looked after. They were also efficiently managed and did all that was expected of them in moving huge volumes of freight in trains of up to 10,000 tons weight, and so did more than their share in hauling NKP's finances out of the depths.

Yard operations were dieselised shortly after the war, and when more road power was required NKP decided in 1948 to have a long look at the all-conquering diesel-electric. The result was the first of only two occasions when a diesel-electric locomotive demonstrator was returned to the makers following trials and an order for steam power placed instead. Taking everything into account, the arithmetic showed that diesel operation would be more expensive than steam using modern locomotives. Hence the "S-3" class delivered by Lima in 1949, that great builder's final order for steam. In 1949 Nickel Plate took over its long-term associate, the Wheeling

& Lake Erie, so obtaining a further 32 generally similar (but not so well looked-after) 2-8-4s, designated class "S4".

Despite the fact that heavy NKP steam-hauled freights hauled by shiny new steam locomotives could often be seen rapidly overhauling New York Central freights pulled by shabby and prematurely ageing diesels on adjacent tracks, the time came when steam had to bow out. By the mid-1950s, the problems of being one out of only two railroads still seriously using steam traction had begun to tell, and by 1960 all the lovely 2-8-4s had been retired. Six are preserved, notably No.759 which is restored to working order and, indeed, crossed the continent with the American bi-centennial "Freedom Train" in 1976.

Left: *NKP westbound "hot shot" freight in the hands of of S-3 Class No.748.*

Below: *Lima's last steam build. NKP Class S-3 had a short life as dieselisation spread in the 1950s. All were gone by 1960.*

booster would be cut in if speed fell below walking pace and cut out when the train had reached the speed of a man's run. Fuel consumption would be of the order of 37 gallons per mile up grade.

In the mountains downhill speeds were limited to 25-30mph (40-50km/h) by curvature, frequently as sharp as 462ft (140m) radius, but passengers hardly found—or find—this portion of the journey tedious having regard to the nature of the views from the car windows. On the few

Above: *No.5921 was one of the 1938 batch of Selkirks which featured improved styling.*

straight sections of line 65mph (108km/h) could be achieved by these locomotives.

The 2-10-4s were able to nego-

tiate these sharp curves by dint of widening the gauge on the curves from 4ft 8½in to 4ft 9¾in (1,435mm to 1,469mm), an exceptional amount, and by giving the leading axle nearly an inch (25mm) of side-play each way as well as providing it with a pair of flange lubricators. In other ways standard North American practice was applied, including a fairly early application of the cast steel one-piece locomotive frame, and the class stood up well to robust usage.

In 1952 diesels took over the running across the mountains and after the 2-10-4s had done a stint on freight haulage across the prairies, they were withdrawn. The last one was cut up in 1959, except for No.5931 (numbered 5934) in the Heritage Park, Calgary, and No. 5935 at the Railway Museum at Delson, Quebec.

S1a 0-8-0 Norfolk & Western Railway (N&W), 1952

Gauge: 4ft 8½in (1,435mm).
Tractive effort: 69,932lb (31,730kg).
Axleload: 67,925lb (30.8t).
Cylinders: (2) 25 x 28in (635 x 711mm).
Driving wheels: 52in (1,320mm).
Heating surface: 2,570sq ft (239m²).
Superheater: 637sq ft (59m²).
Steam pressure: 220psi (15.5kg/cm²).
Grate area: 47sq ft (4.4m²).
Fuel: 30,000lb (13.6t).
Water: 13,000 US gall (49.2m³).
Adhesive weight: 247,000lb (112.1t).
Total weight: 459,000lb (208.3t).
Length overall: 77ft 0½in (23,482mm).

Railroads owe their whole existence to the fact that long trains made up of many conveniently-sized loads can be run economically as one unit. The process of making up loads into trains, which we know as switching is, however, one of the least glamorous, although the most expensive, of all railroad operations. Most railroads responded by doing their switching with elderly locomotives, superannuated from work out on the road.

The Chesapeake & Ohio Railroad was one of the exceptions, and in 1948 had bought 30 modern switching locomotives from Baldwin. These Class "C-16" 0-8-0s had every modern refinement such as locomotive beds with cylinders cast in-situ, overfire jets in the firebox, and Baker

valve gear. Their paint was hardly dry when Chessie decided to dieselise, and in 1950 they offered this nearly new batch of "C-16s" to neighbour Norfolk & Western at a bargain price.

N&W, so good in other ways, had what they considered to be the economical policy of using hand-me-downs for switching, and it turned out that these new yard engines were a revelation. The new owners logically designated their first class of dedicated switching locomotives "S1" and they kept the same numbers 255 to 284. Some minor modifications were made, such as increasing the already quite large fuel and water capacity of the tenders in order to increase the time between servicing. Costs instantly fell and

the speed with which yard operations were performed rose. It was an object lesson in the wrongness of making-do with unsuitable equipment which just happened to be available.

A programme for replacing further obsolete locomotives used for switching was now begun, involving construction of a further series of 45 0-8-0s numbered 200 to 244. The work was done in the company's fabled Roanoke Shops. The new locomotives, classified "S1a", were almost the same as the "S1"s, but water capacity was further increased. The last of them, No.244, put into service in December 1953, is notable as built for a United States Class I railroad.

In accordance with typical

Class YP 4-6-2 Indian Railways (IR), 1949

Gauge: 3ft 8⅜in (1,000mm).
Tractive effort: 18,450lb (8,731kg).
Axle load: 23,500lb (10.7t).
Cylinders: (2) 15¼ x 24in (387 x 610mm).
Driving wheels: 54in (1,372mm).
Heating surface: 1,112sq ft (103m²).
Superheater: 331sq ft (31m²).
Steam pressure: 210psi (14.8kg/cm²).
Grate area: 28sq ft (2.6m²).
Fuel: 21,500lb (9.75t).
Water: 3,000gall (3,600 US) (13.6m³).
Adhesive weight: 69,000lb (31.5t).
Total weight: 218,500lb (99t).
Length overall: 62ft 7½in (19,088mm).

A total of 871 of these beautifully proportioned and capable locomotives were built between 1949 and 1970 for the metre-gauge network of the Indian Railways. The newest members of the class, which still remains virtually intact, were the last express passenger locomotives to be built.

It could be said that whilst

Britain's principal achievement in India was the construction of the railway network the greatest fault in what was done was the division of the system into broad and metre gauge sections of not far off equal size. Even so, 15,940 miles (25,500km) of metre-gauge railways, including many long-distance lines, required to be worked and power was needed

to do it. Strictures rightly applied to the standard "XA", "XB" and "XC" 4-6-2s of the 1920s and 1930s were not deserved by their metre-gauge counterparts, the handsome "YB" 4-6-2s supplied between 1928 and 1950. Nevertheless Indian Railways decided to do what they had done on the broad gauge and go American. Jodhpur, one of the

Above: *A Class "YP" 4-6-2 spreads a pall of black smoke at the head of a Southern Railway metre-gauge express.*

princely states, in those days had still its own railway, and they had received ten neat 4-6-2s from Baldwin of Philadelphia in 1948. Baldwin was asked to produce 20 prototypes of class "YP",

good Norfolk & Western practice, the older engines were modified so that they would be interchangeable with the newer ones. But all was to no avail, for N&W eventually had to follow suit and abolish steam traction. It fell to an S1a to take the last curtain call. The sad day in question was May 7, 1960, at Williamson, Virginia, when eight-year old No.215 (by then renumbered 291) finished a day's switching.

Right: *Another short-lived class, Norfolk & Western's S1a switcher, all of which were retired within nine years. This example is working hard at Shaffers Crossing, close to its Roanoke birthplace.*

similar to those locomotives but slightly enlarged. The new locomotives were also a little simpler, with plain bearings instead of roller ones and eight-wheel instead of high-capacity 12-wheel tenders.

Production orders for the "YP" were placed overseas. Krauss-Maffei of Munich and North British Locomotive of Glasgow got production orders for 200 and 100 respectively over the next five years, but the remainder were built by the Tata Engineering & Locomotive Co of Jamshedpur, India. Running numbers are 2000 to 2870, but not in chronological order. The engines could be regarded as two-thirds full-size models of a standard USA 4-6-2. If one multiplies linear measurements by 1.5, areas by 1.5^2 or 2.25, weights and volumes by 1.5^3 or 3.375 the correspondence is very close. Non-American features include the use of vacuum brakes, chopper type automatic centre couplers in place of the buckeye type, slatted screens to the cab side openings and the absence of a bell.

With so many available, these

locomotives can be found in all areas of the metre gauge system; this stretches far and wide from Trivandrum, almost the southernmost point of the Indian railways, to well north of Delhi, while both the easternmost and westernmost points on Indian Railways are served by metre gauge lines. Recent allocation was as follows; Central Railway — 9; Northern Railway — 101; North-Eastern Railway — 235; North East Frontier Railway — 98; Southern Railway — 199: South Central Railway — 72; Western Railway — 155. The two missing engines were withdrawn after accident damage.

Diesel locomotives are now arriving on the metre-gauge network of India, but the "YP" class still hauls important trains.

Above: *Many passenger trains are still steam-hauled on Indian Railways, and especially on the metre-gauge where Class YP units reigned supreme until recent diesel deliveries.*

Below: *Indian Railways' class "YP" 4-6-2, the last express passenger-hauling steam locomotive to be built in the world.*

EMD GP Series B₀-B₀ Electro-Motive Division, General Motors Corporation (EMD), 1949

Type: Diesel-electric road switcher locomotive.
Gauge: 4ft 8½in (1,435mm).
Propulsion : One EMD 567D2 2,000hp (1,490kW) 16-cylinder turbocharged two-stroke Vee engine and generator, supplying current to four nose-suspended traction motors geared to the axles.
Weight: 244,000lb (108.9t) to 260,000lb (116.0t) according to fittings.
Max. axleload: 61,000lb (27.2t) to 65,000lb (29.0t) according to fittings.
Overall length*: 56ft 0in (17,120mm)*.
Tractive effort: 61,000lb (271kN) to 65,000lb (289kN) according to weight.
Max. speed: 65mph (105km/h), 71mph (114km/h), 77mph (124km/h), 83mph (134km/h) or 89mph (143km/h) according to gear ratio fitted.

*Dimensions refer to the GP20 variant of 1959

For the post-war boom in diesel sales EMD offered a range of models based on three main series. First the "E" series of A1A+A1A express passenger locomotives, secondly the "F" series of Bo-Bo locomotives for freight work, but with optional gear ratios covering passenger work to all but the highest speeds, and thirdly a number of switchers (shunters) and transfer locomotives for work within and between marshalling yards. There was an important difference between the switchers and the other models. In the switchers the structural strength was in the underframe, on which

rested the engine, generator and other equipment. The casing or "hood" was purely protective and had no structural strength. The "E" and "F" series, on the other hand, had load-bearing bodies, or "carbodies", which provided an "engine-room" in which maintenance work could be carried out whilst the train was in motion, and which were more satisfactory aesthetically than a hood. With these models EMD captured about 70 per cent of the North American market. Its ability to do so stemmed from a combination of quality of performance and reliability in the locomotive, low maintenance costs, which were helped by the large number

of parts which were common to the different types, and competitive prices made possible by assembly line methods of manufacture. Full benefit of assembly line methods could only be achieved by limiting the number of variants offered to customers, and this, in turn, helped EMD's competitors to pick on omissions from, or weaknesses in, the EMD range by which to hold on to a share of the market. At first EMD's main theme in its diesel sales talk was the benefit accruing from replacing steam by diesel traction, but as its competitors achieved modest success in finding gaps in the EMD range, more and more was that firm concerned with proclaiming the

superiority of its products over those of its competitors.

To achieve this superiority some changes were made in the range, of which the most important originated in customer enquiries received before the war for a locomotive which was primarily a switcher, but which could also haul branch line trains, local freights and even local passenger trains. To meet this need a small number of locomotives were built with switcher bodies, elongated to house a steam generator, and mounted on trucks (bogies) of the "F" series; these were "road switchers". Construction was resumed after the war, still on a small scale, and with the design adapted to meet individual customer's requirements.

By 1948 EMD's competitors, particularly Alco, were achieving success with a general purpose hood unit for branch line work. For this application, ability to gain access to the working parts was more important than protection for technicians to work on the equipment on the road, and the hoods also gave the enginemen a much wider field of view. In 1948, therefore, EMD offered a branch line diesel, designated "BL", incorporating the 1,500hp (1,120kW) 567B engine, and other equipment including traction motors from the "F" series. These were accommodated in a small semi-streamlined casing, whose main advantage compared with a carbody was the improved view from the cab. There was, however, a

Left: *A pair of GP-series EMD diesel units, typical freight power on Conrail's network.*

Right: *The GP 38-2 standard road-switcher 2,000hp diesel electric locomotive as supplied by General Motors (Canada) for the Canadian Pacific rail system.*

serious snag—the "BL" was too expensive.

EMD then designed a true hood unit for general purpose duties, designated "GP". Richard Dilworth, EMD's Chief Engineer, said that his aim was to produce a locomotive that was so ugly that railroads would be glad to send it to the remotest corners of the system (where a market for diesels to replace steam still existed!), and to make it so simple that the price would be materially below standard freight locomotives.

Although the "GP" was offered as a radically new design, many parts were common to the contemporary "F7" series. The power plant was the classic 567 engine, which like all EMD engines was a two-stroke Vee design; this was simplier than a four-stroke but slightly less efficient. Much development work was devoted over the years to improving the efficiency of the EMD engines to meet

Above: *Sporting the new-cab look, one of the original GP7s, by then over 30 years old, shown in service in 1982 on Canada's Algoma Central Railway.*

the competiton of four-stroke engines. The trucks were of the Blomberg type, a fairly simple design with swing-link bolsters, which were introduced in the "FT" series in 1939 and are still, with changes in the springing system, standard in EMD Bo-Bo models in the 1980s. EMD's success with this long-running design is in contrast to the radical changes which have been made in truck design in other countries over that period.

The cab afforded a good view in both directions, the hood gave easy access to the equipment, and, despite the designer's intentions, EMD's stylists produced a pleasing outline. Electrical equipment was simplified from the "F"

series, but nevertheless it gave the driver tighter control over the tractive effort at starting, and a more comprehensive overall control to suit the wide range of speeds envisaged.

First production series of the new design was the "GP7", launched in 1949. It was an immediate success, and 2,610 units were supplied between 1949 and 1953 to US roads, plus 112 to Canada and two to Mexico—and this at a time when the "F7" was still selling in record numbers.

In 1954 the next development of the 567 engine, the C series of 1,750hp (1,305kW), was introduced into the range, giving the "GP9". This differed in detail from the "GP7", mainly to bring still further reductions in maintenance. By this time the hood unit was widely accepted, and sales of the "GP" at 4,157 established another record. The "GP" was now America's (and therefore the world's) best selling diesel locomotive.

So far the EMD engines had been pressure-charged by a Roots blower driven mechanically from the engine, but with its competitors offering engines of higher power, EMD now produced a turbocharged version of the 567 engine, 567D2, giving 2,000hp (1,490kW). For customers for whom the extra power did not justify the expense of the turbo-blower, the 567D1 at 1,800hp (1,340kW) was availble. Both these models had a higher compression than their predecessors, which, combined with improvements in the fuel injectors, gave a fuel saving of 5 per cent. These engines were incorporated in the "GP20" and "GP18" series, respectively.

By this time US railroads were fully dieselised, and this, combined with a decline in industrial activity, reduced the demand for diesels. EMD therefore launched its Locomotive Replacement Plan. The company claimed that three "GP20s" could do the work of four "F3s", so it offered terms under which a road traded in four "F3s" against the purchase of three "GP20s", parts being reused where possible. It was claimed that the cost of the transaction could be recovered in three to four years, and the railroad then had three almost new units in place of four older ones with much higher maintenance costs. Despite this, only 260 "GP20s" and 390 "GP18s" were sold over 13 years.

The final phase of "GP" development with the 567 engine came in 1961 with the 567D3 of 2,250hp (1,680kW) in the "GP30." The designation "30" was a sales gimmick, based on there being 30 improvements in the new model; it was claimed that maintenance was reduced by 60 per cent compared with earlier types. The "GP30" was in turn succeeded by the "GP35" of 2,500hp (1,870kW). With trade reviving, and many more early diesels in need of replacement, these models achieved sales of 2,281. At this stage the 567 engine was replaced by the 645 with which the "GP" series remains in full production in the 1980s.

The "GP" series with the 567 engine totalled 10,647 units,or about one-quarter of the total of North American diesels, and it established the hood unit as the norm for all future construction.

Gas Turbine B₀-B₀-B₀-B₀ Union Pacific Railroad (UP), 1951

Type: Gas-turbine electric freight locomotive.
Gauge: 4ft 8½in (1,435mm).
Propulsion: One 4,500hp (3,360kW) oil-burning gas turbine driving a generator and supplying direct current to eight nose-hung traction motors.
Weight: 551,720lb (250.3t).
Max. axleload: 68,970lb (31.3t).
Overall length: 83ft 6½in (25,464mm).
Tractive effort: 135,000lb (600kN).
Max. speed: 65mph (105km/h).

Union Pacific is a big railroad; its last three designs of steam engine were all, in some way, the largest or most powerful of their type, and there was a dramatic contrast when the road began to buy off-the-shelf diesels of 1,750hp instead of 6,000hp steam engines. But UP is also a road of contrasts.

One main line crosses deserts where coal and water are scarce, but oil is available; this was an obvious line for dieselisation. In other districts, however, the company owns coal mines, and there the economic case for dieselisation was less clear. In particular, any alternative to the diesel which might burn coal was of interest.

Above: *UP's gas turbine unit No.14 at Salt Lake City in the final years of its life.*

In the post-war surge of interest in the gas turbine, General Electric was well placed, with years of successful steam turbine work behind it. As far back as 1904 it had begun work on gas turbines.

In 1946, development of a gas turbine for locomotive work was begun, and an experimental locomotive appeared in 1948. The attractions of the gas turbine for locomotives were the high power-to-weight ratio, simple mechanical parts and the ability to use low grade fuel. This turbine burned a heavy oil commonly termed "Bunker C", but already work was in progress on the use of pulverised coal in a turbine.

The gas turbine drove a generator, which supplied direct current to eight traction motors of normal design mounted on four bogies, giving the wheel arrangement Bo-Bo-Bo-Bo. The main frame of the body formed the fuel tank, and a boiler was provided to heat the oil in the tank, as it was too viscous to flow when cold. With a horsepower of 4,500, it was the most powerful internal-combustion locomotive in the world, and it soon attracted the attention of UP, to which it was

Below: *Early 4,500hp version of UP's gas turbine electric.*

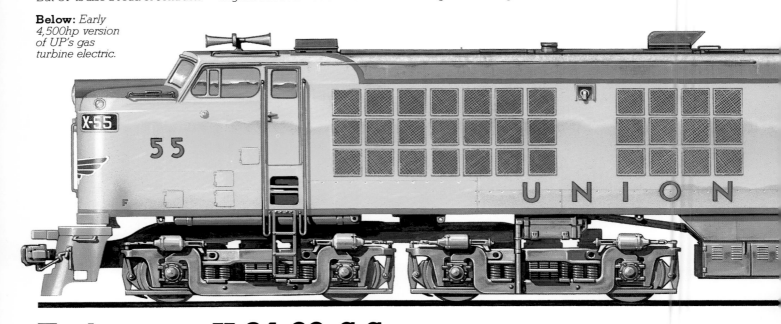

Trainmaster H-24-66 C₀C₀ Fairbanks Morse & Co (FM), 1953

Type: General-purpose diesel-electric locomotive.
Gauge: 4ft 8½in (1,435mm).
Propulsion: One Fairbanks Morse 38D-12 2,400hp (1,790kW) 12-cylinder turbocharged opposed-piston diesel engine and generator supplying six nose-suspended traction motors geared to the axles.
Weight: 375,000lb (170.1t).
Max. axleload: 62,500lb (28.4t).
Overall length: 66ft 0in (20,120mm).
Tractive effort: 112,500lb (500kN).
Max. speed: 65mph (105km/h), 70mph (113km/h), or 80mph (129km/h) according to gear ratio fitted.

Fairbanks Morse of Beloit, Wisconsin, was an engineering firm which had for a long time supplied general equipment to railroads, such as water stand pipes. In the 1930s the firm developed a specialism, an opposed-piston diesel engine, with two pistons in each cylinder, and two crankshafts connected by gearing. This engine was fitted to a number of railcars, but further railway applications were delayed by the US Navy, which took the total production for four years to power submarines. After the war, FM introduced a range of switcher and transfer locomotives, and then in 1950 it produced the "Consolidation" line of carbody or cab units, with a choice of engines rated at 1,600hp (1,190kW), 2,000hp (1,490kW) or 2,400hp (1,790kW), supplying four traction motors. Twenty-two units with the 2,400hp engine were sold in 1952-53, but the market was changing rapidly, and carbody designs were giving way to the more versatile hood-type road switcher.

Fairbanks Morse acted quickly, and in 1953 produced a 2,400hp hood unit designated "H-24-66" (Hood, 2,400hp, 6 motors, 6 axles). It was mounted on two three-motor three-axle bogies of new design. Compared with its competitors everything about it was big—the dynamic brake power, the train heating boiler (if fitted), the fuel supplies, the tractive effort. Although EMD offered a twin-engined 2,400hp carbody unit, the FM engine was the largest then on the market. With some justification, the firm chose the pretentious name "Trainmaster", and showed the first unit at a Railroad Manufacturers' Supply Association Fair at Atlantic City, where it stole the show. This publicity, combined with the impression made by the four demonstrator units, soon brought orders.

The peak year for Trainmaster production followed all too quickly in 1954, when 32 units were built,

but orders then slowed down. Railroads encountered problems with the opposed-piston engine and with the electrical systems. One of the characteristics of EMD service had always been the prompt and thorough attention which was given to faults in the field, but customers found that the smaller FM company could not give such good service. During 1954-55 the firm was still dealing with engine problems, including pistons and bearings, but then came a blow to the future of all FM products.

The Morse family had large holdings in the company, and family feuding cast doubts upon the whole stability of the firm, which led to a takeover by another company. By the time conditions were stable, the diesel market was in the doldrums, and competitors had been busy catching up. One result of this trouble was that Illinois Central decided against

loaned for trials.

Success of these trials brought a quick response. UP was led by a new President, A. E. Stoddard, a convinced "big engine" man to whom the 4,500hp unit appealed, and 10 were ordered. These where delivered in 1952-53; numbered from 51 to 60, they closely followed the design of No. 50, but had a cab at one end only. They went quickly into freight work between Ogden, Utah, and Green River, Wyoming, where their rated tonnage was 4,890. So successful were they that when only six of them had been delivered, a further 15 were ordered.

Thirteen months after the delivery of the 25th gas turbine, UP was sufficiently enthusiastic to take a second plunge, this time with an order for 15 locomotives (later increased to 30) with an 8,500hp turbine. The new design differed from the previous one in its layout, there being two Co-Co units, one carrying the turbine

and generator and the other the control and auxiliary equipment. In addition a converted steam-engine tender was attached as a fuel tank. They took over from the earlier turbines the distinction of being the most powerful internal combustion locomotives in the world—by a considerable margin.

The gas turbine was, by its

Above: *The lead unit of the later 8,500hp three-unit set houses the gas turbine.*

working cycle, inherently less efficient than a diesel, and the key to its ability to better the diesel in running costs was the use of cheaper fuel. However, this heavy oil brought penalties of corrosion

and fouling of the blades, as well as difficulties in handling the viscous fluid. An attempt was made to use liquefied propane gas, but this was expensive and even more difficult to handle than heavy oil. Similarly, blade erosion was the main reason for the attempt to burn coal in a gas turbine being unsuccessful.

Despite the excellent work which the 55 "Big Blows" performed, time was against them. Changes in the petro-chemical industry made Bunker C oil more valuable, whilst developments in diesel locomotives made them more efficient and powerful, and thus more competitive with gas turbines. By the time the turbines needed heavy repairs, UP already had the world's most powerful diesel locomotives in service, and further expenditure on the turbines could not be justified. They were gradually replaced by diesels, and the last of them finished work in December 1969.

placing an order for 50 to 60 units which it had contemplated, an order which could have changed the whole outlook for the model. In the event a total of 105 were sold to eight US railroads, and a further 22 were built in Canada.

Major users were the Norfolk & Western, which acquired 33 Trainmasters as a result of mergers,

and Southern Pacific, which used them extensively on commuter trains. Most of the locomotives ended their days on switching duties, where their high adhesive weight was still appreciated after they had been displaced from main line work by more powerful locomotives from other makers.

A 1,600hp version of the Train-

master, sometimes known as the "Baby Trainmaster" also failed to achieve satisfactory production, with a total of 58 sales. The opposed-piston engine had failed to make the grade in railway work. The fate of the Trainmaster was sealed when, by three years after its introduction, it had failed to achieve a level of sales which

Above: *Two of the prototype "Trainmaster" diesel-electric units coupled together to form a locomotive of 4,800hp, a high figure for diesels of 30 or so years ago.*

made its production economically viable, but for a time it enjoyed well-earned acclaim.

FL9 B₀-A1A

FL9 B_o-A1A New York, New Haven & Hartford RR (New Haven), 1960

Type: Electro-diesel passenger locomotive.

Gauge: 4ft 8½in (1,435mm).

Propulsion: General Motors 1,750hp (1,350kW) Type 567C V-16 two-stroke diesel engine and generator—or alternatively outside third-rail—feeding current to four nose-suspended traction motors geared to both axles of the leading truck and the outer axles of the trailing one.

Weight: 231,937lb (105.2t) adhesive, 286,614lb (130t) total.

Max. axleload: 57,984lb (26.3t).

Overall length: 59ft 0in. (17,983mm).

Tractive effort: 58,000lb (258kN).

Max. speed: 70mph (112km/h).

These unusual and interesting machines, like a number of others, were the result of that famous ordinance of the City of New York prohibiting the use therein of locomotives which emitted fumes. It occurred like this: the New Haven railroad was in the 1950s considering abandonment of its path-finding single-phase electrification, which dates from as early as 1905, and changing over to diesel traction. The only problem was how to run into New York.

New Haven trains used both the Grand Central terminal (of the New York Central RR) and the Pennsylvania Station. Both routes were equipped with conductor rails (of different patterns) supply-ing low-voltage direct current. This corresponded closely to the current produced in the generator of a diesel-electric locomotive and it was suggested that a standard General Motors "FP9" passenger cab unit could be modified easily to work as an electric locomotive when required. The ac electrifi-cation could then be dismantled, yet trains could continue to run without breaking the law. In fact axleload restrictions led to one quite substantial change—sub-stitution of a three-axle trailing truck for the standard two-axle one; hence a unique wheel arrangement. The end product was designated "FL9" and 60 were supplied between 1956 and 1960. The most obvious evidence of their unique arrangements were the two-position retractable collec-ting shoes mounted on the trucks, to cater for New York Central's under-contact conductor rail and Long Island RR's top-contact one. Otherwise the presence of addi-tional low-voltage control gear inside the body was the principal technical difference between an "FP9" and an "FL9".

In the event the New Haven changed its mind over dispensing with the electrification, but the "FL9s" still found employment, surviving long enough to be taken over by the National Railroad Passenger Corporation (Amtrak) in the 1970s. Many locos of what is now a veteran class are still shown on Amtrak's books at the

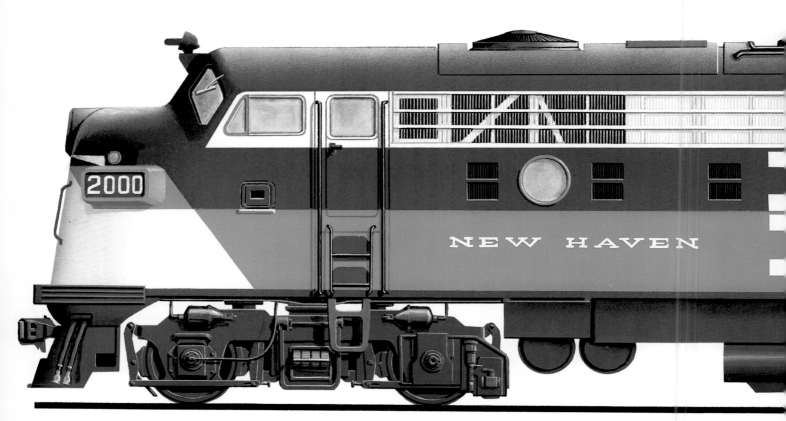

Mv A1A-A1A Danish State Railways (DSB), 1954

Type: Diesel-electric mixed-traffic locomotive.

Gauge: 4ft 8½in (1,435mm).

Propulsion: General Motors Electro-Motive Division Type 567C 1,700hp (1,268kW) 16-cylinder two-stroke diesel engine and generator supplying current to four nose-suspended traction motors, one geared to each of the outer axles of the two bogies.

Weight: 154,280lb (70t) adhesive, 227,675lb (103.3t) total.

Max. axleload: 38,570lb (17.5t).

Overall length: 62ft 0in (18,900mm).

Tractive effort: 39,700lb (176kN).

Max. speed: 83mph (133km/h).

Danish State Railways were not strangers to diesel-electric motive power—their excellent *Lyntog* or "Lightning" trains had been running since the 1930s. By 1954 the time had come to put a tentative toe in the water and order a small batch of five large modern diesels for main line locomotive-hauled pass-enger and freight trains. With commendable good sense they settled on more or less standard locomotives of US design pro-duced by General Motors Electro-Motive Division, then almost the only really experienced diesel locomotive builders in the world. They were actually supplied by the Swedish locomotive-building firm of Nydqvist & Holm, better known as Nohab, who had a

Left: *DSB No.1019 shows clearly its EMD F-series parentage.*

time of writing.

While they exist, the "FL9s" represent a spark of originality in a country whose locomotives were and are much of a muchness (apart from their livery) from Oregon to Florida or Arizona to Maine.

Right: *The New Haven's unique electro-diesel Class FL9 still doing good work as Amtrak No.488, seen at Rensselaer, NY, February 1983.*

Below: *New York, New Haven & Hartford Class FL9 Bo-A1A electro-diesel locomotive. These locomotives could run on current drawn from two types of third rail in New York City.*

licence to produce EMD products in Europe. By taking bits out of EMD's comprehensive Meccano set, Nohab were able quickly to put together a suitable package for DSB. The locomotives, classified "Mv" were basically "F" cab units, but with the car body modified so that there was a driving cab at both ends. To reduce the axleload to the lower values appropriate to Europe, six-wheel trucks each with a central unmotored axle were provided. They were the same as those used on EMD's "E" units, but for differences in the springing. Indeed apart from buffers, screw couplings and a Danish Royal Crown on each end, everything was totally trans-Atlantic.

It was Nohab's secret how much they did themselves and how much came over ready-assembled from EMD, but DSB made it clear they liked what they got by ordering a production batch of 54, more or less identical but with uprated engines developing 1,950hp (1,455kW). This was Class "My". Not only that, but other locomotives subsequently ordered followed the same recipe. Next came 45 of the 1,425hp (1,063kW) "MX" class and then, more recently, 46 of 3,300 to 3,900hp (2,462 to 2,910kW) "MZ" class of 1967-79. Locomotives very similar to the "Mv/My" classes went to Norway, Belgium and Hungary, and many other countries and railway administrations were to follow this excellent principle of buying locomotives off-the-shelf from the most experienced people in the business.

Right: *Mv No.1132 just arrived at the ferry-port of Korsor.*

U25B B₀-B₀ General Electric Company (GE), 1960

Type: Diesel-electric road switcher locomotive.

Gauge: 4ft 8½in (1,435mm).

Propulsion: One GE FDL16 2,500hp (1,870kW) four-stroke 16-cylinder Vee engine and generator supplying four nose-suspended traction motors geared to the axles.

Weight: 260,000lb (118.0t).

Max. axleload: 65,000lb (29.5t).

Overall length: 60ft 2in (18,340mm).

Tractive effort: 81,000lb (360kN) with 65mph gear ratio.

Max. speed: 65mph (105km/h), 75mph (121km/h), 80mph (129km/h) or 92mph (148km/h) according to gear ratio fitted.

If, in the 1920s, one had said to an American locomotive engineer: "The diesel-electric locomotive seems to have great potential; which locomotive manufacturer is capable of exploiting it?" he would almost certainly have said "General Electric", for that company was then building on 30 years' experience of electric traction of all sorts by turning out diesel switchers (shunters) incorporating various makes of engine. However, the prophet would have been wrong, for it was the massive resources of General Motors Corporation thrown into its Electro-Motive Division which sparked off, and largely fuelled, the steam-to-diesel revolution in the United States.

GE was thus destined to take a minor part in the overall process, but within the 25 per cent or so of the market which did not fall to EMD, it has always had a major share. When the American Locomotive Company (Alco) embarked seriously on production of road diesels, it made an agreement with GE to use only GE electrical equipment in its products, in return for which GE agreed not to compete with Alco. From 1940 to 1953 both companies benefited from this agreement; Alco profited from the expertise of the biggest firm in the electric traction business, and GE acquired an easy market for products which it was well qualified and equipped to supply. A second manufacturer, Fairbanks Morse, likewise offered GE equipment in its models.

By the early-1950s, total diesel-isation of the US railroads was certain, and although Alco was well established in the market, its sales ran a poor second to EMD and were not improving. GE then took the plunge; it quietly terminated its agreement with Alco and embarked on development of its own range of large diesels. Although most of its previous diesels had been small switchers, it had in fact built a 2,000hp (1,490kW) Sulzer-engined unit in 1936, which

for 10 years was North America's most powerful single-engined diesel locomotive, and in the post-war years the company had built up an export market in road locomotives.

The essential requirement for GE to enter the home road-diesel market was a large engine. At this time its switchers were fitted with Cooper-Bessemer 6-cylinder in-line and 8-cylinder Vee engines, so the company acquired the rights to develop this engine. Two versions were made, the 8-cylinder developing 1,200hp (895kW) and the 12-cylinder developing 1,800hp (1,340kW).

First outward sign of GE's new venture was a four-unit locomotive, with "cab" or totally-enclosed bodies, two units fitted with the V8 engine and two with the V12. These units were tested on the Erie Railroad from 1954 to 1959, and based on their successful performance the company launched a new series of export models in 1956, designated the

Above: *General Electric U36C 3,600hp (2,690kW) Co-Co diesel-electric locomotive supplied to the Union Pacific Railroad.*

"Universal" series. With the experience gained from V8 and V12 engines, GE now embarked on a major step forward, a 16-cylinder version developing 2,400hp (1,790kW). Two of these engines were installed in Bo-Bo hood units, and were tested on the Erie, covering 100,000 miles (160,000km) in 11 months. Although masquerading under the designation "XP24", denoting 2,400hp export test units, these were in fact destined to be the demonstrators of a new model for the home market.

In 1960, seven years after the ending of its partnership with Alco, GE announced its new model, the 2,500hp (1,870kW) "Universal" Bo-Bo, denoted "U25B". Its most obvious sales point was that it had the highest horsepower of any locomotive on

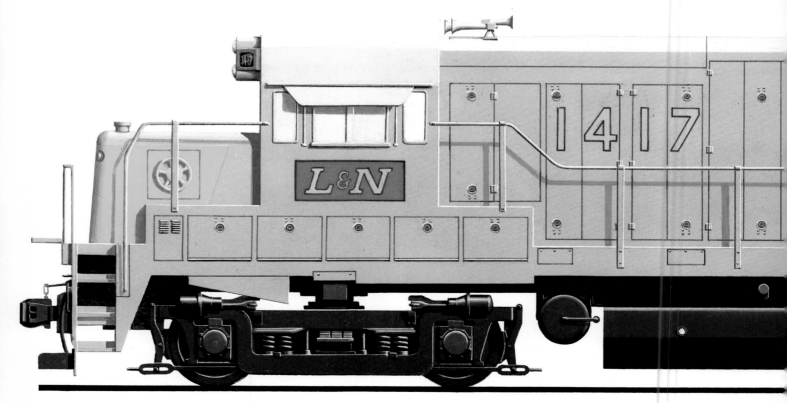

the US market, by 100hp (75kW), but to have any chance of breaking into the EMD/Alco markets, it had to have many attractions which were less obvious, but equally important to customers.

In preparing the design, GE had asked the motive power chiefs of 33 railroads what they liked and disliked in the diesels which they already operated. The costs of operating these units were also analysed, and it was found that repairs accounted for 28.7 per cent of total diesel operating costs. The designers' aim was therefore to improve performance, but at the same time to simplify equipment to make it more reliable and maintenance-free. A major cause of complaint was the air system, both for supplying the engine and for cooling. The incoming air was filtered, and in most contemporary designs the filters needed cleaning at about 2,500 miles (4,000km). Alco designed a self-cleaning mechanical filter. Another complaint was that

air for ventilating the equipment compartments commonly passed through the engine compartment, becoming heated and polluted in doing so. On the "U25B" the air from the fan to the equipment compartment passed through ducting in the main frame, well away from the engine. Another simplification was elimination of electrically-controlled shutters to the radiator ventilating system.

In contrast to these changes much of the electrical equipment was well tried, including the traction motors, and roads which operated Alco locomotives would already have many of the parts in stock. However, there was an electrical innovation—use of modular electronic equipment.

Launching of the new model coincided with unfavourable economic conditions on the railroads, and more than a year passed before any orders came in. The first came from Union Pacific, which was always on the lookout for higher-powered locomotives,

and other roads which had a specific need for higher power followed. Over a period of six years a total of 478 "U25Bs" were sold, not a great number by EMD standards, but sufficient for GE to displace Alco from second place in the US diesel sales league.

It was already established practice for a US road switcher to be offered both as a four-axle and as a six-axle unit, the latter appealing to railroads which needed more adhesive weight or a slightly lower axleload. The "U25C" therefore appeared in 1963, and added a further 113 units to GE sales. With the spread of the "U" designation, someone referred to "U-boats' and the nickname caught on.

The effect on other manufacturers of GE competition was to spur them to modify their own models. Competition was keen, particularly horsepower competition. GE's 16-cylinder engine and its generator were rated modestly, so that uprating would be possible without major alterations (and more spare parts to stock!), and so in 1966 came the 2,800hp (2,090kW) engine, in the "U28B" and "U28C" models.

UP bought 16 "U25Bs", but then ordered a special model to suit the addiction of its motive power chief, D. S. Neuhart, to very powerful locomotives. Already his road was operating 8,500hp (6,340kW) GE gas turbine locomotives, and the builder

now produced a 5,000hp (3,730kW) twin-engined version of the "U25B" mounted on four bogies and weighing 247t; these were the "U50Bs". Later came a simplified Co-Co version of the same power. Neither of these types was entirely successful, and with the coming of standard models of 3,000hp (2,240kW) UP was content to fall into line with other railroads and buy off-the-shelf.

The next landmark in diesel development in the US was the 3,000hp engine, produced by EMD, Alco and GE in 1965-66. The GE models, "U30B" and "U30C", appeared late in 1966, and were followed less than a year later by 3,300hp (2,460kW) versions. In 1969 yet another increase, to 3,600hp (2,690kW), was achieved. The GE decision to use a moderately-rated engine in the first "U-boats" paid good dividends at this time, for whereas GE attained these increases in power by development of the 16-cylinder engine, EMD had to move to 20 cylinders. However, the railroads soon lost their enthusiasm for engines above 3,000hp when they discovered the extra maintenance costs incurred.

In 1976 a further revision of the GE range, known as the "7-series" was accompanied by a change in designation, the 3,000hp Co-Co becoming the "C30-7". With these models GE remains firmly in the US market, and also exports them directly or through overseas associates. There has also been a revival in sales of 3,600hp locomotives.

GE demonstrated that it was possible to compete with EMD. Its models offered some attractive technical alternatives to the EMD products, and by doing so they prevented the larger builder from achieving a monopoly.

Left: *On the Rock Island line at Limon, Colorado, U25C No.213 heads a consist on a March day in 1965.*

Below: *A four-axle "U-boat" road-switcher of the Louisville & Nashville Railroad.*

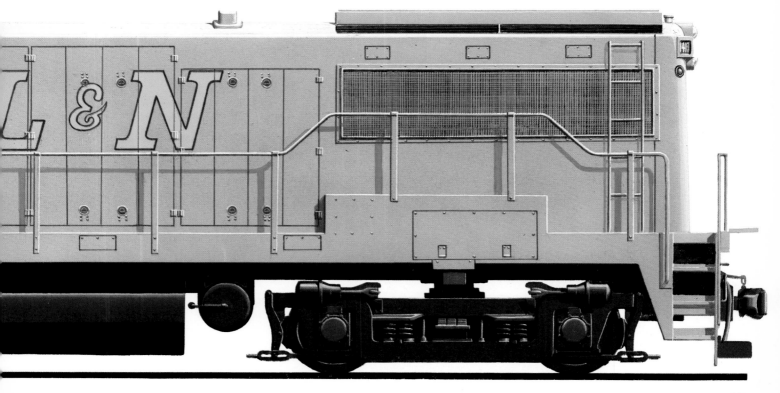

Krauss-Maffei C-C Denver & Rio Grande Western and Southern Pacific Railroads (D&RGW and SP), 1961

Type: Diesel-hydraulic freight locomotive.

Gauge: 4ft 8½in (1,435mm).

Propulsion: Two 2,000hp (1,500kW) four-stroke pressure-charged 16-cylinder Maybach MD870 engines driving through two Voith three-stage hydraulic transmissions, each geared to the axles of one bogie.

Weight: 330,600lb (150t).

Max. axleload: 55,100lb (25t).

Overall length: 65ft 11⁵⁄₁₆in (20,100mm).

Tractive effort: 90,000lb (400kN).

Max. speed: 70mph (113km/h).

During the 1950s the proportion of the world's single-unit diesel locomotives above 2,000hp (1,500kW) which were fitted with hydraulic transmission rose from 4 per cent to 17 per cent due to vigorous development work in West Germany. In 1960, of the world's major diesel users, the United States alone, with more than half the world's 54,000 diesel locomotives, adhered exclusively to electric transmission. Furthermore, diesel-hydraulics were made in West Germany, and the US had imported no locomotives since the earliest days of railways. There was thus a sensation on both sides of the Atlantic when it was announced that two US railroads, the Denver & Rio Grande Western and Southern Pacific, had each ordered three diesel-hydraulic C-C locomotives from Krauss-Maffei of Munich, and furthermore that they would be 4,000hp (2,980kW) units, which

was 1,600hp more than any model a US manufacturer could offer.

D&RGW was the first to approach KM, but to make a viable production run a second order was needed; SP responded. The reasons for this revolutionary step were threefold: diesel-hydraulics gave a much greater horsepower per unit weight than diesel-electrics; German experience showed that with hydraulic transmission adhesion was much improved; and in US experience electrical transmission was the biggest item of repairs in diesels, accounting for up to two-thirds of failures on the road. The improved power-to-weight ratio made it possible to mount two 2,200hp engines in a C-C locomotive.

The engines for the US orders were enlarged versions of the

Above: *Krauss-Maffei's diesel-hydraulic locomotive No.4003 built in 1961 for the Denver & Rio Grande Western.*

Right: *12,000hp provided by three diesel-hydraulics takes a freight over the Rockies on the Rio Grande's Denver to Salt Lake City trans-continental route.*

Maybach units used in most German diesel-hydraulics, and were notable for their speed of 1,500rpm, which was almost 50 per cent more than the highest in an American engine. The rating of 2,000hp was the engine output, and after allowing for the losses in the transmission the power was 3,540hp (2,640kW), which was the figure more truly comparable with a US rating (which is power available for traction).

Each engine was connected by a cardan shaft to a Voith gearbox near the outer end of the frame. From this gearbox an inclined cardan shaft led to a final gearbox on the inner end of the bogie, whence a further cardan shaft led to the axles. The gearbox provided for hydro-dynamic braking, and the controls were pneumatic with provision for multiple-unit working.

The first locomotive completed was D&RGW No. 4001. To test the locomotive in Europe under US mountain railroad conditions,

Left: *Though the hydraulics were quite satisfactory in operation, D&RGW decided not to perpetuate the type in further orders.*

Right: *The second batch of diesel-hydraulics supplied to Southern Pacific were designed as "hood" rather than "cowl" units.*

the makers arranged for No. 4001 to work for a week on the famous Semmering line in Austria, with gradients of 1-in-40 (2½ per cent). On the steepest gradient the locomotive started, and hauled at 16mph (26½km/h), a train of 867t. Only once did the wheels slip, and then only slightly, and the dynamic brake was found to work well.

The six units were duly shipped to the US and put to work in 1961. On the D&RGW the locomotives worked in duplicate or triplicate on trains of 4,000t to 7,000t on 1-in-50 (2 per cent) gradients. Although their work was satisfactory, the road decided not to continue with the experiment, and when the locomotives had covered 200,000 miles (320,000km) they were sold to the Southern Pacific. The latter, by contrast, was sufficiently impressed to order 15 more, which were delivered in 1963. With a total of 21 of the German machines, SP was able to assess their economic and technical performance.

The verdict came in 1968; the hydraulic transmission "could provide a reliable means of propulsion with competitive maintenance costs" but the engines suffered from "complexity of construction and inaccessibility for repairs". Air intake problems arose in tunnels, and the pneumatic controls were troublesome. Some modifications were made, but as the diesel-hydraulics came due for heavy repairs they were withdrawn from service.

This was not quite the end of diesel-hydraulics on the SP, for in 1964 Alco built three C-C versions of its Century series fitted with Voith transmission. These showed promise, but the closure of Alco in 1969 ruled out any possibility of further development.

RDC Single Railcar The Budd Company (Budd), 1949

Type: Self-propelled diesel-mechanical railcar.
Gauge: 4ft 8½in (1,435mm).
Propulsion: Two General Motors Type 6-110, six-cylinder 275hp (205kW) diesel engines mounted beneath the floor, each driving the inside axle of one bogie, via longitudinal cardan shafts and gearing.
Weight: 63,564lb (29t) adhesive, 126,728lb (57.5t) total.
Max. axleload: 31,782lb (14.5t).
Overall length: 85ft 0in (25,910mm).
Max. speed: 85mph (136km/h).

After World War II, the Budd Company made a bid to extend their passenger car-building business using stainless steel construction which had started with the "Pioneer Zephyr" streamline train in 1934 as previously described. By 1948 Budd ranked second in the USA after Pullman and their plan now was to produce not long-distance streamliners but equipment for lesser services—'plug runs', in US vernacular.

To some extent this market had

been explored in the 1920s with the gas-electric "doodlebugs" (qv), but something with a more up-to-date aura and still lower costs was needed. Budd's Vice-President for Engineering, Maj-Gen G.M. Barnes, had heard of a new V-6 diesel engine developed by General Motors for tank propul-

Below: *Thirty years on! A surviving Budd RDC in Amtrak colours at Washington, DC, in May 1982.*

sion. Furthermore, he had had experience of torque-convertor transmission while in the army.

Combined with the weight-saving possibilities of Budd's normal stainless steel construction, a pair of these engines married to two such transmissions would give an excellent self-propelled passenger railcar with an ample power-to-weight ratio of some 8hp/ton. This would provide rapid acceleration from stops and give better than 40mph (64km/h) on a 1-in-

Above: *Many stopping trains in rural Canada were run by RDCs.*

50 (2 per cent) grade as well as a maximum speed as high as would be acceptable to the generality of railroad companies. Disc brakes with anti-slide control would also provide superior stopping power. Moreover, the proposal was to produce the car first, then demonstrate it to the railroads, rather than try to sell a mere idea.

Accordingly, in 1949 a demonstrator RDC (Rail Diesel Car) was built and it performed with impressive reliability. In fact, the Budd RDCs sold so well that by 1956 more than 300 were running. The largest fleet was that of Boston & Maine with 64, while RDCs provided a local train service over more than 924 miles (1,478km) from Salt Lake City to Oakland (San Francisco). The longest RDC service was that of the Trans-Australian Railway from Port Pirie to Kalgoorlie, 1,008 miles (1,613km). Varying amounts of passenger accommodation could be provided in proportion to mail/parcels space according to customers' requirements, while trains could be made up of any

Class WP 4-6-2 Indian Railways (IR), 1946

Gauge: 5ft 6in (1,676mm).
Tractive effort: 30,600lb (13,884kg).
Axle load: 45,500lb (20.7t).
Cylinders: (2) 20¼ x 28in (514 x 711mm).
Driving wheels: 67in (1,705mm).
Heating surface: 2,257sq ft (286.3m²).
Superheater: 725sq ft (67m²).
Steam pressure: 210psi (14.7kg/cm²).
Grate area: 46sq ft (4.3m²).
Fuel: 33,000lb (15t).
Water: 6,000gall (7,200 US) (27m³).
Adhesive weight: 121,500lb (55t).
Total weight: 380,000lb (172.5t).
Length overall: 00ft 00in (00,000mm).

Of only a few classes of steam locomotive amongst those described in this book can it be said (with much pleasure) that all

remain in service, doing the job for which they were made. One of them is this massive broad-gauge (5ft 6in—1,676mm) American-style 4-6-2, the standard express passenger locomotive of the Indian Railways. Class "WP" comprises 755 locomotives, built between 1947 and 1967, with running numbers 7000 to 7754.

The prototypes were a batch of 16 ordered from Baldwin of Philadelphia in 1946, well before Independence, so the decision to go American was not connected with the political changes. It was taken as a result of the satisfactory experience with the American locomotives supplied to India during the war, coupled with unsatisfactory experience with the Indian standard designs of the 1920s and 1930s.

Naturally, the locomotives supplied were built to the usual rugged simple basic USA standards. The provision of vacuum brakes, standard in India, made them even simpler, because a vacuum ejector is a vastly less complicated device than a steam air-pump. An air-smoothed exterior was provided for aesthetic

Above: *India's standard Pacific passenger loco, Class WP No.7080 at Khurda Road, South Eastern Railway, November 1978.*

rather than aerodynamic reasons, giving a solid dependable look

Above: *Chicago & North Western RDCs in a service bay at Chicago, summer 1952.*

number of RDCs without reducing speed or acceleration, or needing extra crew.

Generally speaking, the Budd cars managed to save their own first cost in less than a year by reducing costs and improving revenue. However, many of these results were obtained against a background of compulsion to provide local passenger services. When this compulsion disappeared, as it had generally in the USA by the 1970s, then not even an RDC could be operated cheaply enough to run the service at a profit. Even so, a large number are still in service more than 33 years after the prototype took to the rails, notably in Canada.

No doubt the ever-lasting stainless bodywork and the ease with which replacement engines can be fitted have contributed to this great span, but the main reason for such un-American longevity is the brilliance of execution of the original concept.

to some solid dependable locomotives.

The original batch were designated "WP/P" (P for prototypes) and the production version differed in minor details. During the next ten years further members of the class were supplied from foreign countries as follows:

USA—Baldwin 100
Canada—Canadian
  Locomotive Co 100
Canada—Montreal
  Locomotive Works 120
Poland—Fabryka
  Locomotywim, Chrzanow 30
Austria—Vienna Lokomotiv
  Fabrik 30

There was then a pause until 1963, when India's own new Chitteranjan locomotive building plant began production of the remainder. Some further small modifications to the design were made to facilitate production at this works.

The fleet of "WP"'s work in all parts of the broad gauge network and find full employment on many important express passenger trains, although they have been displaced from the very top assignments by diesels and electrics, also Indian-built. Enormous trains, packed with humanity, move steadily across the Indian plains each headed by one of these excellent locomotives. A crew of four is carried (driver, two firemen and a coal-trimmer) but even with two observers on

Above: *An Indian Railways class "WP" 4-6-2. The letters "CR" on the tender indicate it is allocated to the Central Railway.*

board as well there is ample room in the commodious cab.

Metroliner Two-car Trainset Pennsylvania Railroad (PRR — Pennsy), 1967

Type: High-speed electric
multiple-unit trainset.
Gauge: 4ft 8½in (1,435mm).
Propulsion: Alternating current
at 11,000V 25Hz fed via
overhead catenary, step down
transformer and rectifiers to
eight 300hp (224kW) nose-
suspended motors, one geared
to each pair of wheels.
Weight: 328,400lb (149t).
Max. axleload: 41,880lb (19t).
Overall length: 170ft 0in
(51,816mm).
Max speed: 160mph
(256km/h)*.

*Design speed; yet to be
achieved in normal service.

In the 1960s, the United States
passenger train was at a very low
ebb. Most railroads were reporting
massive deficits on passenger
services as well as a steady loss of
traffic. Over long distances the jet
airliner had a twenty-fold advantage
in time, which hardly affected the
time disadvantage between city
centre and operational terminal,
compared with rail. Over short
distances, though, the opposite
was the case and there seemed a
possibility of the train continuing
to compete, were it not for out-
dated equipment and image.
    One such route was the Penn-
sylvania Railroad's electrified main
line between New York, Philadelphia and Washington, now
known as the North East Corridor. It
was in order to offer better
service on this route that these

remarkable trains came into being.
Possible prototypes had been
acquired from the Budd Company
of Philadelphia in 1958 ("MP 85")
and in 1963 some cars—the Budd
Silverliners—were acquired on
behalf of Pennsy by the City of
Philadelphia.
    Later in the decade the railroad
received some government assistance towards a $22 million scheme
for new high-speed self-propelled
trains plus $33 million for some
improvements to the permanent
way. 160mph (256km/h) operation
was envisaged.
    Orders were placed in 1966
with Budd for 50 (later increased
to 61) stainless steel cars to be
called *Metroliners*. They drove on
all wheels, could attain considerably more than the specified
speed and had a fantastic short-

term power-to-weight ratio of
34hp per tonne. They also had
dynamic braking down to 30mph
(48km/h), automatic acceleration,
deceleration and speed control
using new sophisticated techniques. Full air-conditioning, air-
line-type catering, electrically controlled doors and a public tele-
phone service by radio link were
provided. The order included
parlour cars and snack-bar coaches
as well as ordinary day coaches.
All had a driving cab at one end,
but access between adjacent sets
through a cab not in use was
possible. They were marshalled
semi-permanently in pairs as two-
car units. An over-bold decision
was taken to begin production
straight from the drawing board,
for once, with the Pennsylvania
Railroad suffering from a terminal

Above: *A pair of Metroliner
sets at speed on the Northeast
Corridor main line. These
potentially exciting trains
did not fulfil expectations.*

sickness, its officers did not insist
on the usual Pennsy precaution of
building and testing prototypes
first. As a result, faults galore
again and again delayed entry
into public service until after ill-
fated Penn Central took over in
1968. A single round-trip daily
began at the beginning of 1969
and even then a modification programme costing 50 per cent of
the original price of the trains was
needed to make them suitable for
public service.
    Amtrak took over in May 1971
and a year later 14 daily *Metroliner*
trips were being run and start-to-

Highliner Railcar Illinois Central (IC), 1971

Type: Double-deck electric
railcar for commuter service.
Gauge: 4ft 8½in (1,435mm).
Propulsion: Direct current at
1,500V fed via overhead
catenary to four 160hp (120kW)
traction motors geared to the
axles.
Weight: 130,000lb (59t).
Max. axleload: 32,500lb
(14.75t).
Overall length: 85ft 0in
(25,908mm).
Max. speed: 75mph
(120km/h).

Chicago is even today a great
railroad city, and virtually all the
railroads leading there catered for
people who earned their daily
bread in the downtown area but
lived in the suburbs. The Illinois
Central Railroad was no exception,
the difference being that its service
was for many years the best,
because in 1926 it had been
electrified. Forty years later the
heavyweight cars supplied then
were still soldiering on in a reliable
fashion, but it was considered
that something more up-to-date
was needed.
    By this time it was beginning to
be recognised that the passengers
and the railroads could not
between them pay for commuter
train services and that, if such
service was to continue, financial

Above: *Budd Metroliner self-propelled high-speed club car smartly turned out in the new Amtrak colours.*

stop average speeds as high as 95mph (152km/h) were scheduled. Even so, speeds as high as the announced 150mph were not run in public service, although 164mph (262km/h) was achieved on test; the work done on the permanent way was not sufficient for this, 110mph (176km/h) being the normal limit.

Since then a programme of track work has been carried out over the North East Corridor. At a cost of $2,500 million, this is 75 times as much as the original rather naive proposal, but does include the New York to Boston line. At long last this great work is drawing near to completion, and higher speeds can be envisaged. However, the *Metroliners*, now over 15 years old, have been displaced from the New York-Washington services by "AEM7" locomotives and trains of Amfleet coaches, which are effectively non-powered *Metroliners*. The powered *Metroliners* now work the New York-Philadelphia-Harrisburg route. The original schedule of 2½ hours for the 226 miles (362km) between New York and Washington was never achieved, but (taking 1978 as an example) hourly trains did the run in a very respectable 3 hours (or a minute or two more) with four intermediate stops, an overall average of 75mph (120km/h).

aid would be necessary. In due time, this was forthcoming, and orders were placed with General Steel Industries' St Louis Car Division for a replacement fleet of what were to be called "Highliners", due to cost almost $40 million.

The main difference from the previous multiple-unit cars was that these were to be double-deckers, seating 156 passengers. The advantage of this arrangement lies in the fact that a six-car "Highliner" train (the longest to be operated) seats 96 more people than the 10-car train of its predecessors. The running of longer and taller cars—the first overhead electric double-decker cars in America—meant hundreds of small alterations to tracks, catenary heights and platform edges, but the expense was justified by the advantage gained.

An interesting feature is the hydraulically-operated braking system, actuated by air pressure and controlled either by electrically-operated valves or (as a back-up) by a drop in pressure in the train line in the usual air-brake manner. Each car has a single-arm panto-graph mounted on a low section of roof above the one driving cab. Each axle is driven by a 160hp (120kW) motor and this gives a "Highliner" train of any length a maximum speed 15 per cent greater than the older cars and an acceleration of 1.5mph (2.4km) per second. On the 29-mile (47km) run from Chicago to Richton Park with 30 intermediate stops the plan was to reduce the scheduled time from 60 minutes to around 45.

Passenger comfort was improved by providing full air-conditioning, vinyl-upholstered seats in place of rattan (notorious for snagging nylon tights and stockings) and tightlock couplers. High-level platforms had been in use for many years, but such things as automatic ticket-vending and ticket-collection machines were introduced and stations modernised so that other aspects of the system were improved in line with the trains. Since then the fleet of "Highliners" has been increased to 165, all owned by the Chicago South Suburban Mass Transit District and leased to what is now Illinois Central Gulf.

Left: *At the end of an early morning commuter run, a "Highliner" double-deck electric approaches its Chicago terminal.*

Right: *Despite a decline in patronage of Chicago's commuter railways, Illinois Central "Highliners" are still giving sterling service.*

Class DD40AX "Centennial" D$_o$-D$_o$ Union Pacific Railroad (UP), 1969

Type: Diesel-electric locomotive for heavy freight duty.

Gauge: 4ft 8½in (1,435mm).

Propulsion: Two supercharged two-stroke General Motors 16-cylinder Type 645 engines each of 3,300hp (2,460kW) with integral alternators, feeding eight nose-suspended traction motors.

Weight: 545,270lb (247.5t).

Max. axleload: 68,324lb (31t).

Overall length: 98ft 5in (29,997mm).

Tractive effort: 133,766lb (603kN).

Max. speed: 90mph (144km/h).

If one were to choose the world's number one rail line, a fairly likely candidate would be the central section of the first United States transcontinental railroad, known now by the same name—Union Pacific—as it was when opened in 1869. In the days of steam, UP had the largest and most powerful locomotives in the world, the legendary "Big Boys", to haul the heavy and constant flow of freight across the continental divide. Going west, this began with the famous Sherman Hill (named after General Sherman who was in charge of building UP) out of Cheyenne, Wyoming; it consists of some 40 miles (64km) of 1-in-66 (1.5 per cent) grade.

When diesel traction took over, the power of a steam 4-8-8-4 could be matched or exceeded by coupling locomotive units in multiple, but UP management consistently made efforts to find a simpler solution by increasing the power of each unit. It has been described earlier how gas turbines with their increased power-to-weight ratio were used for a time, and how in the end the ability to buy off-the-shelf from diesel locomotive suppliers proved to have an over-riding advantage.

In the late-1960s, the UP operating authorities once again felt that there should be a better solution than having six or even eight locomotives on one train. General Motors had put together a peculiar 5,000hp (3,730kW) locomotive which they called a "DD35", which was essentially a huge booster unit with the works of two standard "GP35" road-switchers mounted on it. The locomotive ran on two four-axle trucks; these were considered to be hard on the track, but being contained in a mere booster unit could not take the leading position in a train where any bad effects of the running gear would be accentuated. Even so, no one was very keen to put the matter to the test. Only a handful of "DD35s" were sold and those only to Union Pacific and Southern Pacific. UP's track was (and is) superb, however, and it was suggested to GM that a "DD35" with a normal cab hood would be useful. The result was the "DD35A", of which 27 were supplied to UP. It was not disclosed how much saving in cost, allowing for an element of custom-building, there was between two "GP35s" and one "DD35A", but in length at least the former's 112ft 4in (34,240mm) compared with the latter's 88ft 2in (26,873mm).

A centenary in a new country is a great event and when during the late-1960s UP considered how to celebrate 100 years of continuous operation, they decided to do it by ordering a class of prime mover which was the most powerful in the world on a single-unit basis. Again, virtually everything except the chassis of the locomotive came off General Motors shelves, but even so the "Centennials" (more prosaically, the "DD40AXs") are a remarkable achievement.

In the same way that the "DD35A" was a double "GP35", the "DD40AX" was a double "GP40". The 16-cylinder engines of the "GP40" (essentially a supercharged version of those fitted to the "GP35") were uprated from 3,000 to 3,300hp (2,240 to 2,460kW), thereby producing a 6,600hp (4,925kW) single-unit locomotive. This was done by permitting an increased rpm. The result was not only the most powerful but also the longest and the largest prime-mover locomo-

Above: *No.6914 leads a freight at Barstow, Ca, February 1970.*

tive unit in the world. Forty-seven were built between 1969 and 1971, completion of the first (appropriately No. 6900) being pushed ahead to be ready on centenary day. The locomotives had a full-width cab and incorporated all the recent improvements which GM had introduced in the standard range of diesel locomotives. These included the new Type 645 engine, of uniflow two-stroke design like its long-lived predecessor the Type 567. The same cylinder bore and stroke is common to a 1,750hp (750kW) switcher and the 6,600hp (4,925kW) "Centennial". The gen-

Above: *Brand new No.6900 poses for this UP official photo.*

Left: *Do-Do No.6934 waits for orders at Denver, April 1971.*

erator is basically a brushless alternator, but has built-in silicon diode rectifiers to produce direct current suitable for traction motors. Naturally, the control system includes dynamic braking and wheelslip correction features.

The complex electrical system common to all diesel-electric locomotives was improved in these machines by being concentrated in a series of modules which could be isolated, tested and easily replaced if found faulty. In this way, repairs, adjustments or an overhaul could be done under factory conditions. Afterwards this arrangement became standard throughout the whole range of GM locomotives, models with it becoming known as "Dash-2", for example "SD40-2" for an "SD40" with modular electrics.

It could be said that this development proved to be self-destructive to the future of monster diesel-electrics, for a principal advantage of combining two "GP40s" on one chassis was the saving of a lot of electrical control gear. So making the electrics less troublesome made inroads into this advantage, and as a result these dinosaurs are not being repeated, even for Union Pacific. Another factor was the building of the "SD45-2" series with 20-cylinder engines rated at 3,600hp (2,685kW).

After these superb "Centennials", UP once again returned to buying diesel units off-the-shelf like virtually all US railroads and indeed the majority of railways the world over. When a train was called, required power would be calculated on a horsepower per ton basis according to the severity of the route. The most conveniently available units to make up this total horse power would then be coupled up to form the motive power; in these circumstances large special indivisible units are more of a hindrance than a help. Thus the "Big Boys" and the turbines have been superseded, and the "Centennials" submerged by more mundane motive power; even so, the pageant of freight movement up Sherman Hill and across the Divide is still one of the great railway sights of the world.

Below: *Union Pacific Class DD40AX "Centennial". Its genesis as two GP40 units is clear to see from the transverse passage between the two engines.*

Class X C₀-C₀ Victorian Railways (VicRail), 1966

Type: Diesel-electric mixed-traffic locomotive.
Gauge: 5ft 3in (1,600mm) and 4ft 8½in (1,435mm).
Propulsion: General Motors Type 16-567E 1,950hp (1,455kW) Vee 16-cylinder two-stroke diesel engine and generator supplying current to six nose-suspended traction motors geared to the axles.
Weight: 255,665lb (116t).
Max. axleload: 42,980lb (19.5t).
Overall length: 60ft 3in (18,364mm).
Tractive effort: 64,125lb (285kN).
Max. speed: 84mph (134km/h).

It is well known that Australia has a serious railway gauge problem, the various states having in the early days gone their own ways in this respect. The state of Victoria

and its neighbour South Australia were the two which opted for a 5ft 3in (1,600mm) broad gauge. In steam days this meant different designs of locomotive, but with diesels the differences can be minimal, confined almost wholly to the appropriate wheelsets.

These Class "X" diesels of Victorian Government Railways are a case in point because, now that standard-gauge has put a tentacle into the state (notably to connect Melbourne to the Trans-Australian railway as well as over the trunk route from Sydney), they provide haulage over both gauges.

The locomotives are a typical General Motors product—like virtually all VicRail's diesel locomo-

Left: *"X" class diesel-electric locomotive No. X49 arrives in Melbourne with the "Southern Aurora" express from Sydney.*

Class 2130 C₀-C₀ Queensland Railways (QR), 1970

Type: Diesel-electric mineral-hauling locomotive.
Gauge: 3ft 6in (1,067mm).
Propulsion: General Motors Type 16-645E 2,200hp (1,640kW) 16-cylinder Vee two-stroke diesel engine and alternator feeding via solid-state rectifiers six nose-suspended traction motors geared to the axles.
Weight: 215,050lb (98t).
Max. axleload: 35,850lb (16.3t).
Overall length: 59ft 3in (18,060mm).
Tractive effort: 64,500lb (287kN).
Max. speed: 50mph (80km/h).

Queensland's 6,206 mile (9,930km) railway system has been extended recently to serve various mining

operations, and so has rather surprisingly moved into the premier place as regards mileage amongst the Australian state and national administrations. Furthermore, in spite of being mostly laid on narrow-gauge, QR also holds the top place in load hauling. The locomotives that achieve this record are these Class "2130" diesel-electrics. The 11 machines which form the "2130" class are, like 57 per cent of the QR fleet, of General Motors design but built (or at any rate, assembled, under licence) by Clyde Engineering. They also follow US practice in being used as building blocks to form a tractive effort of the power desired.

The most heroic use for these excellent machines is their employment as two groups of three on

the newly built Goonyella line to haul 148-wagon coal trains weighing 11,140t (12,250 US tons) and carrying 8,700t (9,130 US tons) of coal. As the drawgear of the train is not strong enough to take the tractive effort of all six locomotives,

Above: *A 6,600 horsepower couplage of QR Class 2130 diesel electric units.*

Below: *Queensland Railways' Class 2130 diesel-electric locomotive, supplied in 1970.*

tives—and were assembled by GM's Australian licensee, Clyde Engineering Pty of Sydney, New South Wales. This standardisation gives an advantage in that most of the diesel fleet can be run in multiple regardless of class.

Soon after the first six "Xs" had been delivered, Clyde began offering GM's new 645 series engine and this was used for a subsequent batch of 18 supplied in 1970. The power output could thus be increased to 2,600hp (1,940kW) without weight penalty. These were then the most powerful units on the system, but subsequently axleload limits have been raised to 22.5t (24.8 US tons) on certain lines. Hence a further batch of GM Co-Co units (the "C" class) supplied with an installed power of 3,300hp (2,460kW).

One requirement for all Victorian locomotives that possibly defeated General Motors' ability to supply

off-the-shelf was provision of sets of pneumatically-operated token exchange equipment. Under British-style operating rules, some physical token of authority is needed to be on any particular section of single line. The token (or staff) has to be exchanged for another when passing from one

section to the next. The places where this happens often do not coincide with the train's stopping places and the exchange apparatus enables this to be done at speed. Modern electrical methods of signalling are slowly doing away with this picturesque operation, but for the moment it con-

Above: *Victorian Railways' Class X Co-Co diesel-electric Locomotive No.X45,* Edgar H. Brownbill, *supplied by Clyde Engineering in 1970.*

tinues and locomotives however modern have to be equipped to cope.

---

the second group is cut into the centre of the train. These midtrain units are remotely controlled from the lead units without any cable connections between them, by a system of US origin widely-used in North America and known as Locotrol.

The Locotrol system involves a special vehicle marshalled next to the group of units in the centre of the train. This vehicle operates on the principle of sensing the drawbar pull and applying power to the units it controls accordingly. Safety is ensured by having the brakes of the whole train under the control of the driver in the leading unit. Six of the locomotives (Nos. 2135 to 40) are fitted out for use as lead units, with air-conditioned cabs and Locotrol equipment.

The "2130" class is part of a group of generally similar diesel locomotives, 57 in number, all of General Motors origin and numbered in the 21xx and 22xx series, as befits their rating of 2,000hp-plus. The only non-General Motors units of this order of power on the system are the 16 Class "2350" of 2,350hp (1,735kW) supplied by English Electric and used on lines with an axleload limit of 15t. This high-power fleet may be the summit of diesel development in Queensland because plans are afoot to begin electrification of some heavily-used lines.

Left: *A Queensland Railways' coal train hauled by three General Motors Class 2130 diesel-electric locomotives.*

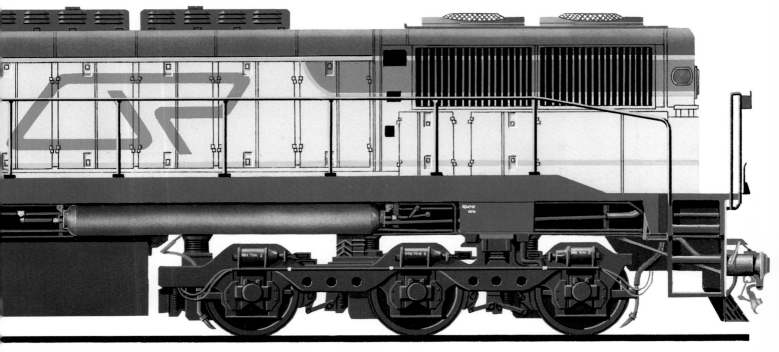

Colonel Teague Mount Washington Cog Railway, 1973

Gauge: 4ft 8¼in (1,428mm).
Tractive effort: 9,540lb (4,329kg).
Axleload: 14,000lb (6.4t).
Cylinders: (4) 9 x 12in (228 x 304mm).
Driving wheels: 24in (609mm).
Heating surface: 655sq ft (61m²).
Steam pressure: 140psi (9.8kg/cm²).
Grate area: 9.5sq ft (8.8m²).
Fuel: 2,000lb (0.9t).
Water: 746 US gall (2.8m³).
Total weight: 38,000lb (17.2t).
Length overall: 21ft 3in (6,477mm).

Above: *Almost brand-new motive power for the Mount Washington,* Col Teague *of 1972.*

The world's first mountain-climbing railway was the cog railroad which to this day in summer ascends the summit of Mount Washington in New Hampshire. During the debate on the granting of its charter, an amendment was sarcastically proposed to allow the promoter, Mr Sylvester Marsh, to continue the line 'on the moon'. This was an indication of how startling the proposal must have been in those days, involving as it did an average inclination of 25 per cent (1-in-4) and a maximum of 37½ per cent (1-in-2⅔).

Marsh himself drew the plans for the first locomotive, which had a conspicuous vertical boiler resembling an old-fashioned pepper-sauce bottle. The official name *Hero* was soon superseded by *Old Peppersass,* a name still proudly borne by the old machine now resting on a display plinth at Base Station.

The current fleet of eight similar 0-2-2-0 locomotives has been produced over almost a century. The

oldest was supplied by the Manchester Locomotive Works, later part of Alco, in 1875, while the newest, No.10 *Colonel Teague,* was completed 'in house' as recently as 1972. This is the only full-size steam locomotive to have been built in the USA during the last 30 years. It is also remarkable in having taken 15 years to construct.

The project was a brainchild of Col Arthur Teague, President of the company, but he died in 1967 and so almost did the idea of building an addition to the then six-strong locomotive fleet. Happily,

a capable master mechanic called Niles LaCross joined the staff the following year. With the aid of ancient but adequate machine tools acquired when big brother Boston & Maine went diesel, LaCross began work on the new locomotive. In between demands on his time for maintaining the existing fleet, slow progress was made. Finally, at the end of the 1972 season, the locomotive was ceremonially named *Colonel Teague* in the presence of a distinguished audience, and made a triumphant ascent of the mountain.

The design is really unlike anything else that runs on rails, not even other steam cog-railway locomotives. Two pairs of quite small cylinders, mounted each side outside the frames, drive crankshafts at each end of the locomotive. The final pinions run loose on the axles and are driven through reduction gearing from the crankshafts. The boiler is steeply inclined downwards so it will be reasonably level when

WDM2 Cₒ-Cₒ Indian Railways (IR), 1962

Type: Mixed-traffic diesel-electric locomotive.
Gauge: 5ft 6in (1,676mm).
Propulsion: Alco 251D 2,600hp (1,940kW) 16-cylinder Vee diesel engine and generator supplying current to six nose-suspended traction motors geared to the axles.
Weight: 279,910lb (127t).
Max. axleload: 47,385lb (21.5t).
Overall length: 58ft 10in (17,932mm).
Tractive effort: 63,000lb (280kN).
Max. speed: 75mph (120km/h).

Above: *WDM2 No.18371 starts the "West Coast Express" out of Erode Junction, Southern Railway, en route from Mangalore to Madras.*

In spite of India being a country with little oil and much coal, the railway authorities had decided by 1960 that diesel traction would have advantages. Although with hindsight, it was a decision that might prove to be an expensive one, they at least went about implementing it in a way that commands admiration. They ignored the temptation succumbed to by so many other "third world" countries, of a big fleet of ready-made diesels, which would have left India for ever in the power of

the suppliers. At the same time they recognised that "do-it-yourself" was not possible without assistance from an overseas manufacturer.

In 1961 then, those entrusted with the project looked over the field and decided that the United States firm Alco Products Inc had the best deal to offer. The agreement provided for Alco to supply technical help as well as complete designs to Indian Railways and, at the start, finished parts for locomotive production at a diesel

locomotive works to be established in Varanasi (Benares), India. When completed, the covered shops had an area over 20 acres (8Ha) in extent, while the whole factory complex, inclusive of a self-contained township, extended to 550 acres (220Ha).

The first 40 locomotives came over from America early in 1962 in completed form, followed in 1963 by a batch sent over in knocked-down condition. Ten years later production was of the order of 75 units per year and

import-content was down from 100 per cent to 25 per cent. The three types which have been or are being produced are the large broad-gauge "WDM2" class (W = broad gauge, D = diesel, M = mixed traffic) described here, a smaller broad-gauge Class "WDM1" and a metre-gauge type,

ascending steep gradients. There are no couplings (except between engine and tender), merely a buffer, nor are there air brakes. Reliance is placed on drum brakes on the crankshafts. The details of the design have stood the test of time, as they were those originated in 1875 by the Manchester Locomotive Works. Such is steam locomotive construction in the USA today.

Above: *Close-up of the curious Col Teague, produced to a 19th-century design for service through to the 21st century.*

smaller still, Class "YDM4". All three have the Alco 251 engine, the difference being in the number of cylinders—16, 12 and 6 respectively for the three classes.

Alco's designation for the "WDM2" is "DL560" and in many ways it is similar to locomotives in the "Century" series. The six-wheel bogies have had to be modified to allow for the broad gauge, but they are of the familiar unsymmetrical pattern, taking account of the necessarily unsymmetrical arrangement of three nose-suspended traction motors. One change is the installation of a combined compressor-exhauster, provided to cater for vacuum-braked trains. Axleload is also lower than for models produced for the North American market. Although Alco went out of locomotive manufacture in 1969, its Canadian associate, previously the Montreal Locomotive Works but now known as Bombardier, is still very much in business and continues to give support to the Indian enterprise.

A scheme to update the "WDM2" design has been proposed, using an alternator in place of a dc generator and replacing the 16-cylinder engine by a 12-cylinder one developing the same horse-power. However, the advantages of building locomotives to the same good design over a long period very often outweigh any advantage accruing from some technical improvement. A factor which occasionally affects sensible judgements is the need on the part of the engineers concerned to be seen to be abreast of the latest techniques, but those in charge of locomotive development in India have so far shown a sensible contempt for such motives.

Left: *Despite the spread of electrification and the huge fleet of steam locos still in service, over 60 per cent of India's freight is now diesel-hauled by units like this Varanasi-built WDM2 No. 17462.*

C630 "Century" C₀-C₀ Alco Products Incorporated (Alco), 1965

Type: Diesel-electric road-switcher locomotive.
Gauge: 4ft 8½in (1,435mm).
Propulsion: One 16-cylinder four-stroke turbocharged 3,000hp (2,240kW) Alco 251E Vee engine and alternator, supplying three-phase current through rectifiers to six nose-suspended traction motors each geared to one axle.
Weight: 312,000lb (141.5t).
Max. axleload: 52,000lb (23.6t), but could be increased to 61,000lb (27.7t) if desired.
Overall length: 69ft 6in (21,180mm).
Tractive effort: 103,000lb (458kN).
Max. speed: 80mph (129km/h) according to gear ratio.

The old-established American Locomotive Company, long known in the trade as Alco, had pioneered one of the most important types of diesel locomotive, the road switcher, when in 1946 it produced a 1,500hp (1,120kW) A1A+A1A hood unit, the first really successful American diesel to be equally at home on switching (shunting) or freight duties. It incorporated the Alco 244 engine, which had per-

formed well in switchers, but which revealed weaknesses under the more arduous conditions of road working.

The 244 was therefore replaced by a new engine, the 251, which officially displaced the 244 from the Alco range in 1956. It was available in 6-cylinder in-line and 12-cylinder Vee formation, to which were added V16 and V18. At first it was installed in existing designs of locomotives, but in

1963 a new range of road switchers was launched, the "Century" series.

Despite the success of its new engine, the position of Alco at this time was increasingly difficult. From 1940 to 1953 the company had an agreement with General Electric that only GE electrical equipment would be used in Alco

Below: *A pair of Santa Fe C630s pausing between duties.*

locomotives, in return for which GE agreed not to compete with Alco in the diesel locomotive market. In 1953 GE withdrew from the agreement, and began to develop its own range of road switchers, which were launched in 1960. This was formidable competition. With the railroads now fully dieselised, the diesel salesman had to convince potential customers that it would pay them to replace their "first generation" diesels by his latest product.

A very strong selling point in any new model must be reduced maintenance costs, and this point was pressed very strongly in support of the Century range. The makers claimed that a saving in maintenance of up to two-thirds could be expected compared with existing 10 year-old designs.

The new series was designated by three figures, of which the first was the number of axles, all powered; the second and third denoted the engine power, in hundreds of horsepower. The first models launched were "C420", "C424" and "C624", of which the two latter were in the range of power which was most

Class 92 1-C₀-C₀-1 East African Railways (EAR), 1971

Type: Diesel-electric mixed-traffic locomotive.
Gauge: 3ft 3⅜in (1,000mm).
Propulsion: Alco Type 251F 12-cylinder four-stroke 2,550hp (1,902kW) Vee-type diesel engine and generator supplying direct current to six nose-suspended traction motors geared to the main axles.
Weight: 218,200lb (99t) adhesive, 251,255lb (114.5t) total.
Max. axleload: 36,370lb (16.5t).

Overall length: 59ft 1in (18,015mm).
Tractive effort: 77,000lb (342kN).
Max. speed: 45mph (72km/h).

Construction of the so-called Uganda Railway was the start of civilisation in what is now called Kenya. Little wood-burning steam engines reached the site of Nairobi in 1895, so beginning the history of a line which for most of its existence has had to struggle to move ever-increasing traffic.

Oil-burning took over from wood in the 1930s, and traffic

Above: *EAR Class 92 hauls empty oil tanks en route to Mombasa.*

popular at this time. The 16-cylinder turbocharged engine developed 2,600hp (1,940kW), with an output from the generator for traction of 2,400hp (1,790kW); in accordance with US practice it was thus designated a 2,400hp model.

In 1964 a new version of the engine appeared, uprated to 2,750hp (2,050kW) by a combination of increased speed and intercooling. This was the most powerful engine on the US locomotive market. At a time when railroads were increasingly attracted by higher-powered locomotives, this was a strong selling point, but it was only strong enough to sell 135 units in the US.

In 1965 there came another increase in engine speed, raising the power to 3,000hp (2,240kW) for traction. More significantly this model, the "C630", had an alternator generating three-phase ac, which was then rectified for supply to the traction motors. This was the first alternator sold by a US manufacturer, and it led to the general adoption of alternators by other builders.

Finally in 1968 the engine power was raised to 3,600hp

(2,690kW), producing the "C636." These increases in power were all achieved with the same 16-cylinder engine. Other variants in the Century range were the "C855" for Union Pacific, a massive Bo-Bo-Bo-Bo with two 2,750hp (2,050kW) engines, and the "C430H", a diesel-hydraulic incorporating two 2,150hp (1,600kW) engines and Voith

Above: *Snowplough-equipped C630 No.703 at Lillooet, British Columbia Railway.*

hydraulic transmission. Neither of these was repeated.

Despite this enterprise, Alco was edged steadily out of second place in the US locomotive market by GE. Major improvements at the Schenectady Works could

not save the day. Orders declined and in 1969 the works was closed. Fortunately for the Alco tradition, the firm's Canadian associate, Montreal Locomotive Works, was in better shape, with continued sales in Canada and Mexico. MLW took over all Alco designs and patents, and in 1982 was still marketing its own versions of the Century series.

---

reached a point where articulated locomotives—the legendary Beyer Garratts—were needed. The efficiency with which traffic was worked by these monsters made what was then called East African Railways a very hard nut indeed for diesel traction to crack. Various studies over the years indicated that there was no case for change, apart from "keeping up with the Joneses", but in the 1960s the administration began to order medium-power units from English Electric of Britain.

By 1970 some progress in dieselisation had been made on peripheral routes, but the main trunk route which climbed steadily from sea level at Mombasa to 9,131ft (2,783m) at Timboroa, en route to Uganda, was still a Garratt stronghold. To find a means of working this traffic economically with diesel traction, EAR went shopping outside Britain, almost for the first time. The result was this Class "92" diesel of Alco design, supplied by the Montreal Locomotive Works. It offered 38

per cent more power than the most powerful diesels then in Kenya.

The Class "92s" were based on the standard Alco product adapted for metre-gauge. To reduce the axleload to a value acceptable on the main line west of Nairobi, not only was it necessary to use six-wheel bogies but an idle pony wheel had to be attached to each bogie also. The arrangement was offered by MLW specially for low axleloads as their "African series" and EAR themselves ordered an even lighter lower-power version (Class "88") for lines with a 12 ton axleload in Tanzania on the same chassis.

In 1976, EAR was divided up among the owning nations, Kenya, Uganda and Tanzania. The Class "92s" went to Kenya, retaining the same classification. Since then a Class "93" Co-Co design of similar power has been imported from General Electric. Advances in design have enabled axleload restrictions to be met without the extra two pairs of pony wheels.

Left: *Standard Alco plus pony wheels to spread the axleload—that's EAR (later Kenya Railways) Class 92.*

Class Dx C₀-C₀ New Zealand Railways (NZR), 1972

Type: Diesel-electric locomotive for mixed traffic.
Gauge: 3ft 6in (1,067mm).
Propulsion: General Electric (USA) 2,750hp (2,050kW) Type 7FDL-12 twelve-cylinder diesel engine and alternator supplying current via solid-state rectifiers to six nose-suspended traction motors.
Weight: 214,890lb (97.5t).
Max. axleload: 35,925lb (16.3t).
Overall length: 55ft 6in (16,916mm).
Tractive effort: 54,225lb (241kN).
Max. speed: 65mph (103km/h).

New Zealand may be a country with a small population as well as a small-gauge railway system, but its railwaymen have always believed in big powerful locomotives. For example, the legendary New Zealand-built "K" class 4-8-4s were as powerful as anything that ran in the mother country, in spite

of an axleload limit only 71 per cent of that in Britain. Similarly, these big "Dx" diesel-electrics have a power output comparable with Britain's standard Class "47s", again within the limits of axleload in proportion as before.

Class "Dx" was the culmination of a dieselisation programme which began in the 1950s—as regards main-line traction units of, say, 750hp plus—with the 40 Class "Dg" A1A-A1A units of 1955. What was called "Commonwealth Preference" in import duties gave British manufacturers a substantial advantage in those days, and the order went to English Electric. The class was lightweight, able to

Left: NZR Class Dx Co-Co diesel-electric loco crosses a trestle viaduct typical of the system, hauling a long freight train.

Below: Class Dx Co-Co diesel electric locomotive as supplied by the General Electric (USA) Co.

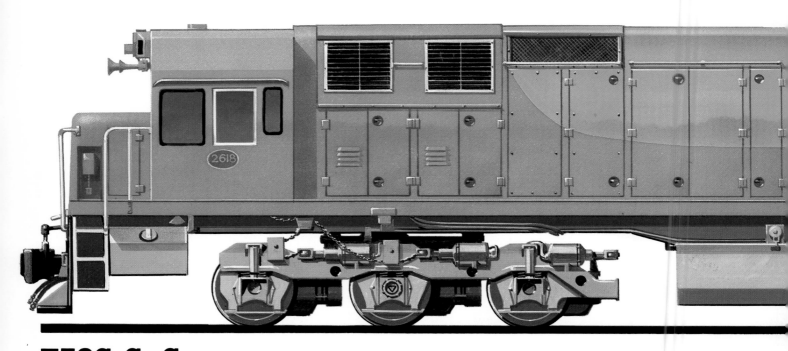

E50C C₀-C₀ Muskingum Electric Railroad (MER), 1967

Type: Unmanned mineral-hauling electric locomotive.
Gauge: 4ft 8½in (1,435mm).
Propulsion: Alternating current at 25,000V 60Hz fed via overhead catenary, step-down transformer and silicon rectifiers to six 830hp (620kW) dc traction motors geared to the driving axles. Control is by automatically generated radio signals received continuously at the terminals and at fixed points elsewhere.
Weight: 390,000lb (177t).
Max. axleload: 65,000lb (29.5t).
Tractive effort: 117,000lb (520kN).
Overall length: 65ft 7in (19,989mm).
Max. speed: 70mph (112km/h).

Railroads are a natural subject for automation but actual automatic railroads hardly exist. There is only one such in the true sense in the whole USA and it feeds the Muskingum River electric power plant near Cumberland, Ohio. Coal is dug about 20 miles (32km) away by a huge dragline excavator known as 'Big Muskie', which has to remove 120ft (36m) of overburden before the coal seam is reached.

In 1967-68 an electric railroad was built to carry coal from the strip-mine to a point from which a conveyor belt feeds the generating plant. High-voltage industrial frequency alternating current was connected up to a lightweight catenary and two electric freight trains soon began moving an average of 18,000 tons of coal

five days a week. Two Co-Co electric locomotives designated type "E50C" had been supplied by General Electric, rather charmingly numbered 100 and 200 respectively as if the Muskingum Electric Railroad intended to have a huge fleet.

The "E50Cs" were based on the chassis and body of a standard GEC Co-Co diesel-electric road-switcher with transformer and special control gear replacing the diesel engine and alternator. A cab is provided complete with engineer's seat, which is normally vacant. The trains are controlled in the loading and unloading areas by a continuous radio signal modulated to give speed commands ranging from 'stop' and 'creep' to '50' mph. The processes at both ends are entirely automatic

although supervised. Air-operated bottom doors on each 100-ton capacity hopper car are controlled by a signal received via a shoe mounted on one of its trucks.

Out on the line, the locomotives encounter a fixed control location preceded by a warning marker at approximately one mile intervals. Each one of these presents a fixed coded response to a detector circuit on the locomotive as it goes by, which determines the speed of the train over the next mile. If the time taken from one control location to the next does not correspond within a reasonable margin to the speed set, then the train will make an emergency stop. This will also occur if the train has run further than a mile without encountering a control location.

192

run over the light rails of the South Island system, where there was an axleload of only 11t (12 US tons).

Between 1955 and 1967, General Motors came in in a very big way with the 74-strong 1,428hp (1,065kW) Class "Da" as the mainstay of the North Island main lines. There were also the 16 lighter GM "Db" class locomotives for North Island branch lines. In 1968 and 1969 the Japanese firm Mitsubishi delivered 60 Class "Dj" Bo-Bo-Bos for the South Island; this class offered 1,045hp (780kW) for an axleload of 10.9t (12 US tons). As a result of these deliveries the last regular steam-hauled train ran in 1972.

It then became apparent that more powerful locomotives could be used to advantage, and the result was this "Dx" class. Very surprisingly NZR went to a fourth source for these magnificent machines. General Electric of USA —not to be confused with GEC Traction of Britain or its subsidiary

Above: *Dx No.5454 heads out of Wellington on a late afternoon seven-car local.*

General Electric (Australia)—supplied 47 of these units during 1972-75. They are used on crack trains on the North Island trunk line between Wellington and Auckland, both passenger and freight.

The design is based on General Electric's standard "U26C" export model.

GEC did not capture the market, though, because subsequent deliveries were from General Motors with both A1A-A1A and Co-Co versions of a similar locomotive (classes "Dc" and "Df" of 67 and 30 units respectively). This in

spite of a debate then in full cry concerning the need for railways at all in a country with such modest transport requirements. In the end the verdict was favourable to railways but not to diesels —instead New Zealand Railways is going ahead with a major programme of electrification which will use indigenous forms of energy.

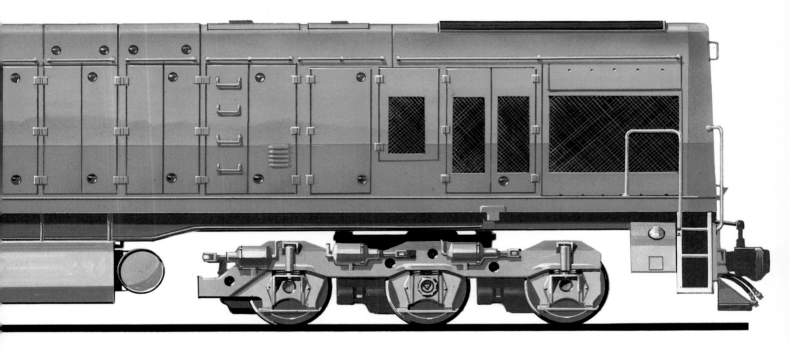

The locomotives normally run at half the rated maximum speed and the 15 empty cars of each train are propelled on the return trip. One train is normally loading while the other makes its out-and-back trip to unload, a complete cycle taking 2¼ hours. Six cycles are performed each weekday, making 90,000 tons weekly, hauled without human intervention except for supervision in case of malfunction.

Right: *Much like any other locomotive, the Muskingum Electric unit even has an engineer's seat—but there's no engineer! This fully-automated mine-to-power station railroad is a fine example of rail's potential in the age of automation.*

SD40-2 Co-Co

Electro-Motive Division, General Motors Corporation (EMD), 1972

Type: Road switcher diesel-electric locomotive.

Gauge: 4ft 8½in (1,435mm).

Propulsion: One EMD 645E3 3,000hp (2,240kW) 16-cylinder turbocharged two-stroke Vee engine and alternator supplying current through silicon rectifiers to six nose-suspended traction motors.

Weight: 368,000lb (167.0t).

Max. axleload: 61,330lb (27.8t).

Overall length: 68ft 10in (20,980mm).

Tractive effort: 83,100lb (370kN).

Max. speed: 65mph (105km/h).

For 50 years the Electro-Motive Division of General Motors has dominated the US diesel market, taking 70 to 75 per cent of total orders. The remainder of the market has been shared between the former steam locomotive builders Alco and Baldwin/Lima, a few smaller firms, and latterly GE, but since 1969 only GE has survived. However, the effect has been that EMD has never had a monopoly, and although the company's success has been due very much to its policy of offering a limited number of off-the-shelf models, it cannot ignore specialist needs of its customers. There has thus been steady development and improvement of the EMD models over the years, directed mainly at increasing power, reducing fuel consumption and maintenance costs, and improving adhesion.

Introduction of the "hood" design "GP7" model in 1949 marked the beginning of the end for the "carbody" unit on which EMD had made its reputation. From then onwards nearly all EMD's road locomotives would be general-purpose machines. There was, however, a variant;

Right: *An Electro-Motive SD40-2 road-switcher diesel-electric locomotive, lettered for the Conrail system, a government-financed grouping of bankrupt railroads in eastern USA.*

the four-axle machines inevitably had a heavy axleload, and EMD therefore offered a six-axle version designated "SD", for "Special Duty". Although the axleload was reduced, the total weight of the locomotive was greater than that of a four-axle machine, and it thus appealed also to roads which had a need for maximum adhesion due to climatic conditions. The pattern thus became established of offering four-axle and six-axle variants of each model.

Elsewhere in this book the "GP" series up to "GP35" is discussed. These are the models with the original 567 engine, and corresponding six-axle "SD" models were also built. By the time this engine was pressed to 2,500hp (1,865kW) for traction, it was reaching its limit, and a new engine was produced with the same piston stroke of 10in (245mm), but with the diameter increased from 8.5in (216mm) to 9¹/₁₆in (230mm). The cylinder volume became 645cu in, thus giving the engine its designation "645". Like the 567 it is a two-stroke engine, and is available with or without turbocharger. A two-

stroke engine requires some degree of pressure-charging to give effective scavenging, and if there is no turbocharger, there is a Roots-type blower driven directly from the engine. There have thus been two lines of development, the turbocharged engine pressed to give successive increases in power, and the engines without turbochargers remaining at 2,000hp (1,490kW), but benefit from mechanical improvements directed at reducing fuel consumption and maintenance costs.

One of the attractions of the diesels which first replaced steam on freight work was that a number of modest-sized units working in multiple under the control of one crew could replace the largest steam engine. These diesels were little bigger than some of the diesel switchers which the roads already operated, and their maintenance was easier than that of overworked steam locomotives

Below: *Southern Pacific SD40-2, one of the later batch with high-adhesion (T) bogies, seen at Luling, Texas, May 1978.*

which were very demanding of attention and needed good quality fuel to give of their best. The diesels could show a reduction in operating costs, even when their higher capital cost was taken into account.

However, when the possible economies from total dieselisation had been achieved, motive power officers looked for other means of effecting economies. With the problems of diesel maintenance now better understood, an attractive idea was to use a smaller number of larger units to achieve the same total power. This was found to save money both in purchase price and in operating costs. EMD's competitors were first in the field with higher horsepower as a selling point, and it was not until 1958 that EMD marketed a 2,400hp (1,790kW) engine in the "SD24" series with which to match the Fairbanks-Morse Trainmaster of 1953. In 1959 EMD produced its 2,000hp (1,490kW) four-axle model, and from then the horsepower race was on.

The 645 engine was launched in 1965 in two versions, the pressure-charged 645E and the turbocharged 645E3. The 645E was made in 8, 12 and 16 cylinder versions, and the 645E3 with 12, 16 and 20 cylinders. These engines were incorporated in a new range of nine locomotives, which included the "GP40" and "SD40" with the 16-cylinder version of the turbocharged engine, giving 3,000hp (2,240kW), and the "SD45" with the 20-cylinder engine giving 3,600hp (2,690kW). This was the first US engine with 20 cylinders, and it brought EMD firmly into the high horsepower stable, some time after Alco and GE had reached 3,000hp. All these new models incorporated a new design of traction motor,

known as "HT-C" (High Traction, three axle). Adhesion was still a major concern to the railroads, and as orders came in for the "Dash-2" range, two trends became apparent: first, that the extra maintenance costs of the 20-cylinder engine and its large turbocharger and radiators were not justified for 600hp more than the 16-cylinder engine could give, and secondly, that the 3,000hp four-axle locomotive, the "GP40", had given trouble with wheelslip and excessive maintenance of its highly-rated traction motors. The high-power model to emerge as the most popular in the range was therefore the "SD40-2", with 3,000hp transmitted through six axles. By the late-1970s this was established as virtually the standard high-power diesel in the US, with sales approaching 4,000 by the end of the decade. The railroad with the largest number was Burlington Northern with about 900, a quarter of its total locomotive stock.

Concurrently the high cost of maintaining a turbocharger compared with a Roots blower had encouraged railroads to purchase large numbers of "GP38-2" units of 2,000hp for duties for which a 3,000hp locomotive was not required, and sales of this model passed 2,000 by 1980.

EMD now tackled the problem of improving adhesion in four-axle locomotives by a wheelslip detector employing Doppler radar, which is sufficiently sensitive to allow an axle to work safely at the limit of adhesion. Engine development made it possible to offer a 3,500hp (2,610kW) 16-cylinder engine, and in 1980 the company launched the "GP50" with the 3,500hp engine on four axles, so that railroads once again had the choice of a high-power locomotive without the expense of six axles.

with improved insulation, and therefore better performance at high power. The six-axle types had a new Flexicoil bogie to give improved riding, and the 3,000hp and 3,600hp engines introduced alternators, instead of generators, to the EMD range. The alternators were more compact than generators, and this assisted the designers in finding space for the larger engines.

With the railroads enthusiastic about high-powered locomotives, the "SD45" was the most popular model in the range, achieving a total of 1,260 sales in six years. The highest-powered four-axle unit in the range, the 3,000hp

GP40, achieved sales of 1,201, and for roads which required a six-axle layout, 883 of the "SD40" were supplied.

These models remained standard until the beginning of 1972 when, with competition from GE still keen, a revision was made of the whole range, known as "Dash 2", from the addition which was made to the class designation, for example, "SD40-2". At this stage no further increase in power was offered, and the alterations were directed at improving fuel consumption and simplifying maintenance by eliminating some of the difficulties encountered with existing locomotives. The most

Above: *A three-unit SD40-2 combination belonging to Canadian National Railways. Note the modified "safety" cab on the second unit.*

important changes were in the electrical control system, which comprises largely plug-in modules of printed circuits which can be changed quickly from stock. Owners of earlier models had encountered difficult in locating electrical faults, and an annunciator was therefore developed which records and stores information about malfunctions in the system.

New high-adhesion trucks were offered in the six-axle models,

F40PH Bₒ-Bₒ Electro-Motive Division, General Motors Corporation (EMD), 1976

Type: Diesel-electric passenger locomotive.
Gauge: 4ft 8½in (1,435mm).
Propulsion: One EMD 645E3 3,000hp (2,240kW) 16-cylinder turbocharged two-stroke Vee engine and alternator supplying current through silicon rectifiers to four nose-suspended traction motors geared to the axles.
Weight: 232,000lb (105.2t).
Max. axleload: 58,000lb (26.3t).
Overall length: 52ft 0in (15,850mm).
Tractive effort: 68,440lb (304kN).
Max. speed: 103mph (166km/h).

The last of the EMD passenger "carbody" diesels was built at the end of 1963, and with passenger traffic declining rapidly, the need for special passenger locomotives seemed to have disappeared. Both EMD and its competitors offered a train-heating steam generator as an optional extra on certain "hood" units, and this met the needs of the railroads which required replacements for ageing "E" or "F" series units.

In 1968, with the railroads' enthusiasm for high-power diesels at its climax, the Atchison, Topeka & Santa Fe Railway proposed to buy from EMD some 20-cylinder 3,600hp (2,690kW) Co-Co locomotives geared for high speed to operate its premier passenger services. The railroad asked that the locomotives should be given a more acceptable appearance for passenger work, and that the

body should have less air resistance at speed than a normal hood unit. The outcome was the "cowl", a casing shaped like an angular version of the old carbody, but differing from it in that the casing does not carry any load. The cowl extends ahead of the cab, giving the front of the cab more protection against the weather than a normal hood.

The model was designated "FP45", and was very similar in its equipment to the "SD45" road switcher. Another variant had a shorter frame resulting from the omission of the steam generator; it was designated "F45".

In 1971 the National Railroad Passenger Corporation (Amtrak) took over most of the non-commuter passenger services in the US, and in 1973 took delivery of its first new locomotives to replace the old "E" and "F" series. By this time, enthusiasm for engines above 3,000hp had declined, so the Amtrak units were similar to the "FP45" but with a 16-cylinder 3,000hp (2,240kW) engine. A total of 150 were delivered in 1973-74. They were equipped with two steam generators mounted on skids, which could easily be replaced by two diesel-alternators when steam-heated stock was replaced by electrically-heated vehicles. In view of the similarity to the "SD40s", these locomotives were classified "SDP40".

Right: *EMD F40PH unit performing commuter service with Chicago's Regional Transportation Authority.*

For a time all was well, but then an alarming series of derailments occurred to the trailing bogies of "SDP40s" whilst negotiating curves. No explanation could be found, but it was clear that the track had been spread or rails turned over by excessive lateral forces. The bogies were only slightly different from those of other EMD "Dash-2" three-axle bogies, but it was the only part of the locomotive on which suspicion could fall.

In the meantime, for shorter-distance routes on which the coaches were already electrically-heated, Amtrak had ordered a four-axle 3,000hp (2,240kW) locomotive, with an alternator for supplying three-phase current at 60Hz for train services driven by gearing from the engine crankshaft. This model is designated "F40PH", and deliveries began in March 1976 when the problem of the "SDP40" derailments was acute. As the well-tried Blomberg truck fitted to the "F40PH" had given no cause for criticism, Amtrak decided that the Co-Co locomotives should be rebuilt as "F40PHs". The frame could be shortened by 16ft, as the steam generator was no longer needed. The "F40PHs"

Below: *Amtrak's standard passenger locomotive is this F40PH "Cowl" Bo-Bo unit built by General Motors' Electro-Motive Division. The F40PHs displaced most of the vintage "F" and "E" series locomotives from Amtrak's principal long-distance trains in the late 1970s.*

built new had a 500kW alternator, which drew a maximum of 710hp from the engine, but for the trans-continental "Superliner" trains an 800kW alternator and larger fuel tanks were needed, so that the "F40PHs" obtained by rebuilding are 4ft longer than the others.

In the fact the rebuilding was nominal, for it cost nearly 70 per cent of the price of a new locomotive, and in effect the "SDP40s" were scrapped when only four to five years old. Amtrak now has a fleet of 191 "F40PH" locomotives.

Many US commuter services are the responsibility of transit authorities, some of whom operate their own trains. A number of these operators bought a shortened version of the unhappy "SD40F", in which the steam

Below: *An FP40H of Toronto's GO Transit on a double-deck train at Scarborough, Ont.*

generator was replaced by an alternator. This is the "F40C", and in this application the engine is uprated to 3,200hp (2,390kW). At the moderate speeds of commuter services, no trouble has been experienced with derailments, but nevertheless when further locomotives were required the transit authorities ordered the four-axle "F40PH", in some cases with the engine uprated to 3,200hp.

197

Class E60CP C₀-C₀ National Railroad Passenger Corporation (Amtrak), 1973

Type: High-speed electric express passenger locomotive.
Gauge: 4ft 8½in (1,435mm).
Propulsion: Alternating current at 12,500V 25Hz (or at 12,500V or 25,000V 60Hz) supplied via step-down transformer with thyristor control system to six 1,275hp (951kW) nose-suspended traction motors geared to the axles.
Weight: 387,905lb (176t).
Max. axleload: 48,490lb (22t).
Overall length: 71ft 3in (21,720mm).
Tractive effort: 75,000lb (334kN).
Max. speed: 85mph (137km/h)*.

*In service. Design speed was 120mph (194km/h).

In the 1970s it became urgent to seek a replacement for the legendary "GG1" electric locomotives which worked the New York to Washington express passenger route. This was not so much on account of difficulties with the "GG1s" themselves—they worked as well as ever. It was more the bad image created by having to admit reliance upon motive power almost 50 years old, plus the fact that the "GG1s" were not suitable for a then impending (but now postponed) modernisation of the power supply, involving a change from a special frequency to the normal industrial frequency.

In order to meet the requirements quickly, General Electric, who had not supplied any passenger electric locomotive to US railroads since 1955, modified a coal-hauling Black Mesa & Lake Powell Railroad locomotive in 1972. The changes involved re-gearing, provision for supplying auxiliary power to the train and (for some of the units) oil-fired steam-heating boilers. The 27 locomotives supplied in 1973 ran well except that the riding at high speeds left something to be desired. So, in the event, the "GG1s" had to be retained to cater for this requirement.

Some "E60CPs" were found employment on lesser duties, others were disposed of to other users; it was left for locomotives of Swedish design and possessing excellent riding qualities, to displace the old faithfuls.

Above: *Amtrak E60P electric locomotive at Newark, New Jersey, with New York-Miami "Silver Star" train, June 1982.*

Right: *Not quite the intended high-speed flyer and GG1 replacement; Amtrak's E60CP class No.963 at Washington, DC on a December day in 1979.*

Class AEM7 B₀-B₀ National Railroad Passenger Corporation (Amtrak), 1980

Type: Electric locomotive for high-speed passenger trains.
Gauge: 4ft 8½in (1,435mm).
Propulsion: Alternating current at 12,500V 25Hz or 60Hz, or at 25,000V 60Hz supplied via overhead catenary, a thyristor control and rectification system to four traction motors geared to each axle using ASEA hollow-shaft flexible drive.
Weight: 199,500lb (90.5t).
Max. axleload: 53,300lb (24t).
Tractive effort: 53,300lb (236kN).
Overall length: 51ft 5¾in (15,700mm).
Max. speed: 125mph (200km/h).

The "Rc" family of electric locomotives, developed by the Allmänna Svenska Elektriska Aktiebolaget (ASEA) organisation initially for Swedish State Railways, bids fair to be the world's most successful electric locomotive. Basically intended for mixed-traffic working, the scope of the design was developed on the one hand to handle express passenger traffic at 100mph (160km/h), while on the other a version has been supplied for hauling heavy iron-ore trains in Arctic regions. Abroad, such widely differing customers as Austria, Norway and the USA have ordered "Rc" derivatives.

One of the reasons for this pre-eminence is that the "Rc1" was the world's first thyristor locomotive design put into service in 1967; ingenuity on the part of other manufacturers was no substitute for years of experience in service. One of the major problems with thyristor locos is to prevent harmonic ripples produced by the thyristor circuits feeding back into the rails and interfering with signalling currents (which also flow in the same rails) and communication circuits generally. ASEA developed sophisticated electrical filters to deal with this problem.

By 1975 development had reached the "Rc4" class, the design of which included a patent system developed by ASEA for countering wheelslip. This automatically reduces the current supplied to any driving motor which begins to creep faster than the others. There are also improvements such as solid-state instead of rotary convertors for power supply to auxiliary apparatus. A total of 150 "Rc4s" were supplied to Swedish railways, plus another 15 with modifications produced for Norway (Class "el 16"), but ASEA's greatest success has occurred in the USA.

The National Railroad Passenger Corporation (better known as Amtrak) had had the problem of finding motive power to replace the superb but now ageing "GG1" class of 1934 already described. The new locomotives were required for use on the New York - Philadelphia- Washington main line, electrified at 11,000V 25Hz. Various substitutes fielded by US industry (which had built very few high-speed electric locomotives since the "GG1s") and one from France were disappointing, but a modified "Rc4" sent over on trial—'our little Volvo' Amtrak's motive-power men called her—proved to be just what the doctor ordered. Accordingly, a fleet of 47 was proposed.

Rather than fight the 'Buy American' lobby in the USA, ASEA sensibly licensed General Motors "Electro-Motive Division to build, using some ASEA parts, what are now known as Class "AEM7". The "AEM7s" have stronger bodies, 25 per cent more power than the demonstrator, and multi-current capability to cover future

Left: *Amtrak high-speed loco of Class AEM7, No.905, hurries through Harrison, New Jersey, with Train 121, the 16.30 New York to Washington Metroliner on September 9, 1982.*

conversions to 25,000V 60Hz, with a certain amount of 12,500V 60Hz.

Maximum speed is much higher at 125mph (200km/h), while the weight has risen by 17 per cent. This is no detriment, since very high axleloads are catered for in the USA by the use of heavy rail, closely-spaced sleepers and deep ballast. Vast sums have recently been expended by Amtrak to bring the North-East Corridor tracks, on which the "AEM7s" are used, up to first-class standards. The performance delivered by the "AEM7s" is what one might expect of a locomotive that can develop three times the power of Amtrak's contemporary "F40PH" diesels.

Below: *Swedish thyristor technology eventually sounded the death-knell for the famed GG1s, in the form of these EMD-built Class AEM7 locos with multi-current capability. No.902 is at Washington, DC.*

LRC B₀-B₀ Via Rail Canada (Via), 1982

Type: High-speed diesel-electric locomotive for matching train with tilting mechanism.

Gauge: 4ft 8½in (1,435mm).

Propulsion: Alco Type 251 16-cylinder 3,900hp (2,910kW) turbocharged four-stroke diesel engine and alternator feeding via rectifiers four nose-suspended direct current traction motors geared to the axles.

Weight: 185,135lb (84t).

Max. axleload: 46,285lb (21t).

Overall length: 66ft 5in (202,692mm).

Max. speed: 125mph (200km/h)*.

*Design speed of train; track limitations at present reduce this to 80mph (128km/h).

Having as its designation carefully chosen letters that read the same in English or French—Light, Rapid, Comfortable or *Leger, Rapide, Confortable* respectively—the designers had to have pointed out to them the letter L might in French just as well stand for *Lourd* or 'heavy'. The fact that an LRC passenger car weighs "only" 57 per cent more than, for example, an HST car of the same capacity in Britain does lend some sharpness to the point made. Similarly the LRC locomotive weighs 20 per cent more than the HST power car. Even so, LRC is an impressive creation, although the many years which have passed in development have seen as many (or more) setbacks and premature entries into service as Britain's APT. Even so, the new trains were due to go into service between Montreal and Toronto in September 1981. A scheduled time of 3hr 40min was originally intended for the 337 miles (539km), 45 minutes better than that offered by their best predecessors, the lightweight "Turbo-trains" in the late-1970s. But by July 1982 the best offered in the timetable was 4hr 25min, with an ominous note "Timings subject to alterations, journeys may be extended by up to 55 minutes", indicating a possible need to substitute conventional equipment.

This note reflects the fact that the LRC trains had to be withdrawn during the Canadian winter of 1981-82, having suffered from fine dry powdery snow getting inside sophisticated equipment. That the improvement in timings has been so relatively modest is due to the effects of heavy freight traffic on the existing track and the speed limits consequently imposed on the LRC. Two sets leased by the USA operator Amtrak have also not given satisfaction, and they have recently been returned to the makers.

Even so, LRC is a well thought out concept with a fourteen-year period of development behind it. An "active" tilting system allowing 8½° of tilt, ½° less than BR's APT, is combined with an advanced level of comfort of passengers. Ample power is available from the locomotives (which, incidentally, do not tilt) for both traction and substantial heating/air-conditioning requirements. One unique detail is the provision of outside loudspeakers so that announcements can be made to intending passengers on station platforms. The current order for Via Rail Canada provides for 22 locomotives and 50 cars. At the present time, however, problems with the cars have led to a surplus of motive power; LRC locomotives have been noted coupled to non-tilting stock on the Toronto to Chicago "International Limited".

Left: *The Via Rail LRC train (LRC—Light, Rapid, Comfortable) which attains its objective by having sophisticated tilting capability—up to 8½°—a low profile and a low centre of gravity. Propulsion is conventional diesel-electric.*

Right: *An early version of the Canadian LRC high-speed train was tried out in the United States by Amtrak but did not find favour.*

Below: *The locomotive of the LRC train developed in Canada by the Montreal firm of Bombardier Inc., between 1978 and 1983.*

SD-50 C₀-C₀

SD-50 C_o-C_o General Motors' Electro-Motive Division (EMD), 1981

Type: High-power multi-purpose diesel-electric locomotive.
Gauge: 4ft 8½in (1,435mm).
Propulsion: One EMD 645F3 3,800bhp (2,840kW) 16-cylinder turbocharged two-stroke Vee diesel engine supplying current through silicon rectifiers to six nose-suspended traction motors geared to the axles.
Weight: 368,000lb (167t).
Max. axleload: 61,340lb (27.9t).
Tractive effort: 96,300lb (426kN).
Overall length: 71ft 2in (21,692mm).
Max. speed: 70mph (112km/h).

The most prolific locomotive manufacturer the world has ever known? Well, it will not be long now, because although Baldwin produced almost 60,000 in 125 years of locomotive building, General Motors' Electro-Motive Division's score currently stands just beyond the 50,000 mark. Of course, EMD is well ahead as regards horsepower, while Baldwin certainly offered greater variety with steam of many wheel arrangements, rack-and-pinion, turbine, as well as straight electric and diesel-electric locomotives of the

two normal Bo-Bo and Co-Co types, amongst others. EMD is not only the main supplier in the USA, having built some 70 per cent of locomotives now running on US Class I railroads, but it also the biggest exporter. Most countries outside the communist world, except for those few with a domestic industry to protect, use General Motors' locomotives.

The present king of the EMD range is the "SD-50" 3,800hp (2,835kW) unit, driven by the 16-cylinder 645F3 engine. This is an improved version of that fitted to the "SD40-2" locomotive already described. The "SD40-2" series, best-seller during the 1970s, is still in the EMD range, but it appears that the "SD-45" series, which gave high horsepowers by using a 20-cylinder version of the 645 series engines, involved their users in high maintenance costs. The "SD-50" series is based on an alternative policy of strengthening and uprating the 16-cylinder engine.

The 12-wheel "SD-50" (the 'dash 2' designation, meaning modular electrics, is now taken as read) is also offered as an eight-wheeler called the "GP-50". An axleload only 6 per cent greater than that of the "SD-50" does not pose too serious a problem as regards

damage to the track, but the reduced weight on the drivers means a 30 per cent lower tractive effort, so that the "GP-50" is more suited to less heavily-graded lines upon which high power output is more significant than maximum tractive effort.

In this connection, EMD in 1981 introduced a considerably more sophisticated anti-wheel slip device than hitherto offered. This is known as the Super Series Adhesion Control System and uses radar to check the ground speed against the speed of revolution of individual pairs of wheels. The torque of each motor is automatically adjusted to keep the rate of wheel creep to a minimal amount. It is claimed that one-third more tractive effort can be produced by a unit which uses this device than one which does not.

In theory, modern electronic technology has something more to offer. For example, by means of microprocessors it would be theoretically possible to make a substantial improvement at the most critical point in the diesel cycle—the moment when the fuel is injected into the cylinder. With solely mechanical arrangements in this area, there must be some compromise with perfection—only too visible in the form of clouds of

filthy black smoke—at different points across the wide range of working. EMD is not revealing any secrets, but a micro-processor test unit has been seen running. One suspects that at this stage the idea is to replace the racks of relays which occasionally malfunction.

Returning to the present, it could be said that the high degree of standardisation and compatibility achieved has eliminated a great deal of variety from the railroad scene. But this has led to one fascinating area of increased interest, due to the ability of railroads to interchange standardised locomotives like freight cars. Even in a single train, the diesel units of two or three railroads and more than one manufacturer—some a long way from their home territory—can often be found. So, even if one can no longer see the wheels go round and the majority of locomotives are the same shape, the colour and style of their finish has a variety which offsets the uniformity.

Right: *In spanking new Conrail livery, EMD SD-50 No.6728 poses for the photographer one snowy morning. This class reverts to the 16-cylinder version of the 645 engine.*

GF6C C_o-C_o British Columbia Railway (BCR), 1983

Type: Heavy duty mineral-hauling electric locomotive for Arctic use.
Gauge: 4ft 8½in (1,435mm).
Propulsion: Alternating current at 50,000V 60Hz fed via overhead catenary and thyristor control system to six traction motors geared to the axles.
Weight: 330,000lb (150t).
Max. axleload: 82,500lb (37.5t).
Tractive effort: 95,180lb (421kN).
Overall length: 68ft 10in (20,980mm).
Max. speed: 68mph (109km/h).

The early-1980s were years when the nuts-and-bolts of North American railroading were undergoing few physical changes. For many lines it was not a case of how many new diesel units to order but how many to put away in storage lines. There were even rumours that General Motors Electro-Motive Division's main plant at La Grange, Illinois, would have to shut down for a time. Of course, when it came to placing locomotives in store, it was the interesting and unusual ones that were put away.

However, significant moves that had been distant dreams or mere ideas in the 1970s were in the 1980s beginning to be possibilities. If any were to happen, the technical face of railroading in North America would change almost overnight and almost out of recognition, just as its commercial and political aspects have

so recently done. Behind all these possibilities lies the huge change in the relative cost of energy obtained from coal compared with energy from oil. And the message is—put railroads under the wires because electrification is the best way to use coal for transportation power.

All sorts of other conditions might also be favourable to electrification. First, government assistance might even be made available. The Department of Transportation has been issuing tentative construction timetables and schedules for suitable electrification projects. Secondly, the main locomotive builders—not surprisingly since diesels can reasonably be regarded as electric locos of the self-generating type—are able to supply suitable power. Thirdly, the risk that heavy additional local taxes might have to be paid on the fixed electrical equipment seems no longer to be valid. Fourthly, the rationalisation which is following the mega-mergers and relaxation of other restraints means there is freedom to concentrate flows of traffic on fewer routes—and electrification needs dense traffic to justify the cost of fixed equipment. Fifthly, with profitability improving, schemes involving big capital investment might no longer be so difficult to finance. Lastly, there is now no argument as to the type of electric current to be supplied to moving trains—that is, it should be the same single-phase 60Hz alternating current that we are supplied

with in our own houses.

So far, it is true, electrification has been the biggest non-event in American railroad history. The USSR, for example, works nearly 60 per cent of its tonne-km electrically, whereas the figure for the USA is only 0.1 or even 0.01 per cent. Even 80 years ago, one could read almost the same arguments as appear above. But coming events cast their shadow before, and one notes with pleasure that General Motors (Canada) has supplied a batch of ac electric locomotives, designated "GF6C" for an 80-mile (129km) branch of the British Columbia Railway opened for traffic in November 1983. This has been built to bring out coal from a place called Tumbler Ridge in the north-eastern corner of the Province, far into the depths of the Canadian north. It is the first main-line electric railway in Canada outside the suburbs of Montreal.

The "GF6C" locomotive has a similar chassis and trucks to a standard diesel-electric road-switcher. There is a full width carbody with a depressed roof in the centre to accommodate the 50kV switchgear, and a transformer and thyristor control system replace the diesel engine and generator assembly. Three locomotives will be used on each 98-car train.

Right: *Canada's first electric locomotives to be built since 1914. The three BCR units are rated at 4,475kW.*

ACE 3000 4-8-2 Coal Oriented Advanced Systems (COALS), 1985

Type: Coal-burning freight locomotive.
Gauge: 4ft 8½in (1,435mm).
Propulsion: Coal-fired gas-producer firebox generating superheated steam at 300psi (21.1kg/cm²) in a fire tube boiler and supplying it first to two high-pressure and then to two low pressure cylinders, driving the four main axles direct by means of connecting and coupling rods.
Adhesive weight: 240,000lb (109t).
Max. axleload: 60,000lb (27.25 t).
Overall length: 458ft 6in (48,312mm).
Max. speed: 70mph (112km/h).

A most startling change in railroad motive power could be just round the corner—steam itself might be on the way back. Of course, most electric railroading is in a sense steam traction, because generators in power stations—even nuclear ones—are generally driven by steam, but the project in question is for a real steam locomotive burning coal directly. The key to the idea is the relative cost of different energy sources. In the 1940s and 1950s, when railroads changed from steam traction to diesel, diesel fuel cost around one-fifteenth of today's price. Coal, on the other hand, then cost only about a quarter of what it does today. Put another way, a dollar spent on coal now buys nearly

four times as much energy as the same sum spent on diesel fuel. It is granted that the steam locomotive will be less thermally-efficient, but there will still be a handsome margin of saving.

The idea that steam traction might have substantially lower costs than diesel is one that takes a little getting used to. Even the most rabid steam fan never claims more than that the diesel takeover battle was a much closer one than the victors ever admit. The big hurdle is to produce a machine that is less labour-intensive and polluting than its predecessors, but which at the same time retains the simplicity and reliability which was steam's greatest asset.

The original proposer of what

was first called the "ACE 3000" project (ACE stands for American Coal Enterprises) was a man named Russ E. Rowlands. He and his design team have borne all these things well and truly in mind because Rowlands, a commodities broker, had had experience in running conventional steam locomotives on diesel-worked railroads. He was the man who put a Nickel Plate 2-8-4, a Reading 4-8-4 and a Chesapeake & Ohio 4-8-4 back on the rails, and naturally most of the original features of the new project are orientated towards solving the problems of servicing. For example, run-of-the-mine coal used as fuel would be supplied ready packaged in 11-ton modules. The

Glossary

Adhesion—the frictional grip between wheel and rail.
Adhesive weight—the sum of driving wheel loads.
Air brake—power braking system with compressed air as the operating medium.
Alternating current (ac)—electric current which reverses its direction flow at rapid and regular intervals.
Alternator—a machine which converts mechanical energy to electrical energy and generates alternating current.
Armature—the rotating part of a direct current electric motor or generator. Contains a number of coils, or windings, which rotate in a magnetic field and are connected to the commutator.
Axlebox—box-shaped housing containing axle bearing.
Ballast—material placed between the sleepers and formation of railway track to distribute the load of passing traffic.
Catenary—supporting cable for the contact or conductor wire of an overhead electrification system.
Circuit breaker—automatic switch for making and breaking an electrical circuit.

Boiler—steam producing unit. Locomotive type consists essentially of a fire box surrounded by a water space in which the combustion of fuel takes place, and barrel containing the flue tubes surrounded by water.
Collector shoe—metal block in contact with conductor rail for collecting current from third rail electrification system.
Common carrier—a transport organization which is not permitted to be selective in the freight accepted for conveyance.
Consist—composition or make-up of a train.
Crank—device for converting rotary to reciprocating motion or vice versa. Consists of an arm, one end of which is fixed to a shaft and the other free to rotate about the axis of the shaft.
Diesel—compression ignition, internal combustion engine.
Direct current (dc)—electrical current which flows in one direction continuously.
Direct drive—direct mechanical connection between output end of prime mover and driving wheels of locomotive.
Drive—transmission of power.

Dynamic braking—system of braking utilizing the braking characteristics of the engine compression, transmission or traction motors.
Eccentric—disc, keyed to axle, whose centre does not coincide with that of the axle. It rotates an eccentric strap, to which is attached the eccentric rod, and imparts reciprocating motion for operating the steam distribution valve.
Exhaust steam—emission of steam from the cylinder after completion of the working stroke.
Expansion of steam—increase in volume of steam in the cylinder after the supply has been cut off. The ability to take maximum advantage of the expansive qualities of steam results in economies in the consumption of fuel and water.
Firebox—part of a steam locomotive boiler where combustion of the fuel takes place.
Flange—projecting edge or rim on the periphery of a wheel or rail.
Frame—foundation or chassis upon which a locomotive is built.
Frequency—number of times a second an alternating electric current reverses its direction of flow.
Gas turbine—rotary internal combustion machine which is driven by gas flow thus causing varied disc(s) mounted on common shaft to turn at high speed.
Gauge—the distance between

running edges or inner faces of the rails of railway track.
Generator—electrical machine which changes mechanical energy. Term generally applied to one which produces direct current.
Grade—slope or inclination to the horizontal of a railway. Expressed as a percentage of unit rise or fall to the horizontal or slope length.
Heating surface—areas of locomotive boiler exposed to heat on one side and available for water evaporation on other.
Hot box—an overheated vehicle axlebox bearing resulting from breakdown of lubricating film between bearing and journal.
Injector—device for forcing water into the boiler of a steam locomotive; also device for feeding atomized fuel oil into cylinder or combustion chamber of a diesel engine.
Journal—area of a shaft or axle supported by a bearing.
Live rail—electrical conductor for transmitting power to locomotives or train on third-rail electrified lines.
Motion—a moving mechanism; the valve gear of a steam locomotive.
Motor generator set—electric motor and generator mechanically coupled for the purpose of converting direct current from one voltage to another.
Multiple unit—two or more locomotives or powered vehicles

locomotive-type boiler and direct-drive compound double-acting cylinders correspond to conventional principles, although the layout proposed has not previously been successful.

An important technical feature is one that has been developed in Argentina and more recently in South Africa. The coal is to be converted to a mixture of water and producer gas before being burnt, by introducing steam into the firebed. The reaction takes place at a modest temperature; consequently clinker does not form. There are two advantages; first, the coal is consumed more thoroughly and so the process is more efficient. Secondly, since the air for combustion is introduced

above the firebed, unpleasant emissions of unburnt fuel in the form of smoke and ash are virtually eliminated, thereby making steam traction acceptable to people who object to black smoke.

To give the machine a long range between water stops, a bulky condensing tender is planned. A sophisticated electronic control system would enable the locomotive to run in multiple with diesel locomotives or another "ACE 3000," and it could be driven from a cab at either end or from another "ACE 3000". The four driving axles are rigidly mounted on the same chassis; the two inner ones have crankshafts and are coupled together by a pair of internal connecting rods. This arrangement

allows for perfect balance to be achieved.

A totally new feature is that a microprocessor will look after combustion of the fuel as well as setting the precise steam thrust on the pistons at every point during each revolution of the wheels. This would cover dynamic braking as well as normal traction, thereby opening a totally new concept of locomotive control. Trials of the computer equipment are to be carried out on the preserved Chesapeake & Ohio Greenbriar 4-8-4 No.614.

A new consortium of American Coal Enterprises, Burlington Northern, Chesapeake & Ohio and Babcock & Wilcox/McDermot International, known as

COALS (Coal-Oriented Advanced Locomotive Systems) is now at work on the project. Substantial savings are promised to any railroad that adopts "new steam"; for that and every other sort of reason the appearance of some hardware is eagerly awaited.

Below: *Could this be the motive power for a future starved of oil supplies? At least the cost of providing infrastructure for running and maintaining a fleet of steam locos would be far less than the huge investment necessary for diesel's other rival—electric traction. Time will tell whether this visionary project has a future.*

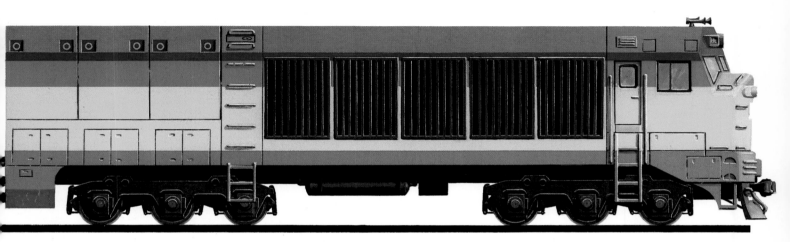

coupled together, or in a train, operated by only one driver.

Narrow gauge—railway track of less than the standard gauge.

Nose-suspended-motor—traction motor mounted on bearings on axle being driven with a "nose" resiliently fixed to a bogie cross member to prevent rotation round axle. Gear on axle is in constant mesh with pinion on armature shaft.

Overhead—catenary and contact wire of a suspended electrical distribution system.

Pantograph—link between overhead contact system and power circuit of an electric locomotive. Simplest form is spring loaded pivoted diamond frame with copper or carbon contact strip.

Pony truck—two-wheel pivoted truck to assist the guidance of a locomotive around curves.

Rack railway—system used on mountain railways (and occasionally elsewhere) where gradients exist too steep for the normal adhesion between wheel and rail to be effective. A pinion on the locomotive engages in a rack fixed to the track. The rack can consist either of a longitudinal series of steel teeth or of rungs of gear-tooth profile fixed to side members like the rungs of a ladder.

Railcar—self-propelled passenger-carrying vehicle.

Rapid transit—system for high-

speed urban mass transport.

Rectifier—a device for converting alternating electric current to direct current.

Regenerative brake—electrical braking system whereby the traction motors of direct current electric locomotives work as generators and feed electrical energy back into supply system.

Relay—remotely controlled electromagnetic switch for low electrical currents.

Rheostatic braking—electrical braking system whereby the traction motors work as generators, the resultant electrical energy being dissipated as heat in resistances.

Roller bearing—hardened steel cylinders located in a cage which revolve in contact with inner and outer races.

Roundhouse—locomotive shed in which the stabling tracks radiate from a turntable.

Safety valve—directly connected to the steam space of all boilers and set to operate automatically at a pre-determined pressure to release excess steam.

Semi-conductor—material used in electric traction rectifiers, whose electrical resistance depends on the direction of the applied voltage. Germanium and silicon are typical examples.

Series-parallel connection—method of connecting traction motors whereby individual motors are connected in series to form

groups and each group then connected in parallel.

Series motor—direct current electrical machine with ideal traction characteristics. Produces a high torque when the vehicle is started and as the load increases the speed drops.

Single-phase—single alternating electric current. One phase of three-phase supply.

Slip—loss of adhesion between driving wheel and rail causing wheels to spin.

Smoke box—extension to barrel at the front end of a locomotive boiler housing the main steam pipes to cylinders, blast pipe, blower ring and chimney.

Supercharge—supply air to the inlet valves of a diesel engine at above atmospheric pressure.

Superheating—increasing the temperature and volume of steam after leaving the boiler barrel by application of additional heat.

Suspension—connecting system, including springs, between vehicle wheel and body, designed to give best possible riding qualities by keeping unsprung weights to a minimum and reducing shock loadings on track.

Tank locomotive—one which carries its fuel and water supplies on its own main frames.

Third rail—non-running rail carrying electrical current to electric locomotive or train.

Three-phase—simultaneous

supply or use of three electrical currents of same voltage, each differing by a third in frequency cycle.

Tire—steel band forming the periphery of a wheel, on which the flange and tread profile is formed.

Train-pipe—continuous air or vacuum brake pipe, with flexible connections between vehicles, through which operation of the train brake is controlled.

Transformer—device which by electromagnetic induction converts one voltage of alternating current to another.

Turbo-charger—turbine, driven by the flow of exhaust gases from a diesel engine coupled to a rotary compressor which supplies air at above atmospheric pressure to the engine-inlet valves.

Vacuum brake—braking system with atmospheric air pressure as operating medium.

Valve gear—mechanism which controls the operation of the steam distribution valve in the steam chest of a locomotive cylinder. Stephenson, Walschaert, Baker and Southern are the valve gears most commonly seen.

Vigilance device—ensures the continued vigilance or alertness of the driver by requiring him to make a positive action at frequent intervals. Failure to do so results in power being cut off and the brakes applied.

Index

Bold figures refer to locomotives mentioned in captions to illustrations

A

Ackroyd-Stuart diesel-electric locomotive No.1 (Alco), **86-7**
Adhesion control system (EMD), **202**
"Aerotrain" (C, RI&P), 18
Agenoria 0-4-0 (Shutt End Railway, Stourbridge), 24-5
Alabama Great Southern Railroad, Ps-4-6-2, 101
"Alaskan", **93**
Alco,
  4300 4-8-2 (SP), 80-1
  800 2-10-10-2 (VGN), 80-1
  9000 4-12-2, **96-7**
  A 4-4-2 (CMSt P&P), **112-3**
  A 4-8-4, 92
  Big Boy 4-8-8-4 (UP), **136-7**
  C630 Century Co-Co **190-1**
  FEF-2 4-8-4 (UP), **126-7**
  J3a 4-6-4 (NYC), **98-9**
  Niagara 4-8-4 (NYC), **152-3**
  No.1 Bo-Bo, **86-7**
  No.2400 0-6-6-0, **58-9**
  No.57156, 1201 2-62T, 76-7
  PA Series A1A-A1A, **156-7**
  Ps-4 4-6-2 (SR), **100-1**
  WDM2 Co-Co (IR), **188-9**
Algoma Central Railway, GP7 Bo-Bo (EMD), **171**
Allen, Horatio, 24
Allmanna Svenska Elektriska Aktiebolaget (ASEA), 199, 202-3
  Alternators, 191
American Civil War, 36-7
American Locomotive Co, see Alco
American Standard Class 4-4-0, 31, **36-7**
Amtrak
  AEM7 Bo-Bo (EMD), **198-9**
  E60CP Co-Co (GE), **198-9**
  F40PH, Bo-Bo (EMD), **197**
  Metroliner Two-car trainset (Budd), **182-3**
"Andrew Jackson" 0-4-0 (B&O), **28**
"Arabian" 0-4-0 (B&O), 28
Articulated locomotives, see Mallet articulated locomotives
ASEA, 199, 202-3
Atchison, Topeka & Santa Fe Railway (AT & SF)
  900 2-10-2, **62-3**
  1300 2-4-6-2, **66-7**
  2900 4-8-4, **148-9**
  3460 4-6-4, **118-9**
  5001 2-10-4 **124-5**
  PA-series A1A-A1A No.51, **156**
  C630 Century Co-Co (Alco), **190**
"Atlantic" 0-4-0 (B&O), **28-9**
Atlantic Class E3sd 4-4-2 (PRR), **54-5**
  Rebuild as Class A-6 (SP), **90-1**
Atlantic City Railroad, Camelback 4-4-2, **48-9**
Attwood, Ellis D, 69
Automatic railraod (MER), 192
Automation, **22-3**

B

Baker's valve gear, 98
Baldwin locomotives (BLW), **39-49, 54-5, 60-5, 68-9, 74-5, 78-9, 83, 84-5, 88-9, 92-5, 104-5, 118-21, 128-9, 140-1, 146-7, 154-5, 158-9, 162-5, 168-9**
Baldwin — De La Vergne diesel engine, 164
Baltimore & Ohio Railroad (B&O),
  "Tom Thumb" 0-2-2, **26-7**
  Grasshopper 0-4-0, **28-9**
  Mud-digger 0-8-0, **30-1**
  "Lafayette" 4-2-0, **32-3**
  Camel 4-6-0, **34-5**
  Nos. 1-3 Bo + Bo, **46-7**
  P-7 President 4-6-2, **102-3**
  F series Bo-Bo (EMD), A&B units, **122**
  Museum, 78, 87
Bangor & Aroostook Railroad (BAR), BL2 Bo-Bo, **160-1**
Barco low water alarm, 121
Batchelder, Asa, 56
Beardmore diesel-electric locomotive No.9000 2-Do-1 (CNR), **106-7**
Beaver Meadows Railroad, Hercules 4-4-0, **31**
Belpaire firebox, 103
Benares locomotive works, 188
Bengal & Assam Railway, 144
Berkshire type locomotive 2-8-4, S-3 (NKP), **166-7**
Bib Boy 4-8-8-4 (U), **136-7**
Bipolar, Class EP-2, 1-B-D-D-B-1 (CMSt P&P), **82-3**
Birmingham & Gloucester Railway, 33
Bowen, H.B., 116-7
Braking systems, 12, 40-1, 132
Bridgton & Saco River Railroad (B&SR), No.7 2-4-4-T, **68-9**
British Columbia Railway,
  C630 Century Co-Co (Alco), **191**
  GF6C Co-Co, **202-3**
British War Department, 1201 2-6-2T, **76-7**
"Broadway Limited", **73**
Brooks Locomotive Works, 30, 51
"Brother Jonathan" 4-2-0 (M&HRR), **25**, 30, 32
Budd Co,
  RDC Single Railcar, **180-1**
  Metroliner Two-car trainset, **182-3**
Bury, Edward, 27

C

Cab Forward, Class AC-4 4-8-8-2 (SP), **104-5**
Cab interior, **14**
Cab-signalling system, 111
California Railroad Museum, Sacramento, 27
Camden & Amboy Railroad,
  "John Bull" 0-4-0 (later 4-2-0), **26-7**
  "John Stevens" 6-2-0, **34-5**
Camel 4-6-0 (B&O), **34-5**
Camelback Class 4-4-2 (ACR), **48-9**
Campbell 4-4-0 (PG&NRR), 30
Canadian Locomotive Cc, 106, 146
Canadian National Railways (CNR),
No.9000 2-Do-1, **106-7**
  U-1f 4-8-2, **146-7**
  U-4 4-8-4, **146-7**
  SD40-2 Co-Co (EMD), **195**
Canadian Pacific Railway,
  GP32-2 Bo-Bo (EMD), **170**
  Royal Hudson 4-6-4 **116-7**
  Selkirk 2-10-4, **166-7**
"Cannonball" express, **95**
Car-body principle, 122
Cascade Tunnel electrification, **158-9**
Casey Jones, 48-9
Centennial DD40AX Do-Do (UP), **184-5**
Centipede 2-Do-Do-2 (SAL), **184-5**
"Central of New Jersey" No.1000 (Alco), 87
Central Pacific Railroad (CPR),
  "El Gobernador' 4-10-0, **40-1**
  "Jupiter" 4-4-0, **37**
Century, C630 Co-Co (Alco), **190-1**
Challenger 4-6-6-4 (UP), **15, 142-3**
Chattanooga Choo-choos, 131
"Cheltenham Flyer;; (GWR), 116
Chesapeake & Ohio Railroad (C&O),
  F15 4-6-2, **52-3**
  H-8 Allegheny 2-6-6-6- **138-9**
  L-2a 4-6-4, **162-3**
  M-1 2-1Co-2-1Co-Bo, **158-9**
Chicago & North Western Railway, 113
  "400" trains, 120
  E4 4-6-4, **120-1**
  RDC Single Railcar (Budd), **181**
Chicago & South Side Rapid Transit, Forney o-4-T, **8-9, 46-7**
Chicago, Burlington & Quincy Railroad (CB&Q),
  05A 4-8-4, **120-1**
  Pioneer Zephyr Three-car train, **108-9**
  "Zephyr", 113, 121
Chicago, Milwaukee St Paul & Pacific Railroad (CMStP&P),
  A 4-4-2, **112-3**
  EP-2 Bi-polar, **82-3**
  F7 4-6-4, **112-3**
Chicago Museum of Science & Industry, 45, 109, 149
Chicago, North Shore & Milwaukee Railroad (North Shore),
  "Electroliner", **134-5**
Chicago Regional Transportation Authority, F40PH Bo-Bo (EMD), **196**
Chicago, Rock Island & Pacific Railroad, **18, 114**
Cincinnati, New Orleans & Texas Pacific Railroad, PS-4 4-6-2, 101
"City of Los Angeles" trainset (UP), **108,** 114
  "City of San Francisco", 114
Civil War, 36-7
Classes of Locomotives,
  0-1A 2-8-2 (CB&Q), **94-5**
  0-5A 4-8-4 (CB&Q), 120-1
  60-3 Shay B-B-B (Sierra Nevada Wood & Lumber Co) **15, 70-1**
  92 1-Co-Co-1 (EAR), **190-1**
  141R Libration 2-8-2 (SNCF), **150-1**
  800 2-10-10-2 (VGN), **80-1**
  1201 2-6-2T (British War Dept), **76-7**
  1300 2-4-6-2 (AT&SF), **66-7**
  2130 Co-Co (QR), **186-7**
  2900 4-8-4 (AT&SF), **148-9**
  3000 2-10-10-2 (AF&SF), **63**
  3460 4-6-4 (AT&SF), **118-9**
  3800 2-10-2 (AT&SF), **63**
  4300 4-8-2 (SP) **80-1**
  5001 2-10-4 (AT&SF), **124-5**
  9000 4-12-2 (UP), **96-7**
  9700 Mikado 2-8-2 (Nippon Railway) **58-9**
  A 4-4-2 (CMStP&P), **112-3**
  A 4-8-4 (NP), **92-3**
  A6 4-4-2 (SP), **90-1**
  AC-4 Cab Forward 4-8-8-2 (SP), **104-5**
  ACE3000 4-8-2 (COALS), **204-5**
  AEM7 Bo-Bo (Amtrak), **198-9**
  BL2 Bo-Bo (BAR), **160-1**
  C16-60 (D&RG), **42-3**
  C19 (D&RG), **42-3**
  C630 Century Co-Co (Alco), **190-1**
  D16sb 4-4-0 (PRR), **50-1**
  DD1 2-B+B-2 (PRR), **64-5**
  DD40AX Centennial Do-Do (UP), **184-5**
  Dc A1A-A1A (NZR), **193**
  Df Co-Co (NZR), **193, 192-3**
  E 2-10-0 (Imperial Russian Government), **78-9**
  E Series A1-A1 (EMD), **114-5**
  E3sd Atlantic 4-4-2 (PRR), **54-5**
  E4 4-6-4 (C&NW), **120-1**
  E50C Co-Co (MER), **192-3**
  E60CP Co-Co (Amtrak), **198-9**
  E60P, **110**
  EL-2 2-8-8-0 (B&O), **59**
  EP1 Bo-Bo (NY, NH&HRR), **60-1**
  EP2 Bi-polar 1-B-D-D-B-1, (CMStP&P), **82-3**
  EP3 (CMStP&P) 83
  F Series Bo-Bo (EMD), **122-3**
  Fla, F2a 4-4-4 (CPR), **100-1**
  F7 4-6-4 (CMStP&P), **112-3**
  F15 4-6-2 (C&O), **52-3**
  F16-F19 4-6-2, 53
  F40PH Bo-Bo (EMD), **196-7**
  FEF2 4-8-4 (UP), 126-7
  F19 Bo-A1A (NY, NH&HRR), **174-5**
  G5s 4-6-0 (LIRR), **103**
  GFC Co-Co (BCR), **202-3**
  GG1 2-Co-Co-2 (PRR), **110-1**
  GP Series Bo-Bo (EMD), **170-1**
  GS2-6 484 (SP), **132-3**
  H4 4-6-2 (GN), **62-3**
  H8 Allegheny 2-6-6-6 (C&O), **138-9**
  I-1 4-6-0 (LS&MSRR), **50-1**
  I-5 4-6-4 (NY, NH&HRR), **128-9**
  J 4-8-4 (N&W), **130-1**
  J1a 2-10-4 (PRR), **140-1**
  J3a 4-6-4 (NYC), **98-9**
  K4 4-6-2 (PRR), **72-3**
    Rebuild as P1 4-6-4 (WAB), **94-5**
  K36 2-8-2 (D&RG), **88-9**
  L 2-6-6-0 (GN), **58**
  L2a 4-6-4 (C&O), **162-3**
  LRC Bo-Bo (Via), **200-1**
  M1 2-1Co-2-1Co-Bo, **158-9**
  M3 Yellowstone 2-8-8-4 (DM&IR), 128-9
  MvA1A-A1A (DSB), **174-5**
  NH/4 2-8-2 (ScSR), **150-1**
  NW2 Bo-Bo (EMD), **134-5**
  P1 4-6-4 (WAB), **94-5**
  Ps-4 4-6-2 (SR), **100-1**
  P7 4-6-2 (B&O), 102-3
  Q 4-6-2 (NZR), **52-3**
  QR1 4-8-4 (NdeM), **154-5**
  RDC Single Railcar (Budd), **180-1**
  RF16 "Shark-nose" Bo-Bo (BLW), **164-5**
  S 1-Do-1 (NYC&HRRR), **56-7**
  S 2-Do-2 (NYC), **64-5**
  S1a 0-8-0 (N&W), **168-9**
  S2 6-8-6 (PRR), **154-5**
  S3 2-8-4 (NKP), **166-7**
  S7 0-10-2 (URR), **118-9**
  S160 2-80 (USATC), **144-5**
  SD40-2 Co-Co (EMD), **194-5**
  SD50 Co-Co (EMD), **202-3**
  T Bo-Bo+Bo-Bo (NYC), **64-5**
  T1 2-10-4 (C&O), 140
  T1 4-4-4-4 (PRR), **140-1**
  U1f 4-8-2 (CNR), **146-7**
  U4 4-8-4 (CNR), **146-7**
  U25B Bo-Bo (GE), **176-7**
  W1 Bo-Do-Do-Bo (GN), **158-9**
  WDM2 Co-Co (IR), **188-9**
  WP 4-6-2 (IR), **180-1**
  X Co-Co (VicRail), **186-7**
  Y6b 2-8-8-2 (N&W), **162-3**
  YP 4-6-2 (IR), **168-9**
  American Standard 4-4-0, 31, **36-7**
  Big Boy 4-8-8-4 (UP), **136-7**
  Camel 4-6-0 (B&O), **34-5**
  Camelback 4-4-2 (ACR), **48-9**
  Centipede 2-Do-Do-2 (SAL), **164-5**
  Challenger 4-6-6-4 (U), **15, 142-3**
  Consolidation 2-8-0 (LVR), **38-9**
  Fairlie 0-6-6-0 (FCM), **66-7**
  Forney 0-4-4R (Chicago & South Side Rapid Transit), **46-7**
  Gas Turbine Bo-Bo-Bo-Bo (UP), **172-3**
  Grasshopper 0-4-0 (B&O), **28-9**
  Krauss-Maffei C-C (D&RGW&SP), **178-9**
  Light Mikado 2-8-2 (USRA), **78-9**
  Little Joe 2-Do-Do2 (SZD), **160-1**
  Macarthur 2-8-2 (USATC), **144-5**
  Mogul 2-6-0 (Rogers), **38-9**
  Mud-digger 0-8-0 (B&O), **30-1**
  Narrow-gauge 0-10-0 (KPR), **84-5**
  Niagara 4-8-4 (NYC), **152-3**
  Norris locomotives **32-3**
  Royal Hudson 4-6-4 (CPR), **116-7**
  Selkirk 2-10-4 (CPR), **166-7**
  Trainmaster H24-66 Co-Co (FM), **15, 172-3**
Clyde Engineering Pty, Sydney (NSW), 186-7
Coal Oriented Advanced Systems (COALS), ACE3000 4-8-2, **204-5**
Cog locomotives,
  G5s 4-6-0 (LIRR), **103**
  Highliner Railcar, **182-3**
Commuter traffic, **20-3**
"Confederation" No.61000, 146
"Consolidation" 2-8-0 (LVR) **38-9**
Construction train, 2
Cooper, Peter, 26
Cooper, Thomas, 27
"Coronation" express (LNER), 132
Couplers, 12
Crampton, Thomas Russell, 34
Crawford mechanical stoker, 72
Cumbres & Toltec Scenic Railroad, **17,** 89

D

Danish State Railways (DSB), MVA1A-A1A (EMD), **174-5**
Davis & Gartner, 28
"Daylight" express 91, **132-3**
"De Witt Clinton" (M&HRR), **28-9**
Delaware & Hudson Canal Co (D&H), "Stourbridge Lion" 0-4-0, **24-5**
Delaware & Hudson Railway (D&H)
  No.1403, "L.F. Loree", 4-8-0, **106-7**
  'Shark-nose', RF16, Bo-Bo, **165**
Denver & Rio Grande Railroad (D&RG)
  D16, C19 locomotives, **42-3**
  F series Bo-Bo (EMD), **123**
  K36 2-8-2, **88-9**
  Krauss-Maffei C-C, **178-9**
"Detroit Arrow", 73
Diesel-electric locomotives, early history, **86-7**
  early examples, **106-9**
Diesel-hydraulic Krauss-Maffei C-C locomotive, **178-9**
Dilworth, Richard M, 122
Distance record-holder for steam, 3460 4-6-4 (AT&SF), **118-9**
"Dominion" express (CPR), 117, 166
Double-Fairlie locomotives, 67
Dreyfus casing, on J3 Hudson, **99**
Dripps, Issac, 26-7
Dual-voltage locomotive, EP1 Bo-Bo (NY, NH & HRR), **60-1**
Duluth, Missabe & Iron Range Railroad (DM&IR), M-3 Yellowstone 2-8-8-4, **128-9**
Duplex fiasco, **140-1**

E

Eames Vacuum Brake Co, 40
East African Railways (EAR), 92 1-Co-Co-1 (Alco), **190-1**
East Broad Top Railroad (EBT) No.14 2-8-2, **68-9**
  Petrol-electric railcar, **91**
Eastwick & Harrison, 31
Edaville Railroad, No.7 2-4-4T, **68-9**
Edison, Thomas, 43
"El Gobernador" 4-10-0 (CPRR), **40-1**
Electric Railway Co, "The Judge", **43**
Electrification, **20,** 202
"Electroliner" Four-car trainset (North Shore), **134-5**
Electro-Motive Company
  M-300 Single-unit railcar, **90-1**
  see also General Motors Corporation, Electro-Motive Division
Electro-pneumatic brakes, 132
Elevated railways, 46-7
"Empire Builder", **12**
"Empire State Express", No.999 4-4-0 (NYC&HRRR), **44-5**
"Empire State Express", J1 4-6-4 No.5280, **99**
Erie Railroad, Triplex 2-8-8-8-2, **74-5**
Essl, Max, 164
"Experiment" 4-2-0 (M&HRR), 25

F

Fairbanks Morse & Co (FM), Trainmaster H-24-66, Co-Co, **15, 172-3**
Fairlie 0-6-6-0 (FCM), **66-7**
Festiniog Railway,
  Double-Fairlie 0-4-4-0, 67
  "Mountaineer" 1201 2-6-2T, **76-7**
Field, Stephen, 43
Ford (Henry) Museum, Dearborn, Mich., 28, 139
Forney P-4-4T (Chicago & South Side Rapid Transit), 8-9, **46-7**
Foster & Rastrick, 24
"Four Aces", No.1111, 4-8-4, 92
"Freedom Train", 133, 167
French National Railways (SNCF), 141R Liberation 2-8-2, **150-1**

G

Galloping Goose railcar (RGS), **17, 124-5**
Garrett & Eastwick, 31
Gas Turbine Bo-Bo-Bo-Bo (UP), **172-3**

Gasoline, see Petrol
"General" 4-4-0, 36, 37
General Electric (USA),
EP1 Bo-Bo (NY, NH&HRR), **60-1**
EP2 Bi-polar 1-B-D-D-B-1 (CMStP&P), **82-3**
No.1 Bo-Bo (Alco), **86-7**
Nos. 1-3 Bo+Bo (B&O), **46-7**
S 1-Do-1 (NYC&HRRR), **56-7**
PA Series A1A-A1A (Alco), **156-7**
W1 Bo-Do-Do-Bo (GN), **158-9**
Little Joe 2-Do-Do-2 (SZD), **160-1**
Gas Turbine Bo-Bo-Bo-Bo (UP), **172-3**
U25B Bo-Bo, **176-7**
Dx Co-Co (NZR), **192-3**
E60CP Co-Co (Amtrak), **198-9**
diesel-electric engines, **176-7**
relationship with Alco, 190-1
General Motors (Canada), 202-3
General Motors Corporation,
2130 Co-Co (QR), **186-7**
Electro-Motive Division,
AEM7 Bo-Bo (Amtrak), **198-9**
BL2 Bo-Bo (BAR), **160-1**
DD40AX Centennial Do-Do (UP), **184-5**
E Series A1A-A1A, **114-5**
F Series Bo-Bo, **16-17, 122-3**
F40PH Bo-Bo, **196-7**
GP Series Bo-Bo, **170-1**
Mv A1A-A1A (DSB), **174-5**
N&SW Series Bo-Bo, 134-5
NW2 Bo-Bo, **134-5**
SD-40-2 Co-Co **194-5**
SD-50 Co-Co, **202-3**
X Co-Co (VicRail), **186-7**
General Steel Industries, St Louis Car Division,
Highliner Railcar (1C), **182-3**
"George Washington", **10**
Gillingham & Winans, 30
"Governor Stanford" 4-4-0 (CPRR), 40
Grand Trunk Western Railroad, 146
Grasshopper 0-4-0 (B&O), **28-9**
Great Northern Railway (GN),
H4 4-6-2, **62-3**
W1 Bo-Do-Do-Bo, **158-9**
Gulf, Mobile & Ohio Railroad, EMD E-series, **115**

H

Hayes, Samuel, 34
Hercules 4-4-0 (Beaver Meadows Railroad), **31**
"Hiawatha", 113, 120, 132
Highliner Railcar (IC), **182-3**
Hill, Jerome, 62
Honesdale (Penn.), 24
Hornsby, Richard & Co, 86
Hudson, William, 38
Hudson type locomotives 4-6-4,
3460 (AT&SF), **118-9**
E4 (C&NW), **120-1**
F7 (CMStP&P), **112-3**
15 (NY, NH&HRR), **128-9**
J3 (NYC), **98-9**
L2a (C&O), **162-3**

I

Illinois Central Railroad,
Highliner Railcar, **182-3**
No.382 4-6-0, **48-9**
WD, **144**
Ingersoll-Rand diesel engines, 86
"International Limited", 106

J

Jervis, John B, 25, 28
"John B Jervis", No.1400, 4-8-0 (D&H), 106
"John Bull" 0-4-0 (later 4-2-0) (Camden & Amboy Railroad), **26-7**
"John Hancock" 0-4-0 (B&O), 28
"John Stevens" 6-2-0 (Camden & Amboy Railroad), **34-5**
Jones, Casey, 48-9
Jubilee, F2a 4-4-4 (CPR), **100-1**
"The Judge" (Chicago Railroad Exposition, 1883), **43**
Jupiter 4-4-0 (CPRR), **37**

K

Kiefer, Paul, 98, 152
"King George V" (GWR), 102
"Klamath" express, **132**
Ko Pei Railway (KPR), Narrow Gauge 0-10-0, **84-5**
Krauss-Maffei C-C (D&RGW&SP) **178-9**

L

Lafayette 4-2-0 (B&O), **32-3**
Lake Shore & Michigan Southern Railroad (LS&MSRR), **50-1**
Lehigh Valley Railroad (LVR), Consolidation 2-8-0, **38-9**
Liberation, 141R 2-8-2 (SNCF), **150-1**
Light Mikado 2-8-2 (USRA), **78-9**
Lima Locomotive Works
60-3 Shay B-B-B, **15, 70-1**
5001 2-10-4 (AT&SF), **124-5**
S3 2-8-4 (NKP), **166-7**
T1 2-10-4 (PRR), **140-1**
Lion 0-4-0 (D&H), **24-5**
Little Joe 2-Do-Do-2 (SZD), **160-1**
Loewy, Raymond, 73, 110
Long Island Railroad,
Petrol-electric railcar, **90**
G5s 4-6-0, **103**
"L.F. Loree", No.1403, 4-8-0 (D&H), **106-7**
Louisville & Nashville Railroad, "U-boat" road switcher (GE), **177**
"Lovatt Eames" 4-2-2 (P&R), **40-1**
Lynton & Barnstaple Railway (L&B), "Lyn" 2-4-2T, **54-5**

M

"Madam Queen", 5001 2-10-4 (AT&SF), **125**
Mallet articulated locomotives,
800 2-10-10-2 (VGN), **80-1**
9000 4-12-2 (UP), **96-7**
1300 (AT&SF), **66-7**
AC-4 Cab Forward 4-8-8-2 (SP), **104-5**
Challenger 4-6-6-4 (UP), **142-3**
history, 142
M3 Yellowstone 2-8-8-4 (DM&IR), **128-9**
No.2400 (B&O), **58-9**
Triplex 2-8-8-8-2 (Erie Railroad), **74-5**
Manchester Locomotive Works, 188, 189
Maryland DoT, F series Bo-Bo (EMD), **123**
Massachusetts Bay Transportation Agency, F series Bo-Bo (EMD), **122**
"Mastodon" 4-8-0 (CPRR), 40
"Matt. H Shay", Triplex 2-8-8-8-2 (Erie Railroad), **74-5**
MCB coupler, 12
Metroliner Two-car trainset (PRR), **182-3**
"Metroliner" (Amtrak), **198**
Mexican Railway (FCM), Fairlie 0-6-6-0, **66-7**
Mikado, 9700 2-8-2 (Nippon Railway), **58-9**
Miller, E.L., 25
Miller, Victor A, 125
Mogul 2-6-0 (Rogers), **38-9**
Mohawk & Hudson Railroad (M&HRR),
"Brother Jonathan" 4-2-0, **25**
"De Witt Clinton", **28-9**
Montrol Locomotive Works, 191
Most powerful locomotive, Allegheny 2-6-6-6 (C&O), **138-9**
Mount Clare 0-8-0 (B&O) 31
Mount Clare Shops, Baltimore, 28-31
B&O Museum, Baltimore, 78
Mount Washington Cog Railway (MWCR), "Colonel Teague" 0-2-2-0, **188-9**
Mountain locomotives, **42-5, 62-3, 76-7, 80-1, 84-5, 104-5, 138-9, 158-9, 188-9**
"Mountaineer", 1201 2-6-2T (Festiniog Railway), **76-7**
Muskingum Electric Railroad (MER), E50C, Co-Co, **192-3**

N

Narrow-gauge locomotives,
0-10-0 (KPR), **84-5**
60-3 Shay B-B-B (Sierra Nevada Wood & Lumber Co), **70-1**
1201 2-6-2T (British War Department), **76-7**
2130 Co-Co (QR), **186-7**
9700 Mikado 2-8-2 (Nippon Railway), **58-9,** 144
C16-60 (D&RG), **42-3**
Dx Co-Co (NZR), **192-3**
Galloping Goose railcar (RGS) **124-5**
K36 2-8-2 (D&RG), **88-9**
"Lyn" 2-4-2T (L&B), **54-5**
Macarthur 2-8-2 (USATC), **144-5**
MacDermot 4-6-2 (Overfair Railroad), **74-5**
NH/4 2-8-2 (SoSR), **150-1**
No.7 2-4-4T (B&SR), **68-9**
No.9 4-6-0 (NCO), **60-1**
No.14 2-8-2 (EBT), **68-9**
Q 4-6-2 (NZR), **52-3**
"The Judge" (Chicago Railroad Exposition), **43**
YP 4-6-2 (IR), **168-9**
National Museum of Transport, St. Louis (Mo), 87, 133, 163
National Museum of Science & Technology, Ottawa, 147
National Railroad Passenger Corporation, see Amtrak
National Railway Museum, Delson (Quebec), 101, 167
National Railways of Mexico (NdeM), QR1 4-8-4, **154-5**
Nevada-California-Oregon Railroad (NCO), No.9 4-6-0, **60-1**
New York Central Railroad (NYC),
J3a 4-6-4, **98-9**
Niagara 4-8-4, **152-3**
T Bo-Bo+Bo-Bo, **64-5**
New York Central & Hudson River Railroad (NYC&HRRR), No.999, "Empire State Express" 4-4-0, **44-5**
New York, New Haven & Hartford Railroad (NY, NH&HRR),
EP1 Bo-Bo, **60-1**
FL9 Bo-A1A, **174-5**
1-5 4-6-4, **128-9**
New York, Ontario & Western Railroad, Mogul 2-6-0, **39**
New Zealand Railways (NZR),
Dx Co-Co, **192-3**
Q 4-6-2, **52-3**
Niagara 4-8-4 (NYC), **152-3**
Nickel Plate Railroad (NKP), S3 2-8-4, **166-7**
Nippon Railway, Class 9700 Mikado 2-8-2, **58-9**
Norfolk & Western Railway,
J 4-8-4, **130-1**
Roanoke (Va) Works, 162
Y6b 2-8-8-2, **162-3**
Norris locomotives, **32-5**
"North Coast Limited", **8,** 93
Northern Pacific Railroad (NP), A 4-8-4, **92-3**
Northern type locomotives, 4-8-4,
05A (CB&Q), **120-1**
2900 (AT&SF), **148-9**
A (NP), **92-3**
GS-2-6 (SP), **132-3**
J (N&W), **130-1**
Niagara (NYC), **152-3**
QR1 (NdeM), **154-5**
Numbers,
1 Bo-Bo (Alco), **86-7**
1-3 Bo+Bo (B&O), **46-7**
1-67 HGe 2/2 (Panama Canal Co), **77**
7 2-4-4T (B&SR), **68-9**
9 4-6-0 (NCO), **60-1**
24 2-6-2 (SRRL), **84-5**
33 "Silver Cliff", **42**
119 (P), **36-7**
147, F15, 4-6-2 (C&O), **52-3**
278, **42**
M-300 Single-unit railcar (Electro-Motive Company), **90-1**
346 "Cumbres", **42-3**
382 4-6-0 (ICRR), **48-9**
481, 487, K36, 2-8-2 (D&RG), **88-9**
611, J, 4-8-4 (N&W), **131**
800 series, FEF, 4-8-4 (UP), **126-7**
999 "Empire State Express" (NYC&HRRR), **44-5**
1000 "Central of New Jersey" (Alco), 87
1027 Camelback 4-4-2 (ACR), **48-9**
1223 D16 4-4-0, **51**
1300-1 2-4-6-2 (AT&SF), **66-7**
1400-1403 4-8-0 (D&H), **106-7**
1406, Ps-4, 4-6-2 (SR), **100**
1601, 1604, 1648, H8 Allegheny 2-6-6-6 (C&O), **138-9**
2400 0-6-6-0 (B&O), **58-9**
2661, 2680, 2685, A, 4-8-4 (NP), **92-3**
2816, 2839, 2850, 2858, 2860, Royal Hudson 4-6-4 (CPR), **115-6**
2928, Fla, 4-4-4 (CPR), **101**
3002, F2a, 4-4-4 (CPR), **100**
3985, Challenger, 4-6-6-4 (UP), **142-3**
4960, Ola, 2-8-2 (CBQ), 94-5
5200, 5280, 5449 4-6-4 (NYC), **98-9**
6001, Niagara, 4-8-4 (NYC), **152-3**
6168, J1, 2-10-4 (PRR), **141**
7000-7754, WP, 4-6-2 (IR), **180-1**
8444, last UP steam locomotive, **126-7**
9000, 9013, 9032 4-12-2 (UP), **97**
9000 2-Do-1 (CNR), **106-7**
M10001 Six-car trainset (UP), **108-9**
Nydqvist & Holm (Nohab), 174-5

O

Ore-car haulage, 128-9, 202-3
"Oriental Limited", 62-3

P

Pacific type locomotives, 4-6-2,
H4 (GN), **62-3**
K4 (PRR), **72-3**
MacDermot, scale replicas, **74-5**
President (B&O), **102-3**
Ps4 (SR), **100-1**
YP (IR), **168-9**
WP (IR), **180-1**
Panama Canal Company, Nos. 1-67, HGe 2/2, **77**
Panama-Pacific Exposition, San Francisco, 19
Pennsylvania Railroad,
D16sb 4-4-0, **50-1**
E3sd 4-4-2, **54-5**
DD1 2-B+B-2, **64-5**
K4 4-6-2, **72-3**
K4 4-6-2, **72-3**
GG1 2-Co-Co-2, **110-1**
J1a 2-10-4, **140-1**
T1 4-4-4-4, **140-1**
S2 6-8-6, **154-5**
Altoona Shops & Museum, 73, 111
Centipede 2-Do-Do-2, **164-5**
"Shark-nose" unite, **164-5**
Metroline Two-car trainset (Budd), **182-3**
Petrol railcar, Galloping Goose, **124-5**
Petrol-electric single-unit railcar M300, **90-1**
Philadelphia & Reading Railroad, Lovatt Eames 42-2, **40-1**
Philadelphia, Germanstown & Norriston Railroad (PG&NRR), Campbell 4-4-0, **30**
"Phoenix" 0-4-0 (SCRR), 25
Pioneer Zephyr Three-car train (CB&Q), **108-9**
"Planet", 26, 32
"Potatoland Special", 160
Prairie type locomotive, 2-6-2, **85-5,** 95
"Puffing Billy", 25
Pullman Standard M10001 Six-car trainset (UP), **108-9**

Q

Queensland Railways (QR), 2130 Co-Co, **186-7**

R

Rack & adhesion locomotive, **77**
Rack & pinion locomotive, **44-5**
Rapid transit systems, **22-3**
Rio Grande Southern Railroad (RGS), Galloping Goose railcar, **17, 124-5**
"Rocket", 27
Rogers, Thomas, 36
Rogers Locomotive & Machine Works, Mogul 2-6-0, **38-9**
"Rotorua Express", 53
Rowlands, Russ F, 204
"The Royal Blue", 103
Royal Hudson 4-6-4 (CPR), **116-7**
"Royal York" (CPR), 116
Russia, Class E 2-10-0, **78-9**
see also Soviet Railways (SZD)

S

St. Louis Car "Electroliner", **134-5**
St. Louis San Francisco Railroad, Class E 2-8-0, **78-9**
Sandy River & Rangeley Lakes Railroad (SRRL), No.24 2-6-2, **84-5**
Santa Fe type locomotive, 900 2-10-2 (AT&SF), 62-3
Science Museum, London, 25
Scindia State Railway (ScSR), NH/4 2-8-2, **150-1**
Seaboard Air Line (SAL), Centipede 2-Do-Do-2, **164-5**
Selkirk 2-10-4 (CPR), **166-7**
"Shark-nose", RF16 Bo-Bo (BLW), **164-5**
Shay 60-3 B-B-B (Sierra Nevada Wood & Lumber Co), **15, 70-1**
Shunting locomotives, see Switching locomotives
"Silver Star" (Amtrak), **198**
Sierra Nevada Wood & Lumber Co, 60-3 Shay B-B-B **15,70-1**
Sleeping-car train, first, M-10001 (UP), **108-9**
Smithsonian Museum, Washington (DC), 25, 27, 101
Snow-plough locomotive, **13**
South Carolina Railroad (SCRR), "Best Friend of Charleston" 0-4-0T, **24-5**
Southeastern Pennsylvania Transportation Authority, 134
"Southern Aurora" express, **186**
Southern Pacific Railroad (SP),
4300 4-8-2, **80-1**
A6 4-4-2, **90-1**
AC4 Cab Forward 4-8-8-2, **104-5**
GS4 4-8-4, **132-3**
Krauss-Maffei C-C, **178-9**
SD40-2 Co-Co, **194**
Southern Railway (of US) (SR), Ps-4 4-6-2, **100-1**
"Southwest Limited", **19**
Soviet Railways (SZD), Little Joe 2-Do-Do-2, **160-1**
Steam turbine locomotive, S2 6-8-6 (PRR), **154-5**
Steam turbo-electric M1 2-1Co-2-1Co-Bo (C&O), **158-9**
Stephenson, George & Robert, 26
Stevens, A.J, 40-1
"Stourbridge Lion" 0-4-0 (D&H), **24-5**
Strasburg Railway Museum, Strasburg (Penn), 73, 103, 111
"Super Chief" express (AT&SF), **16-17,** 119, **148-9**
"Superliner" trains, 197
Switcher locomotives,
C630 Century Co-Co (Alco), **190-1**
GP series Bo-Bo (EMD), **170-1**
NW2 Bo-Bo (EMD), **134-5**
S1a 0-8-0 (N&W), **168-9**
S7 0-10-2 (URR), **118-9**
SD40-2 Co-Co (EMD), **194-5**
U25B Bo-Bo (GE), **176-7**

T

"Texas" 4-4-0, 37
Texas, Class 5001, 2-10-4 (AT&SF), **124-5**
Thyristor control systems, 198-9, 202-3

Tilting high speed train (Via), **200-1**
Timken Roller Bearing Co, 92
"Tom Thumb" 0-2-2 (B&O), **26-7, 29**
Trainmaster H-24-66 Co-Co (FM), **15, 172-3**
Transportation Museum, Roanoke (Va), 131, 139
Triplex 2-8-8-2 (Erie Railroad), **74-5**
"Twentieth Century Limited", 45, **50-1**

U

Union Pacific Railroad (UP), 9000 4-12-2, **96-7**
DD40AX Centennial Do-Do, **184-5**
FEF-2 4-8-4, **126-7**
M10001 Six-car trainset, **108-9**
No.119 4-4-0, **36-7**
NW2 Bo-Bo, **135**
U36C Co-Co (GE), **176**
Big Boy 4-8-8-4, **136-7**
Challenger 4-6-6-4, **15, 142-3**
Gas Turbine Bo-Bo-Bo-Bo, **172-3**
Union Railroad (URR), S7 0-10-2, **118-9**
United States Army Transportation Corps (USATC), Macarthur 2-8-2, **144-5**
S160 2-8-0, **144-5**
United States Railroad Administration (USRA), Light Mikado 2-8-2, **78-9**
Unmanned locomotive, E50C Co-Co (MER), **192-3**

V

Varanasi (Benares) Locomotive Works, 188

Vauclain compound cylinder locomotives, **44-9**
"Vauxhall", 32
Via Rail Canada (Via), LRC Bo-Bo, **200-1**
Victorian Railways (VicRail), X Co-Co, **186-7**
Virginian Railroad (VGN), 800 2-10-10-2, **80-1**
Vulcan Foundry, 66

W

Wabash Railroad (WAB), P1 4-6-4, **94-5**
Walschaert's valve gear, **15,** 53, 58
War locomotives, **76-9, 144-5**
"Washington County Farmer" 4-2-0, 32
"West Point" (SCRR), 28
West Point Foundry, New York, 25, 28
Western & Atlantic Railroad (W&ARR), American Type 4-4-0, **36-7**
Westinghouse air-brake, **12, 40**
Westinghouse motors, 61, 83, 106,, **154-5,** 158, 164
Winans "Camel" 0-8-0, **34-5**
Winans "Camel" 0-8-0, **34-5**
Winans Crab, 30-1
Winton engines, in early EMD E-series, 114-5

Y

Yellowstone wheel arrangement 2-8-8-4, 129

Z

Zephyr style trainsets (CB&Q), **108-9,** 113, 121

Picture Credits

Electricity took the *Olympian* through the Cascade Mountains.